Sir James Outram

Lieut.-General Sir James Outram's campaign in India

1857-1858

Sir James Outram

**Lieut.-General Sir James Outram's campaign in India
1857-1858**

ISBN/EAN: 9783337221751

Printed in Europe, USA, Canada, Australia, Japan

Cover: Foto ©ninafisch / pixelio.de

More available books at **www.hansebooks.com**

LIEUT.-GENERAL SIR JAMES

OUTRAM'S CAMPAIGN IN INDIA,

1857—1858;

COMPRISING

GENERAL ORDERS AND DESPATCHES

RELATING TO THE DEFENCE AND RELIEF OF THE LUCKNOW GARRISON,
AND CAPTURE OF THE CITY, BY THE BRITISH FORCES;

ALSO,

CORRESPONDENCE

RELATING TO THE RELIEF, UP TO THE DATE WHEN THAT
OBJECT WAS EFFECTED BY SIR COLIN CAMPBELL.

Printed for Presentation to Personal Friends of Sir James Outram, who begs that it may be regarded as a Private Communication, and not a Publication.

LONDON:
PRINTED FOR PRIVATE CIRCULATION ONLY,
BY SMITH, ELDER AND CO., 65, CORNHILL.

M.DCCC.LX.

PREFACE.

This volume has been printed for private circulation among the personal friends and comrades in arms of Sir James Outram.

When Sir James Outram, after the fall of Lucknow, assumed the seat in the Supreme Council of India to which he had been appointed some months previously, he found himself overwhelmed with applications from officers who had served under him, for extracts from his General Orders and Official Correspondence, for testimonials to personal services, and for authoritative statements regarding various events connected with the recent campaign.

Unable to reply to these almost incessant requisitions without neglecting his duties as member of Council, Sir James invoked the aid of the Government press; and leaving his friends to make their own extracts, he furnished them with authenticated printed copies of his Despatches.

This concession, however, led to fresh demands. In the Calcutta reprint, the Despatches and other documents were given, without reference to the chronological order of the events they described, and in a form neither pleasant to the eye nor convenient for reference. His friends, therefore, entreated him to consent to their reproduction in this country: urging him to give with them his Correspondence, both epistolary and telegraphic, which he had maintained during the recent stirring events, and which was then scattered through voluminous blue-books, inaccessible newspaper files, and isolated pamphlets and memoirs.

Any *publication* of his despatches and correspondence, Sir James, however, promptly and peremptorily declined; and it was not till after much solicitation that he agreed to have them reprinted at his own expense, for distribution among his more immediate friends: and in making this qualified concession, he stipulated that, with his own Despatches, should be given those of his brother Generals.

But the pressure of his official duties utterly precluded Sir James preparing the promised volume for the press, and he forwarded the materials to his confidential agents, Messrs. Smith, Elder and Co., with a request that they should endeavour " to reduce the chaotic mass to order, ruthlessly commit the rubbish to the flames, print only what was likely to interest the friends to whom the volume was to be presented, and obtain the sanction of the India authorities in England for the distribution of the volume."

Messrs. Smith, Elder and Co. placed Sir James Outram's despatches and correspondence in the hands of a literary gentleman of military knowledge and experience, whom they authorized to exercise his own discretion as to what should be preserved and what rejected; and they requested him to furnish such introductory and connective remarks as he might deem indispensably necessary for the due elucidation of the text.

65, CORNHILL.

INTRODUCTION.

On the 6th February, 1856, the memorable Proclamation was issued by the Indian Government decreeing the annexation of Oude. The execution of the decree was entrusted to Sir James Outram, the British Resident at the Court of Lucknow, and it was carried into effect without resistance. The late Resident became Chief Commissioner of the newly-acquired territory; but he had scarcely succeeded in organizing its civil administration, when failing health compelled him to repair to England. While in this country, he was selected by her Majesty's Ministers for the united military and diplomatic command of the Persian expedition. His appointment as Chief Commissioner of Oude, which the new preferment necessarily vacated, was bestowed on the late Sir Henry Lawrence, and Sir James Outram and his friends believed that he had bidden a final adieu to Oude. But it was otherwise ordered. The Persian war was rapidly brought to a close, and Sir James Outram was, on his return to India, called upon to exercise his military talents in the province he had so recently ruled in peace.

The example set by the mutineers of Meerut and Delhi had been followed by their brethren in other parts of India. Within a month, the whole of Hindostan, from Calcutta to Peshawur, was in a flame, and the sepoy army of Bengal had ceased to exist as a regular and disciplined force. India had been, to a great extent, denuded of British troops; in the first place, owing to the exigencies of the Russian war, and subsequently by having been called upon to furnish the Persian expeditionary force. The utmost energies of the Government were taxed to prevent the communication between Bengal Proper and the Upper Provinces from being effectually interrupted by the rebels, before the arrival of reinforcements; for which requisitions had been made to the Presidencies of Madras and Bombay, to the Governors of Ceylon, Mauritius, and the Cape, and to the officers in command of the expedition then *en route* for China. The territories under the Presidency of Bengal somewhat resemble in shape an hour-glass, of which Allahabad and Benares represent the narrow middle, being straitened by mountains in the west, and the turbulent province of Oude on the east. At these two important towns all the great roads between the upper and lower provinces meet. Benares, the focus of Hindoo fanaticism, was without a European soldier; whilst the Fort of Allahabad, which commands both the Grand Trunk Road and the Ganges and Jumna at their point of junction, was garrisoned by a few sepoys and a body of native artillerymen.

Under these critical circumstances, the Government, leaving the reduction of Delhi to the force which Sir John Lawrence had sent from the Punjaub, concentrated their efforts in hurrying up troops to the nearest points of immediate danger. The affair admitted no delay, for it was obvious that if the native troops in Oude, with or without the support of the warlike chiefs of that country, had made themselves masters of Allahabad—which might have been accomplished, notwithstanding all the efforts of the small body of European pensioners whom Sir Henry Lawrence had, with his wonted promptitude and on his own responsibility, ordered to repair there—the upper and the lower provinces would have been effectually isolated from each other. Happily for us, the mutineers acted neither wisely nor in concert: the mutiny at Lucknow, which occurred on May 30th, was, through the prompt and wise measures of Sir Henry Lawrence, restricted to a portion of the troops; and its result was humiliating to the mutineers, who were driven to ignominious flight, and, instead of hastening to Allahabad, sought sympathy and refuge at the different military stations in Oude. The troops at Benares delayed their *émeute*, till the arrival of Colonel Neill on the 4th of June insured their utter defeat; and though the 6th Regiment at Allahabad, on the same day, murdered their European officers, and perpetrated other atrocities, the surviving English fell back on the fort; for which the wise foresight and promptitude of Sir Henry Lawrence had secured a small European garrison. Here, with the aid of Brasyer's gallant Sikhs, they held their own, till the arrival of Neill, who, on procuring adequate reinforcements from Benares, had started off at the head of a flying column for the release of Allahabad. On the 12th of June he entirely defeated the mutineers, who broke and fled, but his want of cavalry rendered pursuit impossible. Thus Benares and Allahabad were saved, and the communication secured between the latter place and Calcutta.

But Cawnpore was now in the hands of the mutineers, who, under the command of the infamous Nana, had been besieging the gallant Wheeler and his heroic band from June 5th; the British inhabitants of Lucknow, also, were preparing to resist the attack on their position which Sir Henry Lawrence had long seen to be inevitable. Ere Neill could advance to Wheeler's succour, that brave but too confiding officer and his garrison had fallen victims to a fiendish act of treachery; and within a few days of that event the Lucknow garrison had entered on their ever memorable " defence."

On the 30th June, Colonel Neill was superseded by Brigadier-General Havelock, who had recently returned from Persia, where Sir James Outram had obtained for him a divisional command.. General Havelock left Allahabad on this occasion at the head of 2,000 Europeans, consisting of the 64th Regiment, the 78th Highlanders, the Madras Fusiliers, and a company of Royal Artillery; and on the 12th July, he attacked the insurgents, 15,000 strong, capturing eleven guns, and scattering their forces in utter confusion in the direction of Lucknow. In this battle, known by the name of Futtehpore, not a single European was wounded. But while this engagement was taking place, a terrible catastrophe occurred at Cawnpore: Nana Sahib had ordered the murder of all his prisoners. Thus, when Havelock, after having thrice beaten the enemy in the field and captured fifteen of his guns, re-took Cawnpore, cheered by the prospect of rescuing his captive countrymen and countrywomen, he found that he had arrived too late for aught but vengeance.

On the 20th July General Havelock was joined by General Neill at the head of 1,000 Europeans, and the combined force moved on Bithoor, the fort which the British Government had presented to Nana Sahib, and the usual residence of that miscreant. This was found to be evacuated. General Havelock then advanced in the hope of being able to relieve the garrison of Lucknow, who continued resolutely to hold their weak and straggling entrenchment amid dangers that may well have appalled the bravest, and difficulties that were all but insurmountable. On the 29th, he gained a decisive victory over the rebels, 10,000 strong, at Oonao, and on the same day he pushed on to Busserut Gunge, where he gained another victory. But the want of reinforcements, and the influence of the weather, thwarted the efforts of this " hero of antique grandeur," and of his devoted troops. He was at last compelled to fall back and cut his way through the enemy to Cawnpore, where he arrived, with scarcely 900 men, on the 11th September. Here he entrenched himself, while awaiting the arrival of his friend and former chief. Sir James Outram, on his arrival at Calcutta, was at once placed in command of the Dinapore and Cawnpore divisions of the army, and at the same time was nominated to the Chief Commissionership of Oude; which office had then been vacant for some weeks, owing to the lamented deaths of Sir Henry Lawrence and his interim successor Major Banks.

The following Despatches illustrate the events in which Sir James Outram more or less participated subsequently to his nomination to the Dinapore and Cawnpore divisions on August 5th, 1857. But these are not the despatches of Sir James alone: they embrace those of Sir Colin Campbell, Sir Henry Havelock, Sir John Inglis, as well as many of their subordinate officers; and it is the same with the Correspondence.

Had the Editor consulted his own inclinations, he would have interspersed the Despatches and Correspondence in such a manner as to form the whole into a continuous narrative. But, as Sir James Outram sent them home in separate *fasciculi*, the Editor has assumed that he wished them to be printed separately; though in the Parliamentary Blue Books no such technical distinction is maintained.

The Correspondence, it will be seen, does not extend beyond the date on which Sir James Outram took up his position on the plain of Alumbagh, to hold the armed hosts of Lucknow in check until the Commander-in-Chief should be in a position to undertake the capture of that city. There are many who will regret this: but the reason is obvious. Whatever differences of opinion may have existed, after that date, between Sir James and the Governor-General as to questions of policy, up to that period, the most perfect unanimity prevailed among all those on whom it devolved to guard the interests and honour of their country, either in the Cabinet or the Field: had they been brothers, it is impossible that a more affectionate cordiality or a more perfect harmony of views could have characterized their communications. It is gratifying to observe the incessant exertions made by the Governor-General and the Commander-in-Chief to supply Generals Outram and Havelock with the troops of which they stood so urgently in need, and curious to mark the extraordinary value attached to Europeans: even reinforcements of twenty or thirty men are announced by telegraph to the expectant Generals, and the grateful thanks of the latter for such valuable aid are promptly returned by the same agency.

The Editor has, in obedience to his instructions, excised a portion of the Correspondence, both epistolary and telegraphic. He, however, trusts that he has not done so to such an extent as to impair the interest of the volume.

One portion of the Correspondence the Editor may possibly

be blamed by some for suppressing—that referring to the measures adopted and the severe orders issued by Sir James Outram on his way to Cawnpore, with the object of repressing the spirit of vengeance which had displayed itself among our European soldiers; who were too apt to regard every sepoy as a mutineer, and every native inhabitant of hostile villages as a treacherous enemy whom it was just to slay and criminal to spare. The reproduction of what was written on the subject would indeed bring into pleasant relief the equanimity and humanity of the officer whom Lord Canning had selected to reduce the Central Provinces to order, and to be the exponent and enforcer of his own merciful policy; but it would, at the same time, awaken painful reminiscences, and revive incidents which, lamentable as they were, have been greatly exaggerated. Sir James Outram's Orders on these events, though virulently assailed at the time by some newspaper critics, have since met with general approval; and from the first they received the cordial approbation of both Lord Canning and Sir Colin Campbell.

From the Correspondence it will be seen how eager the Commander-in-Chief ever showed himself to protect his Generals from the injustice of the Press. Sir James Outram having been denounced for having retarded the progress of some troops, when at the very time he was straining every nerve to hasten their advance, Sir Colin Campbell, who would probably have allowed a hundred such diatribes to pass unnoticed had they only affected himself, hastened to vindicate the reputation of his Lieutenant through the medium of a General Order.

The Despatches and Correspondence tell their own tale. In a few, but very few, places, the Editor deemed it necessary to introduce some explanatory remarks; but he has made them as brief as possible.

Three plans accompany this volume. The first is a copy of that sent by Sir James Outram to the Alumbagh, along with the instructions he furnished for the guidance of the force which advanced to the second relief of Lucknow, in November, 1857. On this are indicated the route which Sir James Outram marked out for General Havelock's force, and that by which the Commander-in-Chief subsequently advanced. The second exhibits Sir James Outram's position at the Alumbagh; and the third illustrates the final capture of Lucknow by the army under Sir Colin Campbell in March, 1858.

PART I.

GENERAL ORDERS AND DESPATCHES,

RELATING TO

THE RELIEF OF THE GARRISON OF LUCKNOW;

THE

DEFENCE OF THE ALUM BAGH POSITION;

AND

THE SIEGE AND CAPTURE OF THE CITY OF LUCKNOW.

1857-58.

GENERAL ORDERS AND DESPATCHES,

&c., &c.

GENERAL ORDERS BY HIS EXCELLENCY THE ACTING COMMANDER-IN-CHIEF.

Head Quarters, Calcutta, 5th August, 1857.

The following arrangements are directed, with the sanction of the Right Honourable the Governor-General of India in Council:—

Major-General Sir James Outram, K.C.B., Chief Commissioner in Oude, to exercise the Military Command of the united Dinapore and Cawnpore Divisions, until further orders.

Brevet Colonel R. Napier, Chief Engineer, to be Military Secretary and Chief of the Adjutant-General's Department with Sir James Outram.

Captain Huntley R. Garden, Assistant Quartermaster General of the Army, is attached in that capacity to Major-General Sir James Outram's command.

Lieutenant F. H. M. Sitwell, of the 31st Regiment of Native Infantry, to be Aide-de-Camp, and Lieutenant F. E. A. Chamier, of the 34th Regiment of Native Infantry, to be Interpreter and Aide-de-Camp, on the personal Staff of Sir James Outram.

The permanent establishment of Officers of the several Departments of the General Staff belonging to the Dinapore and Cawnpore Divisions, will receive their orders from Major-General Sir James Outram, and be located as he may consider most advisable.

Major-General G. W. A. Lloyd, C.B., is removed from the Divisional Staff of the Army.

By Order of His Excellency the Commander-in-Chief.

W. MAYHEW, *Major*,
Deputy Adjt.-Genl. of the Army.

NOTIFICATION.

FORT WILLIAM.—FOREIGN DEPARTMENT.

Dated the 11th of September, 1857.

The Governor-General in Council is pleased to re-appoint Major-General Sir James Outram, K.C.B., commanding the troops in the Dinapore and Cawnpore Divisions to be Chief Commissioner in Oude, vice Major-General Sir H. Lawrence, K.C.B., demised.

Mr. W. J. Money, C.S., is appointed to act as Private Secretary to Sir James Outram. This is temporary.

G. F. EDMONSTONE,
Secretary to the Government of India.

[Sir James Outram started to join General Havelock at the head of the reinforcements, and *en route* the gallant action was performed by Major Vincent Eyre which is noticed in the following despatches.]

THE DEPUTY ADJUTANT-GENERAL OF THE ARMY TO THE SECRETARY TO THE GOVERNMENT OF INDIA.

Head Quarters, Calcutta,
September 16*th*, 1857.

I have the honour, by desire of the Commander-in-Chief, to forward for submission to the Governor-General in Council, despatches in original from Major-General Sir J. Outram, G.C.B., reporting the operations of a detachment of troops sent under the command of Major V. Eyre, of the Artillery, to dislodge a party of insurgents who had effected a footing in the Doab from the Oude territory, near the village of Koondun Puttee.

2. I am to add that His Excellency concurs in Sir J. Outram's recommendation of Major Eyre, and his detachment, to the favourable notice of Government.

I have, &c.,

W. MAYHEW, *Major*.

The Secretary to the Government of India to the Deputy Adjutant-General of the Army.

With reference to your letter of the 16th instant, forwarding Major's Eyre's report of his successful operations against a party of rebels who crossed from the Oude side of the Ganges into the Doab, I am directed to acquaint you, for the information of His Excellency the Commander-in-Chief, that the Governor-General in Council highly appreciates this further good service rendered by Major Eyre and the detachment under his command, and has noted with satisfaction the energy and sound judgment exhibited by Major Eyre and his officers in the execution of it.

I am, &c.,

R. J. H. BIRCH, *Colonel*.

Major-General Sir J. Outram to the Deputy Adjutant-General of the Army.

Camp Thureedon, Sept. 11th, 1857.

I have the honour to report, for the information of His Excellency the Commander-in-Chief, that on arriving at my camp, Katogun, on the 9th instant, I received definite information that a party of insurgents from Oude, amounting to from 300 to 400, with four guns, had crossed the Ganges near the village of Koondun Puttee, fifteen miles north of Khaga, on the trunk road, between Futtehpore and Allahabad.

Operations against them could be best effected from this encampment, because I could here obtain the most certain intelligence, and my having apparently passed the direct road to them, was likely to throw them off their guard. I accordingly sent orders to halt the leading column, in order to have rested men for the work.

On joining Major Simmons's column at this place, I despatched, under Major Eyre, a party consisting of 100 of her Majesty's 5th Fusiliers, and 50 of her Majesty's 64th Regiment, mounted on elephants, with two guns, and completely equipped with tents, two days' cooked provisions, and supplies for three more.

Captain Johnson's detachment of the 12th Irregulars, consisting of 40 men, made a forced march, and concentrated with Eyre's party at Hutgaon Khas yesterday evening, having completed 40 miles.

For the further proceedings, I beg to refer his Excellency to Major Eyre's despatch. His reputation as a successful leader had already been so well established, that I purposely selected him for this duty, in the perfect confidence that he would succeed.

The importance of this success will, I am sure, be fully appreciated by his Excellency and the Governor-General. I now consider my communication secure, which otherwise must have been entirely cut off during our operations in Oude; and a general insurrection, I am assured, would have followed throughout the Doab, had the enemy not been destroyed, as they were but the advanced guard of more formidable invaders; from which evils having been preserved by Major Eyre's energy and decision, that officer and the detachment under his command are, I consider, entitled to thankful acknowledgments from Government, which I am confident will not be withheld.

Major Eyre to Colonel Napier.

Koondun Puttee, Sept. 11th, 1857.

I am happy to have it in my power to report, for the information of Major-General Sir James Outram, K.C.B., that the expedition he did me the honour of entrusting to my command has been attended with entire success, and the daring invasion of this territory from Oude has been signally punished.

I arrived at Hutgaon last evening at dusk, where I was joined by Captain Johnson's troop of the 12th Irregular Horse, forty in number. As they had marched twenty-four miles, and were in need of rest, I halted till half-past one A.M., when we had the advantage of moonlight to pursue our march to Koondun Puttee, where we arrived at daybreak.

The Oude rebels having been apprised but a short time previously of our advance, had fled precipitately to their boats, about half a mile off. I ordered the cavalry, under Captain Johnson and Lieutenant Havelock, to pursue them, and followed up, myself, with all practicable speed with the infantry and guns. We found the cavalry had driven the enemy into their boats, which were fastened to the shore, and were maintaining a brisk fire on them from the bank above.

On the arrival of the detachments of Hill's 5th Fusiliers and 64th Foot, under Captains Johnson and Turner, the fire of our musketry into the densely crowded boats was most telling ; but the enemy still defended themselves to the utmost, until the guns under Lieutenant Gordon opened fire, when the rebels instantly threw themselves, panic-stricken, into the river. Grape was now showered upon them, and a terrific fusilade from the infantry and cavalry maintained, until only a few scattered survivors escaped. Their numbers appeared to be about 300.

Previously to their plunging into the river, they threw their guns overboard, and blew up one of their boats, which had been boarded by a party of infantry, whereby, I regret to say, one man of Hill's 5th was killed, and ten, more or less, injured (of whom five were Europeans and five natives). All the officers mentioned above distinguished themselves highly ; and the conduct of the men was all that could be desired.

Captain Impey, of the Engineers, and Mr. Volunteer Tarby, have likewise, by their zeal and usefulness, merited my thanks and commendation.

P.S.—Having heard of another party of rebels at a ghaut higher up the river, I have despatched the cavalry to reconnoitre.

Major V. Eyre, Commanding Field Detachment, to Colonel Napier, Military Secretary.

Camp Futtehpore, Sept. 12th, 1857.

I have the honour herewith to forward a correct return of killed and wounded on the late expedition to Koondun Puttee.

In the postscript of my despatch of the 11th instant, I mentioned having sent the forty 12th Irregular Cavalry troopers, under Captain

Johnson, to reconnoitre, and, if possible, to intercept a party of Oude rebels said to have landed at Ukree Ghaut.

They had, however, retreated across the river before Captain Johnson's troop could get at them; but a small fort, which had been recently erected near the ghaut by the rebels, was destroyed by Captain Johnson.

I was informed by Mahomed Zuboor Khan, the Thanadar of Koondun Puttee, that, had not the Oude invaders been checked, and a portion of them destroyed by our troops, it was their intention to have overrun the whole country between Futtehpore and Allahabad, with a view of interrupting our communication and impeding our operations.

He also assured me that the following persons on this side of the river had taken an active part in these disturbances and hostile designs, viz.: Bhunmur Sing, Zemindar of Ukree, Ramsahæ (hæt) of Hutgaon (an active confederate of the former), Seetta Bux and Pulwan Sing, of Burgulla, and Nurlusta Kumaroodeen Hoossain, of Puttee.

I take this opportunity of mentioning that the detachment of the 12th Irregulars had already marched twenty-four miles, when they received the sudden order to join me at Hutgaon, and, although both men and horses had been a whole day without food, they galloped on the whole way to meet me, a distance of nine miles further, guided by that energetic officer, Captain Dawson, of the 1st N. I., who also took a conspicuous part in their subsequent operations.

NOMINAL RETURN *of* KILLED *and* WOUNDED *with the Field Force under command of Major V. Eyre, Artillery, on the* 11*th of September,* 1857.

Her Majesty's 5*th.*—Private Isaac Money, Stephen Lally, Thomas Walker; Charles Helford, slightly burnt; Private William Berant, severely burnt; Corporal Henry Evans, slightly burnt, sword-cut in head.

Artillery.—Tent Lascar, severely burnt; Tent Lascar, bullet wound, severely.

12*th Irregular Cavalry,*—Hossein Bux, slight sword-cut.

Commissariat.—Jemadar of Mahouts, killed.

Camp Followers.—Three (names unknown), severely burnt.

[The following General Order by his Excellency the Commander-in-Chief, with its enclosures, refers to the march of the column on Lucknow, and the arrangements made by the generals.]

GENERAL ORDERS BY HIS EXCELLENCY THE COMMANDER-IN-CHIEF.

Head Quarters, Calcutta,
28*th September,* 1857.

Seldom, perhaps never, has it occurred to a Commander-in-Chief to publish and confirm such an order as the following one, proceeding from Major-General Sir James Outram, K.C.B.

With such a reputation as Major-General Sir James Outram has won for himself, he can well afford to share glory and honour with others. But that does not lessen the value of the sacrifice he has made with such disinterested generosity in favour of Brigadier-General Havelock, C.B., commanding the field force in Oude.

Concurring, as the Commander-in-Chief does, in everything stated in the just eulogy of the latter by Sir James Outram, his Excellency takes this opportunity of publicly testifying to the Army his admiration for an act of self-sacrifice and generosity, on a point, which, of all others, is dear to a real soldier.

The confidence of Major-General Sir James Outram in Brigadier-General Havelock is indeed well justified. The energy, perseverance, and constancy of the Brigadier-General, have never relaxed throughout a long series of arduous operations, in spite of scanty means, a numerous and trained enemy, and sickness in his camp. Never have troops shown greater or more enduring courage than those under the orders of Brigadier-General Havelock.

The force and the service at large are under the greatest obligations to Sir James Outram, for the manner in which he has pressed up the reinforcements to join Brigadier-General Havelock, in the face of much difficulty.

The following orders are confirmed:—

Division order by Major-General Sir James Outram, K.C.B., commanding the Dinapore and Cawnpore Divisions of the Army.

Camp Cawnpore, 16th September, 1857.

1. All Cawnpore divisional reports to be made for

the information of Major-General Sir James Outram, K.C.B., commanding.

2. The force selected by Brigadier-General Havelock, which will march to relieve the garrison of Lucknow, will be constituted and composed as follows:—

INFANTRY.

1*st Brigade.*—Her Majesty's 5th Fusiliers; Her Majesty's 84th Regiment, and detachment 64th Foot attached; 1st Madras Fusiliers;—Brigadier-General J. G. S. Neill, commanding, nominating his own Brigade Staff.

2*nd Brigade.*—Her Majesty's 78th Highlanders; Her Majesty's 90th Light Infantry; Ferozepore Regiment; — Brigadier Hamilton, commanding, nominating his own Brigade Staff.

ARTILLERY.

3*rd Brigade.*—Captain Maude's Battery, Captain Olphert's Battery, Brevet Major Eyre's Battery; Major Cooper to command, nominating his own Staff.

Cavalry.—Volunteer Cavalry, 12th Irregular Cavalry; Captain Barrow to command.

Engineer Department.—Captain Crommelin, Chief Engineer; Lieutenants Limond and Judge, Engineers; Captain Oakes, 8th Native Infantry;—Assistant Field Engineer.

Brigadier-General Havelock, C.B., to command the Force.

The important duty of relieving the garrison of Lucknow had been first entrusted to Brigadier-General Havelock, C.B., and Major-General Outram feels that it is due to that distinguished officer, and to the strenuous and noble exertions which he had already made to effect that object, that to him should accrue the honour of the achievement.

Major-General Outram is confident that this great end, for which Brigadier-General Havelock and his brave troops have so long and so gloriously fought, will now, under the blessing of Providence, be accomplished.

The Major-General, therefore, in gratitude for, and admiration of, the brilliant deeds of arms achieved by Brigadier-General Havelock and his gallant troops, will cheerfully waive his rank in favour of that officer on this occasion, and will accompany the force to Lucknow in his civil capacity, as Chief Commissioner of Oude, tendering his military services to Brigadier-General Havelock as a volunteer.

On the relief of Lucknow, the Major-General will resume his position at the head of the Forces.

By Order of his Excellency the Commander-in-Chief.

W. MAYHEW, *Major*,
Deputy Adjutant-General of the Army.

[The following Field Force After Order, by Major-General Havelock, was not published in General Orders:—]

Cawnpore, 16th September, 1857.

Brigadier-General Havelock, in making known to the column the kind and generous determination of Major-General Sir James Outram, G.C.B., to leave to him the task of relieving Lucknow and rescuing its gallant and enduring garrison, has only to express his hope that the troops will strive, by their exemplary and gallant conduct in the field, to justify the confidence thus reposed in them.

[During the advance of the column the following telegraphic despatches were forwarded to head-quarters, showing the successes achieved:—]

Telegraphic Despatch from General Havelock.
Dated *Bussarut Gunge*, 21st *September*, 1857.

I have to request that you will inform his Excellency the Commander-in-Chief that I was joined by my reinforcements on the 15th and 16th instant.

On the 19th, I crossed first to the island on the Ganges, and then to its left bank, by a bridge of boats, which had been laboriously constructed by Captain Crommelin, Field Engineer. The enemy retired after a very feeble, in fact a nominal, resistance to his position at Mungarwara. The two brigades of my force occupied an alignment, with the right centre behind sand-hills, the centre and left on a plain extending to the road from Lucknow Ghaut to Mungarwara.

My heavy guns and baggage were passed over on the 20th. This morning I attacked the enemy, turned his right, and drove him from his position, with the loss of four guns, two of which, and the regimental colour of the 1st Bengal N. I., were captured by the volunteer cavalry in a charge headed by Sir James Outram. The loss on our side was trifling. The enemy suffered severely—about 120 were sabred by the cavalry.

Telegraphic Despatch from Sir J. Outram to the Governor-General.

Dated Baga Gunge, 22nd September, 1857.

The rebels along the road are flying before our force, which marched twenty miles to-day, and yesterday fourteen miles. Their retreat was too precipitate to enable them to destroy the Bunnee Bridge. Only four guns were taken, but many have been cast into wells, and only four passed the Bunnee Bridge. Firing at Lucknow distinctly heard, and royal salutes by our 24-pounders have been fired by us to announce our approach to our friends.

Telegraphic Despatch from Sir J. Outram to the Governor-General.

Dated Lucknow Residency, 26*th September,* 1857.

Yesterday General Havelock's force, numbering about 2,000 men of all arms, the remainder being left in charge of the sick, wounded, and baggage occupying the Alum Bagh, forced their way into the city under serious opposition. After crossing the Char Bagh bridge the troops skirted the city to the right, thereby avoiding the enemy's defensive works prepared through the entire length of the main street, leading directly to the Residency. Still much opposition had to be encountered ere we attained the Residency in the evening—just in time apparently; for now that we have examined the outside of the defences, we find that two mines had been run far under the garrison's chief works—ready for loading—which, if sprung, must have placed the garrison at their mercy. Our loss is severe, not yet correctly ascertained, but estimated at from four to five hundred killed and wounded. Among the former are General Neill, Lieutenant Well, 40th; Major Cooper, Artillery ; Captain Pakenham, 84th ; Lieutenant Webster, 78th ; Lieutenant Bateman, 64th ; and Lieutenant Warren, 12th Irregular Cavalry. Among the latter, Lieutenant Havelock, Deputy

Assistant Adjutant-General ; Major Tytler, Deputy Quartermaster-General, and many others.

To-day the troops are occupied in taking the batteries bearing on the garrison, which have been held till now assaulted, and continued occasionally to fire on the Residency. Since our junction with the garrison last night many thousands of the enemy have deserted the city. . . . .

I send lists of survivors in the garrison, . . . also list of the dead.

[The notifications and despatches that now follow do not require any elucidation on the part of the editor; for the correspondence following the despatches will fully tell the tale of the relief of Lucknow, when read in connection with the despatches.]

NOTIFICATION.—FORT WILLIAM.

2nd October, 1857.

The Governor-General in Council rejoices to announce that information has been this day received from Major-General Sir James Outram, G.C.B., showing that the Residency at Lucknow was in the possession of Major-General Havelock's Force on the 25th ultimo, and that the garrison is saved.

Rarely has a commander been so fortunate as to relieve, by his success, so many aching hearts, or to reap so rich a reward of gratitude as will deservedly be offered to Major-General Havelock and his gallant band, wherever their triumph shall become known.

The Governor-General in Council tenders to Sir James Outram and to Major-General Havelock his earnest thanks and congratulations upon the joyful result of which a merciful Providence has made them the chief instruments.

The Governor-General in Council forbears to observe further upon information which is necessarily imperfect; but he cannot refrain from expressing the deep regret with which he hears of the death of Brigadier-General

Neill, of the 1st Madras European Fusiliers, of which it is to be feared that no doubt exists.

Brigadier-General Neill, during his short but active career in Bengal, had won the respect and confidence of the Government of India; he had made himself conspicuous as an intelligent, prompt, self-reliant soldier, ready of resource and stout of heart; and the Governor-General in Council offers to the Government and to the army of Madras, his sincere condolence upon the loss of one who was an honour to the service of their Presidency.

By order of the Governor-General of India in Council.

R. J. H. BIRCH, *Colonel*,
Secretary to the Government of India,
in the Military Department.

With reference to the preceding General Order by the Right Honourable the Governor-General in Council, No. 1,543, of this day's date, and in recognition of the heroism of the defenders of the Residency at Lucknow, the Right Honourable the Governor-General in Council hereby orders that—

1. Every officer and soldier, European and native, who has formed part of the garrison of the Residency, between the 29th of June and the 25th of September last, shall receive six months' batta.

2. Every civilian in the Covenanted Service of the East India Company, who has taken part in the defence of the Residency, within the above-named dates, shall receive six months' batta, at a rate calculated according to the military rank with which his standing corresponds.

3. Every uncovenanted civil officer or volunteer who has taken a like part, shall receive six months' batta, at a rate to be fixed according to the functions and position which may have been assigned to him.

4. Every native commissioned and non-commissioned officer and soldier who has formed part of the garrison, shall receive the Order of Merit, with the increase of pay attached thereto, and shall be permitted to count three years of additional service.

5. The soldiers of the 13th, 48th, and 71st Regiments N. I., who have been part of the garrison, shall be formed into a Regiment of the Line, to be called the Regiment of Lucknow, the further constitution of which, as regards officers and men, will be notified hereafter.

R. J. H. BIRCH, *Colonel*,
Secretary to the Govt. of India, Military Department.

By order of his Excellency the Commander-in-Chief,
W. MAYHEW, *Major*,
Deputy Adjutant-General of the Army.

Brigadier-General H. Havelock, to Captain H. W. Norman, Assistant Adjutant-General.

Residency, Lucknow, 30th Sept., 1857.

Major-General Sir J. Outram having, with characteristic generosity of feeling, declared that the command of the force should remain in my hands, and that he would accompany it as Civil Commissioner only, until a junction could be effected with the gallant and enduring garrison of this place, I have to request that you will inform his Excellency the Commander-in-Chief that this purpose was effected on the evening of the 25th instant. But before detailing the circumstances I must refer to antecedent events. I crossed the Sye on the 22nd instant, the bridge at Bunnee not having been broken. On the 23rd, I found myself in presence of the enemy, who had taken a strong position, his left resting on the enclosure of the Alum Bagh, and his centre and right drawn up behind a chain of hillocks. The head of my column at first suffered from the fire of his guns, as it was compelled to pass along the Trunk Road between morasses, but as soon as my regiments could be deployed along his front, and his right enveloped by my left, victory declared for us, and we captured five guns. Sir J. Outram, with his accustomed gallantry, passed on in advance, close down to the canal. But as the enemy fed his artillery with guns from the city, it was not possible to maintain this, or a less advanced position for a time taken up; but it became necessary to throw our right on the Alum Bagh, and refuse our left, and even then we were incessantly cannonaded throughout the 24th; and the enemy's cavalry, 1,500 strong, crept round through lofty cultivation, and made a sudden irruption upon the baggage massed in our rear. The soldiers of the 90th, forming the baggage guard, received them with great gallantry, but lost some brave officers and men, shooting down, however, twenty-five of the troopers, and putting the whole body to flight. They were finally driven to a distance by two guns of Captain Olpherts' battery.

The troops had been marching for three days under a perfect deluge of rain, irregularly fed, and badly housed in villages. It was thought necessary to pitch tents, and permit them to halt on the 24th. The assault on the city was deferred until the 25th. That morning our baggage and tents were deposited in the Alum Bagh, under an escort, and we advanced. The 1st Brigade, under Sir James Outram's personal leading, drove the enemy from a succession of gardens and walled enclosures, supported by the 2nd Brigade, which I accompanied. Both brigades were established on the canal at the brigade of Char Bagh.

From this point the direct road to the Residency was something less than two miles ; but it was known to have been cut by trenches, and crossed by palisades at short intervals, the houses also being all loopholed. Progress in this direction was impossible; so the united column pushed on, detouring along the narrow road which skirts the left bank of the canal. Its advance was not seriously interrupted until it had come opposite the King's Palace, or the Kaiser Bagh, where two guns and a body of mercenary troops were entrenched. From this entrenchment a fire of grape and musketry was opened, under which nothing could live. The artillery and troops had to pass a bridge partially under its influence ; but were then shrouded by the buildings adjacent to the palace of Fureed Buksh. Darkness was coming on, and Sir James Outram at first proposed* to halt within the courts of the Mehal for the night; but I esteemed it to be of such importance to let the beleaguered garrison know that succour was at hand, that, with his ultimate sanction, I directed the main body of the 78th Highlanders and Regiment of Ferozepore to advance. This column rushed on with a desperate gallantry, led by Sir James Outram and myself, and Lieutenants Hudson and Hargood, of my staff, through streets of flat-roofed, loop-holed houses, from which a perpetual fire was kept up, and overcoming every obstacle, established itself within the enclosure of the Residency. The joy of the garrison may be more easily conceived than described ; but it was not till the next evening that the whole of my troops, guns, tumbrils, and sick and wounded, continually exposed to the attacks of the enemy, could be brought step by step within this *enceinte* and the adjacent palace of the Fureed Buksh. To form an adequate idea of the obstacles overcome reference must be made to the events that are known to have occurred at Buenos Ayres and Saragossa. Our advance was through streets of houses such as I have described, and thus each forming a separate fortress. I am filled with surprise at the success of the operation, which demanded the efforts of 10,000 good troops. The advantage gained has cost us dear. The killed, wounded, and missing, the latter being wounded soldiers, who I much fear, some

---

* This point will be found adverted to in the letter from Sir James Outram to the Commander-in-Chief which follows.

or all, have fallen into the hands of a merciless foe, amounted, up to the evening of the 26th, to 535 officers and men. Brigadier-General Neill, commanding 1st brigade; Major Cooper, brigadier, commanding artillery; Lieutenant-Colonel Bazely, a volunteer with the force—are killed. Colonel Campbell, commanding 90th Light Infantry; Lieutenant-Colonel Tytler, my deputy-assistant quartermaster-general; and Lieutenant Havelock, my deputy-assistant adjutant-general, are severely but not dangerously wounded. Sir James Outram received a flesh wound in the arm, in the early part of the action near Char Bagh; but nothing could subdue his spirit; and though faint from loss of blood, he continued to the end of the action to sit on his horse, which he only dismounted at the gate of the Residency. As he has now assumed the command, I leave to him the narrative of all events subsequent to the 26th.

Enclosed is the return of casualties up to that date.

I have, &c.,

H. HAVELOCK, *Brigadier-General,*
Commanding Oude Field Force.

NAMES OF OFFICERS KILLED AND WOUNDED.

KILLED.

General Staff.—Brigadier-General Neill; Brigadier (Major) Cooper, Artillery; Lieutenant-Colonel Bazely, Bengal Artillery.

Artillery.—Lieutenant Crump, Madras Artillery; Assistant-Surgeon Bartrum.

12th Irregular Cavalry.—Lieutenant Warren.

Detachment, Her Majesty's 64th.—Lieutenant Bateman.

Her Majesty's 78th Highlanders.—Lieutenant Webster; Lieutenant Kirby.

Her Majesty's 84th.—Captain Pakenham; Lieutenant Poole.

Her Majesty's 90th Light Infantry.—Lieutenant Moultrie.

WOUNDED.

General Staff.—Major-General Sir J. Outram, G.C.B.; Captain Becher, A.A.G.; Captain Orr, slightly.

Divisional Staff.—Captain Dodgson, A.A.G.; Lieutenant Sitwell, A.D.C.

Field Force Staff.—Lieutenant-Colonel Tytler, D.A.Q.M.G.; Lieutenant Havelock, D.A.A.G.

Engineers.—Captain Crommelin, slightly.

Artillery.—Captain Olpherts, slightly.

Volunteer Cavalry.—Lieutenant Lynch, Her Majesty's 70th, slightly; Lieutenant Palliser, 63rd Bengal Native Infantry, slightly; Lieutenant Swanston, 7th Madras Native Infantry; Lieutenant Birch, 1st Bengal Light Cavalry, severely.

Her Majesty's 5th Fusiliers.—Captain L'Estrange, severely; Captain Johnson, severely.

Her Majesty's 78th Highlanders.—Captain Lockhart, severely; Captain Hastings, slightly; Lieutenant Crowe, slightly; Lieutenant Swanson, severely; Lieutenant Grant, severely; Lieutenant Jolly,

Her Majesty's 32nd (attached), since dead; Lieutenant Macpherson, slightly.
Her Majesty's 84th.—Captain Willis, slightly; Lieutenant Barry, slightly; Lieutenant Oakley, severely; Lieutenant Woolhouse, severely.
Her Majesty's 90th Light Infantry.—Lieutenant-Colonel Campbell, severely; Lieutenant Knight, severely; Assistant-Surgeon Bradshaw, slightly; Lieutenant Preston, slightly.
1st Madras Fusileers.—Lieutenant Arnold, since dead; Lieutenant Bailey, severely.

Extract from a letter addressed by Sir James Outram to his Excellency the Commander-in-Chief.

Alumbagh, 2nd January, 1858.

I trust that you will forgive me for bringing a small personal matter to your private notice which has caused me some slight annoyance, for such consideration as you may think it deserving of.

I perceive from the published despatch of Sir Henry Havelock, describing the operations connected with his entrance into Lucknow for the relief of the garrison, the lamented General therein states that, after taking the Chutter Munzil, we held a conversation, at which I recommended that we should remain where we were, while he advocated pushing on at once, and adopted the latter course.

It seems to me that a dispassionate peruser of the above passage would infer that the relief of the garrison was due to General Havelock's adoption of his own views in preference to mine, and I therefore wish to explain that I proposed a halt, of only a few hours' duration, in order to enable the rear-guard, with which were all our heavy guns, the baggage, and the doolies containing our wounded, to come up, by which time the whole force would have occupied the Chutter Munzil in security, which we were then holding, and from which we could have effected our way to the Residency by opening communication through the intervening palaces;

in a less brilliant manner, it is true, but with comparatively little loss ; at the same time offering to show the way through the street if he preferred it. I submit that the result proved the soundness of my advice. General Havelock pushed on without waiting for the rear-guard, which was consequently cut off for two nights and a day, not effecting its entrance to the entrenchment until the morning of the 27th, and then only at a heavy sacrifice of life, and the loss of a nine-pounder gun and much baggage, and, still more sad to relate, at the cost of the lives of very many wounded officers and men, who were cut up in their doolies. (N.B.—The return of killed during that period was 61, and 77 missing. The latter being the unfortunate wounded.) This disaster would have been prevented, had the rear-guard been allowed to come up before we vacated the Chutter Munzil, as our light artillery from thence would have kept down the fire from the Kaiser Bagh, which was the principal cause of all the casualties. And the wounded were murdered at the entrance of the Chutter Munzil, which we had vacated. . . .

It may seem to your Excellency that I should have made these observations before, and I have therefore to state, that I should certainly have requested the General to modify that passage in his despatch in which he mentions that I was desirous of a halt, had my name appeared in the official original which was forwarded through me by cossid to Captain Bruce, for transmission to your Excellency. But as such was not the case, I can only conclude that it was subsequently interpolated without the knowledge of General Havelock, when (on hearing that the original had miscarried) a copy was furnished which did not pass through my hands.

I am well aware that in surrendering the command to General Havelock, I left him at undoubted liberty to put on record his own impressions regarding the conduct of the operations; but I am sure that if he were alive, he would at once assent to the correctness of what I have above stated.

It is with no desire of controversy, or any wish to reflect injuriously on the illustrious dead, that I mention the above facts for your private information. I think it only due to my professional reputation, however, to put you, my superior officer, in possession of the real facts of the case, because if the despatch, as it stands, gives you the impression (which, I think, I am justified in assuming it might do) that General Havelock accomplished such an achievement as that of the relief of Lucknow, by adopting a course of action contrary to that which I had recommended, it would naturally shake your confidence in me, and lead you, not unreasonably, to doubt my fitness to undertake the conduct of similar, or other military operations.

[In reference to this subject, the editor has received the following communication from an officer of the beleaguered garrison, to whom he submitted the foregoing letter, and from whom he solicited some explanatory information with reference to the amicable difference of opinion here referred to as existing between the two generals:—]

Consult the plans, and bear in mind the circumstances of the case. Generals Outram and Havelock both believed that the garrison was on its last biscuit; and they had been unable to bring with them any provisions beyond the few days' rations the men carried in their havresacks. They came not to *reinforce*, but to *extricate* us. Their object, therefore, was not so much to accelerate their advance to our position as—with the least possible sacrifice of those precious lives on which the safe removal of the garrison must be, in a great measure, dependent—to open and keep open such communications with the Residency as should enable us to be withdrawn with our sick and wounded, women and children. In this view, the concentration of the entire relieving force, under the shelter of the palaces, appeared to Sir J. Outram preferable to pushing on at once, and leaving the rear-guard behind; and he thought it more advisable to open communications with the Residency through the comparatively sheltered courts and gardens of the palaces (which, once occupied, could have been retained as long as was necessary), than to advance through crooked streets of loopholed houses, with the certainty of having either to repass these streets with the enfeebled and encumbered garrison, or to force a passage through the palaces, which the enemy would, in all probability, have by that time reoccupied. And it was a part of Sir J. Outram's plan to facilitate the arrival of the rear-guard at the Chutter Munzil (where he proposed making the halt), by ordering the field guns, then up with the main body, to open such a fire as should effectually divert the enemy's attention, if not altogether silence those guns of the Kaiser Bagh, from which he foresaw the rear-guard must otherwise suffer severely. As it was, the palaces had to be secured and occupied the next or the following day. It was through *them* that the garrison was eventually removed, two months later, by Sir Colin Campbell. Even after the arrival of the Commander-in-Chief's army, and notwithstanding the great extension in all directions which our position had ere then received, this was the only safe or practicable egress. And that it was not only practicable but safe, on the afternoon of September 25th, Sir James Outram, whose local knowledge was considerable, Captain Moorsom, on whose surveys of Lucknow the only accurate plans of the city are based, and Captain Alexander P. Orr, the commandant of a regiment in the late King of Oude's service, and who had for years been familiar with every inch of the locality, had satisfied themselves by a personal reconnaissance. Expecting that the relieving force would enter Lucknow by the regular Cawnpore road, the enemy had made their dispositions accordingly. A portion remained at their old batteries to keep the garrison in play, and prevent its making a diversion in favour of General Havelock; but the overwhelming majority had gone out to hold the barricades, breastworks, batteries, and loopholed houses, extending from the Charbagh bridge to the Residency, which had prepared to resist our relief. On finding that the British troops had, through the local knowledge and under the guidance of Sir James Outram (aided by Captains Moorsom and Orr), been enabled to baffle their arrangements by a flank movement, the sepoys, regular and irregular, began that evacuation of the city which they had completed on the morning of the following day; but the artillery stood to their posts, and the *budmashes*, Rajwarra troops, and matchlockmen hastened to retrieve their mistake by pouring down on the line of route actually adopted. They swarmed in the direction by which the rear-guard must advance to effect a junction with the main body then under the shelter of the neighbouring palaces; and they occupied the streets, and every position commanding the streets that led from the palaces to the Residency, as the casualties too plainly prove. But they had *not* been able to obtain possession of the palaces. These, as I have said, were quite deserted.

Though General Outram afterwards " concurred " in General Havelock's determination to push on without the rear-guard, and to take the street route, instead of that through the palaces, he retained his own opinion to the last. But, as he had voluntarily placed himself under General Havelock, it would have been unbecoming in him to persist in setting up his judgment in opposition to that of his commander. He yielded; but, in doing so, craved permission to lead what he knew must be a fearfully perilous advance.

I scarcely understand what General Havelock meant to express, when referring to his anxiety to let the garrison know that succour was at hand. Mines had certainly been prepared against one or more of our principal positions, the explosion of which might have proved serious. But of the existence of these mines, the relieving force was then ignorant. We were by no means hardly pressed by the enemy, whose attention was amply engaged by the glorious Havelock himself and his brave troops. We had been for some days prepared for the arrival of the relieving force; our ears made us sufficiently acquainted with their actual approach; and our topographical knowledge enabled us to guess pretty accurately the progress they were making, and the positions they had secured.

DIVISION ORDERS.

Lucknow Residency, 26th September, 1857.

The relief of the Lucknow Garrison having last night been accomplished by General Havelock and his brave troops, Major-General Sir J. Outram resumes his position as commander of the forces.

The Major-General heartily congratulates General Havelock, and the troops whom that gallant and distinguished officer has so gloriously led to victory, on their brilliant successes over the hosts that have opposed them since the army crossed the Ganges on the 19th instant. He sincerely believes, that in the history of warfare British valour was never more conspicuously displayed than on the 21st instant, at Mungulwura, on the 23rd at Alumbagh, and on the 25th, when his heroic comrades forced the city bridge and other formidable obstacles which interrupted their passage to the position held by the beleaguered garrison. The Major-General deeply laments the heavy cost at which the relief of our countrymen has been purchased; but the glorious devotion with which the gallant dead, and equally gallant survivors, staked their lives to rescue the Lucknow garrison, will be deeply appreciated by our Queen and our country; and the safety of those whom we, under God's blessing, have been permitted to redeem from a dreadful fate, must be our consolation for the loss of so many of our noble comrades. The Major-General begs to return his most sincere and heartfelt thanks to the General and his gallant army for their glorious exertions, the only acknowledgment of their achievements which it is in his power to render. On General Havelock it will devolve, in his reports to the Commander-in-Chief, to do justice to the army which has so devotedly carried out his orders. But while fully aware that every arm was stimulated by the same brave spirit, the Major-General deems it right to bear his personal testimony to the admirable conduct of such of the troops as acted under his immediate observation. He would especially note the behaviour of the 90th Regiment, who led the advance of the left attack at Mungulwura: that of the Volunteer Cavalry, who charged the artillery of the retiring enemy, and captured two of their guns; that of the 84th and detachment of the 64th attached to it, who led the attack on the enemy's left at Alumbagh; that of Captain Olpherts' battery, who so bravely followed up their retreat on that occasion; and Major Eyre's battery, in opposing the enemy who afterwards bore on their position; that of the 5th Fusiliers and Captain Maude's battery, who led the column on the 25th instant, under a most murderous fire; that of the 1st Fusiliers (Madras), who charged the bridge and battery at the entrance of the city, headed by the gallant assistant adjutant-general, Lieutenant Havelock; and finally, that of the 78th Highlanders, who led the advance on the Residency, headed by their brave commander, Colonel Stisted, accompanied by the gallant Lieutenant Hargood, aide-de-camp to General Havelock; Captain Grant, 1st Madras Fusiliers; Lieutenant Hudson, 64th Regiment, and Lieutenant Chamier, aide-de-camp.

SUPPLEMENTAL ORDER.

The Major-General regrets to find, that in noticing the services of the troops which came under his personal attention, in Division Orders of 26th instant, he omitted to mention the Regiment of Ferozepore and its gallant leader, Captain Brasyer. The Major-General in that order merely referred to what he himself observed, but was well aware that this Regiment was most prominently forward on every occasion. Though happening seldom to be in the same part of the field, he takes blame to himself for having inadvertently omitted to mention their advance with the 90th at Mungulwura, which did come under his personal observation. The time has not yet come for the Major-General to notice the conduct of the troops subsequently to his assuming command, during which period the Sikh Regiment has been incessantly occupied on most important service; but they may rest assured that they, as well as all the corps who have, like them, highly distinguished themselves since, will be brought to prominent notice.

Major-General Sir J. Outram, G.C.B., to His Excellency Sir Colin Campbell, G.C.B., Commander-in-Chief.

Lucknow, 30th September, 1857.

General Havelock having effected his junction with the garrison holding the Residency of Lucknow on the evening of the 25th instant, I, on the following day, resumed command of the troops, issuing the Order,* of which I enclose a copy for his Excellency's information.

I had on the day after leaving Cawnpore sent a note to the Commandant of the garrison, informing him of our approach, and warning him not to be enticed into

---
* Order of September 26, *vide antea*.

weakening his garrison by detaching to our support when he should hear us engaged in the city, lest the enemy should avail themselves of that opportunity to assault his position. This note I have since learnt he received. A copy is enclosed.*

Since we have obtained access to the exterior of the entrenchments, we find that the enemy had completed six mines in the most artistic manner—one of them from a distance of 200 feet—under our principal defensive works, which were ready for loading, and the firing of which must have placed the garrison entirely at their mercy. The delay of another day, therefore, might have sealed their fate.

To force our way *through* the city, would have proved a very desperate operation, if indeed it could have been accomplished.

After passing the bridge, therefore, which is at the entrance, General Havelock took his force by a detour to the right, where but little means comparatively of opposition had been prepared, until he approached the front of the "Kaiser Bagh" (King's Palace), from whence a heavy fire was opened upon us, and from that point (through a limited extent of about a quarter of a mile of street which then intervened before reaching the Residency) the troops were much exposed to the fire of the enemy, occupying the houses on both sides, as well as to some of the besieging guns which had been turned against us, besides being obstructed by ditches which had been cut across the street—all which ob-

---
* *To Brigadier Inglis.*
North Side of the River, 20*th September,* 1857.
The army crossed the river yesterday and, all the material being over, marches to-morrow, and, under the blessing of God, will now relieve you. The rebels, we hear, purpose making a desperate assault upon you as we approach the city, and will be on the watch in expectation of your weakening your garrison to make a diversion in our favour as we attack the city. I beg to warn you against being enticed too far from your works when you hear us engaged. Such diversion as you can make, without in any way risking your position, should only be attempted. J. OUTRAM.

stacles were overcome by the usual gallantry and dash of British troops, but at a heavy cost. The Residency was gained in the evening; and the cheers of our rescued comrades overcame for the time our regrets for the many who had fallen in their cause.

General Havelock's report will acquaint your Excellency with details; my own reports commencing from the following day, when, as the enemy had, during the night, continued to hold his offensive position and to maintain his fire on the entrenchment, it became my first object to occupy or destroy his works; for, independent of the damage caused by his fire to the now crowded garrison, no communication could be held with the city. I, therefore, on the morning of the 26th, ordered the " Captain Bazar " to be cleared, which has heretofore harboured the enemy in vexatious proximity to the garrison, and it was occupied by her Majesty's 32nd Regiment under Brigadier Inglis, capturing five guns, with a loss of one officer (Captain Hughes, 57th L. I.) and two privates killed, and seven privates wounded; thus removing all obstruction from the river side of our position.

On the 27th September, the palaces extending along the line of the river, from the Residency to near the " Kaiser Bagh " ("Tara Kotee," "Chuttur Munzil," and "Forad Buksh"), were occupied for the accommodation of our troops. On the same day, at noon, a party, consisting of 150 men, made a sortie on another of the enemy's positions, and destroyed four guns, at a loss of eight killed and wounded. At daylight on the 28th, three columns aggregating 700 men, attacked the enemy's works at three different points, destroyed ten guns, and demolished by powder explosions the houses which afforded position to the enemy for musketry fire. This has effectually destroyed his attacks excepting on one point, where he has still three guns which it is difficult to get at, but it is not likely the enemy will attempt to maintain that isolated position; and as there has been no fire from thence this morning, it is probable he may have abandoned it. This successful operation was attended by the serious loss of one officer and fifteen men killed and missing, one officer and thirty-one men wounded; the officer killed being Major Simmons, commanding her Majesty's 5th Fusiliers, most deeply regretted by the whole army.

Our present prospects have now to be considered. It was the urgent desire of the Government that the garrison should be relieved, and the women and children, amounting to upwards of 470 souls, withdrawn.

The army of the enemy has been beaten in the open field without difficulty. The resistance was more obstinate in the suburbs, and at great sacrifice the troops forced their way to the garrison in Lucknow. The sick and wounded had been left with the baggage in a strong enclosure, called "Alumbagh," five miles from the Lucknow entrenchment.

In considering the heavy loss at which we forced our way through the enemy, it was evident there could be no possible hope of carrying off the sick, wounded, and women and children (amounting to not less than 1,500 souls, including those of both forces). Want of carriage alone rendered the transport through five miles of disputed suburb an impossibility.

There remained but two alternatives: one to reinforce the Lucknow Garrison with 300 men, and, leaving everything behind, to retire immediately with the remains of the infantry upon the Alumbagh, thereby leaving the garrison in a worse state than we found it, by the addition to the numbers they had previously to feed, of the great amount of our wounded, and of the

300 soldiers, who would barely have sufficed to afford the additional protection that would have been required—without adding such strength as would have enabled them to make an active defence, to repel attacks by sorties, or to prevent the enemy occupying the whole of their old positions. At the same time, it would have been impossible for any smaller force than the remainder of our troops, diminished by those 300 men, to have any hope of making good their way back; and that not without very serious loss. I therefore adopted the second alternative, as the only mode of offering reasonable hope of securing the safety of this force, to retain sufficient strength to enforce supplies of provisions should they not be open to us voluntarily, and to maintain ourselves, even on reduced rations, until reinforcements advance to our relief.

Now that Delhi has fallen and released our forces, two brigades might perhaps be spared for this service. But I am satisfied that even one brigade, with two batteries of artillery, could make good its way to the "Dilkoosha" (a position three miles hence on the Cawnpore side of the canal), the route to which, the rains now being over, will be practicable for artillery by the direct road from Alumbagh.

With such a force established at Dilkoosha, we could without difficulty open out our communication and withdraw the whole, or such portion of our forces as may be desired after re-establishing our authority at Lucknow.

Since my decision has been made, I have received a letter from the Alumbagh, in which it is stated that they are in great want of provisions, but from returns of what they have, it is clear that they are not aware of their resources, which were sufficient for some days. I have, therefore, ordered back the cavalry to join them in the night by a circuitous route, with conditional orders to withdraw to Cawnpore, or to maintain their position, as may be found most practicable. Their only difficulty is provisions, as they are placed in a fortified enclosure, defended by two of our heavy guns, and two 9-pounders, besides other guns taken from the enemy, 250 European soldiers, and a number of convalescents fit to bear arms. I have, &c.,

J. OUTRAM, *Major-General.*

1st October.

P.S.—The cavalry failed to make their way out last night; the enemy being found on the alert, and in such strength beyond our picquets, it was not deemed prudent to attempt to force a passage; consequently this despatch was brought back, and there will be no means of transmitting it at present.

[The foregoing despatch having miscarried, was not received in Calcutta till December 30th; on the 31st, his Excellency the Commander-in-Chief promulgated it to the army with the subjoined General Order by the Right Honourable the Governor-General in Council:—]

GENERAL ORDERS BY HIS EXCELLENCY THE
COMMANDER-IN-CHIEF.

Adjutant-General's Office,
Calcutta, Dec. 31st, 1857.

General Orders by the Right Honourable the Governor-General of India in Council.

Fort William, 30th December, 1857.

The Right Honourable the Governor-General in Council, in directing the publication of the subjoined despatch from Major-General Sir J. Outram, G.C.B., dated the 30th of September, 1857, considers it due to that officer and to others who may have felt disappointment at the omission of it among the despatches which were published in the *Calcutta Gazette Extraordinary* of the 23rd instant, to explain that although earlier in date than those despatches it has been received after them, and that its publication has not been delayed.

His Lordship in Council most fully appreciates the valour of the troops whom that distinguished officer, the late Sir Henry Havelock, aided and supported by Sir James Outram, and by the lamented Brigadier-General Neill, led victoriously through the hosts of the insurgents and in the face of extraordinary difficulties, to the relief of the garrison of Lucknow; and he desires that every officer, non-commissioned officer, and soldier, will accept the assurance of the entire approbation of Government, as offered to each and all individually.

The Governor-General in Council observes with great satisfaction the supplemental order in which Sir James Outram separately brings to notice the services rendered by the Ferozepore Regiment under their gallant leader, Captain Brasyer. The thanks of Government were given to this regiment in the General Order, No. 1625 of the 22nd instant; and his Lordship in Council willingly reiterates his acknowledgments to Captain Brasyer and his officers and men.

A despatch from the Deputy Adjutant-General of the army, dated the 22nd of December, 1857, is also now published. In it, his Excellency the Commander-in-Chief prominently brings to notice the good service performed by the officers of the Volunteer Cavalry, commanded by Captain Barrow, and the Governor-General in Council embraces with much satisfaction this opportunity of publicly recording his sense of the gallant conduct of Captain Barrow and his devoted band, officers and men, ever forward where hard work and danger were to be found.

R. J. H. BIRCH, *Colonel,*
Secretary to the Govt. of India, in the Military Dept.

Division Orders by Major-General Sir James
Outram, G.C.B.

Head-quarters, Lucknow, 5th October, 1857.

The incessant and arduous duties which have devolved on Brigadier Inglis and his Staff since the arrival of the relieving force, had hitherto prevented him from furnishing to the Major-General commanding the usual official documents relative to the siege of the garrison.

In the absence of these, the Major-General could not with propriety have indulged in any public declaration of the admiration with which he regards the heroism displayed by Brigadier Inglis and the glorious garrison he has so ably commanded, during the last three months, and he has been reluctantly obliged to defer, therefore, so long the expression of the sentiments he was desirous to offer.

But the Major-General having at length received Brigadier Inglis' reports, is relieved from the necessity of further silence, and he hastens to tender to the Brigadier, and to every individual member of the garrison, the assurance of his confidence that their services will be regarded by the Government under which they are immediately serving, by the British nation, and by her gracious Majesty, with equal admiration to that with which he is himself impressed.

The Major-General believes that the annals of warfare contain no brighter page than that which will record the bravery, vigilance, fortitude, and patient endurance of hardships, privation, and fatigue, displayed by the garrison of Lucknow; and he is very conscious that his unskilled pen must needs fail adequately to convey to the Right Honourable the Governor-General of India, and his Excellency the

Commander-in-Chief, the profound sense of the merits of that garrison, which has been forced on his mind by a careful consideration of the almost incredible difficulties with which they have had to contend.

The term "illustrious" was well and happily applied by a former Governor-General of India to the garrison of Jellalabad; but some far more laudatory epithet, if such the English language contain, is due, the Major-General considers, to the brave men whom Brigadier Inglis has commanded with undeviating success and untarnished honour, through the late memorable siege; for, while the devoted band of heroes who so nobly maintained the honour of their country's arms under Sir R. Sale were seldom exposed to actual attack, the Lucknow garrison, of inferior strength, have, in addition to a series of fierce assaults gallantly and successfully repulsed, been for three months exposed to a nearly incessant fire from strong and commanding positions, held by an enemy of overwhelming force, possessing powerful artillery, having at their command the whole resources of what was but recently a kingdom, and animated by an insane and blood-thirsty fanaticism.

It is a source of heartfelt satisfaction to the Major-General to be able, to a certain extent, to confer on the native portion of the garrison an instalment of those rewards which their gallant and grateful commander has sought for them, and which he is very certain the Governor-General will bestow in full; and though the Major-General, as regards the European portion of the garrison, cannot do more than give his most earnest and hearty support to the recommendations of the Brigadier, he feels assured that the Governor-General of India will fully and publicly manifest his appreciation of their distinguished services, and that our beloved Sovereign will herself deign to convey to them some gracious expression of royal approbation of their conduct.

Brigadier Inglis has borne generous testimony to the bravery, vigilance, devotedness, and good conduct of all ranks; and to all ranks the Major-General, as the local representative of the British Indian Government, tenders his warmest acknowledgments. He would fain offer his special congratulations and thanks to the European and Eurasian portion of the garrison whom Brigadier Inglis has particularly noticed; but by doing so he would forestall the Governor-General in the exercise of what the Major-General is assured will be one of the most pleasing acts of his official life.

T. F. WILSON, *Captain*,
Officiating Deputy-Assistant Adjutant-General.

[General Inglis's despatch bears the date on which it was first roughly drafted, ten days prior to the date on which, in its revised form, it seems to have been submitted to Sir James Outram.]

Brigadier Inglis, Commanding Garrison of Lucknow, to the Secretary to Government, Military Department, Calcutta.

Dated *Lucknow, 26th September,* 1857.

In consequence of the very deeply-to-be-lamented death of Brigadier-General Sir H. M. Lawrence, K.C.B., late in command of the Oude Field Force, the duty of narrating the military events which have occurred at Lucknow since 29th June last, has devolved upon myself.

On the evening of that day several reports reached Sir Henry Lawrence that the rebel army, in no very considerable force, would march from Chinhut (a small village about eight miles distant on the road to Fyzabad) on Lucknow on the following morning; and the late Brigadier-General, therefore, determined to make a strong reconnaissance in that direction, with the view, if possible, of meeting the force at a disadvantage, either at its entrance into the suburbs of the city, or at the bridge across the Gokral, which is a small stream intersecting the Fyzabad road, about half way between Lucknow and Chinhut.

The force destined for this service, and which was composed as follows, moved out at six A.M., on the morning of the 30th June:—

Artillery.—4 guns of No. — Horse Light Field Battery; 4 guns of

No. 2 Oude Field Battery; 2 guns of No. 3 Oude Field Battery; an 8-inch howitzer.
Cavalry.—Troop of volunteer cavalry; 120 troopers of detachments belonging to 1st, 2nd, and 3rd Regiments of Oude Irregular Cavalry.
Infantry.—300 of H. M.'s 32nd; 150 of the 13th N. I.; 60 of the 48th N. I.; and 20 of the 71st N. I. (Sikhs.)

The troops, misled by the reports of wayfarers, who stated that there were few or no men between Lucknow and Chinhut, proceeded somewhat further than had been originally intended, and suddenly fell in with the enemy, who had up to that time eluded the vigilance of the advanced guard by concealing themselves in overwhelming numbers behind a long line of trees. The European force and the howitzer, with the N. 1., held the foe in check for some time, and, had the six guns of the Oude Artillery been faithful, and the Sikh Cavalry shown a better front, the day would have been won in spite of an immense disparity in numbers. But the Oude artillerymen and drivers were traitors. They overturned the guns into ditches, cut the traces of their horses, and abandoned them, regardless of the remonstrances and exertions of their own officers, and of those of Sir Henry Lawrence's Staff, headed by the Brigadier-General in person, who himself drew his sword upon these rebels. Every effort to induce them to stand having proved ineffectual, the force, exposed to a vastly superior fire of artillery, and completely outflanked on both sides by an overpowering body of infantry and cavalry, which actually got into our rear, was compelled to retire with the loss of three pieces of artillery, which fell into the hands of the enemy, in consequence of the rank treachery of the Oude gunners, and with a very grievous list of killed and wounded. The heat was dreadful, the gun ammunition was expended, and the almost total want of cavalry to protect our rear made our retreat most disastrous.

All the officers behaved well, and the exertions of the small body of volunteer cavalry—only forty in number—under Captain Radcliffe, 7th Light Cavalry, were most praiseworthy. Sir Henry Lawrence subsequently conveyed his thanks to myself who had, at his request, accompanied him on this occasion (Colonel Case being in command of her Majesty's 32nd). He also expressed his approbation of the way in which his staff—Captain Wilson, officiating deputy assistant adjutant-general; Lieutenant James, sub-assistant commissary-general; Captain Edgell, officiating military secretary; and Mr. Couper, Civil Service—the last of whom had acted as Sir Henry Lawrence's aide-de-camp from the commencement of the disturbances—had conducted themselves throughout this arduous day. Sir Henry further particularly mentioned that he would bring the gallant conduct of Capt. Radcliffe and of Lieut. Bonham, of the Artillery (who worked the howitzer successfully until incapacitated by a wound), to the prominent notice of the Government of India. The manner in which Lieutenant Birch, 71st N. I., cleared a village with a party of Sikh skirmishers, also elicited the admiration of the Brigadier-General. The conduct of Lieutenant Hardinge, who, with his handful of horse, covered the retreat of the rear guard, was extolled by Sir Henry, who expressed his intention of mentioning the services of this gallant officer to his Lordship in Council. Lieutenant-Colonel Case, who commanded her Majesty's 32nd Regiment, was mortally wounded whilst gallantly leading on his men. The service had not a more deserving officer. The command devolved on Captain Steevens, who also received a death-wound shortly afterwards. The command then fell to Captain Mansfield, who has since died of cholera. A list* of the casualties on this occasion accompanies the despatch.

It remains to report the siege operations.

It will be in the recollection of his Lordship in Council that it was the original intention of Sir Henry Lawrence to occupy not only the Residency, but also the fort called Muchhee Bhowun—an old dilapidated edifice, which had been hastily repaired for the occasion, though the defences were even at the last moment very far from complete, and were moreover commanded by many houses in the city. The situation of the Muchhee Bhowun with regard to the Residency, has already been described to the Government of India.

The untoward event of the 30th June so far diminished the whole available force, that we had not a sufficient number of men remaining to occupy both positions. The Brigadier-General, therefore, on the evening of the 1st July, signalled to the garrison of the Muchhee Bhowun to evacuate and blow up that fortress in the course of the night. The orders were ably carried out, and at twelve P.M. the force marched into the Residency with their guns and treasure without the loss of a man; and shortly afterwards the explosion of 240 barrels of gunpowder and 6,000,000 ball cartridges, which were lying in the magazine, announced to Sir Henry Lawrence and his officers—who were anxiously waiting the report—the complete destruction of that post and all that it contained. If it had not been for this wise and strategic measure, no member of the Lucknow Garrison, in all probability, would have survived to tell the tale; for, as has already been stated, the Muchhee Bhowun was commanded from other parts of the town, and was moreover indifferently provided with heavy artillery ammunition, while the difficulty, suffering, and loss which the Residency garrison, even with the reinforcement thus obtained from the Muchhee Bhowun, has undergone in holding the position, is sufficient to show that if the original intention of holding both posts had been adhered to, both would have inevitably fallen.

It is now my very painful duty to relate the calamity which befel us at the commencement of the siege. On the 1st July an eight-inch shell burst in the room in the Residency in which Sir H. Lawrence was sitting. The missile burst between him and Mr. Couper—close to both—but without injury to either. The whole of his staff implored Sir Henry to take up other quarters, as the Residency had then become the special target for the round shot and shell of the enemy. This, however, he jestingly declined to do, observing that another shell would certainly never be pitched into that small room. But Providence had ordained otherwise, for on the very next day he was mortally wounded by the fragment of another shell which burst in the same room, exactly at the same spot. Captain Wilson, deputy assistant adjutant-general, received a contusion at the same time.

---

* Not received by Government.

The late lamented Sir H. Lawrence, knowing that his last hour was rapidly approaching, directed me to assume command of the troops, and appointed Major Banks to succeed him in the office of chief commissioner. He lingered in great agony till the morning of the 4th July, when he expired, and the Government was thereby deprived, if I may venture to say so, of the services of a distinguished statesman and a most gallant soldier. Few men have ever possessed to the same extent the power which he enjoyed of winning the hearts of all those with whom he came in contact, and thus ensuring the warmest and most zealous devotion for himself and for the Government which he served. The successful defence of the position has been, under Providence, solely attributable to the foresight which he evinced in the timely commencement of the necessary operations, and the great skill and untiring personal activity which he exhibited in carrying them into effect. All ranks possessed such confidence in his judgment and his fertility of resource, that the news of his fall was received throughout the garrison with feelings of consternation, only second to the grief which was inspired in the hearts of all by the loss of a public benefactor and a warm personal friend. Feeling as keenly and as gratefully as I do the obligations that the whole of us are under to this great and good man, I trust the Government of India will pardon me for having attempted, however imperfectly, to portray them. In him every good and deserving soldier lost a friend and a chief capable of discriminating, and ever on the alert to reward merit, no matter how humble the sphere in which it was exhibited.

The garrison had scarcely recovered the shock which it had sustained in the loss of its revered and beloved General, when it had to mourn the death of that able and respected officer, Major Banks, the officiating chief commissioner, who received a bullet through his head while examining a critical outpost on the 21st July, and died without a groan.

The description of our position, and the state of our defences when the siege began, are so fully set forth in the accompanying memorandum,* furnished by the garrison engineer, that I shall content myself with bringing to the notice of his Lordship in Council, the fact that when the blockade was commenced only two of our batteries were completed, part of the defences were yet in an unfinished condition, and the buildings in the immediate vicinity, which gave cover to the enemy, were only very partially cleared away. Indeed, our heaviest losses have been caused by the fire from the enemy's sharpshooters stationed in the adjoining mosques and houses of the native nobility, the necessity of destroying which had been repeatedly drawn to the attention of Sir Henry by the Staff of Engineers. But his invariable reply was— " Spare the holy places, and private property too, as far as possible ;" and we have consequently suffered severely from our very tenderness to the religious prejudices, and respect to the right of our rebellious citizens and soldiery. As soon as the enemy had thoroughly completed the investment of the Residency, they occupied these houses, some of which were within easy pistol-shot of our barricades, in immense force,

---

* Not received by Government.

and rapidly made loopholes on those sides which bore on our post, from which they kept up a terrific and incessant fire day and night, which caused many daily casualties, as there could not have been less than 8,000 men firing at one time into our position. Moreover, there was no place in the whole of our works that could be considered safe, for several of the sick and wounded who were lying in the Banqueting-hall, which had been turned into an hospital, were killed in the very centre of the building, and the widow of Lieutenant Dorin, and other women and children, were shot dead in rooms into which it had not been previously deemed possible that a bullet could penetrate. Neither were the enemy idle in erecting batteries. They soon had from 20 to 25 guns in position, some of them of very large calibre. These were planted all round our post at small distances, some being actually within fifty yards of our defences, but in places where our own heavy guns could not reply to them, while the perseverance and ingenuity of the enemy in erecting barricades in front of and around their guns in a very short time, rendered all attempts to silence them by musketry entirely unavailing. Neither could they be effectually silenced by shells, by reason of their extreme proximity to our position; and because, moreover, the enemy had recourse to digging very narrow trenches about eight feet in depth in rear of each gun, in which the men lay while our shells were flying, and which so effectually concealed them, even while working the gun, that our baffled sharpshooters could only see their hands while in the act of loading.

The enemy contented themselves with keeping up this incessant fire of cannon and musketry until the 20th July, on which day, at ten A.M., they assembled in very great force all around our position, and exploded a heavy mine inside our outer line of defences at the Water-gate. The mine, however, which was close to the Redan, and apparently sprung with the intention of destroying that battery, did no harm. But as soon as the smoke had cleared away the enemy boldly advanced under cover of a tremendous fire of cannon and musketry, with the object of storming the Redan. But they were received with such a heavy fire that, after a short struggle, they fell back with much loss. A strong column advanced at the same time to attack Innes' post, and came on to within ten yards of the palisades, affording to Lieutenant Loughnan, 13th N. I., who commanded the position, and his brave garrison, composed of gentlemen of the Uncovenanted Service, a few of her Majesty's 32nd Foot and of the 13th N. I., an opportunity of distinguishing themselves, which they were not slow to avail themselves of, and the enemy were driven back with great slaughter. The insurgents made minor attacks at almost every outpost, but were invariably defeated, and at two P.M. they ceased their attempts to storm the place, although their musketry, fire, and cannonading continued to harass us unceasingly as usual. Matters proceeded in this manner until the 10th August, when the enemy made another assault, having previously sprung a mine close to the Brigade-mess, which entirely destroyed our defences for the space of twenty feet, and blew in a great portion of the outside wall of the house occupied by Mr. Schilling's garrison. On the dust clearing away a breach appeared, through which a regiment could have advanced in perfect order, and a few of the enemy came on with the utmost determination, but were met with such a withering flank fire of musketry from the officers and men holding the top of the Brigade-mess, that they beat a speedy retreat, leaving the more adventurous of their numbers lying on the crest of the breach. While this operation was going on another large body advanced on the Cawnpore Battery, and succeeded in locating themselves for a few minutes in the ditch. They were, however, dislodged by hand grenades. At Captain Anderson's post they also came boldly forward with scaling ladders, which they planted against the wall ; but here, as elsewhere, they were met with the most indomitable resolution, and the leaders being slain, the rest fled, leaving the ladders, and retreated to their batteries and loopholed defences, from whence they kept up, for the rest of the day, an unusually heavy cannonade and musketry fire. On the 18th August, the enemy sprung another mine in front of the Sikh lines with very fatal effect. Captain Orr (unattached), Lieutenants Mecham and Soppitt, who commanded the small body of drummers composing the garrison, were blown into the air ; but providentially returned to earth with no further injury than a severe shaking. The garrison, however, were not so fortunate. No less than eleven men were buried alive under the ruins, from whence it was impossible to extricate them, owing to the tremendous fire kept up by the enemy from houses situated not ten yards in front of the breach. The explosion was followed by a general assault of a less determined nature than the two former efforts, and the enemy were consequently repulsed without much difficulty. But they succeeded, under cover of the breach, in establishing themselves in one of the houses in our position, from which they were driven in the evening by the bayonets of her Majesty's 32nd and 84th Foot. On the 5th September, the enemy made their last serious assault. Having exploded a large mine, a few feet short of the bastion of the 18-pounder gun, in Major Apthorp's post, they advanced with large heavy scaling ladders, which they planted against the wall, and mounted, thereby gaining for an instant the embrasure of a gun. They were, however, speedily driven back with loss by hand-grenades and musketry. A few minutes subsequently they sprang another mine close to the Brigade-mess, and advanced boldly ; but soon the corpses strewed in the garden in front of the post bore testimony to the fatal accuracy of the rifle and musketry fire of the gallant members of that garrison, and the enemy fled ignominiously, leaving their leader—a fine-looking native officer—among the slain. At other posts they made similar attacks, but with less resolution, and everywhere with the same want of success. Their loss upon this day must have been very heavy, as they came on with much determination, and at night they were seen bearing large numbers of their killed and wounded over the bridges in the direction of cantonments. The above is a faint attempt at a description of the four great struggles which have occurred during this protracted season of exertion, exposure, and suffering. His Lordship in Council will perceive that the enemy invariably commenced his attacks by the explosion of a mine, a species of offensive warfare, for the exercise of which our position was unfortunately peculiarly situated, and had it not been for the most untiring vigilance on our part, in watching and blowing up their mines before they were completed, the assaults would probably have been much more numerous, and might, perhaps, have ended in the capture of the place. But by countermining in all directions, we succeeded in detecting and destroying no less than four of the enemy's subterraneous advances towards important positions, two of which operations were eminently successful, as on one occasion not less than eighty of them were blown into the air, and twenty suffered a similar fate on the second explosion. The labour, however, which devolved upon us in making these counter-mines, in the absence of a body of skilled miners, was very heavy. The Right Honourable the Governor-General in Council will feel that it would be impossible to crowd, within the limits of a despatch, even the principal events, much more the individual acts of gallantry which have marked this protracted struggle. But I can conscientiously declare my conviction, that few troops have ever undergone greater hardships, exposed as they have been to a never-ceasing musketry fire and cannonade. They have also experienced the alternate vicissitudes of extreme wet and of intense heat, and that, too, with very insufficient shelter from either, and in many places without any shelter at all. In addition to having had to repel real attacks, they have been exposed night and day to the hardly less harassing false alarms which the enemy have been constantly raising. The insurgents have frequently fired very heavily, sounded the advance, and shouted for several hours together, though not a man could be seen, with the view, of course, of harassing our small and exhausted force, in which object they succeeded, for no part has been strong enough to allow of a portion only of the garrison being prepared in the event of a false attack being turned into a real one. All, therefore, had to stand to their arms, and to remain at their posts until the demonstration had ceased; and such attacks were of almost nightly occurrence. The whole of the officers and men have been on duty night and day, during the eighty-seven days which the siege had lasted up to the arrival of Sir J. Outram, G.C.B. In addition to this incessant military duty, the force has been nightly employed in repairing defences, in moving guns, in burying dead animals, in conveying ammunition and commissariat stores from one place to another, and in other fatiguing duties too numerous and too trivial to enumerate here. I feel, however, that any words of mine will fail to convey any adequate idea of what our fatigue and labours have been—labours in which all ranks and all classes, civilians, officers, and soldiers have all borne an equally noble part. All have together descended into the mine, all have together handled the shovel for the interment of the putrid bullock, and all, accoutred with musket and bayonet, have relieved each other on sentry, without regard to the distinctions of rank, civil or military. Notwithstanding all these hardships, the garrison had made no less than five sorties, in which they spiked two of the enemy's heaviest guns, and blew up several of the houses from which they had kept up their most harassing fire. Owing to the extreme paucity of our numbers, each man was taught to feel, that on his own individual efforts alone, depended, in no small measure, the safety of the entire position. This consciousness incited every officer, soldier, and man, to defend the post assigned to him with such desperate tenacity, and to fight for the lives which Providence had entrusted to his care with such dauntless determination, that the enemy, despite their constant attacks, their heavy mines, their overwhelming numbers, and their incessant fire, could never succeed in gaining one single inch of ground within the bounds of this straggling position, which was so feebly fortified, that had they once obtained a footing in any of the outposts, the whole place must inevitably have fallen.

If further proof be wanting of the desperate nature of the struggle which we have, under God's blessing, so long and so successfully waged, I would point to the roofless and ruined houses, to the crumbled walls, to the exploded mines, to the open breaches, to the shattered and disabled guns and defences, and, lastly, to the long and melancholy list of the brave and devoted officers and men who have fallen. These silent witnesses bear sad and solemn testimony to the way in which this feeble position has been defended. During the early part of these vicissitudes, we were left without any information whatever regarding the posture of affairs outside. An occasional spy did indeed come in with the object of inducing our sepoys and servants to desert; but the intelligence derived from such sources was, of course, entirely untrustworthy. We sent our messengers, daily calling for aid and asking for information, none of whom ever returned until the twenty-sixth day of the siege, when a pensioner named Ungad came back with a letter from General Havelock's camp, informing us that they were advancing with a force sufficient to bear down all opposition, and would be with us in five or six days. A messenger was immediately despatched, requesting that on the evening of their arrival on the outskirts of the city, two rockets might be sent up, in order that we might take the necessary measures or assisting them while forcing their way in. The sixth day, however, expired, and they came not; but for many evenings after, officers and men watched for the ascension of the expected rockets, with hopes such as make the heart sick. We knew not then, nor did we learn until the 29th August—or thirty-five days later—that the relieving force, after having fought most nobly to effect our deliverance, had been obliged to fall back for reinforcements, and this was the last communication we received until two days before the arrival of Sir James Outram on the 25th September.

Besides heavy visitations of cholera and small-pox, we have also had to contend against a sickness which has almost universally pervaded the garrison. Commencing with a very painful eruption it has merged into a low fever, combined with diarrhœa; and although few or no men have actually died from its effects, it leaves behind a weakness and lassitude which, in the absence of all material sustenance, save coarse beef and still coarser flour, none have been able entirely to get over. The mortality among the women and children, and especially among the latter, from these diseases and from other causes, has been perhaps the most painful characteristic of the siege. The want of native servants has also been a source of much privation. Owing to the suddenness with which we were besieged, many of these people who might perhaps have otherwise proved faithful to their employers, but who were outside the defences at the time, were altogether excluded. Very many more deserted, and several families were consequently left without the services of a single domestic. Several ladies have had to tend their children, and even to wash their own clothes, as well as to cook their scanty meals entirely unaided. Combined with the absence of servants, the want of proper accommodation has probably been the cause of much of the disease with which we have been afflicted. I cannot refrain from bringing to the prominent notice of his Lordship in Council, the patient endurance and the Christian resignation which have been evinced by the women of this garrison. They have animated us by their example. Many, alas! have been made widows, and their children fatherless in this cruel struggle. But all such seem resigned to the will of Providence, and many, among whom may be mentioned the honoured names of Birch, of Polehampton, of Barbor, and of Gall, have, after the example of Miss Nightingale, constituted themselves the tender and solicitous nurses of the wounded and dying soldiers in the hospital.

It only remains for me to bring to the favourable notice of his Lordship in Council the names of those officers who have most distinguished themselves, and afforded me the most valuable assistance in these operations. Many of the best and bravest of these now rest from their labours. Among them are Lieut.-Colonel Case and Captain Radcliffe, whose services have already been narrated; Captain Francis, 13th N. I. —who was killed by a round shot—had particularly attracted the attention of Sir H. Lawrence for his conduct while in command of the Muchhee Bhowun; Captain Fulton, of the Engineers, who was also struck by a round shot, had, up to the time of his early and lamented death, afforded me the most invaluable aid; he was indeed indefatigable; Major Anderson, the chief engineer, though from the commencement of the siege incapable of physical exertion from the effects of the disease under which he eventually sank, merited my warm acknowledgments for his able counsel; Captain Simons, commandant of Artillery, distinguished himself at Chinhut, where he received the two wounds which ended in his death; Lieutenants Shepherd and Arthur, 7th Light Cavalry, who were killed at their posts; Captain Hughes, 57th N. I., who was mortally wounded at the capture of a house which formed one of the enemy's outposts; Captain McCabe, of the 32nd Foot, who was killed at the head of his men while leading his fourth sortie, as well as Captain Mansfield, of the' same corps, who died of cholera—were all officers who had distinguished themselves highly. Mr. Lucas, too, a gentleman volunteer, and Mr. Bryson, of the Uncovenanted Service—who fell when on the look-out at one of the most perilous outposts—had earned themselves reputations for coolness and gallantry.

The officers who commanded outposts—Lieutenant-Colonel Master, 7th Light Cavalry; Major Apthorp, 41st N. I.; Captain Sanders, 41st N. I.; Captain Boileau, 7th Light Cavalry; Captain Germon, 13th N. I.; Lieutenant Aitken and Lieutenant Loughnan, of the same corps; Captain Anderson, 25th N. I.; Lieutenant Graydon, 44th N. I.; Lieutenant Langmore, 71st N. I.; and Mr. Schilling, Principal of the Martinière College, have all conducted ably the duties of their onerous position. No further proof of this is necessary than the fact which I have before mentioned, that throughout the whole duration of the siege the enemy were not only unable to take, but they could not even succeed in gaining one inch of the posts commanded by these gallant gentlemen. Colonel Master commanded the critical and important post of the brigade mess, on either side of which was an open breach, only flanked by his handful of riflemen and musketeers. Lieutenant Aitken, with the whole of the 13th N. I., which remained to us with the exception of their Sikhs, commanded the Bayley Guard—perhaps the most important position in the whole of the defences ; and Lieutenant Langmore, with the remnant of his regiment (the 71st), held a very exposed position between the Hospital and the Water Gate. This gallant and deserving young soldier and his men were entirely without shelter from the weather, both by night and by day.

My thanks are also due to Lieutenants Anderson, Hutchinson, and Innes, of the Engineers, as well as to Lieutenant Tulloch, 58th N. I., and Lieutenant Hay, 48th N. I., who were placed under them to aid in the arduous duties, devolving upon that department. Lieutenant Thomas, Madras Artillery, who commanded that arm of the service for some weeks, and Lieutenants Macfarlane and Bonham rendered me the most effectual assistance ; I was, however, deprived of the services of the two latter who were wounded, Lieutenant Bonham no less than three times, early in the siege. Captain Evans, 17th B. N. I., who, owing to the scarcity of Artillery officers, was put in charge of some guns, was ever to be found at his post.

Major Lowe, commanding her Majesty's 32nd Regiment ; Captain Bassano, Lieutenants Lawrence, Edmonstone, Foster, Harmer, Cooke, Clery, Browne, and Charlton, of that corps, all have nobly performed their duty. Every one of these officers, with the exception of Lieutenants Lawrence and Clery, have received one or more wounds of more or less severity. Quartermaster Stribbling, of the same corps, also conducted himself to my satisfaction.

Captain O'Brien, her Majesty's 84th Foot; Captain Kemble, 41st N. I.; Captain Edgell, 53rd N. I.; Captain Dinning, Lieutenant Sewell, and Lieutenant Worsley, of the 71st N. I.; Lieutenant Warner, 7th Light Cavalry; Ensign Ward, 48th N. I. (who, when most of our Artillery officers were killed or disabled, worked the mortars with excellent effect); Lieutenant Graham, 11th N. I. ; Lieutenant Mecham, 4th Oude Locals; and Lieutenant Keir, 41st N. I., have all done good and willing service throughout the siege, and I trust that they will receive the favourable notice of his Lordship in Council.

I beg particularly to call the attention of the Government of India to the untiring industry, the extreme devotion, and the great skill which have been evinced by Surgeon Scott (Superintending Surgeon), and Assistant-Surgeon Boyd, of her Majesty's 32nd Foot ; Assistant-Surgeon Bird, of the Artillery; Surgeon Campbell, 7th Light Cavalry; Surgeon Brydon, 71st N. I.; Surgeon Ogilvie, sanitary commissioner ; Assistant-Surgeon Fayrer, civil surgeon; Assistant-Surgeon Partridge, 2nd Oude Irregular Cavalry ; Assistant-Surgeon Greenhow ; Assistant-Surgeon Darby, and Mr. Apothecary Thompson, in the discharge of their onerous and most important duties.

Messrs. Thornhill and Capper, of the Civil Service, have been both wounded, and the way in which they, as well as Mr. Martin, the deputy-commissioner of Lucknow, conducted themselves, entitles them to a place in this despatch. Captain Carnegie, the special assistant-commissioner, whose invaluable services previous to the commencement of the siege I have frequently heard warmly dilated upon, both by Sir H. Lawrence and by Major Banks, and whose exertions will probably be more amply brought to notice by the civil authorities on some future occasion, has conducted the office of provost-marshal to my satisfaction. The Reverend Mr. Harris and the Reverend Mr. Polehampton, assistant-chaplains, vied with each other in their untiring care and attention to the suffering men. The latter gentleman was wounded in the hospital, and subsequently unhappily died of cholera. Mr. McCrae, of the Civil Engineers, did excellent service at the guns, until he was severely wounded. Mr. Cameron, also, a gentleman who had come to Oude to inquire into the resources of the country, acquired the whole mystery of mortar practice, and was of the most signal service, until incapacitated by sickness. Mr. Marshall, of the road department, and other members of the Uncovenanted Service, whose names will, on a subsequent occasion, be laid before the Government of India, conducted themselves bravely and steadily. Indeed, the entire body of these gentlemen have borne themselves well, and have evinced great coolness under fire.

I have now only to bring to the notice of the Right Honourable the Governor-General in Council the conduct of the several officers who composed my Staff :—Lieutenant James, sub-assistant Commissary-General, was severely wounded by a shot through the knee at Chinhut, notwithstanding which he refused to go upon the sick list, and carried on his most trying duties throughout the entire siege. It is not too much to say that the garrison owe their lives to the exertions and firmness of this officer. Before the struggle commenced, he was ever in the saddle, getting in supplies, and his untiring vigilance in their distribution after our difficulties had begun, prevented a waste which otherwise, long before the expiration of the eighty-seven days, might have annihilated the force by the slow process of starvation.

Captain Wilson, 13th N. I., officiating deputy-assistant adjutant-general, was ever to be found where shot was flying thickest, and I am at a loss to decide whether his services were most invaluable owing to the untiring physical endurance and bravery which he displayed, or to his ever-ready and pertinent counsel and advice in moments of difficulty and danger.

Lieutenant Hardinge — an officer whose achievements and antecedents are well known to the Government of India—has earned fresh laurels by his conduct throughout the siege. He was officiating as deputy-assistant quartermaster-general, and also commanded the Sikh portion of the cavalry of the garrison. In both capacities his services have been invaluable, especially in the latter, for it was owing alone to his tact, vigilance, and bravery, that the Sikh horsemen were induced to persevere in holding a very unprotected post under a heavy fire.

Lieutenant Barwell, 71st N. I., the fort-adjutant and officiating major of brigade, has proved himself to be an efficient officer.

Lieutenant Birch, of the 71st N. I., has been my aide-de-camp throughout the siege. I firmly believe there never was a better aide-de-camp. He has been indefatigable, and ever ready to lead a sortie, or to convey an order to a threatened outpost under the heaviest fire. On one of these occasions, he received a slight wound on the head. I beg to bring the services of this most promising and intelligent young officer to the favourable consideration of his Lordship in Council.

I am also much indebted to Mr. Couper, C.S., for the assistance he has on many occasions afforded me by his judicious advice. I have, moreover, ever found him most ready and willing in the performance of the military duties assigned to him, however exposed the post or arduous the undertaking. He commenced his career in her Majesty's service, and consequently had had some previous experience of military matters. If the road to Cawnpore had been made clear by the advent of our troops, it was my intention to have deputed this officer to Calcutta to detail in person the occurrences which have taken place, for the information of the Government of India. I still hope that when our communications shall be once more unopposed, he may be summoned to Calcutta for this purpose.

Lastly, I have the pleasure of bringing the splendid behaviour of the soldiers, viz., the men of H. M.'s 32nd Foot, the small detachment of H. M.'s 84th Foot, the European and Native Artillery, the 13th, 48th, and 71st Regiments N. I., and the Sikhs of the respective corps, to the notice of the Government of India. The losses sustained by H. M.'s 32nd, which is now barely 300 strong; by H. M.'s 84th, and by the European Artillery, show at least that they knew how to die in the cause of their countrymen. Their conduct under the fire, the exposure, and the privations which they have had to undergo, has been throughout most admirable and praiseworthy.

As another instance of the desperate character of our defence, and the difficulties we have had to contend with, I may mention that the number of our artillerymen was so reduced, that on the occasion of an attack, the gunners, aided as they were by men of H. M.'s 32nd Foot, and by volunteers of all classes, had to run from one battery to another wherever the fire of the enemy was hottest, there not being nearly enough men to serve half the number of guns at the same time. In short, at last, the number of European gunners was only twenty-four, while we had, including mortars, no less than thirty guns in position.

With respect to the native troops, I am of opinion that their loyalty has never been surpassed. They were indifferently fed, and worse housed. They were exposed—especially the 13th Regiment—under the gallant Lieutenant Aitken, to a most galling fire of round shot and musketry, which materially decreased their numbers. They were so near the enemy, that conversation could be carried on between them; and every effort, persuasion, promise, and threat, was alternately resorted to in vain, to seduce them from their allegiance to the handful of Europeans, who, in all probability, would have been sacrificed by their desertion. All the troops behaved nobly, and the names of those men of the native force who have particularly distinguished themselves have been laid before Major-General Sir James Outram, G.C.B., who has promised to promote them. Those of the European force will be transmitted in due course for the orders of his Royal Highness the General Commanding-in-Chief.

In conclusion, I beg leave to express, on the part of myself and the members of this garrison, our deep and grateful sense of the conduct of Major-General Sir J. Outram, G.C.B.; of Brigadier-General Havelock, C.B.; and of the troops under those officers, who so devotedly came to our relief at so heavy a sacrifice of life. We are also repaid for much suffering and privation by the sympathy which our brave deliverers say our perilous and unfortunate position has excited for us in the hearts of our countrymen throughout the length and breadth of her Majesty's dominions. I have, &c.,

J. INGLIS, *Colonel, H.M.'s 32nd Brigade.*

MAJOR-GENERAL OUTRAM, COMMANDING CAWNPORE AND DINAPORE DIVISIONS, TO MAJOR-GENERAL MANSFIELD, CHIEF OF THE STAFF.

Camp Alumbagh, 25th Nov., 1857.

SIR.—I have the honour to acquaint his Excellency the Commander-in-Chief with the proceedings of this Force since the 30th of September, the date of my last despatch.

General Havelock has commanded the Field Force occupying the palaces and outposts, and Brigadier Inglis has continued in command of the Lucknow garrison: an arrangement that has proved most convenient.

The first work required was to open a roadway through the palaces for the heavy train, which had been brought into one of the gardens on the 27th September, and by the 1st October was safely parked within the entrenchment.

Contrary to the expectations expressed in my last despatch, the enemy, relying on the strong position of their remaining battery, (the one known as "Phillips' Battery,") continued to annoy the garrison by its fire, and to maintain there a strong force. Its capture, therefore, became necessary, and this was effected on the 2nd October, with the comparatively trifling loss of two killed and eleven wounded; a result which was due to the careful and scientific dispositions of Colonel Napier, under whose personal guidance the operation was conducted. Three guns were taken and burst; their carriages destroyed; and a large house in the garden, which had been the enemy's stronghold, was blown up.

With a view to the possibility of adopting the Cawnpore road as my line of communication with Alumbagh, Major Haliburton, 78th Highlanders, commenced on the 3rd to work from house to house with the crow-bar and pick-axe.

On the 4th, this gallant officer was mortally wounded; and his successor, Major Stephenson, of the Madras Fusiliers, disabled. During the whole of the 5th, these proceedings were continued; but on the 6th they were relinquished, it being found that a large mosque, strongly occupied by the enemy, required more extensive operations for its capture than were expedient; therefore, after blowing up all the principal houses on the Cawnpore road, from which the garrison had been annoyed by musketry, the reconnoitring party gradually withdrew to the post in front of Phillip's Garden, which has since been retained as a permanent outpost, affording comfortable accommodation to H. M.'s 78th Highlanders, and protecting a considerable portion of the entrenchment from molestation, besides connecting it with the palaces occupied by General Havelock. During the foregoing operations, the enemy, recovering from their first surprise, commenced to threaten our position in the palaces and outposts by mining and assaults. As there were only a few miners in the garrison, and none with the field force, the enemy could not be prevented from exploding three mines, causing us a loss of several men; and, on the 6th, they actually penetrated into the palaces in considerable numbers.

But they paid dearly for their temerity, being intercepted and slain at all points. Their loss on that day was reported in the city to have been 450 men.

A company of Miners, formed of volunteers from the several corps, was placed at the disposal of the chief engineer, which soon gave him the ascendancy over the enemy, who were foiled at all points, with the loss of their galleries and mines, and the destruction of their miners in repeated instances.

The Sikhs of the Ferozepore regiment have zealously laboured at their own mines, and though separated only by a narrow passage (16 feet wide) from the enemy, have, under the guidance and direction of the Engineer department, defended and protected their position.

The outpost of her Majesty's 78th Highlanders, under Captain Lockhart, has also been vigorously assailed by the enemy's miners. Its proximity to the entrenchment made it convenient to place it under the charge of the officiating garrison engineer, Lieutenant Hutchinson, under whose skilful directions the enemy have been completely out-mined by the soldiers of her Majesty's 78th Regiment.

I am aware of no parallel to our series of mines in modern war : twenty-one shafts, aggregating 200 feet in depth, and 3,291 feet of gallery have been executed. The enemy advanced twenty mines against the palaces and outposts ; of these they exploded three, which caused us loss of life, and two which did no injury ; seven have been blown in ; and out of seven others the enemy have been driven, and their galleries taken possession of by our miners—results of which the Engineer department may well be proud. The reports and plans forwarded by Sir Henry Havelock, K.C.B., and now submitted to his Excellency, will explain how a line of gardens, courts, and dwelling-houses, without fortified *enceinte*, without flanking defences, and closely connected with the buildings of a city, has been maintained for eight weeks in a certain degree of security; but notwithstanding the close and constant musketry fire from loopholed walls and windows, often within thirty yards, and from every lofty building within rifle range, and notwithstanding a frequent though desultory fire of round shot and grape from guns posted at various distances, from 70 to 500 yards! This result has been obtained by the skill and courage of the Engineer and Quartermaster-General's departments, zealously aided by the brave officers and soldiers, who have displayed the same cool determination and cheerful alacrity in the toils of the trench, and amidst the concealed dangers of the mine, that they had previously exhibited when forcing their way into Lucknow at the point of the bayonet, and amidst a most murderous fire.

But skilful and courageous as have been the engineering operations, and glorious the behaviour of the troops, their success has been in no small degree promoted by the incessant and self-denying devotion of Colonel Napier—who has never been many hours absent by day or night from any one of the points of operation—whose valuable advice has ever been readily tendered and gratefully accepted by the executive officers—whose earnestness and kindly cordiality have stimulated and encouraged all ranks and grades, amidst their harassing difficulties and dangerous labours.

I now lay before his Excellency, Brigadier Inglis' report of the proceedings in the garrison, since its relief by the force under my command, since the capture of the enemy's batteries, and the occupation of the palaces nd posts.

The position occupied by the Oude Field Force relieved the garrison of the entrenchment from all molestation on one-half of its *enceinte*—that is, from the Cawnpore road to the commencement of the river front; and the garrison, reinforced by detachments of the 78th and Madras Fusiliers, was enabled to hold as outposts three strong positions commanding the road leading to the Iron Bridge, which have proved of great advantage, causing much annoyance to the enemy, and keeping their musketry fire at a distance from the body of the place.

The defences, which had been barely tenable, were thoroughly repaired, and new batteries were constructed to mount thirteen additional guns.

The enemy, after the capture of the batteries, adopted a new system of tactics. Their guns were withdrawn to a greater distance, and disposed so as to act, not against the defences, but against the interior of the entrenchment.

The moment they were searched out and silenced by our guns, their position was changed, so that their shot ranged through the entrenchment; and but for the desultory nature of their fire, might have been very destructive.

Under the care of the Superintending Surgeon, Dr Scott, the hospital was securely barricaded without detriment to ventilation.

From the Rev. J. P. Harris, chaplain of the garrison, the sick and wounded received the most marked and personal kindness. His spiritual ministrations in the hospital were incessant; his Christian zeal and earnest philanthropy I have had constant opportunity of observing since my arrival in Lucknow; and but one testimony is born to his exertions during the siege and to the personal bravery he displayed in hastening from house to house in pursuit of his sacred calling, under the heaviest fire. Daily he had to read the funeral service over numbers of the garrison, while exposed to shot, shell, and musketry.

Order was established in the magazine under Captain Thomas, the garrison-commandant of artillery and commissary of ordnance; and under Dr. Ogilvie, sanitary commissioner, the Conservancy department effected great and visible improvements in the condition of the entrenchments, beside removing the horrible collection of filth and putrid carcasses which had accumulated in the palaces taken possession of by the relieving force.

I cannot conclude this report without expressing to His Excellency my intense admiration of the noble spirit displayed by all ranks and grades of the force since we entered Lucknow. Themselves placed in a state of siege,—suddenly reduced to scanty and unsavoury rations,—denied all the little luxuries (such as tea, sugar, rum, and tobacco,) which by constant use had become to them almost necessaries of life,—smitten, in many cases by the same scorbutic affections and other evidences of debility, which prevailed amongst the original garrison,—compelled to engage in laborious operations,—exposed to constant danger, and kept ever on the alert,—their spirits and cheerfulness, and zeal and discipline, seemed to rise with the occasion. Never could there have been a force more free from grumblers, more cheerful, more willing, or more earnest.

Amongst the sick and wounded, this glorious spirit was, if possible, still more conspicuous than amongst those fit for duty.

It was a painful sight to see so many noble fellows maimed and suffering, and denied those comforts of which they stood so much in need.

But it was truly delightful, and made one proud of his countrymen, to observe the heroic fortitude and hearty cheerfulness with which all was borne.

My cordial acknowledgments are due to Brigadiers Hamilton and Stisted, and to their Brigade Staff— Captains Spurgin and Bouverie — for the efficient disposition of their troops under General Havelock's orders and direction, and the vigilance with which they have guarded their extended position.

The glorious reputation which his defence of Lucknow has won for Brigadier Inglis, leaves little room for further commendation of the able manner in which that defence has been continued, — the vigour with which the defences of his garrison have been improved and extended—and the unceasing vigilance which rendered every effort of the enemy to assail him utterly hopeless. I cordially concur in, and second his recommendation to the favourable notice of his Excellency the Commander-in-Chief, of the several officers named in his despatch.

To the gallant Brigadier Eyre, commanding the Artillery, whose victories at Arrah and Jugdespore have already given him a European reputation; to the brave Captains, Olpherts, of the Bengal Artillery, and Maude, of the Royal Artillery, commanding batteries; to Lieutenant Thomas, commissary of ordnance; and to the officers and men of the combined force of Artillery, my hearty and sincere thanks are due. The duties which have fallen on them have been most arduous, and have been carried through with the zeal and gallantry which have ever distinguished their noble arm of the service.

Captain Crommelin, commanding the Engineer Department, has had to undertake very important duties of a novel and difficult nature, without trained Sappers and without any establishment of trained subordinates, and with a very small staff. Under these disadvantages, combined with the very serious one of ill health, Captain Crommelin, aided by the executive department, converted the open arcaded halls of the palace into secure barracks, and has kept aloof the enemy's miners.

To Captain Crommelin, to his gallant and energetic second in command, Lieutenant Hutchinson, to Lieutenants Russell and Limmond, and the officers and men recommended by Captain Crommelin, I am very greatly indebted.

I have particularly to recommend to his Excellency's notice Lieutenant-Colonel Purnell, commanding her Majesty's 90th Light Infantry, who throughout these operations has had charge of the advanced garden and its dependent posts, which have been exposed to the unceasing attack of the enemy. For the very able manner in which these posts have been held, Colonel Purnell deserves the highest praise.

Captain Brasyer, commanding the Regiment of Ferozepore, and Captain Lockhart, commanding her Majesty's 78th Highlanders, have each maintained a difficult position with the most perfect success. These officers, to whom I must also add Captain Shute, commanding detachment of her Majesty's 64th Regiment, have gallantly led their men in every sortie.

To Captain Willis, commanding H. M.'s 84th Regiment; Captain Galwey, commanding Madras Fusiliers; and Lieutenant Meara, commanding H. M.'s 5th Regiment (Fusiliers), I must tender my acknowledgments. Captain Barrow, commanding Volunteer Cavalry, Captains Johnson and Hardinge, commanding Irregular Cavalry, though precluded from acting in their proper capacity, have zealously volunteered for every service in which they or their men could be useful, and have maintained posts, or furnished working parties, with cheerful alacrity.

To Captain Garden, Assistant Quartermaster-General; to Captain Hardinge, Officiating Deputy

Quartermaster-General; Captain Moorsom, Deputy Assistant Quartermaster-General, my thanks are particularly due; and also to Captains Alexander, Orr, and Carnegy, for their services at the head of the Intelligence Department;—notwithstanding the complete hostility of the country, many trustworthy messengers have been furnished, by whom communications have been safely carried to Alumbagh and Cawnpore. Captain Moorsom, of H. M.'s 52nd Regiment, having surveyed the city and environs of Lucknow previous to the outbreak of hostilities, has constantly been able to render most important service, and is a very bold and intelligent officer.

The Commissariat arrangements have been most efficiently conducted under Captain Macbean, attached to the Oude Field Force, and Lieutenant James, attached to the garrison; and I have to thank them for their valuable services.

I beg to recommend to particular notice the excellent arrangements made for the care of the sick by the Medical Department, under Superintending Surgeon J. Scott, whose energy and zeal have been unremitting in the performance of his arduous duties.

I have further to recommend to his Excellency's notice Lieutenant Hudson, of her Majesty's 64th Regiment, Deputy Assistant Adjutant-General; and Lieutenant Hargood, Madras Fusiliers, Aide-de-Camp on the Staff of the late Sir H. Havelock; also the officers of my divisional and personal staff.

To Major North, General Havelock's Deputy Judge-Advocate-General, and subsequently one of the prize agents, my thanks are due for the readiness and success with which he established and superintended the manufacture of Enfield rifle cartridges.

This valuable service was rendered without any relaxation of his other duties, in the prosecution of which he met with a wound.

The pleasing duty now remains of acknowledging my obligations to my personal staff.

To Colonel Napier, Military Secretary, chief of the Adjutant-General's department, for the efficient support I have ever received from him throughout these operations, and whose gallantry in the field was as conspicuous as his able guidance of the engineering operations above detailed was valuable.

I have much pleasure in making favourable mention of the services of Captain Dodgson, Assistant Adjutant-General, who has afforded me every assistance; also Captain Gordon, Deputy Judge Advocate-General.

My aides-de-camp—Lieutenants Sitwell and Chamier—have rendered me most constant and zealous aid. I was unfortunately deprived of Lieutenant Sitwell's services on the 25th September, owing to a contusion received early in the day; and again, on returning from the garrison, from a severe wound on the 17th November. Lieutenant Chamier has attended at my side in the field throughout every operation.

My thanks are due also to my private secretary, Mr. W. J. Money, who has accompanied the army in the field, in addition to his valuable services in his civil capacity.

I have to acknowledge the services of Captain Dawson and Lieutenant Hewett, orderly officers.

I was glad to avail myself of the services of Mr. George Couper, Civil Service, who volunteered to perform the duties of an aide-de-camp during our stay in the garrison and on the night of our retiring from it.

It is with the deepest regret that I have to record at the head of the gallant and distinguished officers who have so zealously and ably aided these operations, and whose loss their country has to deplore, the name of the lamented Sir Henry Havelock, on whose merits it would be superfluous for me to dwell. Worn out by toils and exposure, he lived but long enough to witness the end for which he had fought so nobly, and to receive the valued token conveyed to him of the approbation of his Sovereign.

Colonel Campbell, of Her Majesty's 90th Light Infantry, who, in my former despatch, was returned as wounded, has since died. In him, England has lost a most gallant and distinguished officer.

By the fall of the gallant officers—Major Haliburton, Her Majesty's 78th; Major Simmons, Her Majesty's 5th Fusiliers; and Major Stephenson, of the Madras Fusiliers, the country and service have sustained a very heavy loss.

I have also, with sorrow, to record the loss of the many other valuable officers and soldiers who have fallen in the performance of their duty during the course of these operations, which have involved a total loss (subsequently to those reported in General Havelock's despatch, of the 28th October,) of 6 European officers, 1 Native officer, and 120 rank and file killed; 27 European officers, 7 Native, and 382 rank and file wounded; total 551 killed and wounded.

I have, &c.,

J. OUTRAM, *Major General,*
Comdg. Cawnpore and Dinapore Divisions.

[Sir James Outram's despatch contained a mass of enclosures referring to three entirely distinct series of operations. Some of them describe the measures adopted with a view to the extrication and recovery of the rear-guard of General Havelock's force, which had been left behind on the afternoon of September 25th, and was not finally brought within the entrenchments till the morning of the 27th. Others detail the various operations by which, under Sir James Outram's instructions, Generals Havelock and Inglis extended their lines, secured their position, relieved themselves of the inconvenient pressure of the enemy, and reorganized the Ordnance and Commissariat departments. The remainder are descriptions of the preparations made by Sir James Outram for facilitating the successful advance of the forces which he had requested might be sent to assist him in effecting the safe removal of the original Lucknow garrison, and of the various important operations by which that force (under the command of Sir Colin Campbell) was so materially aided in its advance.

As originally published in General Orders, these despatches are intermingled with little regard to chronological sequence. Their reproduction in this dislocated form would render them unintelligible to the general reader, and of little value to the historian. The editor has, therefore, assumed the responsibility of arranging them. He here subjoins those which refer to the first two of the series of operations above mentioned. Those relating to the measures by which Sir James Outram assisted Sir Colin Campbell in effecting his ever-memorable entry into Lucknow in November, 1857, will be found in their proper place. It will be observed that the dates of the enclosures to Sir James Outram's despatch of the 25th November bear, in general, little relation to the dates of the operations they describe. Under the pressure of incessant and arduous labours, performed in the presence of a vigilant enemy of overwhelming strength, few officers had time for the preparation of formal reports of past achievements. The stern duties of the present hour were all-engrossing. And many weeks elapsed ere some of the reports were received. They have, therefore, been arranged not according to the dates they bear, but as nearly as possible in the order of the operations they narrate.

The editor would earnestly recommend those of his readers who desire fully to comprehend the subjoined despatches, to combine their perusal with a careful study of the plans at the end of the volume.]

Colonel R. Napier, Military Secretary, &c., to Major-General Sir James Outram, G.C.B., Commanding the Forces.

Lucknow, 16th October, 1857.

On the 25th ultimo, Colonel Campbell reported to you, that he, with a small party of the 90th, not exceeding 100 men and almost all the wounded, the heavy guns, and a large number of ammunition waggons, were in the walled passage in front of the Mootee Mchal Palace, which position he should be obliged to hold for the night, as he was invested by the enemy, and could not advance without reinforcements.

On the morning of the 26th, a detachment of 250 men, under command of Major Simmons, 5th Fusiliers and part of the Ferozepore regiment under Captain Brasyer, were sent by your orders to reinforce Colonel Campbell, under the guidance of Captain Moorsom.

They had judiciously occupied a house and garden between Colonel Campbell's position and the palace; but as they were unable to move from their position, I received your orders to proceed to their assistance, with a further reinforcement of 100 men of Her Majesty's 78th Highlanders, under Colonel Stisted, two guns of Captain Olpherts' battery, and Captain Hardinge's Sowars.

Captain Olpherts strongly objected to his guns being taken, and on considering the reason that he offered, I took it upon myself to dispense with them, merely taking spare bullocks. Captain Olpherts accompanied me as a volunteer. As I had reason to believe that I could open a communication through the palace, which would bring me near the position of the guns, I took Mr. Cavanagh, an intelligent civilian acquainted with the locality, examined the palace as far as was practicable, and obtained sufficient knowledge of it to form my plan of operations.

I then led the party by one of the side outlets of the palace along the river bank to Major Simmons' position, under a smart fire from the enemy, from which, however, we received little damage.

Under cover of the night, all the sick and wounded were quietly and safely transported along the river bank to the entrenchment, by a path practicable for camels and doolies, but quite impracticable for guns. Captain Hardinge made several journeys to bring up fresh doolies, until every sick and wounded man was removed. He also took away the camels laden with Enfield ammunition. One of our 24-pounders, which had been used on the previous day against the enemy, but the working of which had ceased, owing to the musketry fire poured upon it, was left in an exposed position; but it was extricated in a very daring and dexterous manner by Captain Olpherts, aided by Captain Crump. (killed), and Private Duffy, of the Madras Fusiliers.

At 3 A.M., the whole force proceeded undiscovered through the enemy's posts, until the leading division had reached the palace; and the heavy guns and waggons were safely parked in the garden which I had reconnoitred on the preceding day. The enemy were aroused too late to prevent the operation; but made an attack on the rear-guard, which was ineffective.

I remained with Colonel Purnell to secure the position thus gained with trifling loss. A large body of sepoys was discovered in a walled garden connected with that which contained our heavy guns, by men of H. M.'s 90th, 5th Fusiliers, and 32nd, who gallantly charged in, led by Colonel Purnell, 90th, and Captain McCabe, 32nd, and almost annihilated the sepoys, securing the garden itself as the rear of our position Measures were immediately taken to open a road for the guns through the palace, and by the 1st instant, every gun and waggon was safely lodged in the entrenchment.

It now remains for me to bring to your favourable notice the officers commanding corps and detachments—Colonel Stisted, 78th; Captain Brasyer' Sikhs; Captain Lowe, 32nd. The late lamented Major Simmons gave me very valuable aid.

To Colonel Purnell's lot fell the more difficult duty of commanding the rear-guard and of securing the position when gained. In the whole of the operations his assistance and support were of the greatest value.

Lieutenant Fraser, of the Artillery, was left, on the 26th, by the fall of Brigadier Cooper, in charge of the heavy guns, and though wounded, his exertions assisted greatly in extricating the unwieldy train.

I must beg most particularly to bring to your notice Captain Olpherts, of the Bengal Artillery. Without his unfailing determination, skill, and fertility of resource, we should never have been able to withdraw the 24-pounder, but at the cost of a very heavy loss of life. From first to last his assistance has been invaluable, and cannot be too highly praised.

To Captain Hardinge's continued exertions is due the safe removal of the wounded and camels, with rifle ammunition.

My Assistant-Adjutant-General, Captain Dodgson, gave me every assistance. Captain Moorsom was here, as everywhere, a sagacious and daring guide. Captain Sitwell attended me zealously through the night.

Captain Olpherts recommends Private Duffy for the Victoria Cross, for his gallantry in extricating the 24-pounder gun under a very heavy fire of musketry, and I beg strongly to second his recommendation.

I have deeply to lament the loss of the gallant Captain Crump, Madras Army, killed whilst extricating the 24-pounder.

I have, &c.,
R. NAPIER, *Colonel*,
Military Secretary, &c.

Brigadier J. Inglis, Commanding the Garrison, to Colonel Napier, Military Secretary, &c.

Lucknow, 22nd October, 1857.

For the information of Major-General Sir J. Outram, G.C.B., commanding the division, I have the honour to enclose two reports from officers commanding sortie parties, giving an account of their proceedings whilst so employed.

Both these officers carried out my orders in a most satisfactory manner, and were most successful in the excellent of the duties entrusted to them. I have, &c.,

J. INGLIS, *Brigadier*,
Commanding Garrison of Lucknow.

Lieutenant R. H. M. Aitken, Commanding Treasury Guard, to Captain Wilson, Deputy-Assistant-Adjutant-General, Lucknow.

Lucknow, 21st October, 1857.

I have the honour to state, for the information of Brigadier Inglis, commanding the garrison, the proceedings of a party of the regiment under my command, on the night of the 25th, and morning of the 26th of September, which ended in the capture of the Taree Kotee.

On the evening of the 25th, after the first column of the relieving force arrived, I heard the shouts of the second column in the city in the direction of the gaol, and thinking they might get entangled in the lanes and might suffer from the guns under the Clock Tower, I took twelve armed sepoys of the regiment, with pickaxes and shovels, for the purpose of clearing away, if possible, the battery under the Clock Tower. We got over without opposition, as the head of the second relieving column was by this time in the lane and close up to the guns. As I thought this a good opportunity to occupy at least a portion of the Taree Kotee, I took upon myself the responsibility to take the sepoys through a door made in the wall by the insurgents. We advanced some distance quietly without meeting any one. At last, in a court-yard, we came upon a small body, eight in number, and took them prisoners, without firing a shot. I left the sepoys in charge of a havildar in this court-yard for the night, and reported the circumstance for the information of Brigadier Inglis, who ordered me to occupy the Taree Kotee with a stronger body in the morning.

Early next morning, we advanced to the bank of the river, and shot a few of the insurgents, who attempted to swim the river. At this time I observed a body of men on the top of a building with a gateway. We attempted to get in by breaking in the principal gate, which was barricaded; but found this impossible. Havildar Ramnarain Pande, however, succeeded in breaking down one of the small doors at the side of the gate, and was the first man who made an entrance. We killed some five or six men in the gateway, and others having got into the rooms above, and on the terraces which run towards the Fureed Buksh. A party of the 32nd came up at this time, under a sergeant, and some twenty-five men altogether were shot and bayoneted. We had two sepoys wounded, and one man of the 32nd was killed. I ought to mention that Captain Lowe, of her Majesty's 32nd, arrived with some men after we had got into the rooms, he having been employed driving the insurgents out of the Captain's Bazaar. All the sepoys behaved well, and I beg to bring to the notice of the Brigadier the gallant conduct of Lieutenant Cubitt, who was most forward throughout the affair.

Unfortunately three of our sepoys were wounded by the Europeans of the second relieving column on the night of the 25th, after we got over the battery under the Clock Tower, they having been mistaken for insurgents.

Captain E. W. D. Lowe, Commanding H. M.'s 32nd Regiment, to Brigadier J. Inglis, Commanding Lucknow Garrison.

City Residency, Lucknow, Sept. 27th, 1857.

I have the honour to acquaint you that, agreeably to your instructions, I proceeded yesterday morning in command of 150 men of the 32nd Regiment for the purpose of clearing the Captain's Bazaar, and adjoining posts, occupied by the enemy.

The party was in three divisions; the first, under Captain Bassano, on the right; the second, in reserve, under Captain Hughes, 57th N. I. (atached to the regiment); and the third, under Lieutenant Lawrence. The first and second advanced under cover of the thick bushes between our trenches and the road, whilst the third, passing through Innes' Outpost, came out on the road, through the houses in front, taking two small guns as they entered it, and which they dismounted from their carriages. The enemy were taken quite by surprise, and fled precipitately to the river, leaving a 6-pounder gun in the road. They were pursued by our men, and were nearly all shot or drowned in endeavouring to swim the river. Lieutenant Lawrence then led his party towards the iron bridge, and most gallantly succeeded in capturing a 9-pounder gun, just as a second round of grape was about to be fired at them. This gun having been brought away, they returned, and we took possession of the ruined mosque and, clearing the Captain's Bazaar, killed some of the enemy there, and captured an 18-pounder gun and four small guns (two of them without carriages).

I then proceeded to the Taree Kotee with part of the men; but found it unoccupied. A gate by the river leading into the Furah Buksh palace was then forced, and several of the enemy inside killed. We were here met by a party of the 13th Native Infantry, under Lieutenant Aitken, who had come in by another entrance. Having your orders not to proceed further in this direction, I withdrew the men.

Captain Hughes had, in the meantime, led a party again towards the iron bridge, and killing a great number of the enemy in the houses about, spiked two large mortars, which, however, he was unable to bring away. He was, I regret to say, dangerously wounded whilst forcing the door of a house. As the party retired, they blew up a large magazine of the enemy's powder.

The object contemplated having been obtained, not without loss, as the adjoining return will show, I withdrew the parties to the Residency, leaving guards at the ruined mosque and Taree Kotee.

In conclusion, I beg to bring prominently to your notice the great zeal and gallantry displayed by all engaged,—both officers and men,—so equally that it would be invidious to particularize any one; but Lieutenant Lawrence has, however, begged me to report the distinguished bravery of Corporal Samuel Cole, and Private Michael Power, in charging and capturing the 9-pounder gun.

Lieutenant Innes, of the Engineers, accompanied the party throughout, and afforded me every assistance.

Brigadier J. Inglis, Commanding the Garrison of Lucknow, to Colonel R. Napier, Chief of the Staff, &c.

Lucknow Garrison, 12th Nov., 1857.

I have the honour to request that you will do me the favour to submit to Major-General Sir James Outram, G.C.B., commanding the forces, the following record of events in this position since the arrival of the army under his command, on the 25th of September.

On the following morning, I received instructions to place under the orders of Major Haliburton, 78th Highlanders, as strong a detachment as I could spare from the garrison, in order to strengthen the rear-guard which had been left at Mr. Martin's house, in charge of the heavy guns that had arrived with the force. I accordingly detailed a party of 100 men of the 32nd Foot, under the command of Captain Lowe, who was accompanied by Captain Bassano, Captain McCabe, and Lieutenant Cooke of the same corps. This detachment remained all day in position with the rear-guard, and on the following morning it covered the extreme rear, on the march into the "Fureed Buksh," whence Captain McCabe led a party of volunteers, composed of the 5th, 32nd, and 90th Regiments, into a garden, and routed the enemy with great slaughter. Early the next day, this detachment, having performed the arduous duties assigned them, returned to my garrison. In these operations, the 32nd Regiment had one sergeant and one private killed, and two sergeants and two privates wounded. Captain Lowe also received a severe wound.

The report of the several sorties made under the direction of the Major-General commanding the forces, and in which detachments from this garrison have borne (I would fain hope) a distinguished part, have been so fully detailed by the officers who commanded on these occasions, that I need not enter further on the subject than to express my admiration of the gallant and devoted behaviour of both officers and men.

As soon as these operations were terminated, I turned my attention to the state of the batteries and defences of this position, many of which were in a very dilapidated state, as the Major-General is aware, especially the part called the brigade mess, at either flank of which was an open breach, neither of which we had ever been able to repair or strengthen, or even adequately to defend. But the large number of doolie bearers placed at my disposal by the Chief of the Staff, and the increased strength of the garrison, enabled me to carry on the works with vigour, and to materially strengthen all my critical positions.

Since the arrival of the force, a large mound and a Musjid adjacent to Innes' post were taken possession of by the late Lieutenant Graydon, and have been made defensible, as they completely overlook and command the iron bridge, and approach therefrom. A description of the works that have been carried out is fully given in the appended memorandum by the Engineer officer. Great praise is due to the great professional skill, the persevering energy, and the untiring personal activity displayed by Lieutenant Hutchinson, under whom the works have been carried out.

Owing to the extreme paucity of numbers attached to the garrison magazine, and the harassing duties which have devolved on this establishment during this very protracted siege, it has necessarily always been in a somewhat unsatisfactory state, and I gladly seized the opportunity to remodel it. With this end in view, I directed Lieutenant Thomas, in charge of the magazine, to remove it to the Post-office compound, as affording the most convenient site for piling shot and collecting together the various materials appertaining to this department. This duty has been ably performed by Mr. Conductor Bewsey, officiating sub-conductor, under the directions of Lieutenant Thomas, and I have now the pleasure to report that all the spare shot and shell have been collected, gauged, and piled. The spare muskets and musket barrels have also been collected, and a large supply of cartridges, wads, fuzes, quick and slow matches, have been prepared. The establishment have besides been employed in repairing sponge staffs, grummetting shot and shell, and in collecting wood, iron, lead, and other materials from the Fureed Buksh and other places. The ordnance drivers have also rendered assistance in removing guns and mortars, and in erecting and repairing batteries and issuing stores.

The buried treasure, amounting to nearly twenty-five lakhs of rupees is being exhumed, and placed again under the charge of the civil authorities.

The Commissariat arrangements made in garrison, under the directions of Sir James Outram, G.C.B., have involved a considerable reduction in rations, and this deprivation, coming as it did upon the garrison at the end of so long a siege, in addition to the want of malt liquor and spirits, has borne somewhat heavily on every one; but all have sustained the deprivation cheerfully, and none more so than the women, whose admirable conduct I have alluded to in a former despatch. An appended memorandum, furnished by the garrison commissariat officer, enters fully into the commissariat arrangements that have been made.

The great number of wounded which accompanied the major-general's force into this position, speedily increased the number of patients from 130 to 627, and as nearly all arrived without bedding, and as there was besides but a small supply of medicine, it became necessary to make every arrangement to meet these wants. In order to provide the requisite shelter, two large double-pole tents have been pitched close to the hospital portico, and a large room in the Begum Kotee made over for the accommodation of wounded officers. The buildings in the Central Sikh Square were also assigned to the remaining portion of the sick and wounded. Old tents have been cut up for bedding, and the patients have been made as comfortable as circumstances would admit; and I am sure that Sir James Outram, G.C.B., will have viewed, with the same satisfaction as myself, the excellent arrangements which have been made by that indefatigable officer, Superintending-Surgeon Scott.

During the period which this report embraces, the proceedings of the enemy have been marked by much less activity than heretofore.

Several of their guns, however, have been moved across the river, whence they have kept up a desultory cannonade, which has been silenced on most occasions by a few rounds of our heavy ordnance.

Their musketry fire has, however, occasionally been so heavy, especially by night, as to induce a belief that they intended an attack; but these demonstrations have rarely lasted for any lengthened period, though they have rendered it necessary that every man should be under arms for the time. Owing to the repairs made to our defences, and the increased cover obtained thereby, our casualties on these occasions have been but few.

Among the officers belonging to this garrison, who have fallen since the advent of the major-general's force, I deeply regret to have to record the loss of Captain Hughes, of the 57th Regiment N. I., doing duty with her Majesty's 32nd Foot, who was mortally wounded at the attack of a house which formed one of the enemy's outposts. Captain McCabe, her Majesty's 32nd Foot, a most distinguished officer, has also fallen; he received his death-wound while leading his fourth sortie. Lieutenant Graydon, too, of the 44th Regiment N. I., an officer of great merit, was mortally wounded while assisting in barricading his post.

Of the officers attached to this garrison who have had opportunities of distinguishing themselves, I would beg to bring to notice the gallant conduct of Captain Lowe and Lieutenant Lawrence, of her Majesty's 32nd Foot, who have each led a sortie; Lieutenant Hardinge, officiating deputy quartermaster-general, who headed two sorties; Lieutenant Aitken, accompanied by Lieutenant Cubitt, of the 13th Regiment N. I., who led a party of his regiment to a successful attack on a barricaded gateway held by the enemy; Major Apthorp and Captain Kemble, 41st Regiment N. I.; Lieutenants Huxham (wounded slightly in two places) and Ouseley, 48th Regiment N. I.; Lieutenant Warner, of the 7th L. C.; Lieutenant Cooke, her Majesty's 32nd Foot; and Lieutenant Mecham, of the Madras Army—also accompanied sorties and distinguished themselves.

Neither must I omit to record my appreciation of the gallant bearing of the Engineer officers—Lieutenants Anderson, Hutchinson, and Innes—who accompanied the storming parties.

My thanks are due to the officers commanding outposts, who have continued to evince the same vigilance and gallantry that have characterized their conduct throughout this memorable siege.

I have already expressed my inability to do justice to the behaviour of the troops, both European and native, and I can therefore only say that they have continued to exhibit the same gallantry under fire, and the same patience under suffering and privation as heretofore.

The several officers who compose my staff have continued to render me every assistance, and have given me every satisfaction in their several departments.

Lastly, I beg to express my grateful acknowledgments to the Major-General commanding the forces for the additional force placed at my disposal, composed of detachments of the Artillery, Volunteer Cavalry, 1st Madras Fusiliers, and 78th Highlanders; all of whom have borne themselves as becomes British soldiers. I have also to add my deep sense of the valuable counsel and advice which I have received from yourself on all occasions.

I have, &c.,

J. INGLIS, *Brigadier,*
Commanding Lucknow Garrison.

NOMINAL ROLL OF OFFICERS ATTACHED TO THE LUCKNOW GARRISON, KILLED AND WOUNDED between the 25th September and the 10th November, 1857.

KILLED.

Artillery.—Lieutenant D. C. Alexander.

WOUNDED.

H.M.'s 32nd Regiment.—Captain E. W. D. Lowe, severely; Captain B. McCabe, dangerously (since dead); Lieut. J. Edmonstoune, slightly; Lieutenant Browne, very slightly (and again severely); Assistant-Surgeon E. Darby, severely.

13th Regiment Native Infantry.—Lieutenant Cubitt, slightly, twice.

44th Regiment Native Infantry.—Lieutenant J. Graydon, mortally (since dead).

48th Regiment Native Infantry.—Lieutenant G. C. Huxham, severely (since dead); Lieutenant Dashwood, severely (since dead).

57th Regiment Native Infantry.—Captain Hughes, dangerously (since dead).

Civil Service.—J. B. Thornhill, Esq., mortally (since dead); — Boulderson, Esq., slightly.

MEMORANDUM *regarding the Sortie of the 27th September.*

Chutter Munzil, 8th November, 1857.

On the 26th September, I was warned by Brigadier Inglis to lead a party from the brigade mess, and having taken the guns in its front, to circle leftwards, taking or destroying all the guns on the way we should reach our own position at the Jail or Taree Kotee. The party, however, that was told off for this purpose on the 26th, was required to help in the heavy guns and rear-guard from the Mootee Mehal, and the sortie was, therefore, temporarily deferred.

Having next morning mentioned the proposed sortie to Lieutenant Anderson, Garrison Engineer, at the Furced Buksh, he stated his opinion of the advisability of the sortie debouching from the Jail and going in rear of the square house and proceeding thence in a direction parallel to the road, by which plan we would start fair from our own ground, probably hit on the enemy's usual route, and take the guns in rear.

The sortie having been re-arranged for the afternoon of the 27th, Lieutenant Anderson proposed to guide it himself. The party was (as I learned on reaching the first house attacked) commanded by Major Stephenson, of the Madras Fusiliers, and the party to explode the guns consisted of artillerymen under the command of Captain Evans. Two sepoys of the 13th Native Infantry accompanied us, under my orders, with picks, to help in knocking down obstacles, should it be necessary.

Lieutenant Anderson led the party out by the Taree Kotee and Jail, and rear of the square house to the building now forming the left of the Highlanders' position. The enemy being in possession of it, it was attacked; but the party never appeared to enter the rooms and clear them; it only remained in or rushed through the court-yards and passages, shooting or bayoneting such of the enemy as voluntarily came out.

The correct place for debouching from the house was on the same side only further advanced, as that at which we had entered it, and, as I afterwards found, Lieutenant Anderson was waiting there to lead the men out, as soon as they should have taken possession of the house. But waiting for no guidance, they left the house at the point which they reached on rushing through it, and immediately found themselves on the road. Hearing a call for an engineer officer, I went forward, and found the party on the road in front of an embrasure which was shortly afterwards charged, and the gun taken. Not forty men were present for the first ten minutes, and although Captain Evans and my two sepoys were there, the rest of the explosion party were among the absentees. After waiting ten minutes and Major Stephenson getting impatient, Captain Evans, hopeless of the arrival of the bursting party and material, spiked the gun. This was no sooner done than they arrived, and the subsequent attempt to blow up the gun was a failure, from the vent being filled up by the spike. During the attempt to burst the gun, an officer (Captain Galwey, I believe), came to report the capture of two other guns, the spiking of one of them, and the necessity for reinforcement. Major Stephenson having advanced towards them asked me where we were, and what was to be done. As to what was to be done, on inquiry from Captain Evans, it appeared that the men had drunk all the water reserved to moisten the clay to tamp the guns, so that, in fact, he could not burst them, and there were no spikes with which to spike them. I therefore said that, wherever we might go, we could destroy no more guns, and that, consequently, our return to the entrenchment seemed to me advisable. As to the place where we were, I said, I thought we were at the battery on the left of the Cawnpore road, which opinion was also expressed by Mr. Cavanagh; Mr. Phillips, our real guide, being unable to give any opinion at all. To make certain of the locality, I told Major Stephenson I would cross the road and reconnoitre, which I accordingly did, and found that my conjecture had been correct. On my return, the party had commenced its return to the entrenchments, which it effected by nearly the same route as that by which it had advanced.

The party which remained with Lieutenant Anderson, at the house first attacked, prevented the enemy still on it from doing us much injury on our return, otherwise our loss might have been most serious. The separation of the whole party into the two bodies, which was the previous cause of the failure in destroying the guns, is entire attributable to an advance having been made from that house without the direction of the proper guide. J. McLEOD INNES, *Lieut. Engineers.*

NOTE.—This sortie was designed to attack the garden battery, and it appears from the experience gained in a subsequent attack (1st, 2nd, and 3rd November) that the strength of the party was quite inadequate to accomplish the object required. The real cause of the failure in bursting, instead of spiking, the guns taken possession of, appears to have been the delay in bringing up the bursting party.

Had the house, alluded to by Lieutenant Innes, been taken possession of, instead of being merely passed through, and measures taken to reconnoitre the ground in advance before the party proceeded, it is probable that the result would have been more satisfactory, and that at all events the captured guns would have been effectually destroyed; but without a much larger body of men, the complete conquest and destruction of the whole garden battery could not have been accomplished.

J. C. ANDERSON, *Lieut.*,
Garrison Engineer.

Captain M. Galwey, Commanding 1st Madras Fusiliers, to the Deputy-Assistant Adjutant-General.

Lucknow, November, 1857.

In reply to your letter, dated 4th November, 1857, number and subject as per margin,* I have the honour to state as follows.

About 2 P. M., on the 27th September, 1857, the Madras Fusiliers, were ordered to parade for a sortie under command of Major Stephenson, commanding the same regiment, for the purpose of taking some guns in the enemy's Cawnpore battery.

The regiment was told off in three divisions, the strength of it not admitting of a larger number. Captain Fraser had command of No. 1, Captain Galwey No. 2, and Captain Raikes of No. 3 division; Lieutenant and Adjutant Gosling, Lieutenants Beaumont and Cleland, and Lieutenant the Honourable J. Fraser, 1st Bengal Native Infantry, doing duty with the Fusiliers, fell in with the regiment. A few men of her Majesty's 32nd Regiment, under Lieutenant Warner; 7th Bengal Corps, Captain Kemble, 41st Bengal Native Infantry; Lieutenant Huxham, 48th Bengal Native Infantry; Lieut. Anderson, Bengal Engineers; and Lieutenant Mecham, 27th Madras Native Infantry, accompanied the party.

The party proceeded in strict silence out of the Bailey Gate to the garden opposite, and passed through a door to the right, about half way down to the garden, which led through bye-paths till it reached the road, at which place there was a considerable street fire from loop-holes and from the tops of houses and from the guns of the enemy in position. A charge was made at the nearest gun through long grass, ruins, small breaches in walls, and a broad ditch. Our men entered by the embrasure, and the enemy immediately abandoned this gun. A considerable delay occurred in making preparations for bursting this gun, which, however, ultimately proved a failure, as some person had spiked it previously and in the hurry of the moment. During this time a party of No. 1 Division, under Captain Fraser, proceeded to reconnoitre a little further, when they came on another battery of the enemy, consisting of a

---

* No. 147.—Directing a report to be made of a sortie by the troops under command of Major Stephenson, Madras Fusiliers, on the 27th September, 1857.

24-pounder and an 18-pounder gun. These were abandoned; but the enemy being all round, and keeping up such a fire on his party, Captain Fraser sent back to Major Stephenson to say he required a reinforcement. On this, Captain Galwey, of No. 2 division, proceeded with a few men. On reaching the spot, he found from the number of the enemy (which he calculated from their heavy fire) that the position could not be held without a further reinforcement. The battery was surrounded with high walls, and apparently with no outlets. Captain Galwey returned, and reported this to Major Stephenson. It was now discovered that we had with us no means by which we could destroy or dismantle the guns; so Major Stephenson directed the advance party to fall back on him, which, however, they did not then do. Captain Fraser spoke in the highest terms of the gallantry of Sergeant Lister, Madras Fusiliers, who spiked the 24-pounder; and of Corporal William Dowling, Her Majesty's 32nd Regiment, who spiked the 18-pounder gun, being at the same time under a most heavy fire from the enemy.

Finding it impossible to burst the first gun, Major Stephenson left a party under a subaltern to protect that gun, and proceeded with Captain Raikes' division No. 3, which he had kept with him, to the advanced battery, which, as before stated, was surrounded with high walls. At this time Sergeant Lister, previously mentioned as having spiked a gun under heavy fire, was killed. Major Stephenson called on some of the volunteers or guides to point out the way to the next battery; but no one knew the way, or seemed at all aware of our locality, and at this time firing being heard in our rear, Major Stephenson was compelled to retire by the way we came, it being quite impossible to go forward without guides. The three guns were left spiked, owing to want of means to destroy them. On the return of the party, it was exposed to a very destructive fire from the enemy, from the tops of houses and loop-holes, and from want of means it was most difficult to take away our killed and wounded. One sergeant, severely wounded, and since dead, must have been left on the ground, had not a private of the 32nd Regiment, in the most gallant manner, with the assistance of Captain Galwey, taken him up and carried him to a place of safety. Lieutenant Huxham, 48th Bengal Native Infantry, was wounded.

I enclose a return of the killed and wounded of the 1st Madras Fusiliers on this occasion.

Lieut. A. C. Warner, Adjutant, 7th Light Cavalry, to Captain Wilson, Officiating Deputy-Assistant Adjutant-General, Lucknow Garrison.

Lucknow, 7th November, 1857.

Agreeably to instructions received, I have the honour to report as follows:—

In consequence of there being no available officers with Her Majesty's 32nd Regiment, I was selected to command a party of that corps on the 27th September, in a sortie, for the purpose of capturing some of the enemy's guns, in a battery opposite to our Cawnpore battery.

We paraded about 2 P. M. with the Madras Fusiliers, and marched out of the Bailey Guard Gate, my party in advance, the whole under command of Major Stephenson, of the Madras Fusiliers. We proceeded through the Taree Kotee, across the road in rear of the Clock Tower, and then took ground to our right. Immediately we had crossed the road, we became exposed to the enemy's fire, and made a rush across a large court-yard through a doorway to our right. After passing through a succession of narrow streets and holes in the wall, we arrived at the Cawnpore road. We then came on one of the enemy's guns, which was firing grape down the Cawnpore road. I took my party to one side of the embrasure, and on receiving the word of command, we rushed in, headed by Major Stephenson. The enemy abandoned their gun, and a naick of the 13th Regiment, Kalka Tewaree, spiked it. We then endeavoured to burst it; but owing to the absence of water and other materials failed.

While we were attempting to burst this gun, a party of men under Captain Fraser, of the Madras Fusiliers, went on to another battery of the enemy's which was further in advance.

Shortly after this, the party under my command went with Captain Galwey and some of his men to reinforce Captain Fraser. On arriving near his position, we found the enemy in great force on all sides of us, keeping up a very heavy fire. We then retreated by order of Major Stephenson, on the main body. One of the Madras Fusilier serjeants being badly wounded, Captain Galwey, Lieutenant Mecham, 27th Madras Native Infantry, Private Smith, her Majesty's 32nd, and myself, with great difficulty, managed to get him back to the main body. This private was, I regret to say, killed in the retreat. Major Stephenson then ordered us to retreat, which was done by the same route by which we had advanced. During the retreat, we were exposed to a heavy fire from the houses. The conduct of Corporal Coony and Private Smith, of the 32nd, who were both killed, was most noble.

I enclose a return of the killed and wounded of her Majesty's 32nd Regiment on this occasion.

Lieutenant J. C. Anderson, Garrison Engineer, to Colonel R. Napier, Military Secretary, &c.

Lucknow, 19*th October,* 1857.

Sortie on 29*th September, from the left square Brigade Mess, for the object of destroying the enemy's guns, left in front of Brigade Mess, in front of Cawnpore Battery, and on the left of Cawnpore Road.*

The sortie proceeded simultaneously with two others, one from the Sikh square, to the right of the brigade mess, and another from the redan towards the iron bridge, led by Captain McCabe, her Majesty's 32nd Regiment, with a few of the men of his regiment, who had, during the siege, been on duty on the posts opposite the position to be attacked.

The whole strength of the sortieing party was 200 men, with a reserve of 150 men.

At daylight the party issued from an opening in the brigade mess wall, and formed up under cover of a wall which runs parallel to the other at the distance of a few paces. The advance was then made in file, the men having to scramble over the debris of a house which had been blown down on a former occasion, and a rush made direct on the enemy's 18-pounder guns, which lay behind a breast-work, at the distance of 80 yards from the brigade mess. The gunners fired two rounds at us when we made our appearance, but before they could fire again, we had scaled their battery and driven them to flight. We then proceeded to force a building immediately to the left of the gun. The lower story was quickly occupied. Captain McCabe, the gallant leader of many former sorties, was mortally wounded in the operation, and some delay having in consequence occurred, a few of the enemy in the upper story had time to kill and wound several of our men before they were attacked and bayonetted. After the house had been taken possession of a picquet of twenty-five men was left to hold it, while the main body of our men proceeded along a narrow lane, under command of Major Simmons, her Majesty's 5th Fusiliers, to occupy two large buildings, about 60 and 80 yards, respectively, in advance of the first, with several other smaller buildings adjoining; the loss to the enemy in all being probably above thirty men. On our side we had the misfortune to lose Major Simmons, who was killed by a musket shot while leading his men into the most advanced building. We had now progressed to a position from which we had a view of the enemy's 18-pounder gun in front of the Cawnpore battery. It lay in a lane running towards the Cawnpore road, the end of which was barricaded and loopholed, and directly in line with it, on he opposite side of the road, the enemy occupied a house from which they kept up a hot musketry fire on our position.

I then sent for the reserve, and desired that an officer of rank might be sent to command the whole party. General Sir J. Outram, having become acquainted with our progress, sent word that, unless further advance could be made without danger of considerable loss, the design of proceeding against the enemy's gun, now in our view, should be abandoned, and that the party should retire after destroying in succession the houses we had taken possession of. After consulting with Captain Evans, attached to the artillery, who had meanwhile destroyed the enemy's gun, which we left at the first house, and also a 6-pounder gun in its neighbourhood, I returned a reply to the General that further advance could not be made without considerable loss, and I proceeded to demolish the three large houses we held, commencing with the one furthest in advance, and withdrawing the party gradually to the rear. This operation, in which 13 barrels of powder were expended, destroyed the principal musketry cover of the enemy against our defencet between the brigade mess and Cawnpore battery, and the destruction of the guns in front of the latter, together with that affected by the sortieing parties acting in conjunction with us to the right, has relieved a considerable portion of our work from serious annoyance.

The party returned about 9.30 A.M.

RETURN of CASUALTIES—*Sortie from left square Brigade Mess, on 29th September,* 1857.

Lucknow, 19th October, 1857.

	Killed.	Wounded.
Her Majesty's 5th Fusiliers:—		
Major Simmons	1	0
Rank and File	0	6
Her Majesty's 32nd Regiment:—		
Captain McCabe	0	1 (since dead)
Rank and File	1	2 do.
Total	2	9

J. C. ANDERSON, *Lieutenant,*
Garrison Engineer.

Major C. Apthorp, Commanding the Reserve, to Captain Anderson, Engineers.

Lucknow, 20th October, 1857.

Agreeably to your request, I have the honour to forward a report of the proceedings of the party as per margin,* under my command, during the sortie of the 29th ultimo. We assembled in the third Sikh square a little before daybreak, as a reserve to an attacking party under command of Captain Hardinge, who, when he had taken the guns in front of the brigade mess, advanced to his right to take a gun situated in a strong position in the middle of a lane, to the left front of Mr. Gubbins' house. He placed his men in a flanking position, and came to me for a party to advance and take some houses to the right and left of the lane, from which there was a heavy fire. I advanced through the breach in the Sikh square, with Lieutenant Ouseley, 48th Regiment Native Infantry, Lieutenant the Honourable J. Fraser, and thirty-five men, and led them up the lane to the front of the enemy's stockade. I took up a position with four or five men, and fired on several of the enemy who were trying to escape. Lieutenant Ouseley, the Honourable J. Fraser, and several men, got over the stockade, and the party under Captain Hardinge came forward, and the gun, a 6-pounder, pointed towards him, was taken possession of. One of our men was killed as we reached the stockade, and one wounded a short time after. Fourteen or fifteen of the enemy were killed, nine of them in two huts to the right and left of the lane. I left this party of the reserve under command of the Honourable J. Fraser, and went back to the remainder of the reserve, which I found had advanced from the Sikh square, under Captain Galwey, and we proceeded down the lane and took up a forward position in a house which Captain Forbes, 1st Light Cavalry, and his Sikh orderly had examined and reported empty. There was a strong party of the enemy to our left front, who kept up a heavy fire. I placed part of the men under Captain Galwey in front of the house; another party, under

---

* One major, two captains, three lieutenants, 100 men 1st Madras Fusiliers.

Captain Forbes, took possession of the upper story of the house; and I detached a third party to take possession of a barricade across the street a little to our right front. Our loss here was one killed and one wounded. Five or six of the men from this position got into a large house still further in advance, and I went and examined the house, and found, after getting into the lower story, that the enemy had begun two mines, the shafts of which were sunk to a considerable depth. I reported this to Lieutenant Innes, the executive engineer, who on examination, decided on blowing them up. Being short of men, I ordered a party of ten, under Sergeant-major Donovan, to come down our centre bastion and occupy the house where the mines were. He remained in charge till the mines were blown up. During the time I was thus occupied, Lieutenant Ouseley rendered great service by capturing a gun, which had checked the advance of the party to which he was attached, by being planted at the end of a very narrow lane, about 60 or 70 yards long. Lieutenant Ouseley, accompanied by Sergeant Higgins and four men of the 1st Madras Fusiliers, went through a number of houses and narrow passages, to the right of the lane, and finding their further progress stopped by a very high and steep bastion, where they distinctly heard the voices of the enemy, they ascended it, led by the above-named officer, found it unoccupied, and rushed across it into a house from which they fired down upon and killed two out of some forty men assembled below them; and raising a cheer routed the enemy, and took possession of the gun, without losing a man, or giving the enemy the power of discharging the piece to which drag-ropes were attached, to enable it to be pulled round the nearest corner, should we attempt to charge it. A party of eight or ten men from Captain Galwey's position, under Lieutenant Cleveland, reinforced Lieutenant Ouseley, and after the gun had been removed they retired and the bastion was blown up. Afterwards two small guns were found in a lane close to this battery, and taken possession of by Lieutenants Ouseley and Aitken, 13th Regiment Native Infantry. The three were dismantled from their carriages and were sent into the garrison, and the carriages broken up and burnt. Our loss at this point was one killed and two wounded, one of the latter being Mr. Lucas, whose zeal and gallantry on every occasion during the siege every one has heard of. About 11 o'clock we returned into garrison, having examined and cleared the guns from the whole of the front of Mr. Gubbins' house. We had not time or men to examine the houses in front of our centre bastion, which I much regret, as there are constant reports from the men, that mining is going on ; but I have no good reason to suppose so, as I have invariably, when called, found the houses unoccupied, and heard no noises that would lead me to suppose that mining was going on.

I have, &c.,
C. APTHORP, *Major*,
Commanding the Reserve.

Lieutenant J. C. Anderson, Garrison Engineer, to Captain Wilson, Deputy Adjutant-General, Lucknow Garrison.

Post Office, 28th October, 1857.

I have the honour to forward, for the brigadier's information, and for transmission to Colonel Napier, reports of the three sorties which took place on the 29th ultimo.

These reports were prepared by Colonel Napier's order, conveyed in a demi-official note.

Lieutenant G. Hardinge, Commanding Irregular Cavalry, &c., to Colonel R. Napier, Chief of the Staff.

Lucknow, 22nd October, 1857.

Agreeably with your orders, I have the honour to report that the undermentioned parties were made over to me to take the guns to the front and right of the brigade mess and Sikh square:—

	Men.
Her Majesty's 32nd Regiment, under Lieutenant Cooke	20
Her Majesty's 78th Highlanders, under Captain Lockhart	140
1st Madras Fusiliers, under Captain Galwey	90
Total	250

We fell in and filed out of the breach in the Sikh square at daybreak of the 29th September, 1857.

The advance consisted of her Majesty's 32nd; main body, her Majesty's 78th Highlanders; reserve, of 1st Madras Fusiliers. The Engineers under Lieutenant Innes, Artillery under Lieutenant J. Alexander; Major Apthorp (whose report I enclose), Captain Forbes, and Lieutenant Ouseley, knowing the ground, accompanied the reserve.

We formed silently under cover of some broken ground. The first gun, a brass 12-pounder, was taken by her Majesty's 32nd with a cheer. By keeping to the right of the embrasure we avoided the discharge. Lieutenant Cooke and Private Keilly were first at the gun.

The 32nd occupied a house in rear of the gun, and enabled the Artillery to burst it unmolested.

The 78th Highlanders, led by Captain Lockhart, who was slightly wounded, then charged a gun to the right. The covering party of the first gun, and a considerable body of the enemy, rallied round this gun. Sergeant James Young, 78th Highlanders, the first man at the gun, bayonetted one of the enemy's gunners while re-loading, and was severely wounded by a sword-cut.

I ordered up a party of the 1st Fusiliers under Lieutenant the Hon. J. Fraser, to take the enemy in rear, and a number of them were killed here and in the houses in the neighbourhood. Hand grenades were used with good effect.

Proceeding further to the right, opposite Mr. Gubbins' house, our further progress was stopped by a small gun and some wall-pieces at the end of a narrow lane.

Lieutenant Ouseley, 48th N. I., and Lieutenant Aitken, 13th N. I., took these pieces in flank, after a difficult detour, by getting into a house above them, and with a cheer and volley routed the enemy. This manœuvre was most skilfully and gallantly executed. Sergeant Higgins, with four men of the Madras Fusiliers, and Private Browne, 32nd, are stated to have been the first men at the gun. Mr. Lucas, a volunteer, well known for his bravery, was mortally wounded here.

Major Apthorp and Captain Forbes, with the Fusiliers under Captain Galwey, occupied the houses commanding the pieces which were brought away. Two shafts of a mine were here discovered and blown up.

The batteries and barricades were completely burnt and destroyed. Working parties of the Sikh Cavalry, under Lieutenant Graham, and sepoys of the 13th N. I., under Lieutenant Aitken, did good work.

I enclose Lieutenant Innes' report. Under cover of the houses blown up, the party fell back unmolested.

One heavy gun was burst, three smaller ones and some wall-pieces brought in.

Our loss was four killed and eleven wounded, including Mr. Lucas and Captain Lockhart.

MEMORANDUM *of* DEMOLITIONS *effected by the Party under Captain Hardinge, on the 29th September,* 1857.

Lucknow, 21st October, 1857.

The party for demolition consisted of six miners of her Majesty's 32nd Regiment, with a fatigue party of six men supplied from the troops under Captain Hardinge's guidance. It carried six barrels of powder, with the requisite supply of hose, port-fire, and slow-match.

The house that covered the first gun taken, being the first selected for demolition, I accordingly laid in it a charge of two barrels. This done, Captain Hardinge pointed out the two next places which he proposed to destroy. They were houses in which the enemy were said to be, and to eject whom would have been attended with no benefit, but probably with a considerable loss of life. One house being in a dilapidated condition, I laid one barrel of powder against the middle of its outer wall; the other was strong, and I therefore lodged two barrels against its wall in a similar position.

These charges being laid, it was decided to defer the explosions till the time should arrive for retiring, when they should be fired in a reverse order to that in which the charges were laid.

On the capture of the guns by the reserve, I lodged a barrel of powder at the stockade where they had been, and fired it. The demolition was successful.

I had thus laid out all the six barrels, when Major Apthorp, in command of the reserve, reported the discovery of a house with mines in it, leading probably to the bastion and out-houses at Mr. Gubbins' compound. I mentioned the want of powder; but Lieutenant Graham arriving and reporting that more powder had been placed at my disposal, I requested to have four barrels sent me. On proceeding to examine the house and mines, I found that there were two shafts, but no galleries. No mines then had to be destroyed, only the house, in which, therefore, I lodged and fired two barrels of powder, bringing down the side of the house facing the entrenchments.

The time for the party to retire having now arrived, I fired the mines mentioned in paragraph 2, in a reverse order to that in which the charges had been laid. As the explosion did not occur till the rear guard was on the entrenchment side of the buildings successively demolished, the inspection of the results could not be made on the site of the building destroyed; but as well as observation from a tolerably short distance could enable a decision to be arrived at, all the demolitions were successful.

J. McLEOD INNES, *Lieutenant, Engineers,*
In charge of the Demolition Party.

REPORT *of a* SORTIE *made on the 29th September,* 1857, *towards the Iron Bridge.*

Lucknow, 22nd October, 1857.

On the morning of the 29th ultimo, I was directed by Lieutenant General Sir James Outram, G.C.B., to proceed as guiding officer, with a column (strength as per margin),* under the command of Captain Shute, her Majesty's 64th Regiment.

The principal object of the expedition was to destroy a 24-pounder gun, situated on a mound about 200 yards from Mr. Hill's shop, which had been doing immense injury in the garrison during the siege.

The party started from Innes' out-post about daybreak, and took and spiked two mortars and four Zemindaree guns of small calibre, destroying the carriages of the latter. The guns were placed on the roads leading towards the iron bridge, and past Mr. Hill's shop, and the column had to traverse a distance of 1,200 yards from the outpost before reaching the last gun. The party then returned about 300 yards, and quitted the road to reach the 24-pounder gun above mentioned. It was taken possession of, and the houses near having been occupied, it was destroyed successfully.

I regret, however, to add that the column sustained considerable loss in consequence of an order with reference to occupying the houses in its rear leading to the iron-bridge not having been carried out.

J. GRAYDON, *Lieutenant* 44th *Regiment N.I.*
Guiding Officer to Captain Shute's Column.

---

* Strength of Captain Shute's Column:—H.M.'s 32nd Regiment, 1 officer and 12 men; H.M.'s 64th Regiment, 2 officers and 21 men; H.M.'s 84th Regiment, 3 officers and 110 men. Total—6 officers and 143 men.

CASUALTY RETURN *of a Party of H.M.'s 32nd Regiment under Lieut. Edmondstoune, on the 29th of September,* 1857.

Lucknow, 30th September, 1857.
1 officer, Lieutenant Edmondstoune, wounded.
1 corporal, wounded (since dead).
Total—1 officer wounded, 1 corporal wounded.

E. W. D. LOWE, *Captain,*
Commanding 32nd Regiment.

RETURN *of the Number of Casualties which took place in H.M.'s 84th and 64th Regiments in the Sortie of the 29th September,* 1857.

Lucknow, 21st October, 1857.
Captain Shute's (against the iron-bridge):—

	Killed.	Wounded.
Her Majesty's 84th Regiment	8	8
Her Majesty's 64th Regiment	2	13

F. A. WILLIS, *Captain,*
Commanding H.M.'s 84th Regiment.

Colonel R. Napier, Military Secretary, &c., to Major General Sir James Outram, G.C.B., Commanding the Forces.

Lucknow, 5th October, 1857.

On the 1st instant, I received your orders to take the enemy's battery in the position called Phillip's Garden, near the Cawnpore Road. For this object you placed at my disposal the following troops:—

Detachments of her Majesty's 5th Fusiliers; 32nd; 64th; 78th; and 90th regiments; and the Hon. East India Company's 1st Madras Fusiliers, under Major Haliburton, her Majesty's 78th; Captain Shute, her Majesty's 64th; and Captain Raikes, Madras Fusiliers,—amounting to 568 men; Lieutenant Limond, Engineers, and Lieutenant Tulloh, Acting Assistant Field Engineer, attended the column with a party of five Miners of her Majesty's 32nd Regiment, and a party of Artillery, under Sergeant Smith, with means of bursting guns.

In the afternoon of the 1st, the column formed in the road leading to the Paen Bagh, and advanced through the buildings near the gaol, occupied the mass of houses on the left and front of Phillips' Garden, under guidance of Mr. Phillips the former occupant, and the enemy were driven from some houses and a barricade on the left of our advance, by fifty men of the Madras Fusiliers, led by Lieutenant Groom under a sharp fire of musketry, in a very spirited manner.

The houses in front were strongly barricaded, and in many cases the doors were bricked up; it was, therefore, late before we had worked a way to a point from whence we could command the enemy's position. A party of the enemy was driven out, and a row of loop-holes was commenced immediately, and the ground examined right and left. Attempts to penetrate the garden to the left were ineffectual; to the right an opening was obtained, which disclosed that the enemy's batteries were separated from us by a deep narrow lane, some twelve or fifteen feet below the garden; the latter was surrounded by a deep mud wall, with buildings attached. The face of the battery was scarped and quite inaccessible without ladders. A heavy fire was kept up from the face of the battery, and the lane was flanked by a strong barricade. As it was dark, and a direct attack would be certain to cost many lives, I determined to wait till day-light before assaulting the battery. The position was duly secured, and the men occupied the buildings for the night.

In the morning, after giving the men breakfast, and arranging with the artillery to open fire from the entrenchment, the troops advanced. A severe fire was opened from the barricade, flanking the lane on the right; but Major Haliburton detached Lieutenant Creagh, Madras Fusiliers, with a party to turn the barricade by the Cawnpore Road, which was effectually done. The troops then doubled out through the lane, and forced a way through the stockade into the enemy's batteries; the 5th Fusiliers and detachment 64th in advance, under Lieutenant Brown, supported by the Madras Fusiliers and her Majesty's 32nd. The enemy was immediately driven from the battery, and Phillips' house occupied without further opposition. A picquet being left in possession, the troops advanced on the guns which had been withdrawn to the end of the garden and to the streets adjoining, and captured two 9-pounders, and one 6-pounder gun, driving off the enemy who defended them with musketry and grape. The guns were immediately dragged to the garden and burst, their carriages completely destroyed, and their ammunition sent to the entrenchment. Phillips' house was blown up by a party under Lieutenant Innes, Engineers, and at dark the troops withdrew to their position of the previous night.

In all the arrangements I was most fortunate in having the aid of that very able and brave officer, Major Haliburton, her Majesty's 78th Highlanders, who deserves particular notice.

I beg to recommend to your favourable notice Captain Shute, her Majesty's 64th, and Lieutenant Brown, 5th Fusiliers, who led the party into the battery, and were foremost in capturing the two 9-pounders. I also beg to recommend to your notice Private McHale, her Majesty's 5th Fusiliers, who was the first man at the capture of one of the guns.

Lieutenant Limond, of the Engineers, was very active in the duties of the Engineer Department, and in reconnoitring the enemy's position. Captain Dawson and Lieutenant Hewett attended me zealously as Field Orderly Officers throughout the operations; and Mr. Cavanagh, Superintendent Chief Commissioner's Office, accompanied the party as a guide, and was always to be found at the front.

The guns were destroyed by Sergeant Smith with the party of Artillery.

The position of this battery was so inaccessible, and the locality so little known, that the enterprise of taking it was considered by the experienced chief engineer of the garrison as one of very serious difficulty. Owing to our laborious investigation of its position, which enabled us to obtain command of it from the adjacent mass of buildings, I was able to take it at the comparatively small loss of 2 killed and 11 wounded.

I have only to add, that, although I have mentioned the names of those officers who had the good fortune to be at the points of attack, yet the conduct of the whole of the officers and men was in every way deserving of your commendation; they were most eager to assault the battery on the night of the 1st, but I restrained them, as I was convinced shat I could effect the desired end without the serious loss that would have then been incurred.

Their attack when made was carried out with their unfailing gallantry.

It is impossible to estimate the loss of the enemy.

I am, &c.

R. NAPIER, *Colonel,*
Military Secretary, &c.

Lieutenant G. Hardinge, commanding Irregular Cavalry, &c., to Colonel R. Napier, Chief of the Staff.

Lucknow, 5th November, 1857.

Agreeably to your order I have the honour to report, that on the 2nd ultimo, the undermentioned party was put under my command for taking the guns to the right of the Cawnpore road:—

Her Majesty's 32nd, Lieut. Cooke . . . 68 Men
Her Majesty's 84th Regiment . . . . 12 „
Madras Fusiliers . . . . . . 15 „
Artillery . . . . 7 „

On coming up to the batteries, we found the enemy had deserted them, and withdrawn one or two guns. They had burst a very heavy gun on the Cawnpore road, and another, an iron 18-pounder, had the muzzle blown off. I had this destroyed after burning the batteries and blowing up a large mosque, in which four barrels of powder were placed.

I withdrew the party unmolested, the enemy only firing from some distant houses. One man of her Majesty's 32nd Regiment was wounded.

Lieutenant Graham and twenty Sikh Cavalry formed the working party.

Major-General H. Havelock, Commanding Oude Field Force, to Captain Dodgson, Acting Military Secretary.

Lucknow, 21st November, 1857.

I have much pleasure in forwarding for submission to Major-General Sir James Outram, G.C.B., the accompanying report from Colonel R. Napier, chief of the Staff, detailing the late operations at the advanced posts in the palace of Fureed Buksh.

I am, &c.

H. HAVELOCK, *Major-General,*
Commanding Oude Field Force.

Colonel R. Napier, Military Secretary, &c., to Captain Hodson, Deputy-Assistant Adjutant-General, Oude Field Force.

Lucknow, 20th November, 1857.

The Chief Engineer of the Oude Field Force being wounded at the time of our arrival at Lucknow, and further prevented, until the 1th ultimo, from personally attending to his duties, by an accidental lameness produced by his arduous exertion in constructing the bridge at Cawnpore for the passage of the Force across the Ganges, there devolved upon me many duties not appertaining to my office, which it is proper that I should report through you, as I believe no officer except myself is acquainted with all that has taken place, and the course of those duties gave me an opportunity of noticing the valuable services of officers which could not otherwise be brought to Major-General Havelock's knowledge.

On the morning of the 27th ultimo, the escort with the heavy train, occupied the range of palaces called the Chuttur Munzil and Fureed Buksh.

Major-General Havelock is aware that these palaces afford the only shelter that our troops could have occupied, and that as mere shelter they give excellent accommodation; but, as a military position they have very great disadvantages. The northern face is well protected by the River Goomtee; but the east and south-east faces are surrounded by buildings and in contact with the city,

Captain Crommelin's plan, which he will submit with his report of the engineer operations, illustrates the preceding remarks.

The position was too extensive for our force, nearly all of which was occupied in guarding it; but it was susceptible of no reduction, so that most desirable as it was that we should have occupied some of the exterior buildings as flanking defences, we were unable to do so, but were obliged to confine ourselves to the palaces and gardens, and to erect precautionary defences against any means of annoyance the enemy could devise. Lieut.-Colonel Purnell, of her Majesty's 90th, being in command of the rear-guard on the 27th, I requested him to assume command of the palace garden and buildings adjacent to it. On the 28th the palace buildings extending in the direction of the Khas bazaar were explored by Captain Moorsom, who with a party of fifty men of the 90th and 5th Fusiliers, gallantly drove the enemy out at the point of the bayonet, killing a considerable number, with the loss of one man of her Majesty's 90th. Captain Moorsom then placed a picquet in a house commanding the Cheena and Khas bazaars. On the 3rd instant, the enemy sprang a mine under the garden-wall, which merely shook it without bringing it down. On the 5th, they exploded a second mine, which effected a considerable breach, and appeared in some force with the intention of making an assault; but on the head of the column showing itself on the breach, a well-directed fire from her Majesty's 90th caused it to retreat precipitately and with considerable loss. The enemy also burned down one of the gateways of the garden, making a second practicable breach, at which they occasionally appeared to fire a shot or two. Lieut.-Colonel Purnell had retrenched both these breaches, which it became evident that the enemy had no real intention of assaulting; but they exposed the garden to a severe musketry fire from commanding buildings on the right, called the Hern Khana; it, therefore, became necessary to open trenches of communication, which were commenced by Lieut.-Colonel Purnell and his officers. On the 6th, the enemy blew up the picquet overlooking the Cheena and Khas bazaars, causing us a loss of three men, and in the confusion that ensued penetrated in considerable numbers into the palace, where many of them were destroyed. They are said to have lost 450 men! The remainder were driven back, but continued to occupy a part of the palace buildings which had been in our possession. Of these, the nearest to us is a mosque commanded by our buildings, but giving several easy means of access to our position. On the 8th, the enemy attacked from the mosque our nearest picquets; but were repulsed with loss. In order to prevent a repetition of this annoyance, I examined carefully, in company with Lieut.-Colonel Purnell and Captain Moorsom, the buildings connecting us with those of the enemy, and we succeeded in penetrating to a vault under their position, where, screened by the obscurity, we could see the enemy closely surrounding the entrance, and hear them in considerable numbers overhead. A charge of two barrels of powder was lodged in the vault, and was fired by Lieutenant Russell, of the Bengal Engineers. The effect was complete; many of the enemy were blown up, and their position greatly injured, whilst we obtained a command over the streets leading to the Khas and Cheena bazaars better and more secure from molestation than our previous one. This post was immediately and securely barricaded by Captain Crommelin, of the Engineers, who this day resumed his duties as chief engineer, and the value of his services was immediately apparent. Though our position was improved by this explosion, the possession of the mosque was absolutely necessary to our security. I accordingly determined to re-capture it, and on expressing my wishes to Lieut.-Colonel Purnell, that officer himself accompanied me with a small party of the 90th and Madras Fusiliers. The enemy, fifty or sixty in number, were surprised and rapidly driven out with very trifling loss on our side, and the position immediately barricaded and secured by Captain Crommelin; it has ever since formed a good connection between the picquets of the advance garden and the quarters of Brasyer's Sikhs, and all attempts of the enemy to molest it have been ineffective. It falls within Captain Crommelin's province to report in detail the various operations by which our difficult position, in close contact with the city, occupied by a numerous and persevering enemy, has been defended and protected.

I beg to bring to the notice of Major-General Havelock the excellent services performed by Lieutenant-Colonel Purnell, who has commanded in the advance garden and its outposts since their occupation. Much of the trench work by which it was rendered unassailable has been executed by his men, and under his superintendence, directed by the Engineer Department. On all occasions he has given the cordial and able co-operation of a most brave and accomplished officer. Captain Grant, of the Madras Fusiliers, has commanded the post of the Mosque, from the 11th of October to the 2nd of November, when he was severely wounded. He maintained the post under a constant and close musketry fire, and repeated attacks by mining, with cool courage and judgment; both these qualities were required to avoid real and to disregard the imaginary dangers of mines, and Captain Grant has displayed them in an eminent degree.

The daring and intelligent Captain Moorsom has been engaged in most of the above operations, and has given very valuable assistance.

Captains Rattray and Wade have shown themselves excellent commanders of outposts.

I have, &c.,
R. NAPIER, *Colonel*,
Military Secretary, &c.

Lieutenant G. Hutchinson, Engineers, Director of Works, to Colonel R. Napier, Engineers, Military Secretary, &c. &c.

Lucknow, 21st November, 1857.

I have the honour to forward a plan and memorandum showing Captain Lockhart's post and work done by the engineer department at that post.

MEMORANDUM *of* WORK *executed at Captain Lockhart's Post, from the first possession of it until the 21st of November,* 1857.

Barricades were at once and primarily erected at all outlets and loopholes cut along all the walls.

Doorways of communications were opened between the three main houses, which originally were distinct buildings, and such arrangements made as enabled us to command to the utmost the ruins on the right and left of position.

A cannon-proof barricade was erected across the Khas Bazar, communicating with 84th post, and an embrasure opened through it for a gun; a second barricade was afterwards placed across the Cawnpore road.

The enemy commenced mining against us (at H) on the left of our position, about six days after our occupying the post. We sunk a shaft preparatory to driving a gallery to meet them; but before we could complete the shaft, the enemy exploded a very large charge of powder, some ten feet short of our outer enclosure wall, which had the effect of shaking down the wall and filling up our shaft by the masses of earth thrown into the air and descending into our shaft. I regret to say we lost one man in this shaft. By some fatality, though the men on duty and at the mine saw the enemy's train burning, and volumes of smoke issuing out of the houses from which they knew the enemy were mining, they did not move from the spot, but merely sent to report to their officer. We were prepared for the explosion, and had the enclosure all ready barricaded off, so that the enemy gained nothing by the mine.

From this time up to within the last six days, we have been almost constantly at work day and night, countermining against them.

Our general success has been very good, having held our ground with an expenditure of but 200 lbs. of powder, and resisted numerous attacks of the enemy's miners.

On two particular occasions our success was more than usual. A gallery driven, from our shaft C, intercepted a gallery of the enemy's, and our explosion completely cut off some 12 feet of it; so that the next morning, on breaking into the portion so cut off, we dug out, or rather dragged out, four dead bodies, the enemy's miners having been completely cut off in a tomb as it were, for the gallery they were in was not broken down, but stopped up by our explosion.

In the second case our operations commenced from shaft D.

We broke into their gallery some 12 feet from our wall about twelve o'clock at night, and Sergeant Day, our superintending miner, remained below, assisted by others, holding the entrance to their gallery until I arrived.

On entering the enemy's gallery, I took Corporal Thompson, of the 78th Highlanders, with me, and observing the apparently great length of the enemy's mine, proceeded cautiously to extinguish the lights, so as to keep ourselves in darkness as we advanced. At this time the enemy were in the mine at or near their shaft, which, contrary to their usual practice, they evidently wished to hold uninjured. They generally fill them in at once when we take their gallery.

I proceeded, extinguishing the lights, until I distinctly saw the enemy at the far end, and to advance further would be to advance in a blaze of light. I therefore lay down and waited, as our preparations above, carried on under Lieutenant Tulloch, were not yet ready. Whilst lying there, I saw a sepoy with musket at trail advance down the mine, and when within 40 feet of him, fired at him. My pistol missed fire, and before Corporal Thompson could hand me his pistol, the sepoy had retreated. After remaining some time longer, I placed another man with Corporal Thompson, and went up to get an officer down, as I felt it required a very steady man down here to support us. While we were laying the charge and making various arrangements, which utterly precluded our watching against an enemy's advance, Lieutenant Hay, of the 78th Highlanders, then commanding the picquet, kindly volunteered and took up my old post. Lieutenant Tulloch and Sergeant Day quickly got the powder down, and all arrangements ready, when we withdrew Lieutenant Hay behind the partial barricade we had formed; and whilst here, still watching with Corporal Thompson, he got two shots at another man who attempted to come down the mine, and apparently wounded him. The enemy made no more attempts to come down the mine, but went outside their building, and came over our heads, apparently with the intention of breaking through. After some quarter of an hour's walking over head, they, I conclude, could not find the direction of the mine, and retreated into the house.

Our charge of 50 lbs., which I had laid outside our barricade, and 82 feet up to the enemy's gallery, was soon tamped, and the charge fired by Lieutenant Tulloch. The charge being laid with 9 feet of sand-bag tamping behind it, and none in front, the main force of the powder acted towards the enemy's shaft, but it took down 40 feet backwards towards us, leaving us 40 feet to use as a listening gallery. I deduce the enemy's mine to be 200 feet long and upwards, from the reconnoitring of Lieutenant Hay and myself before we commenced laying our charge, and from the position of the house it came from. The gallery had numerous air-holes, and was thoroughly ventilated.

I was much indebted to Lieutenant Hay and Corporal Thompson in this business, and also to Lieutenant Tulloch, who himself also fired the mine—a somewhat difficult task, as our bore being short, he had to retreat some 60 feet through the enemy's gallery and ours, and then up the shaft. Such is a brief account of our mining operations. The total length of gallery work run is 500 feet, and five shafts averaging 12 feet deep, with a drain of 5 feet each.

The 9-pounder gun I placed in position in the house on the left of our position, as shown in plan, and it was useful in silencing the fire of a gun of the enemy's firing from a stockade up the lane.

In concluding this report, I would respectfully bring to your notice the valuable assistance rendered by Sergeant Day, of the 32nd, who was in charge of the mines, and until Lieutenant Tulloch was posted to the position, acted direct under my orders. His zeal and quiet, steady management of the raw recruits under him has been most commendable.

I would also bring to your notice the unremitting zeal and attention to his work manifested by Lieutenant Tulloch, since he has been in charge of the post; and during the period of my acting here, Lieutenant Tulloch has almost entirely—unassisted by me—carried on our system of mines most successfully.

I have, &c.,
G. HUTCHINSON, *Lieut., Engineers,*
Director of Works.

NAMES *of* OFFICERS KILLED *and* WOUNDED *with General Havelock's force since leaving Cawnpore to* 29*th September,* 1855, *in addition to the names already published in Government General Order, No.* 1,625, *of* 1857.—"*Extraordinary Gazette*" *of the* 23*rd December,* 1857.

KILLED.

Her Majesty's 5*th Fusiliers.*—Lieutenant E. F. Haig.
Her Majesty's 90*th Light Infantry.*—Lieutenant J. J. Nunn.

WOUNDED.

Her Majesty's 5*th Fusiliers.*—Lieutenant J. W. D. Adair; Lieutenant W. M. Carter (since dead).
Her Majesty's 78*th Highlanders.*—Captain R. Bogle.
Her Majesty's 90*th Light Infantry.*—Brevet Major J. Perrin, Captain A. A. Becher, 40th N. I. (since dead); Lieutenant N. Grahame (since dead).

NOMINAL ROLL of *European Officers Killed and Wounded from* 29*th September to* 21*st October, in Field Force.*

Artillery.—Lieutenant Fraser, September 30th, slightly wounded.

1*st Madras Fusiliers.*—Major Stephenson, October 4th, slightly wounded; Captain Fraser, October 5th, severely wounded; Captain Galwey, October 5th, slightly wounded; Lieutenant Græme, October 5th, mortally wounded (since dead); Lieutenant Barclay, October 21st, slightly wounded.

5*th Fusiliers.*—Captain Scott, October 6th, slightly wounded,

78*th Highlanders.*—Major Haliburton, October 4th, mortally wounded (since dead); Dr. McMaster, October 15th, slightly wounded.

84*th Foot.*—Lieutenant Gibaut, October 6th, mortally wounded (since dead).

90*th Foot.*—Captain Denison, October 6th, severely wounded; Captain Bingham, October 6th, severely wounded; Captain Phipps, October 6th, severely wounded.

Regiment of Ferozepore.—Lieutenant Cross, October 6th, severely wounded.

[Having secured his troops in as perfect safety as the nature of the locality permitted, and reorganized the various military departments, Sir James Outram directed his attention to the arrangements by which he could most effectually facilitate the advance of the force for which he had applied, to effect the removal of the Lucknow garrison. In the " correspondence " which follows these despatches will be found the minute instructions which, with illustrative plans of the city and its environs, he forwarded to the Alumbagh for the guidance of " the officer commanding the relieving force." And in this division of the volume are detailed the several arrangements made by Sir James Outram for enabling that force to communicate with his own, as well as the co-operative measures by which he undertook that the latter should share the labours of the former, and minimize the perils of its advance. How effectually the promises made by Sir James Outram in behalf of his own troops were fulfilled, is shown in the reports of General Havelock, Brigadier Eyre, Colonel Napier, Captain Crommelin, and Lieutenants Hutchinson, Limond, Hall, and Russell. But as these will probably be read with greater interest after the despatch in which Sir Colin Campbell describes the brilliant achievements of his own force, to which the operations of the Lucknow troops were ancillary, precedence is here given to that document. When perusing this despatch, the reader should consult Plan No. I.]

His Excellency the Commander-in-Chief to the Right Hon. the Governor-General.

Head Quarters, Shah Nujjeef, Lucknow, 18th Nov. 1857.

MY LORD,—I have the honour to apprise your Lordship that I left Cawnpore on the 9th November, and joined the troops under the command of Brigadier-General Hope Grant, C.B., the same day, at Camp Buntara, about six miles from Alumbagh.

There being a few detachments on the road, I deemed it expedient to wait till the 12th before commencing my advance.

On that day I marched early for Alumbagh, with the following troops:—Naval Brigade, eight heavy guns; Bengal Horse Artillery, ten guns; Bengal Horse Field Battery, six guns; heavy field battery Royal Artillery; detachments Bengal and Punjaub Sappers and Miners; H.M.'s 9th Lancers; detachments 1st, 2nd, and 5th Punjaub Cavalry and Hodson's Horse; H.M.'s 8th, 53rd, 75th, and 93rd Regiments of Infantry; 2nd and 4th Punjaub Infantry. Probable total—700 cavalry, 2,700 infantry.

The advance guard was attacked by two guns and a body of about 2,000 infantry. After a smart skirmish, the guns were taken, Lieut. Gough, commanding Hodson's Irregular Horse, having distinguished himself very much in a brilliant charge, by which this object was effected.

The camp was pitched on that evening at Alumbagh. This place I found to be annoyed to a certain extent by guns placed in different positions in the neighbourhood.

I caused the post to be cleared of lumber and cattle, and placed all my tents in it.

I made my arrangements for marching without baggage when I should reach the park of Dilkoosha, and the men were directed to have three days' food in their haversacks. I changed the garrison at Alumbagh, taking fresh men from it, and leaving H.M.'s 75th Regiment there, which had been so much harassed by its late exertions.

On the 14th I expected a further reinforcement of 600 or 700 men, who joined my rear-guard, after my march had commenced, in the morning of that day.

As I approached the park of Dilkoosha, the leading troops were met by a long line of musketry fire.

The advance guard was quickly reinforced by a field battery and more infantry, composed of companies of H.M.'s 5th, 64th, and 78th Foot, under the command of Lieutenant-Colonel Hamilton, H.M.'s 78th Highlanders, supported by the 8th Foot. After a running fight of about two hours, in which our loss was very inconsiderable, the enemy was driven down the hill to the Martinière, across the garden and park of the Martinière, and far beyond the canal.

His loss was trifling, owing to the suddenness of the retreat.

The Dilkoosha and Martinière were both occupied, Brigadier Hope's brigade being then brought up and arranged in position in the wood of the Martinière, at the end opposite the canal, being flanked to the left by Capt. Bourchier's field battery and two of Capt. Peel's heavy guns.

Shortly after these arrangements had been made, the enemy drew out a good many people, and attacked our position in front.

He was quickly driven off, some of our troops crossing the canal in pursuit.

On this occasion the 53rd, 93rd, and a body of the 4th Punjaub Sikhs, distinguished themselves. Two very promising young officers lost their lives : Lieutenant Mayne, Bengal Horse Artillery, Quartermaster-General's Department ; and Captain Wheatcroft, Carabineers, doing duty with H.M.'s 9th Lancers.

All the troops behaved very well.

With the exception of my tents, all my heavy baggage, including provisions for fourteen days for my own force and that in Lucknow, accompanied me on my march across the country to Dilkoosha, covered by a strong rear-guard, under Lieutenant-Colonel Ewart, of H.M.'s 93rd Highlanders. This officer distinguished himself very much in this difficult command, his artillery, under Captain Blunt, Bengal Horse Artillery, assisted by the Royal Artillery, under Colonel Crawford, R.A., having been in action for the greater part of the day. The rear-guard did not close up to the column until late next day, the enemy having hung on it until dark on the 14th.

Every description of baggage having been left at Dilkoosha, which was occupied by H.M.'s 8th Regiment, I advanced direct on Secunderbagh early on the 16th.

This place is a high-walled enclosure of strong masonry, of 120 yards square, and was carefully loopholed all round. It was held very strongly by the enemy. Opposite to it was a village, at a distance of 100 yards, which was also loopholed and filled with men.

On the head of the column advancing up the lane to the left of the Secunderbagh, fire was opened on us. The infantry of the advance guard was quickly thrown into skirmishing order to line a bank to the right.

The guns were pushed rapidly onwards, viz., Captain Blunt's troop Bengal Horse Artillery, and Captain Travers's Royal Artillery heavy field battery.

The troop passed at a gallop through a cross fire from the village and Secunderbagh, and opened fire within easy musketry range in a most daring manner.

As soon as they could be pushed up a stiff bank, two eighteen-pounder guns, under Captain Travers, were also brought to bear on the building.

Whilst this was being effected, the leading brigade of infantry, under Brigadier the Honourable Adrian Hope, coming rapidly into action, caused the loopholed village to be abandoned, the whole fire of the brigade being then directed on the Secunderbagh.

After a time a large body of the enemy who were holding ground to the left of our advance, were driven by parties of the 53rd and 93rd, two of Captain Blunt's guns aiding the movement.

The Highlanders pursued their advantage, and seized the barracks, and immediately converted it into a military post, the 53rd stretching in a long line of skirmishers in the open plain, and driving the enemy before them.

The attack on the Secunderbagh had now been proceeding for about an hour and a half, when it was determined to take the place by storm, through a small opening which had been made. This was done in the most brilliant manner by the remainder of the Highlanders, and the 53rd and the 4th Punjaub Infantry, supported by a battalion of detachments under Major Barnston.

There never was a bolder feat of arms, and the loss inflicted on the enemy after the entrance of the Secunderbagh was effected was immense; more than 2,000 of the enemy were afterwards carried out.

The officers who led these regiments were Lieutenant-Colonel Leith Hay, H.M.'s 83rd Highlanders; Lieutenant-Colonel Gordon, H.M.'s 93rd Highlanders; Captain Walton, H.M.'s 53rd Foot; Lieutenant Paul, 4th Punjaub Infantry (since dead); and Major Barnston, H.M.'s 90th Foot.

Captain Peel's royal naval siege train then went to the front, and advanced towards the Shah Nujjeef, together with the field battery and some mortars, the village to the left having been cleared by Brigadier Hope and Lieutenant-Colonel Gordon.

The Shah Nujjeef is a domed mosque, with a garden, of which the most had been made by the enemy. The wall of the enclosure of the mosque was loopholed with great care. The entrance to it had been covered by a regular work in masonry, and the top of the building was crowned with a parapet. From this and from the defences in the garden an unceasing fire of musketry was kept up from the commencement of the attack.

This position was defended with great resolution against a heavy cannonade of three hours. It was then stormed in the boldest manner by the 93rd Highlanders, under Brigadier Hope, supported by a battalion of detachments under Major Barnston, who was, I regret to say, severely wounded, Captain Peel leading up his heavy guns with extraordinary gallantry within a few yards of the building to batter the massive stone walls. The withering fire of the Highlanders effectually covered the naval brigade from great loss, but it was an action almost unexampled in war. Captain Peel behaved very much as if he had been laying the *Shannon* alongside an enemy's frigate.

This brought the day's operations to a close.

On the next day communications were opened to the left rear of the barracks to the canal, after overcoming considerable difficulty. Captain Peel kept up a steady cannonade on the building called the mess-house. This building, of considerable size, was defended by a ditch of about twelve feet broad, and scarped with masonry, and beyond that a loopholed mud wall. I determined to use the guns as much as possible in taking it.

About 3 P.M., when it was considered that men might be sent to storm it without much risk, it was taken by a company of the 90th Foot, under Captain Wolseley, and a picquet of H.M.'s 53rd, under Captain Hopkins, supported by Major Barnston's battalion of detachments, under Captain Guise, H.M.'s 90th Foot, and some of the Punjaub Infantry, under Lieutenant Powlett. The mess-house was carried immediately with a rush.

The troops then pressed forward with great vigour, and lined the wall separating the mess-house from the Motee Mahal, which consists of a wide enclosure and many buildings. The enemy here made a last stand, which was overcome after an hour, openings having been broken in the wall, through which the troops poured with a body of sappers, and accomplished our communications with the Residency.

I had the inexpressible satisfaction shortly afterwards of greeting Sir James Outram and Sir Henry Havelock, who came out to meet me before the action was at an end.

The relief of the besieged garrison had been accomplished.

The troops, including all ranks of officers and men, had worked strenuously, and persevered boldly in following up the advantages gained in the various attacks. Every man in the force had exerted himself to the utmost, and now met with his reward.

It should not be forgotten that these exertions did not date merely from the day that I joined the camp, the various bodies of which the relieving force was composed having made the longest forced marches from various directions to enable the Government of India to save the garrison of Lucknow; some from Agra, some from Allahabad, all had alike undergone the same fatigues in pressing forward for the attainment of this great object. Of their conduct in the field of battle, the facts narrated in this despatch are sufficient evidence, which I will not weaken by any eulogy of mine.

I desire now to direct the attention of your Lordship to the merits of the officers who have served under my orders on this occasion.

I cannot convey to your Lordship in adequate terms my deep sense of the obligations I am under to Major-General Mansfield, Chief of the Staff, for the very able and cordial assistance he has afforded me and the service during these operations, and how admirably the very many and important duties belonging to his situation have been performed—for which his high talents and experience of service in this country so peculiarly fit him.

I have also to express my very particular acknowledgments to Brigadier-General Hope Grant, C.B., who was in immediate command of the division by which this service was effected. His activity in carrying out the details has been admirable, and his vigilance in superintending the outpost duties has been unsurpassed.

My thanks are peculiarly due to Brigadier the Hon. Adrian Hope, who commanded the advance of the force; as also to Captain Peel, C.B., of the Royal Navy, who has distinguished himself in a most marked manner.

I desire to bring to the favourable notice of your Lordship the officers commanding brigades and regiments, and those who have been in the performance of staff duties, or who have been marked out by brigadiers :—

Brigadier Crawford, Royal Artillery, commanding the Artillery; Brigadier Little, commanding the Cavalry; Brigadier Greathed, commanding 3rd Infantry Brigade; Brigadier Russell, commanding 5th Infantry Brigade (severely wounded); Lieut. Lennox, Royal Engineers, acting chief engineer; Lieut. Vaughan, Royal Navy, and Capt. Maxwell, Bengal Artillery, attached to the Naval Brigade; Major

Turner, commanding the Bengal Artillery (to this officer my most particular acknowledgments are due; he has few equals as an artillery officer); Captain Travers, commanding Royal Artillery; Captains Remmington and Blunt, commanding troops of Bengal Horse Artillery; Captains Middleton, Royal Artillery, and Bourchier, Bengal Artillery, commanding horse field batteries; and Captain Longden, Royal Artillery, commanding the mortar battery.

It is impossible to draw a distinction between any of these officers. They all distinguished themselves, under very arduous circumstances; and it was highly agreeable to me to be present on this first occasion when the Bengal and Royal Artillery were brought into action together under my own eyes. I wish also to mention Lieut. Walker, Bengal Artillery, in command of a demi-field battery; Lieuts. Ford and Brown, who successively took up the command of the heavy field battery of Royal Artillery, under Captain Hardy, on the death of that lamented officer; and Lieut. Bridge, who commanded two guns of the Madras Horse Artillery with great ability. I have further to bring to your Lordship's notice Lieut. Scott, Madras Engineers, who commanded the Sappers and Miners.

I would also bring to favourable notice the following officers in command of corps or detachments:—Major Ouvry, H. M.'s 9th Lancers; Major Robertson, military train; Captain Hinde, H. M.'s 8th Regiment; Lieutenant-Colonel Wells, 23rd Fusiliers; Lieutenant-Colonel Gordon, 93rd Highlanders, in temporary command of H. M.'s 53rd Regiment; Lieutenant-Colonel Hale, H. M.'s 82nd Regiment; Lieutenant-Colonel Leith Hay, 93rd Highlanders; Lieutenant-Colonel Hamilton, 78th Highlanders, commanding 1st battalion of detachments; Major Barnston, H. M.'s 90th Regiment, commanding 2nd battalion of detachments (dangerously wounded); and Captain Guise, H. M.'s 90th Regiment, who succeeded Major Barnston in his command.

Lieutenants Watson, Probyn, Younghusband, and Gough, respectively commanding detachments of the 1st, 2nd, and 5th Punjaub Cavalry, and Hodson's Horse; Captain Green, commanding 2nd Punjaub Infantry; Lieutenant Willoughby, who succeeded to the command of the 4th Punjaub Infantry on his three seniors in the corps being severely wounded; Lieutenant Ryves, who commanded the 4th Punjaub Infantry from the evening of the 16th; Major Milman, 5th Fusiliers, and Lieutenant-Colonel McIntyre, 78th Highlanders, in command of detachments employed in the advance on Dilkoosha and the Martinière; Lieutenant-Colonel Ewart, 93rd Highlanders, who commanded at the barracks; Captains Dawson, 93rd Highlanders, Rolleston, H. M.'s 84th Regiment, and Hopkins, 53rd Regiment, and Lieutenants Fisher and Powlett, 2nd Punjaub Infantry, who commanded separate detachments or posts, and whose services have for the most part been noted in the body of the despatch.

It remains for me to express my high sense of the services performed by the Assistant Adjutant-General of the Army, Captain Norman, who on this, as on every other occasion, highly distinguished himself.

I have further to express my warm thanks to all the officers serving on the general and personal staff of myself and Major-General

Mansfield, as named below, but especially to Colonel Berkeley, H. M.'s 32nd Regiment, who attended the Chief of the Staff in the field, and who displayed remarkable activity and intelligence; to Major Alison, Military Secretary (who unfortunately lost his arm); to Captain Sir David Baird, Bart., my first aide-de-camp; and to Lieutenant Hope Johnstone, Deputy Assistant-Adjutant-General to the Chief of the Staff.

The remaining officers of this Staff were Lieutenant G. Algood, deputy assistant-quartermaster-general; Captains Maycock and Carey, officiating deputy assistant-quartermaster-generals; Captain Rudman, acting assistant-adjutant-general of her Majesty's Forces; Captain Hatch, deputy judge-advocate-general; Captains Alison and Foster, my aides-de-camp; Captain Metcalfe, interpreter; and Lieutenant Murray, aide-de-camp to the Chief of the Staff.

Mr. Cavenagh, of the Uncovenanted Civil Service, who came out from Lucknow in disguise to afford me information at the imminent risk of his life, has won my most especial thanks, and I recommend him most cordially to the notice of your Lordship.

Lord Seymour was present throughout these operations, and displayed a daring gallantry at a most critical moment.

I concur most fully in the commendations that have been bestowed by General Grant and officers commanding staffs on their respective staffs as named below, but I would especially draw attention to the services of Captain Cox, H. M.'s 75th Regiment, brigade major of the 4th Brigade, and Lieutenant Roberts, Bengal Artillery, deputy assistant-quartermaster-general; Captain W. Hamilton, H. M.'s 8th Lancers, deputy assistant-adjutant-general; Captain the Hon. A. H. Anson, H. M.'s 84th Regiment, aide-de-camp; and Lieutenant Salmond, 7th Light Cavalry, acting aide-de-camp to Brigadier-General Grant; Captain H. Hammond, Bengal Artillery, brigade major of Artillery (severely wounded); Captain H. Le G. Bruce, Bengal Artillery, who succeeded Captain Hammond; Brevet-Major W. Barry, and Lieutenant A. Bunny, staff officers of Royal and Bengal Artillery, respectively; Lieutenant G. E. Watson, Bengal Engineers, brigade major of Engineers; Captain H. A. Sarel, 17th Lancers, brigade major of Cavalry; and Captains Bannatyne, H. M.'s 8th Foot, and Lightfoot, 84th Foot, brigade majors of the 3rd and 5th Brigade; also Lieutenant Stewart, Bengal Engineers, superintendent of the electric telegraph, who accompanied the force, and made himself particularly useful throughout.

I must not omit to name in the most marked manner Subadar Gokul Singh, 4th Punjaub Rifles, who, in conjunction with the British officers, led the 4th Punjaub Rifles at the storming of Secunderabagh in the most daring manner.

Captain A. D. Dickens, deputy assistant-commissary-general, and Lieutenant W. Tod Brown, deputy commissary of ordnance, have both distinguished themselves exceedingly in carrying on the intricate duties of their departments with very scanty establishments to meet the great demands upon them.

Brigadier-General Grant has made favourable mention of Surgeon J. C. Brown, M.D., Bengal Horse Artillery, whose great exertions have been deserving of all praise. He has since become superintending surgeon of the force.

The number of officers mentioned in this despatch may appear large, but the force employed was composed of many detachments, and the particular service was calculated to draw forth the individual qualities of the officers engaged.

Annexed is a return of casualties; and a list of officers, non-commissioned officers, and soldiers who have been brought to my notice as having particularly distinguished themselves, will be separately forwarded.

I have the honour to be, my Lord, your Lordship's most obedient humble servant,

(Signed)   C. CAMPBELL, *General, Commander-in-Chief.*

LIST OF OFFICERS KILLED.

General Staff.—Lieutenant-Colonel G. Biddulph, head of intelligence department; Lieutenant A. O. Mayne, deputy assistant-quartermaster-general.

Naval Brigade.—Midshipman M. A. Daniel.

Artillery Brigade.—Captain W. N. Hardy, Royal Artillery.

Cavalry Brigade.—Captain G. Wheatcroft, 6th Dragoon Guards, doing duty with Military Train.

3rd Infantry Brigade.—Lieutenant T. Frankland, 2nd Punjaub Infantry.

4th Infantry Brigade.—Captain J. Dalzell, H. M.'s 93rd Highlanders; Captain J. T. Lumsden, 30th Native Infantry, interpreter to H. M.'s 93rd Highlanders; Lieutenant Dobbs, 1st Madras Fusiliers.

5th Infantry Brigade.—Ensign W. T. Thompson, H. M.'s 82nd Regiment.

LIST OF OFFICERS WOUNDED.

Staff.—General Sir C. Campbell, G.C.B., commander-in-chief, slightly; Brigadier D. Russell, commanding 5th Brigade, severely; Major A. Alison, military secretary, severely; Captain F. M. Alison, A. D. C. to Commander-in-Chief, slightly; Captain the Hon. A. Anson, A. D. C. to General Grant, C.B., slightly; Lieut. C. J. Salmond, orderly officer to General Grant, slightly.

Naval Brigade.—Captain J. C. Gray, Royal Marines, slightly; Lieutenant M. Salmon, Royal Navy, severely; Midshipman Lord A. P. Clinton, Royal Navy, slightly.

Artillery Brigade.—Major F. F. Pennycuick, Royal Artillery, slightly; Captain H. Hammond, Bengal Artillery, severely; Captain F. Travers, Royal Artillery, slightly; Lieutenant W. G. Milman, Royal Artillery, slightly; Lieutenant A. Ford, Royal Artillery, slightly; Assistant-Surgeon H. R. Veale, Royal Artillery, severely.

Cavalry Brigade.—Lieutenant R. Halkett, Hodson's Horse, severely.

3rd Infantry Brigade.—Ensign J. Watson, 2nd Punjaub Infantry, dangerously.

4th Infantry Brigade.—Captain B. Walton, H. M.'s 53rd Regiment, severely; Lieutenant A. K. Munro, H. M.'s 53rd Regiment, dangerously; Lieutenant T. C. Ffrench, H. M.'s 53rd Regiment, slightly; Major R.

Barnston, H. M.'s 90th Regiment, dangerously; Lieutenant F. C. Wynne, H. M.'s 90th Regiment, severely; Ensign H. Powell, H. M.'s 90th Regiment, severely; Lieutenant-Colonel J. A. Ewart, H. M.'s 93rd Highlanders, slightly; Captain F. W. Burroughs, H. M.'s 93rd Highlanders, slightly; Lieutenant R. A. Cooper, H. M.'s 93rd Highlanders, severely; Lieutenant E. Welch, H. M.'s 93rd Highlanders, severely; O. Goldsmith, H. M.'s 93rd Highlanders, severely; Lieutenant S. E. Wood, H. M.'s 93rd Highlanders, severely; Ensign F. R. McNamara, H. M.'s 93rd Highlanders, slightly; Lieutenant W. Paul, 4th Punjaub Infantry, dangerously (since dead); Lieutenant J. W. McQueen, 4th Punjaub Infantry, severely; Lieutenant F. F. Oldfield, 4th Punjaub Infantry, dangerously (since dead).

5th Infantry Brigade—Lieutenant H. Henderson, H. M.'s 23rd Fusiliers, slightly; Lieutenant-Colonel C. B. Hale, H. M.'s 82nd Regiment, slightly.

(Signed)   H. W. NORMAN, *Captain*,
Assistant Adjutant-General of the Army.

Head Quarters, Camp Alumbagh, 25th November, 1857.

MY LORD,—In continuation of my report of the 18th, I have the honour to apprise your Lordship that the left rear of my position was finally secured on the night of the 17th instant by the building called Banks' House having been seized by a party of the 2nd Punjaub Infantry (Sikhs) specially employed for that purpose. Brigadier Russell and Lieutenant-Colonel Hale distinguished themselves much in completing the chain of posts on the 17th and 18th in that direction, the enemy having been very vigilant on that point, and kept up an unceasing fire on all the buildings occupied by Brigadier Russell, and on the barrack occupied by 300 of the Highlanders under Lieutenant-Colonel Ewart.

Brigadier Russell having been unfortunately severely wounded on the afternoon of the 18th December, I placed the lamented Colonel Biddulph in command of his line of posts. He was killed almost immediately afterwards when making his dispositions for the attack of the hospital.

Captain Bourchier, of the Bengal Artillary, distinguished himself by the intelligent and able support he afforded Lieutenant-Colonel Hale, H. M.'s 82nd Foot, on that officer succeeding Colonel Biddulph.

These very difficult and tedious operations, conducted as they were under a most galling fire in cramped suburbs, reflect much credit on all the officers and men concerned, and secured the position.

The same afternoon, the enemy made a smart attempt on the picquets covering the centre of the line.

I supported them with a company of H. M.'s 23rd and another of H. M.'s 53rd Foot, not having any more infantry at my disposal.

Captain Remmington's troop of Horse Artillery was brought up and dashed right into the jungle with the leading skirmishers, and opened fire with extraordinary rapidity and precision.

Captain Remmington distinguished himself very much.

I superintended this affair myself, and I have particular pleasure in drawing your Lordship's attention to the conduct of this troop on this occasion as an instance of the never-failing readiness and quickness of the Horse Artillery of the Bengal Service.

During the next three days I continued to hold the whole of the country from the Dilkoosha to the gates of the Residency; the left flank having been secured in the manner above mentioned, with a view to extricating the garrison, without exposing it to the chance of even a stray musket-shot.

From the first all the arrangements have been conducted towards this end. The whole of the force under my immediate command being one outlying picquet, every man remained on duty, and was constantly subject to annoyance from the enemy's fire; but such was the vigilance and intelligence of the force, and so heartily did all ranks co-operate to support me, that 1 was enabled to conduct this affair to a happy issue, exactly in the manner originally proposed.

Upon the 20th, fire was opened on the Kaiserbagh, which gradually increased in importance till it assumed the character of regular breaching and bombardment.

The Kaiserbagh was breached in three places by Captain Peel, R.N., and 1 have been told that the enemy suffered much loss within its precincts. Having thus led the enemy to believe that immediate assault was contemplated, orders were issued for the retreat of the garrison through the lines of our picquets at midnight on the 22nd.

The ladies and families, the wounded, the treasure, the guns, it was thought worth while to keep; the ordnance store, the grain still possessed by the commissariat of the garrison, and the State prisoners, had all been previously removed.

Sir James Outram had received orders to burst the guns which it was thought undesirable to take away, and he was finally directed silently to evacuate the Residency of Lucknow at the hour indicated.

The dispositions to cover their retreat and to resist the enemy, should he pursue, were ably carried out by Brigadier Hon. Adrian Hope; but I am happy to say the enemy was completely deceived, and he did not attempt to follow. On the contrary, he began firing on our old positions many hours after we had left them. The movement of retreat was admirably executed, and was a perfect lesson in such combinations.

Each exterior line came gradually retiring through its supports till at length nothing remained but the last line of infantry and guns with which 1 was myself to crush the enemy if he had dared to follow up the picquets.

The only line of retreat lay through a long and tortuous lane, and all these precautions were absolutely necessary to insure the safety of the force.

The extreme posts on the left under Lieutenant-Colonel Hale, of H. M.'s 82nd Regiment, Lieutenant-Colonel Wells, of H. M.'s 23rd Foot, and Lieutenant-Colonel Ewart, of H. M.'s 93rd Highlanders, made their way by a road which had been explored for them after I considered the line had arrived, with due regard to the security of the whole that their posts should be evacuated.

It was my endeavour that nothing should be left to chance; and the conduct of the officers in exactly carrying out their instructions was beyond all praise. During all these operations from the 16th instant, the remnant of Brigadier Greathed's brigade closed in the rear, and now again formed the rear-guard as we retired to Dilkoosha.

Dilkoosha was reached at four A.M. on the 23rd instant by the whole force. I must not forget to mention the exertions of the cavalry during all the operations which have been described.

The exertions of Brigadier Little and of Major Ouvry, respectively of the Cavalry Brigade and the 9th Lancers, were unceasing in keeping up our long line of communication and preserving our extreme rear beyond the Dilkoosha, which was constantly threatened. On the 22nd, the enemy attacked at Dilkoosha; but was speedily driven off under Brigadier Little's orders.

The officers commanding the Irregular Cavalry—Lieutenants Watson, Younghusband, Probyn, and Gough—as well all the officers of the 9th Lancers, were never out of the saddle during all this time, and well maintained the character they have won throughout the war.

I moved with General Grant's division to Alumbagh on the afternoon of the 24th, leaving Sir James Outram's division in position at Diskoosha, to prevent molestation of the immense convoy of the women and wounded, which it was necessary to transport with us. Sir James Outram closed up this day without annoyance from the enemy.

I have, &c.,

C. CAMPBELL, *General, Commander in Chief.*

LIST OF OFFICERS KILLED AND WOUNDED.

KILLED.

4th Brigade—Lieutenant Benjamin Sandwith, H.M.'s 84th Regiment.

WOUNDED.

Artillery—Lieut. H. E. Harington, Bengal Artillery, severely.

GENERAL ORDER BY HIS EXCELLENCY THE COMMANDER-IN-CHIEF.

Head-quarters, La Martinière, Lucknow, 23rd Nov., 1857.

The Commander-in-Chief has reason to be thankful to the force he conducted for the relief of the garrison of Lucknow.

Hastily assembled, fatigued by forced marches, but animated by a common feeling of determination to accomplish the duty before them, all ranks of this force have compensated for their small number, in the execution of a most difficult duty, by unceasing exertions.

From the morning of the 16th, till last night, the whole force has been one outlying picquet never out of fire, and covering an immense extent of ground, to permit the garrison to retire scathless and in safety, covered by the whole of the relieving force.

That ground was won by fighting as hard as it ever fell to the lot of the Commander-in-Chief to witness, it being necessary to bring up the same men over and over again to fresh attacks; and it is with the greatest gratification his Excellency declares that he never saw men behave better.

The storming of Secundra Bâgh and Shah Nujeef has never been surpassed in daring, and the success of it was most brilliant and complete.

The movement of retreat of last night, by which the final rescue of the garrison was effected, was a model of discipline and exactness. The consequence was, that the enemy was completely deceived, and the force retired by a narrow tortuous lane, the only line of retreat open, in the face of 50,000 enemies, without molestation.

The Commander-in-Chief offers his sincere thanks to Major-General Sir James Outram, G.C.B., for the happy manner in which he planned and carried out his arrangements for the evacuation of the Residency of Lucknow.

By Order of his Excellency the Commander-in-Chief,

W. MAYHEW, *Major*,
Deputy Adjutant-General of the Army.

[The subjoined despatches describe the preparations Sir James Outram had made to enable him to co-operate with Sir Colin Campbell, and the series of movements by which this active co-operation was afforded.]

Major-General H. Havelock, Commanding Oude Field Force, to Colonel R. Napier, Chief of the Staff, &c., to Major-General Sir James Outram, G.C.B.

Lucknow, 16th November, 1857.

I beg to report, for the information of Major-General Sir James Outram, G.C.B., the complete success of the operations in which the troops of my division were employed under his own eye this evening, in capturing a succession of houses in advance of the Palace of Fureed Buksh.

I have given in the margin* the details of detachments employed. The nature of the enterprise may be shortly described as follows:—

The progress of the relieving force under his Excellency the Commander-in-Chief was anxiously watched, and it was determined that as soon as he should reach the Sikunder Bagh, about three miles from the Residency, the outer wall of the advance garden of the palace, in which the enemy had before made several breaches, should be blown in by mines previously prepared; that two powerful batteries erected in the enclosure should then open on the insurgent defences in front, and after the desired effect had been produced, that the troops should storm two buildings known by the names of the Hern Khana, or Deer-house, and the Steam Engine-house. Under these, also, three mines had been driven.

It was ascertained, about 11 A.M., that Sir Colin Campbell was operating against the Sikunder Bagh. The explosion of the mines in the garden was therefore ordered. Their action was, however, comparatively feeble, so the batteries had the double task of completing the demolition of the wall, and prostrating and breaching the works and the buildings beyond it. Brigadier Eyre commanded in the left battery; Captain Olpherts in the right; Captain Maude shelled from six mortars in a more retired quadrangle of the palace. The troops were formed in the square of the Chuttur Munzil, and brought up in succession through the approaches, which in every direction intersected the advance garden. At a quarter-past three two of the mines at the Hern Khana exploded with good effect. At half-past three the advance sounded. It is impossible to describe the enthusiasm with which this signal was received by the troops. Pent up in inaction for upwards of six weeks, and subjected to constant attacks, they felt that the hour of retribution and glorious exertion had returned.

Their cheers echoed through the courts of the palace, responsive to the bugle sound, and on they rushed to assured victory. The enemy could nowhere withstand them. In a few minutes the whole of the buildings were in our possession, and have since been armed with

---

* 5th Fusiliers, 160, under Lieutenant Meara; 64th Regiment, 48, Captain Shute; 84th Regiment, 160, Captain Wills; 78th Regiment, 142, Captain Lockhart; 90th Light Infantry, 181, Lieut.-Colonel Purnell; Regiment of Ferozepore, 100, Lieutenant Cross. Reserve, 200 from 5th Fusiliers, 78th Highlanders, and Regiment of Ferozepore. Each column being accompanied by a party of Miners with tools and powder bags, under command of an Engineer officer.

cannon, and held against all attack. It will be seen by the enclosed return that the loss has been small.

I received throughout the operations the most effective aid from my Staff—Lieutenant Hudson, acting deputy-assistant adjutant-general; Lieutenant Moorsom, 52nd Light Infantry, acting deputy-assistant quartermaster-general; Lieutenant Hargood, 1st Madras Fusiliers, my aide-de-camp; and Lieutenant C. W. Havelock, 12th Irregular Cavalry, my orderly officer.

The officers of Artillery—Brigadier Eyre, and Captains Olpherts and Maude—have earned my best thanks.

I must commend all the officers in charge of detachments; but most prominently Lieutenant-Colonel Purnell, 90th Light Infantry, whose conduct throughout the affair evinced the most distinguished gallantry, united to imperturbable coolness and the soundest judgment; as well as to Lieutenants Russell, Hutchinson, and Limond, of the Engineers, and Captain Oakes (attached), who showed the way to several points of attack.
I have, &c.,
H. HAVELOCK, *Major-General*,
Commanding Oude Field Force.

Major-General H. Havelock, commanding Oude Field Force, to Captain Dodgson, Assistant Adjutant-General.

Lucknow, 19th November, 1857.

I beg to forward, for submission to Major-General Sir James Outram, G.C.B., the accompanying report of Captain Crommelin, field engineer, with plans, and rejoice in this opportunity of testifying to the merits of this officer, and his untiring industry when the state of his health has permitted his exertions to be fully developed.
I have, &c.,
HENRY HAVELOCK, *Major-General*,
Commanding Oude Field Force.

Captain Crommelin, Chief Engineer, Oude Field Force, to Captain Hudson, Deputy Assistant Adjutant-General, Oude Field Force.

Camp Alumbagh, 25th November, 1857.

In continuation of my letter, dated 12th inst.,* I have the honour to report, for the information of the Major-General commanding the Oude Field Force, upon the " Final Engineering offensive operations " at the Palace and Gardens of the Chuttur Munzil.

The Cavalier Battery, alluded to at the conclusion of my previous report, was completed during the night of the 13th inst., and was armed with the heavy guns on the morning of the 14th, viz., the day

---

* This letter is not amongst the published despatches.

originally appointed for the storming of the Hern Khana, Engine-house, and King's Stables.

During the night of the 13th, 29 charges of powder (each 25 lbs. in weight,) were laid in chambers that had been previously prepared for them under the foundation of the east face of the advance garden wall, and immediately in front of the Cavalier Battery. These charges were intended for the demolition of that part of the wall that screened the engine-house, stables, and the other adjacent buildings that were to be breached from the guns of the battery. I would here remind you that our attack was postponed from the morning of the 14th to that of the 16th. The charges of powder were thus exposed, in common canvas bags, for more than forty-eight hours, to the damaging influence of a very damp, sandy soil; so that when they were exploded, their effect, owing to the deterioration of the powder, was only sufficient to shake and split the wall in several places, and to form a small breach. The wall, however, was so much injured that the artillery had an easy task in battering down as much as was necessary. The charges, I may mention, were half as large again as those recommended by Sir W. Pasley (our best practical authority on this as well as most other points of engineering detail), and were such as had been successfully used by myself at Peshawur in a precisely similar case.

During the night of the 12th and 13th the trench (d, d) was widened for the passage of guns; screens were also constructed in the advanced garden; and other precautionary measures taken to protect our force against any musketry fire that might be poured in through the breaches in our own wall.

During the 15th, the three mines that had been prepared for the formation of breaches in the Hern Khana were loaded and tamped. These mines were sprung on the afternoon of the 16th. That at the north-west corner of the building effected the breach by which the right and centre columns of attack entered. Lieutenant Hall, in his report, erroneously states that this breach was made by the 18-pounder gun at the barricade.

The centre mine failed to explode, owing, I imagine, to some wet sand having been dislodged from the roof of the mine by the concussion of our artillery, and having fallen upon the powder-house.

The left charge, which was the largest, exploded; but it proved to be ten feet short of the building, and consequently effected no breach or injury. This error in the position of the charge is not to be wondered at, when it is considered—1st, that we could not, by the most careful survey, satisfy ourselves as to the exact position of the Hern Khana; and, 2nd, that we could not survey the mine itself with the prismatic compass, as no lights would burn owing to the foulness of the air near the end of a gallery that had been carried to the (I believe) unprecedented length of 289 feet without the aid of air-pipes.

On the morning of the 16th, everything was ready for the attack upon the Hern Khana, engine-house, and stables. Copies of instructions, the details of which had been prepared by myself, from memoranda drawn out by Colonel Napier (chief of the staff), were handed over to each of the five officers commanding the storming parties, and to the engineer officers accompanying them; and these instructions were further explained, by the aid of plans, to several of the commanding officers.

For an account of the operations of the storming parties, I must refer to the enclosed reports (in original) of Lieutenants Hutchinson, Russell, Limond, and Hall, with the remark that the duties of the officers under my command appear to me to have been rapidly and efficiently carried out.

I must also refer to a separate report by Lieutenant Hutchinson, directing engineer, upon the engineering operations, from the 16th of November to the hour of our evacuation of the Bailey Guard Entrenchment and Chuttur Munzil Palace—confinement to my quarters owing to an injury of the leg having prevented my superintending them personally.

It now remains for me to bring to the favourable notice of the Major-General commanding, those officers and men of the Engineer Department who have rendered good service; and in the first place, I trust it may not be considered out of order, that I here thankfully record my acknowledgment of the assistance that has always been afforded me by my experienced brother officer, Colonel Napier, military secretary and chief of the staff to Major-General Sir James Outram, G.C.B., who notwithstanding the pressure of his other important duties, was ever ready to aid me with his valuable counsel and advice, to meet my constant demands for workmen and materials, and to superintend and direct the works during the last month of our operations, when I was disabled from personally superintending them myself.

Lieutenant G. Hutchinson, of Engineers, deserves very great credit for the most able manner in which he discharged the duties of directing engineer of the works during the last ten days of our operations. His services, as one of the engineers of the original garrison, will be duly reported by the proper authority.

Lieutenant Russell, of Engineers, has rendered me very efficient aid as brigade-major of engineers; his constant and unwearying exertions, both by night and by day, merit my best thanks and the highest praise.

Lieutenant Limond, the only other engineer officer under my command, has also proved himself a very able and energetic officer, and has rendered very excellent service. To him, and to Lieutenant Russell, was entrusted the general supervision of all the works from the time that I was disabled until the appointment of Lieutenant Hutchinson as directing engineer—a period of about three weeks.

The officers and volunteers who have acted in the capacity of assistant field engineers have, without exception, given me their best and readiest assistance; but I may with justice more conspicuously notice the names of Captain Oakes, 8th N. I.; Lieutenant Hall, 1st Bengal Fusiliers; Mr. Goldsworthy, Volunteer Cavalry; and of Mr. Cavanagh, superintendent of the chief commissioner's office.

Sergeants Duffy and Connell, assistant overseers in the Department of Public Works, have proved most useful, and their duties in supervising workmen and collecting materials, &c., have been most cheerfully and efficiently performed.

I cannot close this report, without noticing, in the most favourable manner, the important services performed by the undermentioned soldiers as superintendents of miners :—Acting-Sergeant Cullimore, of her Majesty's 32nd Regiment; Acting-Sergeant Banetta, of her Majesty's 32nd Regiment; Acting-Sergeant Farrer, of her Majesty's 32nd Regiment; Coporal Dowling; Corporal Hosay, Madras Fusiliers; Private Baylan, of her Majesty's 5th Fusiliers.

Their duties have been of a very dangerous and arduous character, and have invariably been performed to my complete satisfaction.

I have, &c.,
W. A. CROMMELIN, *Captain*,
Chief Engineer, Oude Field Force.

Lieutenant G. Hutchinson, Engineers, Director of Works, to Captain Crommelin, Chief Engineer.

Lucknow, 21st November, 1857.

I have the honour to forward Lieutenant Limond's statement regarding the sortie party he led; also that of Lieutenant Hall.

With reference to my own party, I have to state, that starting from the Garden Picquet-house, Captain Shute and myself led the party to foot of stockade, which we scaled, and that then I turned off at once for the house called Captain Orr's, and in unison with Lieutenant Hall and Lieutenant Hay, who accompanied me, commenced carrying out our instructions. Up to this time not a man had been lost. Captain Shute led his men on beyond the Hern Khana, and took a garden and a gun.

Our mines exploded short; but the mine from the Garden Picquet decidedly shook and damaged the wall.

Lieutenant M. Hall, Assistant Field Engineer, to Captain Hutchinson, Directing Engineer.

Hern Khana, 21st November, 1857.

I have the honour to report, for the information of Captain Crommelin, field engineer, that in accordance with his instructions, I accompanied the right column of attack on the Hern Khana, under Captain Willis, 84th Regiment, on the 16th instant.

Immediately after the explosion of the Barricade Mine, we sallied out and made for the part of the building where it was intended the right breach should have been made. On arriving at the wall of the Hern Khana, we found the crater of the mine, about ten feet short of the wall which remain uninjured. We therefore turned to the left, and entered the Hern Khana by the left breach, which had been made by the 18-pounder gun at the barricade at end of lane.

On getting into the Hern Khana we turned to our right, passed across the open square and immediately commenced loopholing the wall which commands the street dividing our position from the Kaiser Bagh. On your arrival I reported myself to you.

Lieut. D. Limond, Engineers, to Captain Crommelin, Chief Engineer, Oude Field Force.

Lucknow, 21st November, 1857.

According to orders, Lieutenant Chalmers, Assistant Field Engineer, and myself, accompanied the detachment of the 90th Light Infantry, on the attack upon the Engine-house. Keeping to the left on passing that building, we found the rebels evacuating the same, and followed them up to the most advanced building, the Overseer's house, which I at once directed to be barricaded. The enemy opened on it with guns from the Kaiser Bagh, and the house was then abandoned and burnt by Colonel Purnell's orders. The east wall of the Barahduree enclosure was at once loopholed, and the windows to the south blocked up with sand-bags. During the night a battery for three light guns was constructed at the southern extremity of the lane, between the King's stables, and Barahduree enclosure. The doors and windows of the Engine-house facing the river were also barricaded. During the night a trench-covered communication was opened to the advanced garden, none being necessary between the Engine-house and King's stables.

Lieut. J. Russell, Brigade-Major of Engineers, to Captain Crommelin, Chief Engineer.

I have the honor to report that, according to order, Captain Oakes, Assistant Field Engineer, and myself, accompanied the detachment under command of Captain Lockhart, Her Majesty's 78th, on the 16th instant, in the attack upon the King's stables.

The detachment was drawn up in a line in the front trench of the advance garden, and on the order for the advance being given, we crossed the parapet of the trench and the breach in our front and doubled across the open to the King's stables, on reaching which some confusion occurred, for the lower part of the breach that had been made by our guns was some 4 feet from the ground; and not seeing any easy mode of egress, Captain Lockhart led the way into the enclosure of the steam-engine house on the left, and was followed by many of his men.

On his mistake being pointed out, however, he returned, and in company we entered the court-yard of the stables, which we found deserted. The men of the detachment followed us as quickly as they could.

Our orders were to man the walls of the stables on the side of the enemy; but the latter were retreating fast, pressed by our troops from the Hern Khana, on seeing which many of the detachments to which I was attached rushed across the road without orders and joined in the pursuit.

At Captain Lockhart's request, I went to recall these men, and on my return I found that he had occupied the Barahduree and other buildings in rear of the King's stables. Measures were immediately adopted for securing our position; but in a short time the portion of Captain Lockhart's detachment was withdrawn, and the post left to the charge of a detachment of Her Majesty's 90th, under Colonel Purnell.

During the night of the 16th, Lieutenant Limond, of Engineers, and myself, constructed a battery for three guns, which opened fire towards the Kaiser Bagh on the morning of the 17th.

[The next despatch by Brigadier Vincent Eyre, C.B., records the services of the Garrison Artillery between September 26th and the date of the Commander-in-Chief's arrival at Lucknow in November, 1857. But as its most interesting passages refer to the aid rendered by that Artillery in facilitating Sir Colin Campbell's advance, it has been deemed advisable to postpone it to this place.]

Major V. Eyre, Commanding Artillery Brigade, to Colonel R. Napier, Chief of the Staff, with the force under Major-General Sir J. Outram.

Camp Alumbagh, near Lucknow, 8th January, 1858.

The publication of Major-General Sir J. Outram's despatches having brought to light the accidental omission of any detailed report from the Artillery brigade under my orders, I gladly avail myself of his kind permission to fill up the blank, which I do the more readily since it affords me a fitting opportunity of placing on record publicly, my own professional testimony of the signal services rendered by those whom it was my good fortune to command during the recent operations at Lucknow.

2. On the lamented death of Brigadier Cooper, on the 26th September, I succeeded to the command of the brigade, and during my subsequent severe illness, my place was temporarily filled by Captain Olpherts.

3. Owing partly to these changes, and partly to the constant occupation which the daily exigencies of the service demanded from officers and men in the artillery, written reports were not expected, and hence it may have heretofore escaped mention, that, for two special acts of gallantry on the 25th September, both Captain Maude, R.A., and Captain Olpherts, B.A., commanding field batteries, were rewarded by the late Major-General Sir H. Havelock, K.C.B., with the much-coveted distinction of the Victoria Cross.

4. I hope I shall be pardoned for this passing allusion to a fact so gratifying to the pride of the combined artillery arms of England and India, which, in this campaign, have for the first time encountered the enemies of their common country side by side in friendly emulation.

5. Never, I firmly believe, were field batteries exposed to a severer trial than that which attended the penetration of Lucknow on that memorable day! On Captain Maude, who was in advance, devolved the difficult task of silencing the enemy's guns which defended the bridge leading to the city. This he accomplished under a murderous cross fire of grape and musketry, with a loss of one-third of his men;

and it was for his nerve and coolness on this occasion, (but for which the army could not have advanced) that Major-General Sir J. Outram, who was an eye-witness of his conduct, recommended him for the high distinction above recorded.

6. Captain Olpherts was almost simultaneously earning similar laurels by the conspicuous gallantry with which he assisted her Majesty's 90th Light Infantry, led by the lamented Colonel Campbell, in the capture of two guns on our right under a heavy fire of grape; carrying them off in triumph, attached to his spare limbers, through a most galling cross fire of musketry, from the loopholes of neighbouring houses and walled gardens.

7. To narrate our whole proceedings on that day would involve too lengthy details, suffice it therefore to say that, after crossing the bridge, we met no serious obstacle until coming under the fire of grape and musketry from the King's palace and the adjacent buildings on our left, and of round shot and shell from the guns across the river on our right.

8. As our force pushed on towards where the beleaguered garrison at Lucknow were anxiously expecting deliverance, each battery in turn unlimbered on the road, to silence, if possible, the enemy's guns, and thus protect the advance of the main column. While thus engaged, the gunners stood firm and undaunted like so many targets for the enemy's concealed sharp-shooters and grape shot, which latter ploughed up the ground on all sides, committing fearful havoc, as our list of casualties sufficiently testifies.

9. It was late at night ere the entire main body got out of fire; but two heavy guns, under Lieutenant J. M. Fraser, together with some thirty ammunition and store carts, having remained at the Motee Munzul, with a party of her Majesty's 90th, under Colonel Campbell, to protect the rear guard and wounded, were unable to accomplish a junction with the main body until the morning of the 27th. The position of the 14-pounder gun was one of great peril, from which it was with difficulty extricated, chiefly through the able and energetic measures of Captain Olpherts, who had been sent back to render assistance, as very fully described and acknowledged by Colonel Napier in that officer's report, already published.

10. It was here that those brave and lamented officers, Brigadier Cooper, B.A., and Captain Crump, M.A., his Brigade Major, fell victims to their noble zeal. Here also it was that Private Duffy, of the 1st Madras Fusiliers, a volunteer with the artillery, earned the Victoria Cross by his cool intrepidity and daring skill in assisting to extricate one of the guns from its desperate position. Colonel Napier also speaks in high terms of Lieutenant Fraser's exertions on this occasion.

11. On succeeding to the command of the brigade, I appointed Lieutenant Fraser my Brigade Major, and found him most efficient; in fact I cannot speak too warmly of his soldierly zeal and devotion, which, thenceforward down to the present time, I have had constant opportunities of witnessing, and I regard him as a young officer of the highest promise.

12. Being myself prostrated by fever for several weeks after our relief of the Lucknow Garrison, the temporary command of the artillery was most effectively exercised by Captain Olpherts, whose

well-tried abilities always prove equal to every emergency. During the interval of seven weeks that elapsed until the happy arrival of his Excellency the Commander-in-Chief's force, the artillery was chiefly occupied in defensive warfare against foes whose numerical strength and advantages of position, enabled them to surround and worry us at every point.

13. Owing to the paucity of our numbers from casualties, and the great extent of our position, this involved a very great amount of labour for the artillery, who were on continuous duty at their guns without any relief, besides working hard in the construction of fresh batteries whenever required. Under all their fatigues, privations, and dangers, the best spirit prevailed from first to last among the men, who considered no sacrifices too great for the accomplishment of the noble end in view, viz., the deliverance of their countrywomen and wounded comrades from the worst of fates.

14. It is satisfactory too to be able to state that the Native Establishments attached to the field batteries, consisting of gun lascars, horse and bullock drivers, syces, and grass-cutters, behaved most loyally, and, though suffering as severely as any of the troops in killed and wounded, none deserted ! Sirdar Driver Gungoo and Naik Darsun, of the syce drivers (killed by a round shot) both of No. 12 Light Field Battery, were particularly noted for their loyal devotion.

15. On the 16th November, the near approach of the Commander-in-Chief's force was the signal for renewed offensive operations on our side. These have been already alluded to in the late Sir H. Havelock's despatch of that date. Our object was to drive the enemy from certain strong positions which he occupied between us and the advancing columns, and in this we entirely succeeded, thereby greatly facilitating the junction of the two forces, and saving the valuable lives of our soldiers.

16. The batteries which had been for some time previously constructed for this purpose, were concealed behind a lofty wall forming the boundary of our position in that quarter. On them were mounted four 18-pounder iron guns, one 8-inch iron howitzer, four 9-pounder field guns, and two 24-pounder field howitzers, under the skilful direction of Captain Olpherts, Lieutenants Fraser and Smithett (the latter twice wounded and distinguished on several occasions), and Staff Sergeant Melville, of the 1st Company, 5th Battalion. In position behind were six 8-inch mortars under Captain Maude, R.A., most ably assisted by Lieutenants Maitland, R.A., and Simpson and Ward, of Bengal Native Infantry, the two latter being volunteers, well instructed in artillery science.

17. At the appointed time large openings were effected by the united force of mines and breaches in the screen wall in our front, and the batteries opened an excessively hot fire for three hours on the buildings beyond, which were occupied in considerable force by the enemy. Sufficient impression having been thus made, and mines having been exploded by the engineers in several contiguous quarters, storming parties rushed out at 3 P.M., and quickly carried all before them with trifling loss.

18. During the night the artillery pushed forward their heavy guns to the advanced positions thus gained, when some batteries were rapidly constructed from which to open on the King's Palace, now within easy

breaching distance. On the 17th, our 8-inch howitzer shelled the Tara Kotee and Mess House with great effect, setting fire to the former and materially assisting the attack of the advancing force on the opposite side, although perhaps unknown to them, as it must have been difficult for them to distinguish our distant fire from that of the enemy.

19. On the 18th, a junction having been effected between the two forces on the previous night, a joint bombardment took place of the King's Palace, in the outer wall of which several large breeches were rapidly effected, and great havoc made in the principal building behind it. This was continued at intervals, on the two following days, with great loss of life to the enemy crowding within, as was subsequently ascertained, and there can be little doubt that, had it suited our plan of operations, we might have at once walked into the place and occupied the palace with comparatively little loss. But the great object we had in view having been triumphantly accomplished, in the safe rescue of the sick, wounded, and women from their recent perils, any longer delay at Lucknow was considered inexpedient until they should be safely conducted beyond the reach of their merciless foes; and on the night of the 22nd, we effected our final evacuation of the entrenchment.

20. Measures had been previously adopted for the removal or destruction of all our spare ordnance, ammunition, and military stores. This entailed no ordinary amount of labour and physical endurance on the part of those to whose lot it fell to convey so many ponderous carriages by manual force through the narrow and intricate mazes of Chuttur Munzil and Furhut Bux Palaces—a duty in which the artillery were cheerfully aided by their infantry comrades, who on all occasions have volunteered their services, both for ordinary labour and also for the higher obligations of manning the guns when circumstances required.

21. Our hearty acknowledgments are also due to our scientific brethren of the engineers, for their cordial and effective co-operation, to which we are no doubt indebted greatly for whatever success has attended our efforts.

22. Lieutenant Thomas, Madras Artillery, Commissary of Ordnance, I always found indefatigable in his duties, which were latterly very severe, as on him devolved the laborious preparations for removing our magazine and destroying such guns and military stores as we were unable to carry away. With a very small establishment he effected all this as satisfactorily as could be expected. Lieutenant J. Alexander, Artillery, of the Lucknow Garrison, also worked zealously with the guns in position, and deserves creditable mention.

23. Before concluding this report, I wish to record the excellent services rendered to the artillery by Captain Evans, of the Bombay infantry, who commanded with great credit several guns in position in the entrenchment, and whose zeal and devotion were conspicuous. Also those of Lieutenant Ouseley, of the Bengal Native Infantry, who likewise attached himself to the guns and rendered himself extremely useful.

24. Surgeon Irvine and Assistant-Surgeon J. J. Clarke, are also particularly deserving of mention for praiseworthy zeal in the discharge of their professional duties.

25. Lieutenant Delafosse, infantry, one of the few survivors of the Cawnpore massacre, was attached as a volunteer to Captain Olphert's battery, and behaved with great gallantry on the 25th September, as well as in the previous engagements at Mungulwar and Alumbagh. I regret to add, that the privations and trials he thus for a second time endured in a beleaguered garrison, at length broke down his enfeebled frame and obliged him to proceed with the sick to Cawnpore.

26. Among the non-commissioned officers whose conduct most commended itself to notice, were Sergeant Major Bird and Staff Sergeant Roddy, of the 2nd Company 3rd Battalion, and Staff Sergeant Melville, of the 1st Company 5th Battalion. The latter had twice distinguished himself before in Arrah. I beg most earnestly to recommend them to the consideration of superior authority.

27. Sergeant-Major Lamont, of the Royal Artillery, fell gloriously at his gun on the 25th of September, deeply lamented by the whole Artillery brigade. He was a first-rate and most gallant soldier, and must have attained honour and distinction had he survived.

28. Lieutenant D. Gordon, who had assisted me most zealously in working the heavy guns in the actions of Mungulwar and Alumbagh, was left behind at the latter place in command of a portion of the heavy battery, as also Lieutenant G. M. Clerk, with two 9-pounder field guns of Captain Olpherts' battery, and I understand they were able to render material assistance in the defence of that important position. I have, &c.,

VINCENT EYRE, *Major*,
Commanding Artillery Brigade, Oude Force.

P.S.—The last sentence had scarcely been penned when I was startled by the announcement that poor Lieutenant D. Gordon has been just killed in the Alumbagh by a round shot. I deeply regret the loss of this most amiable and excellent young officer.

[On the 21st and 22nd November, the Commander-in-Chief issued the following General Orders expressive of his admiration of the original garrison :—]

GENERAL ORDERS BY HIS EXCELLENCY THE
COMMANDER-IN-CHIEF.

*Head-quarters, Shah Nujeef, Lucknow,
21st Nov., 1857.*

Although the Commander-in-Chief has not yet had time to peruse the detailed report of Brigadier Inglis, respecting the defence made by the slender garrison under his command, his Excellency desires to lose no time in recording his opinion of the magnificent defence made by the remnant of a British Regiment, her Majesty's 32nd, a company of British Artillery, and a few hundred sepoys, whose very presence was a subject of distrust, against all the force of Oude, until the arrival of the reinforcement under Major-Generals Sir J. Outram, G.C.B., and Sir H. Havelock, K.C.B.

The enduring constancy of this small garrison, under the watchful command of the Brigadier, has, under Providence, been the means of adding to the prestige of the British army, and of preserving the honour and lives of our countrywomen.

There can be no greater reward than such a reflection, and the Commander-in-Chief heartily congratulates Brigadier Inglis and his devoted garrison on that reflection belonging to them.

The position occupied by the garrison was an open entrenchment, the numbers were not sufficient to man the defences, and the supply of artillerymen for the guns was most inadequate. In spite of these difficult circumstances, the Brigadier and his garrison held on; and it will be a great pleasure to the Commander-in-Chief to bring to the notice of the Government of India the names of all the officers and soldiers who have distinguished themselves during the great trial to which they have been exposed.

The Commander-in-Chief congratulates Sir James Outram and Sir Henry Havelock on having been the first to aid Brigadier Inglis.

The Governor-General in Council has already expressed his opinion on the splendid feat of arms by which that aid was accomplished.

Head-quarters, Shah Nujeef, 22nd Nov., 1857.

When the Commander-in-Chief issued his Order of yesterday with regard to the old garrison of Lucknow, his Excellency was unaware of the important part taken in aid of the soldiers by the civil functionaries who happened to be at the Residency when it was shut in by the enemy.

His Excellency congratulates them very heartily on the honour they have won in conjunction with their military comrades. This is only another instance that in danger and difficulty all Englishmen behave alike, whatever their profession.

[The following General Orders and Despatches refer to the gallant occupation of the Alumbagh by Lieutenant-Colonel McIntyre and Major Sibley, between the 25th September and 25th November:—]

GENERAL ORDERS BY HIS EXCELLENCY THE
COMMANDER-IN-CHIEF.

Adjutant-General's Office, Calcutta, 22nd *Feb.*, 1858.

By the Honourable the President of the Council of India in Council.

Fort William, 15th *February*, 1858.

The Honourable the President of the Council of India in Council is pleased to direct the publication of the following despatch from Major-General Sir J. Outram, G.C.B., commanding, dated 16th January, 1858, transmitting reports relative to the occupation and defence of the post of Alumbagh, under Brevet Lieutenant-Colonel McIntyre, 78th Highlanders, and of the operations of the Artillery of his force, commanded by Major V. Eyre, Bengal Artillery.

2. His Honour in Council tenders his warm acknowledgments to the several officers named in these reports, as well as to the officers and men engaged, for the good services rendered by them.

108

Major-General Sir J. Outram, G.C.B., Commanding in Oude, to Major H. W. Norman, Deputy-Adjutant-General of the Army.

Camp Alumbagh, 16th January, 1858.

In consequence of my having received no report from the officer commanding at Alumbagh, the services of the garrison and of particular officers have not been brought to the notice of his Excellency the Commander-in-Chief.

I therefore beg leave to submit, for the information of his Excellency a report recently received from Major McIntyre, her Majesty's 78th Regiment, of the occupation and defence of Alumbagh, from the 25th September, when he was placed in command of that post by the late Major-General Sir H. Havelock, K.C.B., until the arrival of his Excellency the Commander-in-Chief's force.

During the earlier portion of Major McIntyre's occupation of Alumbagh, whilst cut off from communication with Cawnpore, uncertain of the fate of the rest of the force from the moment when he lost sight of it in the suburbs of Lucknow, and surrounded by a numerous enemy, his command was one of grave and anxious responsibility, and the firm and able manner in which he used his small resources to repulse the attack of the enemy, to strengthen his defences, and overcome the difficulties of his situation, and the cheerful conduct of the troops under laborious duties, merit my cordial acknowledgments, and will, I feel sure, meet with his Excellency's approbation.

I beg to second, most strongly, the recommendation which Major McIntyre makes in favour of his second in command, Major Sibley, who commanded at Alumbagh, during three weeks, whilst Major McIntyre was on the sick list; also of the several officers of the Staff or commanding detachments favourably mentioned by Major McIntyre.

I also beg permission to submit Brigadier Eyre's report of the artillery operations of the Oude Field Force, from the 21st September to the 24th November, which I have recently received. I beg now to recommend the several officers mentioned by Brigadier Eyre, whose names have not already been submitted for the favourable notice of Government, for their service under their distinguished commander; particularly Lieut. A. Fraser, brigade major of Artillery, whose name, I regret to find, was omitted, but whose gallantry and very zealous services deserved favourable notice.

Captain Evans, of the Bombay Native Infantry, doing duty with the Artillery, was of much service in the Artillery park, at the evacuation of the Residency of Lucknow.

Lieutenant T. N. Haward, of the Artillery, performed good service as commissary of ordnance at Cawnpore, and during the march to Alumbagh.

Lieutenant J. Anderson, of the Engineers, commanding engineer of the Lucknow garrison, though confined to his couch by illness, never ceased to exert himself to supply the engineer department with materials; and Lieutenant J. M. Innes gave very valuable aid in the mining operations until he was also disabled by ill-health and fatigue.

The services of Captain Maycock, deputy-assistant-quartermaster-general, were highly appreciated by the late Sir H. Havelock, and his personal attendance on myself during the march to Alumbagh in the actions of the 21st and 23rd September, deserved my thanks and commendation. I have, &c.,

J. OUTRAM, *Major-General,*
Commanding in Oude.

Major and Brevet Lieut.-Col. McIntyre, 78th Highlanders, to Colonel R. Napier, Chief of the Staff, with the Force under Major-General Sir J. Outram.

Camp near Alumbagh, 3rd January, 1858.

Having been directed to report upon the circumstances attending the occupation and defence of the Alumbagh, I have the honour to state, for the information of the Major-General commanding, that on the advance of the force on Lucknow, on the 25th of September last, under the late Major-General Sir Henry Havelock, K.C.B., I was appointed by that officer to the command of the place, with detachments of regiments, consisting of about 280 Europeans, some Sikhs, and four guns. In it were placed the sick of the force, amounting to 128 men, of whom 64 were wounded, the baggage, commissariat, treasure chest, reserve ordnance park, and a large quantity of small arm ammunition.

The native followers, Government and otherwise, could not have amounted to fewer than between four and five thousand persons, with an enormous number of cattle of various descriptions. The supply of food for the native followers did not exceed the consumption of a few day, and we had little or nothing for the cattle but what could be procured by foraging parties. Fortunately, some crops of rice and other grain, nearly ripe, were on the ground sufficiently near to enable us to gather them, under the protection of our guns. As these became consumed, the sufferings of the native followers from want became, I regret to say, very great. Everything that could be thought of was done to alleviate them. Driven by starvation to seek for food too far in advance of our foraging parties, numbers were cut up by the enemy who surrounded us. The efforts made to relieve their wants from Cawnpore were, for a considerable time, unsuccessful, as even quill communications by cossids failed to reach their destination; however, on the 7th of October, a convoy of provisions, escorted by a party of 250 men and two guns, and commanded by Major Bingham, her Majesty's 64th Regiment, reached us from Cawnpore, and on the 25th of the same month a large convoy, intended for Lucknow, escorted by 500 men and four guns, under the command of Major Barnston, her Majesty's 90th Regiment, reached the Alumbagh. Those enabled me to relieve, to a certain extent, the wants of the native followers. One hundred and fifty men of Major Bingham's party were ordered to remain to reinforce the garrison, and 100 to return to Cawnpore by a forced night march to escort return cattle.

Major Barnston's detachment was ordered after having rested for a day or two to return to Cawnpore. As the enemy had, however, appeared in very great numbers, and had become more daring than usual, I took upon myself the responsibility of detaining them, which turned out fortunately, for in a day or two I received an order to do so permanently. This gave me a force of 900 Europeans and ten guns, which enabled me to increase my foraging parties, and their range.

To take steps for the immediate defence of my post was my first care, and I made use of every available means to accomplish it. Subsequently more permanent works were ably constructed by Lieutenant Judge, of the engineers, assisted by Mr. Tait, civil engineer, attached to that department. Only the bastions, however, at the angles and a banquette beside, were completed, and the mango topes cut down in all directions round the post.

The enemy constructed batteries at different periods, at five different points around us, and their fire was at times exceedingly annoying and destructive to the native followers and cattle, from their necessarily crowded state; but I am happy to say that during the period of our holding the position, forty-nine days, one European soldier only was killed and two wounded.

Jellalabad, occupied in force by the enemy with cavalry, infantry, and four guns, formed a sixth and dangerous neighbour; but on two occasions only did they bring out their guns and open fire, and they were then soon silenced.

A two-gun battery at the Yellow-house,*   *   *   * and silenced by our Artillery fire, under the able direction of Captain Moir, of the Bengal Artillery, was repaired during the night; but on a repetition of our fire, was again silenced, and eventually the enemy withdrew their guns from it.

The duty was at first very severe on both officers and men, but was performed most cheerfully by both. Much praise is due to the artillery and men attached, on whom it was even more severe than on the others.

From about the 3rd to the 22nd of October, in consequence of my illness, the command of the post devolved on Major Sibley, of her Majesty's 64th Regiment, in charge of the treasure chest, the next senior officer, from whom I, on all occasions, received every assistance.

I trust the Major-General will not think it presumptous on my part to bring to his notice the names of those officers (in addition to those already mentioned) who were most conspicuous in the performance of their duties, and deserve much credit. They are—Captain Maycock, deputy-assistant quarter-master general; Lieutenant Gordon, Bengal Artillery, who commanded the detachments of artillery until the arrival of Captain Moir; Lieutenant Sandwith, her Majesty's 84th Regiment, acting field engineer, (Lieutenant Sandwith was subsequently killed in Lucknow); Lieutenant Haldane, her Majesty's 64th Regiment, acting field engineer; Lieutenant Morland, acting staff officer, 1st Bengal Fusiliers.

The unwearied attention of Surgeon Innes, of her Majesty's 84th Regiment, and Surgeon Dominichetti, of her Majesty's 75th Regiment,

---

* Copy illegible.

to the sick and wounded, and their exertions on entering the Alumbagh with sixty-four wounded men, deserve the greatest praise.

May I be permitted to add, that I on every occasion received the greatest assistance from Caption Moir, of the Artillery, who was ever at his post.

I have, &c.,
J. McINTYRE, *Major*,
78th *Highlanders, and Brevet Lieutenant-Colonel.*

[Before concluding this portion of the despatches, the editor has thought it advisable to interpolate here General Orders which relate to the first relief by General Havelock, and the final removal of the garrison by Sir Colin Campbell.]

GENERAL ORDERS BY HIS EXCELLENCY THE
COMMANDER-IN-CHIEF.

Adjutant-General's Office, Calcutta, Dec. 12, 1857.

By the Right Honourable the Governor-General of India in Council:—

Fort William, 8th December, 1857.

The Right Honourable the Governor-General in Council has received from Brigadier Inglis, of her Majesty's 32nd Regiment, lately commanding the garrison in Lucknow, the subjoined report of the defence of the Residency in that city, from the first threatened attack upon it on the 29th of June, to the arrival of the force under Major-General Sir J. Outram, G.C.B., and the lamented Major-General Sir H. Havelock, K.C.B., on the 25th of September.

The divisional order of Major-General Sir James Outram upon the report accompanies it.

The Governor-General in Council believes that never has a tale been told which will so stir the hearts of Englishmen and Englishwomen, as the simple, earnest narrative of Brigadier Inglis.

It rightfully commences with a soldier's testimony, touchingly borne, to the chivalrous character and high deserts of Sir Henry Lawrence, the sad details of whose death are now made known.

There does not stand recorded in the annals of war an achievement more truly heroic than the defence of the Residency at Lucknow, described in the narrative which follows.

That defence has not only called forth all the energy and daring which belong to Englishmen in the hour of active conflict; but it has exhibited continuously, and in the highest, degree, that noble and sustained courage which, against enormous odds and fearful disadvantages, against hope deferred, and through unceasing toil and wear of body and mind, still holds on day after day and triumphs.

The heavy guns of the assailants, posted, almost in security, within fifty yards of the entrenchments,—so near indeed that the solicitations, and threats, and taunts, which the rebels addressed to the native defenders of the garrison, were easily heard by those true-hearted men; the fire of the enemy's musketry, so searching that it penetrated the innermost retreat of the women and children, and of the wounded; their desperate attempts, repeatedly made, to force an entry after blowing in the defences; the perpetual mining of the works; the weary night watching for the expected signal of relief; and the steady waste of precious lives until the number of English gunners was reduced below that of the guns to be worked:—all these constitute features in a history which the fellow-countrymen of the heroes of Lucknow will read with swelling hearts, and which will endure for ever as a lesson to those who shall hope, by treachery, numbers, or boldness in their treasoa, to overcome the indomitable spirit of Englishmen.

A complete list of the brave men who have fallen has not yet reached the Governor-General in Council; but the names mentioned in Brigadier Inglis' report are, in themselves, a long and sad one.

Amongst those who have nobly perished in this protracted struggle, Sir Henry Lawrence will occupy the first place in the thoughts of his fellow-countrymen. The Governor-General in Council has already given expression to the deep sorrow with which he mourns the loss of that distinguished man. But the name of Sir Henry Lawrence can never rise up without calling forth a tribute of honour and admiration from all who knew him.

The Governor-General in Council has also to deplore the loss of Major Banks, an officer high in the confidence of the Government of India, and who, with the full approval of the Governor-General in Council, had succeeded to the charge of Chief Commissioner upon Sir Henry Lawrence's death; of Lieutenant-Colonel Case, Her Majesty's 32nd Regiment, who was mortally wounded while leading on his men at Chinhut on the 29th of June; of Captain Radcliffe, whose conspicuous bravery attracted the attention of Sir Henry Lawrence on that occasion; of Captain Francis, who was also especially noticed by Sir Henry Lawrence for his gallant conduct while in command of the Muchhee Bhowun; of Captain Fulton, of the Engineers, whose indefatigable exertions are thankfully recorded by Brigadier Inglis; of Major Anderson, the chief engineer, who, contending against deadly sickness, did not cease to give his valuable aid to his commander; of Captain Simons, Artillery, mortally wounded at Chinhut; of Lieutenants Shepherd and Arthur, 7th Light Cavalry, killed at their posts; of Captain McCabe, Her Majesty's 32nd, who fell while leading his fourth sortie; of Captain Mansfield, of the same corps, who fell a victim to cholera.

The Governor-General in Council laments also to

find in this melancholy record the names of Mr. Lucas, a traveller in India, and of Mr. Bryson. These two gentlemen, acting as volunteers, received charge of one of the most dangerous outposts, and held it at the cost of their lives.

The good services of Her Majesty's 32nd Regiment throughout this struggle have been remarkable.

To the watchful courage and sound judgment of its commander, Brigadier Inglis, the British Government owes a heavy debt of gratitude; and Major Lowe, Captain Bassano, Lieutenants Edmonstoune, Foster, Harmar, Lawrence, Clery, Cooke, Browne, and Charlton, and Quartermaster Stribbling, of this corps, and Captain O'Brien, of Her Majesty's 84th Regiment, are praised by their superior as having severally distinguished themselves. Of the 7th Light Cavalry, Colonel Master, to whom was entrusted the command of a most exposed post, Captain Boileau, and Lieutenant Warner, are entitled to the thanks of the Governor-General in Council.

The Governor-General in Council recognizes with pleasure the distinction accorded to Major Apthorp, Captains Kemble and Saunders, Lieutenants Barwell and Keir, of the 41st N. I., as well as to Captain Germon and Lieutenant Aitken, of the 13th N. I., the latter of whom commanded an important position in the defences with signal courage and success; to Captain Anderson, of the 25th, and to Lieutenant Graydon, of the 44th N. I.

His Lordship in Council desires to acknowledge the excellent service of Captain Dinning and Lieutenant Sewell, of the 71st N. I.; and of Lieutenant Langmore, of the same regiment, who held continuously a post open to attack, and entirely without shelter for himself or for his men by night or by day; as well as of Lieutenant Worsley, of the same corps; of Lieutenant Tulloch, 58th N. I.; of Lieutenant Hay, 48th N. I., who was placed under the Engineers to assist in the arduous duties of that department; and of Ensign Ward, of the same regiment, who, when the officers of Artillery were mostly disabled, worked the mortars with good effect; also of Lieutenant Graham, of the 11th N. I., and of Lieutenant Mecham, of the 4th Oude Irregulars.

Of the native officers and men of the 13th, 48th, and 71st Regiments of N. I., who have been amongst the defenders of the Residency, it is difficult to speak too highly. Their courageous constancy under the severest trials is worthy of all honour.

The medical officers of the garrison are well entitled to the cordial thanks of the Government of India. The attention, skill, and energy evinced by Superintending Surgeon Scott; Assistant-Surgeon Boyd, her Majesty' 32nd Foot; Assistant-Surgeon Bird, of the Artillery; Surgeon Campbell, 7th Light Cavalry; Surgeon Brydon, 71st N. I.; Surgeon Ogilvie, sanitary commissioner; Assistant-Surgeon Fayrer; Assistant-Surgeon Partridge, 2nd Oude Irregulars; Assistant-Surgeons Greenhow and Darby; and of Mr. Apothecary Thompson, are spoken of in high terms by Brigadier Inglis.

To Dr. Brydon, especially, the Governor-General in Council would address his hearty congratulations. This officer, after passing through the Cabul campaign of 1841-42, was included in the illustrious garrison who maintained their position in Jellalabad. He may now, as one of the heroes of Lucknow, claim to have witnessed and taken part in an achievement even more conspicuous as an example of the invincible energy and enduring courage of British soldiers.

The labours of the officers of Engineers—Lieutenants

Anderson, Hutchinson, and Innes; and of the Artillery —Lieutenant Thomas (Madras), and Lieutenants Macfarlane and Bonham, receive, as they deserve, honourable mention, which the Governor-General in Council is glad to confirm by his cordial approval.

The services rendered by Mr. McRae, civil engineer; Mr. Schilling, principal of the Martinière; and by Mr. Cameron, a gentleman who had visited Oude for commercial purposes, merit the especial thanks of the Government of India.

The Governor-General in Council has read with great satisfaction the testimony borne by Brigadier Inglis to the sedulous attention given to the spiritual comforts of his comrades by the Reverend Mr. Polehampton and the Rev. Mr. Harris. The first, unhappily, has not survived his labours.

The officers of the Staff have rendered excellent service. That of Lieutenant James, sub-assistant commissary-general, calls for the especial thanks of the Government of India. This officer, although severely wounded at Chinhut, resolutely continued to give valuable aid to the Brigadier; and it is mainly owing to his forethought and care that the supplies of the garrison have sufficed through the hardships of the sieges.

Captain Wilson, 13th N. I., deputy assistant adjutant-general, has evinced courage, activity, and sound judgment in a very high degree.

Lieutenant Hardinge, officiating as deputy quartermaster-general, as well as commanding the Sikh Cavalry of the garrison, has proved himself worthy to bear his soldier's name.

Lieutenant Barwell, 71st N. I., Fort adjutant, is honourably mentioned; and Lieutenant Birch, of the 71st N. I., who acted as aide-de-camp to Brigadier Inglis throughout the siege, has discharged his duties in a manner which has called forth emphatic praise from his commander.

The officers of the Civil Service have not been behind their military brethren in courage and zeal. The assistance rendered by Mr. Couper to Brigadier Inglis, as previously to Sir Henry Lawrence, has been most valuable.

Messrs. Thornhill and Capper were wounded during the siege ; and Mr. Martin, deputy commissioner, and Captain Carnegie, assistant commissioner, have earned the special thanks of Brigadier Inglis.

To all these brave men, and to their brother officers and comrades of every rank and degree, European and native, who have shared the same dangers and toils with the same heroic spirit, the Governor-General in Council tenders his warmest thanks.

The officers and men of her Majesty's Regiments must receive their full measure of acknowledgment from a higher authority than that of the Governor-General in Council; but it will be the pleasing duty of his Lordship in Council to express to her Majesty's Government, and to the Honourable Court of Directors of the East India Company, in the strongest terms, the recommendation of them to that favour for which Major-General Sir James Outram so justly pleads.

Meanwhile, it is a gratification to the Governor-General in Council to direct, in a General Order of this day, that the rewards and honours therein specified shall be at once awarded to the officers and men of the two services, and to the civilians respectively.

This notice must not be closed without mention of those noble women who, little fitted to take part in such scenes, have assumed so cheerfully and discharged so earnestly their task of charity in ministering to sickness and pain. It is likely that to themselves the notoriety of praise publicly given may be distasteful; yet, tho

Governor-General in Council cannot forego the pleasure of doing justice to the names of Birch, Polehampton, Barbor, and Gall, and of offering to those whose acts have so adorned them, his tribute of respectful admiration and gratitude.

The history of the defence of the Residency of Lucknow does not end with the narrative of Brigadier Inglis. But no full reports of the course of events at Lucknow subsequently to the junction of Sir Henry Havelock's force with the defenders, or of the final and effectual relief by the advance of the Commander-in-Chief, have yet been received. It is known, however, that the success which has carried joy to so many aching hearts has been clouded by the death, within the last few days, of one of the first soldiers of India, Major-General Sir Henry Havelock.

The Governor-General in Council deeply deplores the loss of this able leader and truly brave man, who has been taken from the service of his country at a time when he can least be spared, though not before he had won for himself lasting renown, and had received at the hands of his Sovereign the gracious and prompt recognition of his merits.

R. J. H. BIRCH, *Colonel*,
Secretary to the Govt. of India, Mily. Depart.

GENERAL ORDERS BY HIS EXCELLENCY THE COMMANDER-IN-CHIEF.

Adjutant-General's Office,
Calcutta, 28th Dec., 1857.

General Orders by the Right Honourable the Governor-General of India in Council.

Fort William, 22nd *December,* 1857.

The Right Honourable the Governor-General in Council is pleased to direct the publication of the accompanying despatches relating to the first relief of the garrison of Lucknow, which have lately reached Government.

These despatches contain an account of the proceedings of the force under the command of the late Major-General Sir H. Havelock, K.C.B., before he forced his way into the city, as well as of the various operations carried on under Major-General Sir James Outram, G.C.B., after a junction had been effected with the garrison of the Residency on the 25th of September, until the arrival of the relieving force under his Excellency General Sir Colin Campbell.

They show how thoroughly this gallant band has sustained the reputation of British soldiers for courage, discipline, and determination, whether in the plain, in the hand-to-hand struggle of the street-fighting, or in the more wearying labours of the siege.

The Governor-General in Council has already had the satisfaction of acknowledging the obligations of the Government of India to Sir James Outram; but his Lordship in Council cannot deny himself the pleasure of expressing again his appreciation of Sir James Outram's eminent services, and his respect for the generous and soldier-like feeling which prompted Sir James to abstain from assuming the position due to his superior rank, and to leave in the hands of Sir Henry Havelock the completion of the undertaking which the latter had successfully begun.

To Brigadier Inglis, the Governor-General in Council can give no higher praise than to say, that during the continuance of the siege, after Sir James Outram had assumed the chief command in the Residency, his ability, energy, and vigilance were worthy of the lasting reputation which his conduct of the defence has secured to him.

Sir James Outram has acknowledged the efficient cooperation which he had from Brigadiers Hamilton and Stisted   To these officers, as well as to Captain Bouverie, and Captain Spurgin, serving on the Brigade Staff, the Governor-General in Council desires to offer his hearty thanks for the good services they have done.

His Lordship in Council conveys to Major Eyre, who had already established a claim on the gratitude of the Government; to Captain Maude, Royal Artillery; to Captain Olpherts, Bengal Artillery; to Lieutenant Thomas, Commissary of Ordnance; and to the officers and men of the combined force of Artillery, the assurance of the satisfaction with which he has received the evidence of their zeal and gallantry.

The labours that devolved upon the Engineer Department, have been of a most important and difficult nature, and the Governor-General in Council begs to assure Captain Crommelin, commanding the Engineers; Lieutenant Hutchinson, second in command; Lieutenants Russell and Limond; the officers and men attached to, as well as those who volunteered to work with, the department—his appreciation of the courage, skill, and energy with which they bore their very arduous part in the siege.

Lieutenant-Colonel Purnell, commanding H. M.'s 90th Light Infantry, deserves praise for the able manner in which he held an advanced post, exposed to the unceasing attacks of the enemy; and to Captain Brasyer, commanding the Regiment of Ferozepore; to Captain Lockhart, commanding H. M.'s 98th Highlanders; to Captain Shute, commanding a detachment of H. M.'s 64th, who have each maintained a difficult post with complete success; to Captain Willis, commanding H. M.'s 84th; to Captain Galwey, commanding Madras Fusiliers; and to Lieutenant Meara, commanding H. M.'s 5th Fusiliers, the Governor-General in Council tenders his hearty thanks.

His Lordship in Council acknowledges with pleasure the cheerful alacrity with which Captain Barrow, commanding Volunteer Cavalry; Captains Johnson and Hardinge, commanding Irregular Cavalry, have come forward to volunteer their services on every opportunity: the latter officer having also rendered good service as Deputy Quartermaster-General.

The thanks of Government are due to Captain Garden, Assistant Quartermaster-General; and to Captain Moorsom, H. M.'s 52nd Regiment, Deputy Assistant Quartermaster-General, for the zeal they have exhibited in their various departments; as also to Captains Alexander, Orr, and Carnegy, for their able services at the head of the Intelligence Department; and to Captain Macbean and Lieutenant James, for the efficient manner in which, under their superintendence, the Commissariat arrangements have been carried out.

The Governor-General in Council has great satisfaction in acknowledging the excellent provision made for the care of the sick by the Medical Department under Superintending-Surgeon J. Scott; and his Lordship in Council desires especially to tender his warm thanks to the Rev. Mr. Harris, for the personal courage displayed by that gentleman in the discharge of his sacred duties, and for the unremitting assiduity with which he, throughout the siege, has sought to allay the sufferings and provide for the comfort of the sick and wounded.

The Governor-General in Council offers to Major North, Deputy Judge-Advocate-General; to Captain Hudson (H. M.'s 64th), Deputy Assistant-Adjutant-General; and to Lieutenant Hargood (Madras Fusiliers), serving on the Staff of the late Sir Henry

Havelock, the thanks they have merited by efficient discharge of their respective duties.

The support rendered to the force, both in the field and throughout the very intricate and difficult engineering operations of the defence, by Colonel Napier, Military Secretary and Chief of the Adjutant-General's Department, has been most valuable, and his Lordship in Council desires to assure Colonel Napier, that his ability and exertions are fully appreciated by Government.

The Governor-General in Council has much satisfaction in acknowledging the services of Captain Dodgson, Assistant-Adjutant-General; Captain Gordon, Deputy Judge-Advocate-General; Lieutenants Sitwell and Chamier, on the Personal Staff of, and Mr. Money, Private Secretary to, Sir James Outram; of Captain Dawson, and Ensign Hewitt, Orderly Officers; and of Mr. G. Couper, of the Civil Service, who volunteered to perform the duties of Aide-de-Camp.

In addition to those whose names have been more prominently brought to notice, the Governor-General in Council desires to convey his hearty thanks to all officers, non-commissioned officers, and men, who have been engaged in the operations referred to in these despatches, for the valour they have displayed in the field, for the firmness with which they have maintained their position in the city, and for the cheerful, willing, and earnest manner in which they have discharged all the various duties and borne the privations imposed upon them, under circumstances of extraordinary difficulty and hardship.

It will be a gratification to the Governor-General in Council to bring the eminent services of Major-General Sir J. Outram's force, officers and men, to the favourable notice of her Majesty's Government and of the

Honourable Court of Directors by the first opportunity. Meanwhile, the Governor-General in Council directs, by a separate order of this date, that the donation batta already granted to the garrison under Brigadier Inglis, shall be extended to Major-General Sir J. Outram's force.

The Governor-General in Council cannot conclude this notice of the events connected with the relief of Lucknow, without expressing his deep regret at the heavy loss which England has suffered by the fall of so many able officers and gallant men.

His Lordship in Council has already recorded his sense of the high worth of those true soldiers, Sir Henry Havelock and Brigadier-General Neill. Their names will be cherished with honour by their fellow-countrymen.

He now has to lament the untimely death of Colonel Campbell, her Majesty's 90th Light Infantry, than whom the Queen's service possessed no more gallant or promising officer.

Major Haliburton, her Majesty's 78th Highlanders; Major Cooper, Artillery; Major Simmons, her Majesty's 5th Fusiliers; Major Stephenson, Madras Fusiliers; and many other brave men amongst their comrades, have died in the discharge of their duty; and in memory of these the Governor-General in Council desires to record his tribute of sorrow and gratitude.

R. J. H. BIRCH, *Colonel*,
Secretary to the Govt. of India, in the Military Dept.

With reference to Government General Order, No. 1625 of this date, the Right Honourable the Governor-General in Council is pleased to direct that every officer and soldier, European and native, who formed part of the force under command of Major-

General Sir James Outram, G.C.B., shall be allowed a donation of six months' batta, as already authorised for the troops composing the late garrison of Lucknow.

R. J. H. BIRCH, *Colonel*,
Sec. to the Govt. of India in the Mily. Dept.

By order of his Excellency the Commander-in-Chief.

W. MAYHEW, *Lieut.-Colonel*,
Adjutant-General of the Army.

[The accompanying extract of a letter will show the pious care taken lest the remains of the gallant Havelock might be desecrated by the enemy.]

George Couper, Esq., to G. F. Edmonstone, Esq.
Alumbagh, 23rd December, 1857.

I am directed to state, for the information of the Right Hon. the Governor-General in Council, that with the view of preventing the desecration of Sir Henry Havelock's grave, in the event of a contingency—unforeseen at present—calling for the operation of this division elsewhere, the Chief Commissioner has directed every trace of the mound to be carefully obliterated, so that the spot may be imperceptible to an uninitiated observer. As it is not impossible, however, that the Government of India, or that of England, may desire, on a future occasion, to have the lamented General's remains removed from their present resting-place to a holier and more honoured cemetery, I am directed to enclose a plan of the Alumbagh, showing the exact position of the grave, in order that no possible doubt regarding the locality may arise hereafter.

THE DEFENCE OF THE ALUMBAGH.

[On the 25th November, 1857, Sir Colin Campbell proceeded towards Cawnpore with the women and children, sick and wounded, and the greater portion of the effective garrison of Lucknow, leaving Sir James Outram with a force of 4,000 men, constituting the First Division of the redistributed army, to hold Lucknow and its armed hordes in check, until his Excellency should be in a position to wrest that city from the enemy.

The position assigned to Sir James Outram embraced the walled enclosures of the Alumbagh, which had been so gallantly maintained for two months by Lieut.-Col. McIntyre and Major

Sibley. The name of that small post became conventionally assigned to the whole of Sir James Outram's position, and a grievous popular misconception has thus arisen respecting the difficulties encountered, and the services rendered, by the First Division during the three months they confronted the population of Oude in arms against them; and by thus finding occupation for many thousands of fighting men, prevented them from assailing Cawnpore.

The general impression is, that between the relief of Lucknow in November, 1857, and its final capture in March, 1858, Sir James Outram occupied the small walled and fortified enclosure of the Alumbagh. This misconception has been greatly strengthened by the circumstance that the despatch in which Sir James Outram recapitulated the services of his division was never published in General Orders, and it has been adopted by several able writers otherwise well informed, who have undertaken to narrate the history of the Indian mutinies.

Under these circumstancess, the editor has deemed it advisable slightly to invert the order of Sir James Outram's despatches from the Alumbagh, and give precedence to the one in which, when on the eve of engaging in those final operations in which he was destined to play a conspicuous and dangerous part, he availed himself of what might possibly be his last opportunity to do justice to the brave troops with whom he had been so long associated.]

Despatch from Governor-General to the Court of Directors.

[*Forwarding Despatch from Commander-in-Chief, dated 12th March, with Enclosure from Major-General Outram, dated 28th February; which through some oversight had not been published in General Orders in India.*]

To the Honourable the Court of Directors of the East India Company.

Allahabad, April 30th, 1858.

I have the honour to transmit the accompanying copy of a letter from the deputy adjutant-general of the army, No. 138 A, dated 12th March, 1858, forwarding a report from Major-General Sir J. Outram, G.C.B., noticing the behaviour of the troops under his command during the few months previous to the capture of Lucknow.

2. It will be observed that Sir J. Outram specially commends Colonel C. A. F. Berkley, of her Majesty's 32nd Regiment, his military secretary.

3. His Excellency the Commander-in-Chief has expressed his entire satisfaction at the manner in which Sir J. Outram fulfilled the expectations which led to his being selected to maintain the position in Alumbagh, and recommends to favourable notice as well the Major-General who commanded there as the officers who executed his orders.

4. I very cordially join in the Commander-in-Chief's well-merited commendation of Sir James Outram, and of the officers and troops under his command.

I have, &c.,

CANNING.

The Deputy Adjutant-General of the Army to the Secretary to the Government of India, Military Department, with the Governor-General.

Head Quarters, Camp before Delhi,
Lucknow, 12th March, 1858.

I have the honour, by direction of the Commander-in-Chief, to forward for the favourable consideration of the Right Honourable the Governor-General a copy of a despatch dated the 28th ultimo, from Major-General Sir James Outram, G.C.B., in which he brings to prominent notice the behaviour of the troops under his immediate command during the last few months.

2. It is matter of great satisfaction to his Excellency, that his expectations with regard to the security of the position selected for Sir James Outram have been so amply justified. The Commander-in-Chief was always convinced that under the able command of the Major-General, the troops left in the vicinity of Lucknow according to the policy of Government, were exposed to no military risk.

3. His Excellency is exceedingly gratified by the report of the disci-

pline of the troops of the 1st division, and he recommends to the favorable notice of his Lordship, the Major-General who commanded, and the officers who executed his orders.

I have, &c.,
H. W. NORMAN, *Major*,
Deputy Adjutant-General of the Army

Major-General Sir J. Outram, G.C.B., Commanding First Division, to the Deputy-Adjutant-General of the Army.
Dated Camp Alumbagh,
28th February, 1858.

1. My separate despatches have from time to time apprised his Excellency the Commander-in-Chief of the several affairs we have had with the enemy, and of my sense of the services which have been rendered on those occasions by the officers and men under my command.

2. But I am desirous of expressing to his Excellency in a more connected form, the very deep obligations under which they have placed me throughout the whole period we have been associated together—obligations which I am certain his Excellency and the Government of India will feel to be theirs also; and I trust it will not be deemed presumptuous or superfluous if, on the eve of more active operations, which may probably involve a severance of the ties that now unite us, I venture to submit to his Excellency's favourable notice, the admirable conduct of a force, which though it has been strictly enjoined by his Excellency to limit itself to defensive operations, and though its casualties have been few, has held an important position, and by its steadiness and bravery, rendered what I venture to hope will be regarded as a very valuable service to the State.

3. Circumstances demanded that, on the relief of Lucknow, his Excellency should withdraw his army to

other districts, certainly for months, possibly for the greater part of a year. But it was deemed of paramount importance that a military footing should be retained in Oude during his Excellency's absence, however protracted that might prove; and to the division which it has been my honour and good fortune to command, was allotted the task of maintaining, for an indefinite period, the honour of the British arms, and of representing the authority of the British Government in this province.

4. It was considered advisable, both on political and strategic grounds, that we should remain in close proximity to the capital. The position assigned us was within a mile and a half of the suburbs of Lucknow. Our advanced posts were within gunshot range of the outworks of a vast city, swarming with hosts of mutinous sepoys, with Nujeebs the undisciplined but well-armed soldier of the rebel Government, with many thousand city "budmashes," the armed and turbulent scum of a population of 700,000 souls, and with numerous bands of feudal retainers of the chieftains and great zemindars of Oude, whose normal state for the last fifty years has been one of warfare.

5. The enemy thus ranged against us, and certain to receive large accessions from the sepoys dispersed in other parts by the victorious forces of his Excellency, had the resources of the entire province at their disposal; while our supplies had to be derived periodically from Cawnpore, a distance of 45 miles: they were known to be well furnished in artillery, and to be strong in cavalry, an arm in which we were ourselves lamentably deficient:—and they were animated by every motive of hostility and vengeance that could be supplied to men conscious of having irretrievably committed themselves by the inflammatory exhortations of Hindoo and Mahomedan fanatics of reputed sanctity, and by the scornful

taunts to which they were subjected by the spirited mother of the boy-king.

6. Such was the position assigned to the 1st division on the 27th of November last; and to enable it to perform the duties that must devolve on it, his Excellency increased its strength to 4,442 men of all arms, Europeans and natives. See below.

But his Excellency is aware that, of this nominal force, a detachment 540 strong (subsequently reinforced by 100 Europeans) was ordered to be kept at Bunnee, 12 miles off, where, though of service in keeping open our rear, and preserving the bridge over which the army had to return when advancing to the reduction of Lucknow, they were obviously of little use to this division in the special duty assigned to it of holding the plain of Alumbagh.

CORPS.	Details.	
	Europeans.	Natives.
Artillery	332	108
CAVALRY.		
Military Train	221	—
Volunteer Cavalry	67	—
12th Irregular Cavalry	3	40
Oude Irregular Cavalry	1	37
INFANTRY.		
5th Fusiliers	526	—
84th Foot	431	—
75th Foot	355	—
78th Highlanders	439	—
90th Light Infantry	591	—
1st Madras Fusiliers	411	—
Ferozepore Regiment	5	295
Madras Sappers	4	110
27th Madras Native Infantry	9	457
Total	3,395	1,047
Grand Total, Europeans and Natives	4,442	

7. Our original force was therefore in reality considerably less than 4,000 of all ranks. Of these the forts of Alumbagh and Jellalabad absorbed about 600

men, brigade and camp duties 450 more, and thus, after deducting sick and wounded, there remained of all arms and ranks (European and native) little more than 2,000, available for action during the absence of the convoys (averaging 450 men) which we had fortnightly to send to Cawnpore. These were on the road for about two-thirds of each month; and of their departure and return the enemy were of course as well informed as ourselves.

8. The military topography of the locality, and our grazing exigencies, rendered it impossible to reduce the circumference of our camp, and its outworks, to less than 10 miles and 1,200 yards.* And on our small force there devolved the duty not only of defending this large and incompact position against a foe who could have brought large bodies of troops to bear against us simultaneously at several distant points, but of supplying foraging parties, and of being prepared to move out beyond our limits to meet the enemy, whenever by his attempts to cut off our communications, to menace Bunnee or Cawnpore, or by other hostile demonstrations, he might render such an operation necessary.

9. Between the 27th November and the 12th February, his Excellency had, at great inconvenience to himself, sent us reinforcements, European and native, to the extent of 1,216 men, together with several pieces of ordnance. And on the 12th and 13th February, he furnished us with a body of sappers and miners, amount-

---

* MEMORANDUM.

Length of Lines from Picquet to Picquet, enclosing the Position defended by 1st Division.

Jellalabad to Alumbagh	4,400 yards.
Alumbagh to left front village	2,600 ,,
Left front to left rear village	3,900 ,,
Left rear village to rear picquet	2,400 ,,
Rear picquet to Jellalabad	5,500 ,,
Total yards	18,800

Or a total of 10 miles and 1,200 yards.

W. R. MOORSOM, *Lieutenant, Deputy Quartermaster-General.*

ing to about 1,200 men. Of these 700 were undrilled, yet they were most acceptable, and may be considered an equivalent for the 75th Regiment, of which we were deprived on the following day. On the 22nd our strength was further increased by the 1st Bengal Fusiliers, numbering 587 of all ranks. And on the 24th we were additionally reinforced by two squadrons of Dragoons, a troop of Horse Artillery, and Hodson's Horse.

10. But in bringing the claims of this division to his Excellency's consideration, I think it but fair to remind him, that when on the 22nd December we moved out to surprise a strong force of the enemy threatening to cut off our communications, our reinforcements amounted to only 340 details and recruits; that when, on the 12th January we repulsed 30,000 of the enemy, our reinforcements aggregated less than 600; and that the Sikh Cavalry, with the accompanying European details, which reached us with the return convoy on the 16th January, only arrived in time to see us again inflict on the foe a still heavier repulse.

11. Although the successes which the division has achieved, whenever it has come into contact with the enemy, were purchased at the very trifling loss of a few casualties on our side on each occasion, the troops are, I consider, not less deserving of credit for the unflinching front with which they have withstood and held in check an enemy numbering such odds.*

* MEMORANDUM.

Strength of the Enemy on the 26th of January, 1858, as ascertained by Captain Alexander Orr, of the Intelligence Department.

37	Regiments of Sepoys, including Oude Force	.	27,550
14	Ditto of new Levies	.	5,400
106	Ditto of Nujeebs	.	55,150
26	Ditto of Regular and Irregular Cavalry	.	7,100
	Camel Corps	.	300
	Total	.	95,500

ARTILLERY.

Guns of all sorts and calibres, not including wall pieces, and the guns brought from Futtehpore, 131. Number of artillerymen not known. The above is

12. That their gallant demeanour was the cause of our remaining comparatively unmolested, I have no doubt. For though we have only had five engagements of sufficient importance to be reported to his Excellency, the enemy has frequently, and of late with increasing frequency, appeared in force, with the evident intention of simultaneously assaulting us at different points; but on finding us prepared to receive him, he has deemed it prudent to relinquish his designs, and remained satisfied with replying from a distance to the accurate fire of our artillery, from which it could easily be seen he sustained considerable loss.

13. These manifestations have not only been more numerous, but have been characterized by a greater boldness, within the last fortnight, a fact susceptible of easy explanation. The vast and daily augmenting accumulation of stores of all kinds lately forwarded to this camp in view of the impending operations, have greatly excited the alarm of the enemy; and it has become obvious to him that by the dispersion of this division, and the destruction of our material, he can alone hope to avert, or even delay, the terrible retribution that awaits him at the hands of the Commander-in-Chief.

14. It is almost superfluous to say, that where men have behaved so well in the field as the troops of the 1st Division, they must have been in a high state of discipline. Such has, indeed, been the case; and their admirable conduct must be held all the more praiseworthy when we consider the extreme exposure and dis-

exclusive of the armed followers of the Talookdars and Zemindars still at Lucknow on the 26th of January, amounting, at the lowest calculation, to 20,000 men, exclusive of the armed budmashes of the city, and exclusive also of four or five regiments that fled to Lucknow from Futtehghur with three to five guns, amounting to certainly not less than 3,000. The total aggregate of hostile forces at Lucknow on the 26th January, not less than 120,000 of all arms. Since that date several of the Zemindaree troops have left; but their place has been much more than supplied by the regiments ordered in from the district.

comfort the whole of them have had to endure from the loss of their warm clothing, and our deficiency of tentage, and that most of them had already sustained much privation during the seven weeks they were besieged in Lucknow.

15. This gratifying state of matters, as his Excellency will readily imagine, has been in no small degree due to the kindness, care, and attention which the officers of all arms and ranks have bestowed on their men, and to the earnest anxiety with which they have endeavoured at all times to promote their comfort and provide for their amusement.

16. From first to last, all alike, officers and men, have acquitted themselves most admirably; and I cannot therefore refrain from this recapitulation of the services of my comrades, and that before the commencement of the approaching operations—lest it may be out of my power to testify hereafter to their devotion, discipline, and bravery.

17. I am certain that neither his Excellency nor their country will forget the heroic troops whom it has been my proud privilege to command; and to his Excellency's kind consideration I now commend them. In doing so I must crave permission to depart from the usual formality of making special recommendations, for I feel that to do so would involve injustice to all those officers whose names might be omitted. As a matter of course I am under the very deepest obligations to the Commandants of Brigades, Regiments, Detachments, and Outposts, and to the members of the Divisional Brigade and personal Staff, for the zealous, earnest, and most valuable aid they have rendered me on all occasions. But I feel that my obligations are equally great to every officer in the force; for every officer has exerted himself

as if the safety and reputation of the force depended exclusively on his individual exertions.

18. There is, however, one officer in whose favour I am bound to depart from the rule of silence which I have prescribed for myself. I refer to Colonel Berkeley, of her Majesty's 32nd Regiment, who has since the 25th November been continuously on my Staff, either in the capacity of Military Secretary and head of the Adjutant-General's Department, or in that of Acting Deputy Quartermaster-General, and whose invaluable services I have not hitherto had an opportunity of adequately bringing to his Excellency's notice. Colonel Berkeley has discharged with signal ability and zeal the duties of both the offices in which he has acted. Both in the camp and in the field he has rendered me the most hearty co-operation; and in action with the enemy his personal gallantry has been most conspicuous. He possesses, to an extent I have rarely seen equalled, the power of securing the confidence, acquiring the respect, and winning the personal regard of those with whom he is thrown into contact; and to the combined firmness and tact with which Colonel Berkeley has discharged his duties, do I attribute, in no small degree, the satisfactory state of matters to which I have had the honour of soliciting his Excellency's attention.

     I have, &c.,
      J. OUTRAM, *Major-General,*
       Commanding 1st *Division.*

[The subjoined despatches refer to the several actions in which the First Division was engaged, while defending the position of the Alumbagh.]

GENERAL ORDERS BY HIS EXCELLENCY THE COMMANDER-IN-CHIEF.

Adjutant General's Office,
Calcutta, 7th January, 1858.

By the Right Honourable the Governor-General of India in Council.

Fort William, 5th January, 1858.

The Right Honourable the Governor-General in Council has much satisfaction in publishing the following report of a successful attack made by a portion of the troops under command of Major-General Sir James Outram, G.C.B., on a body of the enemy in the neighbourhood of his camp, on the 22nd December last. His Lordship in Council concurs in the commendation given by his Excellency the Commander-in-Chief to Sir James Outram and the officers and men under his command on the occasion.

The Deputy Adjutant-General of the Army, to the Secretary to the Government of India, Military Department.

Head-quarters, Camp Poora, December, 1857.

I have the honour, by desire of the Commander-in-Chief, to enclose for the information of the Right Honourable the Governor-General of India in Council, copy of a despatch of the 23rd instant, from Major-General Sir J. Outram, G.C.B., reporting the circumstances of a successful attack made upon a portion of the enemy in the neighbourhood of his camp by a detachment of the troops under the major-general's command, in which four guns were captured; and I am to state that his Excellency considers the whole affair to have been extremely well conducted, and to reflect much credit on the troops engaged.

I have, &c
H. W. NORMAN, *Major,*
Deputy Adjutant-General of the Army.

Major-General Sir J. Outram, G.C.B., Commanding Troops in Oude, to the Deputy Adjutant-General of the Army.

Camp before Lucknow, 23rd December, 1857.

I have the honour to report, for the information of his Excellency the Commander-in-Chief, that I had yesterday an affair with the enemy at a village called Guilee, three miles hence, situated a little to the right of the road to Dilkhoosha.

I had been informed two days previously, by my spies, that the enemy contemplated surrounding my position, in order to cut off supplies, stop all foraging expeditions, and to intercept my communication with Bunnee. With this object they despatched a force to Guilee, which took up a position between that village and Budroop, which places are about a mile distant from each other.

On the evening of the 21st instant, I learnt that the rebels had been reinforced, and that their strength amounted to about 4,000 infantry, 400 cavalry, and 8 field guns.*

Having ascertained that a space of about half a mile intervened between their position and the gardens skirting the canal and the Dilkhoosha, I moved out at 5 A.M., in the hope of surprising them at day-break, and intercepting their retreat to the city, with a force detailed in the accompanying divisional order, which I have this day issued, and to which I beg to refer his Excellency for all details, and for the terms in which I express my appreciation of the conduct of the troops on the occasion.

The main body of the enemy being on the march considerably in advance, retreated to the city by a detour to the left, out of our reach, and concealed by intervening topes of trees, on hearing the attack on their rear; but the loss of four horse artillery guns, much ammunition, besides elephants and baggage, and some fifty or sixty men slain, will, I think, deter the enemy from again venturing beyond their defensive works, or at any rate from attempting, for some time to come, to carry out their plan of surrounding this camp within a too limited circumference; and I have great hopes that the success of this expedition will be productive of good effect in restoring confidence to the neighbouring inhabitants.

DIVISION ORDER ISSUED BY MAJOR-GENERAL SIR JAMES OUTRAM, G.C.B.

Camp Alumbagh, 23rd December, 1857.

1. Major-General Sir James Outram has much pleasure in recording in division orders, his satisfaction with the conduct of the officers and men (quoted in margin),† under the command of Brigadier Stisted,

---

* Since ascertained to have been only 4; all of which were captured.

† 2 9-pounder guns, R. A., Captain Maude; 4 ditto 2nd co. 3rd batt., B.A., Captain Olpherts; 112 military train, Major Robertson; 50 volunteer cavalry, Captain Barrow; 36 irregular cavalry, Lieuts. Hay and Graham; 400 H.M.'s 5th Fusiliers, Colonel Guy; 103 H.M.'s 75th Regiment, Captain Brooks; 156

engaged yesterday in the skirmish at Guilee, in which four guns and twelve waggons filled with ammunition were captured.

2. The right column, under the command of Lieutenant-Colonel Purnell, her Majesty's 90th Regiment, consisting of detachments of the 78th and 90th Regiments, and of the Ferozepore Regiment of Sikhs, excited his admiration by the gallant way in which, with a cheer, they dashed at a strong position held by the enemy, and from which they were met by a heavy fire. Regardless of the overwhelming numbers and six guns reported to be posted there, the suddenness of the attack, and the spirited way in which it was executed, resulted in the immediate flight of the enemy, with hardly a casualty on our side.

3. Colonel Guy, in command of the left column consisting of 400 men of her Majesty's 5th Fusiliers, under the guidance of Lieutenant Moorsom, deputy-assistant quartermaster-general, was equally successful in his simultaneous attack on the adjacent village of Guilee, in which, and the adjoining tope, two guns were captured.

4. The enemy were now rapidly followed up across the plain by the Volunteer Cavalry, under Captain Barrow, until they found refuge in a village, from which they opened a fire of grape and musketry. They were, however, speedily dislodged, by the assistance of two of Captain Olphert's guns, under the command of Lieutenant Smithett, and changing their line of retreat, they endeavoured to reach the city by the way of the Dilkhoosha.

5. The Military Train, under Major Robertson, having been, however, despatched to make a flank movement, followed them up so rapidly that they dispersed their cavalry, and drove their guns into a ravine, where they were captured, the leading horses, of which the traces were cut, only escaping.

6. The Major-General was particularly pleased with the very cool and soldier-like behaviour of the Military Train. Far ahead of the infantry, and unable to remove the guns which were captured, they were menaced in their front by a large body of fresh troops from the city, and attacked on their right flank by the main body of the enemy, consisting of about 2,000 infantry, who had commenced their march previously to our attack, and who, on hearing their rear assailed, also changed their route to one in the direction of the city, but on seeing their guns in possession of so small a force as that under Major Robertson, made demonstrations of an attempt to regain them; but by the bold front shown by the Military Train, and the gallant advance of their skirmishers, they were held at bay, until the arrival of a party of the 5th Fusiliers and two 9-pounder guns, under Captain Olpherts, completely secured the capture of the guns, and enabled a working party of the Madras Sappers, under the command of Lieutenant Ogilvie, to extricate them from the ravine into which they had been

---

H.M.'s 78th Highlanders, Captain Lockhart; 108 H.M.'s 84th Regiment, Captain O'Brien; 270 H.M.'s 90th Light Infantry, Captain Guise; 150 regiment of Ferozepore, Captain Brasyer; 40 Madras Sappers, Lieut. Ogilvie. Total— 6 9-pounder guns, under Captain Olpherts; 190 cavalry, under Major Robertson; 1,227 infantry, under Brigadier Stisted; right column, under Lieut.-Col. Purnell, H.M.'s 90th Light Infantry; left column, under Colonel Guy, 5th Fusiliers; reserve, under Lieut.-Colonel Hamilton, H.M.'s 78th Highlanders.

driven. Captain Hutchinson, chief engineer, on this, as on several other occasions during the day, afforded much valuable assistance.

7. The Major-General has to thank Lieutenant-Colonel H. Hamilton, commanding the reserve, for the good position taken up by him, which, with the fire of the two guns under Lieutenant Simpson, which were most judiciously posted, was of great assistance in checking the advance of the enemy during the protracted operations of removing the captured guns.

8. Sir James Outram has also to express his acknowledgments to Brigadiers Hamilton and Eyre, who were left in charge of the camp, and with the small force at their disposal checked the dispositions for an attack which the enemy was commencing with their skirmishers on the left flank, until the return of the force to camp caused them to abandon their intentions.

9. It will be the pleasing duty of the Major-General to make his Excellency the Commander-in-Chief acquainted with the successful result of yesterday's operations, and his approbation of the conduct of all those concerned in them.

SUPPLEMENT TO DIVISION ORDERS.

In publishing to the troops under his command the return of casualties which occurred in the skirmish at Guilee on the 22nd instant, a well as the return of ordnance captured, the Major-General is happy to have to record his approval of the conduct of Staff-Sergeant Roddy who was in command of the two guns attached to Colonel Guy's column and whom his commanding officer, Captain Olpherts, has mentioned for the able way in which he brought his guns into action, and the good service he rendered in covering the rapid advance of the column.

Major Robertson has also brought to his notice the great assistance he received on every occasion from Captain Lane, 5th Bengal Light Cavalry; and Lieutenant Rich, her Majesty's 9th Lancers, attached to the Military Train.

GENERAL ORDERS BY HIS EXCELLENCY THE COMMANDER-IN-CHIEF.

Adjutant-General's Office, Calcutta, Feb. 4, 1858.

By the Right Honourable the Governor-General of India in Council.

Fort William, 29*th January,* 1858.

The Right Honourable the Governor-General of India in Council is pleased to direct the publication of the following despatch from Major-General Sir James Outram, G.C.B., reporting the repulse of a large body of the enemy, who made an unsuccessful attack on his position on the 12th instant.

His Lordship in Council expresses his entire satisfaction with the manner in which Major-General Sir J. Outram, G.C.B., has conducted this affair, and with the behaviour of our troops engaged on the occasion.

The Assistant Adjutant-General of the Army to the Secretary to the Government of India, Military Department.

Head-Quarters, Camp, Fettehghur, 19th January, 1858.

I have the honour, by desire of the Commander-in-Chief, to enclose for the information of the Right Honourable the Governor-General in Council, copy of a despatch* from Major-General Sir James Outram, G.C.B., reporting the repulse of a large body of the enemy, who made an unsuccessful attack on his position on the 12th instant.

2. Sir James Outram's dispositions appear to have been made with such forethought as to enable him to inflict considerable loss on the rebels without unnecessarily exposing his own troops.

I have, &c.,
D. M. STEWARD, *Captain,*
Assistant-Adjutant-General of the Army.

Major-General J. Outram, Commanding in Oude to General W. R. Mansfield, Chief of the Staff of the Army in the East Indies.

Camp, Alumbagh, 12th January, 1858.

I have the honour to inform his Excellency the Commander-in-Chief that the rebels of Lucknow attacked my position this morning, and were repulsed with considerable loss.

In consequence of reports that Mansoob Allie was collecting men and receiving reinforcements from Lucknow to intercept my communications, I sent a stronger escort than usual with my convoy now on its way from Cawnpore, consisting of 450 infantry, 4 guns, and 80 cavalry.

The rebels were encouraged by this reduction of my force to meditate an attack, of which I received information for several days, and yesterday evening more definite accounts led me to expect them at sunrise this morning. I therefore made such dispositions of my force and outposts as were necessary, and the troops breakfasted at daybreak, and were all in readiness.

About sunrise this morning, large masses of the enemy were seen on

---

* Dated 12th of January, 1858.

my left front, and they gradually spread round the whole front and flanks of my position, extending from opposite to our left rear outpost to near Jellahabad on our right, a distance of at least six miles, and they amounted, at the lowest estimation, to 30,000 men.

As soon as their movements were decidedly in advance, the brigades—the right mustering 713 and the left 733 Europeans, and 100 men of the regiment of Ferozepore—were formed in front of their lines.

The enemy first advanced upon my left front and flank, covered by a large body of skirmishers, on which I detached two regiments of the left brigade to support the outposts, and extended in skirmishing order on their flanks, whilst the third regiment was held in reserve; at the same time Major Olpherts, with four horse battery guns, supported by a detachment of the military train, was directed to check the enemy on my left rear, where their cavalry showed in the greatest strength. The volunteer and native cavalry were drawn up to protect the rear of the camp, which at this time appeared to be threatened.

The right brigade remained on its ground.

As soon as the enemy were fairly within range they were exposed to a severe fire of artillery from Alumbagh, and from the advanced batteries of my outposts on the left front and centre, and fled with the utmost precipitation without having come within musket range, except at the left centre outpost commanded by Captain Down, 1st Madras Fusiliers, where a considerable number entered a grove of trees usually occupied by our outlying picquets, from which they were driven in a few minutes by the skirmishers of the outpost.

On the left rear, Major Olpherts moved out his guns at a gallop, and advancing well to his front, completely drove off and dispersed a very large body of infantry and cavalry which was endeavouring to penetrate to our rear, turning them back towards the city, and doing much execution by the fire of his guns on their masses at 500 yards.

At this time I received a report that Alumbagh and my right advanced outpost of Jellalabad were threatened; and on proceeding to the right I found that the enemy had brought three horse artillery guns, supported by an immense mass of infantry, against the picquet which connects my right with Jellalabad, and which had been strengthened to 100 men with two guns. I moved the regiment of Ferozepore and the 5th Fusiliers, with two guns of Moir's Bullock Battery, from the right brigade to the front, taking the enemy in flank and driving them back. They were then exposed to the fire of Maude's guns from Alumbagh, which played upon them with great effect.

About this time the enemy again advanced on the left front and flank, their cavalry on this occasion being more to the front than before. A party of the latter galloped up to the rifle-pits in front of the left advanced outpost; but Alexander's and Clarke's guns opened on them and drove them back in confusion.

About the same time the enemy on the right, again advancing from the heavy cover of groves and villages into which they had retreated, reopened their guns on the Jellalabad picquet, but were finally silenced and driven off by the fire of Moir's two guns, which had been sent to the picquet to reinforce it, and to replace the two guns originally there, which had been withdrawn to Jellalabad.

Simultaneously with the attack above described, the enemy advanced upon Alumbagh, and established themselves in the nearest cover, notwithstanding that they were seen to suffer severely from the artillery and rifle fire. About noon they also advanced into the open ground, and were immediately dispersed and driven back by the fire of Maude's guns and the riflemen from Alumbagh.

By four o'clock P.M. the whole of the enemy had disappeared, and retired to the city or to their original positions in the gardens and villages in our front.

Nothing could exceed the eagerness of the troops to come in contact with the rebels, nor their disappointment at their precipitate flight to the cover of their works the moment the guns opened and our line of skirmishers advanced.

The artillery made excellent practice on the masses of the enemy, and in reply to the fire from their batteries, which was maintained on our outposts and Alumbagh with little intermission.

The casualties amount to one officer slightly, three privates slightly, and two severely wounded.

I take this opportunity of sending a return of casualties during the last fortnight, including to-day's.

The steadiness of the troops, and the promptitude with which my orders were carried out by my officers, gives me every assurance that the enemy's attack, if it had been as formidable as their forces were numerous, would have been as signally defeated.

I have, &c.,
J. OUTRAM, *Major-General,*
Commanding in Oude.

NUMERICAL RETURN *of Casualties in the Field Force, under the command of Major-General Sir J. Outram, G.C.B., from* 29*th December up to the present date.*

Camp Alumbagh, 12*th January,* 1858.

DETAIL.	KILLED.			WOUNDED.			REMARKS.
	Officers.	Privates.	Total.	Officers.	Privates.	Total.	
Artillery..................	*1	0	1	0	§2	2	* Lieut. Gordon, 1st Co., 5th Batt., 9th Jan., 1858.
H. M.'s 5th Fusiliers...	0	†1	1	0	0	0	† 29th Dec., 1857.
„ 75th Foot......	0	0	0	‡1	0	1	‡ 12th Jan., 1858, Lieut. Hennessy, 34th N.I.
1st Madras Fusiliers...	0	0	0	0	2	2	12th Jan., 1858.
Regt. of Ferozepore ...	0	0	0	0	2	2	Ditto ditto.
Total............	1	1	2	1	6	7	§ 1 wounded, Dec. 30,1857. 1 ditto, Jan. 12, 1858.

J. OUTRAM, *Major-General,*
Commanding 1*st Division.*

GENERAL ORDERS BY HIS EXCELLENCY THE
COMMANDER-IN-CHIEF.

Adjutant-General's Office,
Calcutta, February 18, 1858.

By the Honourable the President of the Council of India in Council.

Fort William, 12*th February,* 1858.

In continuation of G. G. O., No. 182 of the 29th January, 1858, the Honourable the President of the Council of India in Council has much satisfaction in publishing the following despatch from Major-General Sir J. Outram, G.C.B., commanding in Oude, reporting the result of an attack made on his position by the enemy on the 16th January, 1858.

Major-General Sir J. Outram, G.C.B., Commanding in Oude, to General Mansfield, Chief of the Staff of the Army in the East Indies.

Camp Alumbagh, 17*th January,* 1858.

I have the honour to report, for the information of his Excellency the Commander-in-Chief, that the enemy made an attack on my position yesterday, similar to that reported in letter of the 12th instant, except that, though they did not show in such general strength, their attack was more bold than before. In the morning they made a sudden attack on the Jellalabad picquet, and were received with a heavy fire, which drove them back immediately, leaving on the ground their leader, a Hindoo devotee representing Hunnoman, who was advancing bravely at their head, and several killed and wounded, whom they were unable to carry off. As they were seen removing many bodies, their loss must have been severe. Two 9-pounders, under Captain Moir, were sent down to support the picquet, and completed the expulsion of the enemy from the cover in its front.

On the left front and left the enemy advanced skirmishers and threatened during the greater part of the day, suffering severely whenever they ventured within range. After dark they assembled in great strength in front of my left advanced village outpost, commanded by Major Gordon, 75th Regiment, and attacked it with a large body of infantry, who were allowed to approach within eighty yards of the post, when they were received with discharges of grape from three guns, and a heavy fire from the rifles of the post, which inflicted very severe loss and drove them off immediately. Some shells from an eight-inch mortar expedited their retreat. The Enfield rifles, and Captain Maude's guns in Alumbagh, had several opportunities of inflicting severe loss on the enemy, which were promptly taken advantage of. A large body of cavalry showed on my left rear, and were safely left to the vigilance of Captain Olpherts, who watched and kept them in check with his four horse battery guns, supported by a detachment of the Military Train under Captain Clarke.

The casualties of my force during the day amounted to—

  1 Bombardier, killed;
  7 European infantry, wounded;
  1 Gunner, wounded by a fall from his gun.

The judgment and coolness with which Major Gordon defended his post, deserve much praise; he was ably supported by Lieutenant Clarke, commanding the battery.

Much credit is also due to Lieutenant Wynne, of her Majesty's 90th, who commanded the Jellalabad picquet.

Also to Lieutenant-Colonel Smith, commanding the post; and Captain Maude, commanding the artillery at Alumbagh.

To Captain Rattray, commanding the infantry; Lieutenant Gully, commanding the battery of No. 1 advanced outpost on the left; and to the officers and men of their posts for their vigilance and alertness in checking and punishing the enemy at every opportunity.

         H. W. NORMAN, *Major*,
      Deputy Adjutant-General of the Army.

[The following despatch, not having been published, is supposed to have miscarried:—]

Major-General Sir J. Outram, G.C.B., to the Deputy Adjutant-General of the Army.

        Camp Alumbagh, February 17*th*, 1858.

The events that have occurred since my last report, dated the 17th ultimo, have been of no great importance. The enemy have received information of the continual passage of troops and stores along the Cawnpore road, and evince a nervous restlessness which betrays itself in constant assemblies of large bodies of men, both cavalry and infantry, and demonstrations of attacks which a few rounds from our nearest guns have in general put an immediate end to. Although these threatened attacks have cost us but very few casualties, they are excessively harassing to the troops, whom I am obliged constantly to turn out and keep under arms.

On the 15th instant a strong body of horsemen, supported by infantry, were observed moving towards our left rear. As a convoy was on the road, and a most violent dust storm favourable for them to approach it unobserved was blowing, I ordered out two of Captain

Olpherts' horsed guns, and a troop of the Military Train, to observe their movements. And on a further report of the enemy's increasing strength being made, I supported them with the rest of the battery, the remainder of the Military Train, a detachment of Wale's Horse, and her Majesty's 90th Light Infantry.

In the meanwhile a portion of the enemy's cavalry and infantry, escorting a person in a palanquin, having advanced well into the open, Captain Olpherts' two guns and the troop of the Military Train galloped to the front and opened on them with grape, killing and wounding several and dispersing the remainder. I have since been informed that it was the Moulvie himself who headed this party, and that he was severely wounded. We lost one havildar of Gun Lascars.

On the 16th instant the enemy filled their trenches with as many men as they could hold, and assembled in vast numbers under the topes in their rear, while at the same time a body of cavalry and infantry was detached to threaten our left flank. During the morning they made repeated demonstrations of advancing to attack, but their courage apparently as often failed them, and they almost immediately returned to their position. About 5.30 they suddenly issued in clouds of skirmishers from their trenches, advancing for some distance towards our batteries posted on the left and centre of our line, and after opening a smart fire of musquetry on the outposts of the left front village, they advanced towards it in large bodies. They were repulsed by the picquet, consisting of two hundred men of the 90th Light Infantry, under command of Lieutenant-Colonel Smith, of that regiment, after losing a good many men, while the 90th had three wounded. As soon as it was dark, they concentrated a very heavy musquetry fire on the north and east faces of the Alumbagh, which they continued for about two hours, but which fortunately did us no harm. They did not all finally retire till 8.30 P.M. Their loss must have been severe, as their flashes gave an excellent line for our guns, which opened on them with shrapnel shell and grape. Our loss during the last two days has been one killed and three wounded.

To-day they moved about two thousand infantry towards our right rear, apparently with the intention of interrupting the Engineer working parties. I sent three troops of the Military Train, two guns, and a squadron of Wales' Horse, in that direction, and the enemy withdrew towards the city. During their absence, the enemy made a partial advance towards our right and left picquets, but were driven back by the artillery fire.

The reports from the city state that it is their intention to harass us by continually annoying us in this way, and that attacks are every day to be made from all quarters. This obliges me to keep all my picquets very strong, and, added to this, continually turning out, and latterly the almost daily call for escorts for convoys returning to or coming from Bunnee, renders the duty excessively harassing to the troops.

I beg to enclose a return of casualties of this force from the 17th January to the 17th February, 1858.

I have, &c.

J. OUTRAM, *Major-General*,
Commanding 1st Division.

GENERAL ORDERS BY HIS EXCELLENCY THE COMMANDER-IN-CHIEF.

Adjutant General's Office, Calcutta, 9th March, 1858.

By the Right Honourable the Governor-General of India.

Camp, Allahabad, 1st March, 1858.

The Right Honourable the Governor-General of India has much satisfaction in publishing the following report, by Major-General Sir J. Outram, G.C.B., of the repulse of an attack on his position at Alumbagh, on the morning of the 21st February, 1858, in which the arrangements made by Sir J. Outram were most judicious and effectual, and the conduct of the troops engaged was highly creditable to them.

Major-General Sir J. Outram, G.C.B., commanding 1st Division, to the Deputy Adjutant-General of the Army.

Camp Alumbagh, 21st February, 1858.

I have the honour to report that this morning the enemy attacked my position, and with the usual result.

2. Having filled all their trenches with as many men as they would hold, and placed large masses of infantry in the topes all along our front in support of them, they commenced a simultaneous movement round about our flanks, at the same time threatening the whole length of our position, and attacking the north-east corner of the Alumbagh, and also the picquet and fort of Jellalabad, against which they brought 4 guns.

3. I, immediately on perceiving their intention, reinforced the posts of Alumbagh and Jellalabad, which easily repulsed the attacks made on them, and inflicted much loss on the assailants, who had advanced under cover of long grass and underwood, within grape shot range of both these posts.

4. I detached about 250 cavalry and 2 field guns to the rear of the fort of Jellalabad, under command of Captain Barrow, Volunteer Cavalry, where they suddenly came on about 2,000 of the enemy's cavalry. Our guns immediately opened on them, killing several, which caused them to withdraw to the immediate vicinity of the infantry attacking the fort, in number about 5,000; they remained there until the attack was abandoned, when they all withdrew towards the city.

5. The attack on our left flank was made by about from 8,000 to 10,000 infantry and 500 cavalry, to oppose whom I sent out the

remaining 4 field guns available, supported by the military train (120 in number) under command of Major Robertson, of the military train, keeping the 2nd Infantry Brigade in reserve. The cavalry and guns soon drove back the enemy's cavalry, and their infantry then halted, and on the guns being turned on them soon commenced to retreat also, being followed up by us until within range of their batteries.

6. A large convoy was on the road at the time, the escort required for which materially crippled our small cavalry force, and prevented anything more being effected than frustrating their attempts to gain our rear and molest our convoy.

7. The reports from the city state the enemy to have lost 60 killed and 200 wounded in their attack on Alumbagh, and about 80 or 90 killed or wounded in front of Jellalabad. This was exclusive of their loss on the left flank, and along our front, where our heavy artillery had constant opportunities of firing shell and shrapnel into the midst of their moving masses. I consider their loss to have been heavier than on any of their previous attacks.

8. I have the pleasure to state that, as on all former occasions, the conduct of the troops engaged, both officers and men, was admirable.

9. Majors Tinling, 90th Light Infantry, and Nicholson, Royal Engineers, commanded respectively at Alumbagh and Jellalabad, and defended their posts with much spirit. Major Nicholson particularly praises the energy with which Lieutenant Ford, of the Royal Artillery, opposed the fire of the enemy's four guns with the only gun that could be brought to bear on them.

10. Our loss amounted to nine wounded. A nominal roll is transmitted herewith.

I have, &c.,
J. OUTRAM, *Major-General,*
Commanding 1st *Division..*

Head-Quarters, Camp, Cawnpore, 24th *February,* 1858.

Forwarded by order of the Commander-in-Chief, to the Secretary to the Government of India, Military Department, for the information of the Right Honourable the Governor-General.

H. W. NORMAN, *Major,*
Deputy-Adjutant-General of the Army.

GENERAL ORDERS BY HIS EXCELLENCY THE COMMANDER-IN-CHIEF.

Adjutant-General's Office, Calcutta, March 25, 1858.

By the Right Honourable the Governor-General of India.

Camp Allahabad, 8th *March,* 1858.

The Right Honourable the Governor-General has great pleasure in publishing the accompanying despatch from Major-General Sir James Outram, G.C.B., reporting the particulars of an unusually resolute attack on his position, on the 25th of February, 1858, and of its gallant repulse by the troops under his command, to whom, as well as to their distinguished leader, his Lordship offers his thanks for the good service rendered on this occasion.

Major-General Sir J. Outram, G.C.B., Commanding 1st Division, to the Deputy-Adjutant-General of the Army.

Camp, Alumbagh, 26th February, 1858.

I have the honour to report the particulars of the repulse of a determined demonstration, which the enemy made on our position yesterday, the 25th instant.

2. The principal attack was on our right, against which twenty-four regiments of regular infantry, six Nujeeb corps, 1,000 cavalry, and eight guns moved out from the enemy's trenches; of this number, about one-half, with two guns, advanced towards our right rear, and having occupied the "topes" immediately to the east of Jellalabad, commenced shelling that post heavily, evidently in the hope of igniting the large quantity of combustible stores at present collected there, while the remainder held in support of the villages and "topes" directly in front of the enemy's outworks.

3. Large bodies of infantry and cavalry, with three guns, simultaneously menaced our left, and the trenches in front of our position were occupied in force.

4. Soon after ten A.M., I moved out with detachments of artillery, cavalry, and infantry, as per accompanying return, to intercept the column which had opened its guns on Jellalabad, having previously sent Barrow's Volunteers and Wale's Horse round, viâ Nowrungabad, to co-operate in their rear.

5. As we advanced, a portion of the enemy's reserve made a demonstration against our left; but were speedily driven back, and afterwards held in check by the four guns of Remmington's Troop, supported by a squadron of the 7th Hussars, under Colonel Hagart and by Brasyer's Sikhs.

6. The column then moved forward, flanked on the left by Brigadier Campbell, with the native cavalry, which pushed on in advance to intercept the enemy's retreat, which owing to their having heard the fire of Remmington's guns, proved more sudden than we had anticipated. The manœuvre was completely successful, and speedily converted their retreat into a rout, Brigadier Campbell's detachment assailing them on one side, while Barrow's and Wale's Horse appeared on the opposite quarter, and the Military Train, under Captain Robertson, dashed into the middle of the flying enemy and captured their

two guns. The rapidity of their flight prevented the infantry from taking a prominent part in the action. At one P.M., when we finally left the field, the foe had vanished.

7. In the meantime the hostile forces on the left of my position had retired before the very effective fire of Moir's guns, not liking the look of the arrangements which had been prepared by Brigadier Franklyn, who had been left in command of the camp, for their reception.

8. Judging from the corpses which strewed the field where the cavalry had charged, and from the dense masses upon which our guns repeatedly opened, the enemy's casualties must have been heavy. Our loss consisted of four men killed, five officers, and twenty men wounded.

9. My cordial acknowledgments are due to all the officers and men who conducted and took part in these operations, but especially to the military train, whose brilliant charge excited the enthusiasm of all who witnessed it.

10. Colonel Berkeley, my able and zealous military secretary, whose knowledge of the ground was of great service to Brigadier Campell in cutting off the enemy's retreat, was wounded while gallantly charging at the head of Hodson's Horse, as was Lieutenant Moorsom while rendering to Barrow and Wale assistance similar to that which Colonel Berkeley afforded the Brigadier.

11. About four, P.M., the enemy again moved out against us. On this occasion they directed their principal efforts against our left, and evinced more spirit and determination than they had hitherto done. Repeatedly they advanced within grape and musket range, and as they ever met with a warm reception from our guns and Enfields, especially from those of the left front picquet, commanded by Major Master, of the 5th Fusiliers, they must have suffered severely.* They renewed their fire from to time during the night; but solely, I believe, with the object of covering the parties engaged in moving their dead. Our loss in this subsequent operation amounted to one man killed and fourteen wounded. In all five men killed and thirty-five officers and men wounded.

12. The conduct of the troops throughout the entire day and night was excellent at every point, and merits the highest commendation.

The usual returns of ordnance captured and of casualties are hereby forwarded.

I have, &c.,
J. OUTRAM, *Major-General,*
Commanding 1st *Division.*

---

* Information has since been received, which states the enemy's loss throughout the day to have been between 400 and 500.

PART II.

THE FINAL CAPTURE OF LUCKNOW.

THE

FINAL CAPTURE OF LUCKNOW.

[WHILE Sir James Outram was engaged in the way we have seen, in keeping the insurgents at bay in the vicinity of Lucknow, the Commander-in-Chief had been busily collecting reinforcements for the final capture of that city and the subjugation of the revolted chiefs. The arrangements for surrounding the mutineers were most carefully made, and when the time arrived for striking the final blow, Sir Colin Campbell advanced at the head of 18,000 magnificently appointed men. General Franks and Brigadier Hope Grant had been doing good service in the meanwhile, and so soon as the Commander-in-Chief's force reached the Alumbagh, Sir James Outram led the advanced division of the army of retribution across the Goomtee, and took post to the east of Lucknow. The rest of the glorious story is told by the despatches themselves.]

GENERAL ORDERS BY HIS EXCELLENCY THE COMMANDER-IN-CHIEF.

Adjutant-General's Office,
Calcutta, April 16, 1858.

By the Right Honourable the Governor-General of India.

Allahabad, April 5, 1858.

The Right Honourable the Governor-General having now received the despatches from his Excellency the

Commander-in-Chief, giving an account of the re-taking of Lucknow by the force under his Excellency's personal command, is pleased to publish them for general information.

In December last, it became the grateful duty of the Governor-General in Council to promulgate in General Orders, the announcement of the relief of the garrison of Lucknow, so admirably achieved by General Sir Colin Campbell, G.C.B., and the rescue of the women and children, sick and wounded, long beleaguered there. It is now the Governor-General's privilege to convey to his Excellency the tribute of his highest admiration, of his most cordial congratulations, on the capture of the strong city of the rebels.

From the 2nd till the 16th of March, a series of masterly operations took place, by which the Commander-in-Chief, nobly supported in his well-laid plans of attack by the ability and skill of the general officers, and by the indomitable bravery and resolution of the officers and men of all arms, drove the rebels successively from all their strongly fortified posts, till the whole fell into the possession of our troops.

That this great success should have been accomplished at so little cost of valuable lives, enhances the honour due to the leader who has achieved it.

It is a pleasure to the Governor-General to acknowledge publicly the services of the General and other officers who took part in the capture of Lucknow.

During the last days of the operations, the Nepaulese force, under Maharajah Jung Bahadoor, was associated with the army under General Sir Colin Campbell's command.

To the distinguished leader of that force, the Maharajah Jung Bahadoor, the Governor-General desires to express his thanks for the hearty co-operation which the

Commander-in-Chief received from his Highness, and for the gallant bearing of his Highness' troops.

To Major-General Sir James Outram, G.C.B., the Government of India is under a new debt of gratitude. After having held the exposed post of Alumbagh for more than three months, in the face of powerful bodies of rebels, whose attacks he never failed to repel, Sir James Outram has further greatly distinguished himself at the head of the 1st Division, by the brilliant and thoroughly complete manner in which he executed the duties entrusted to him. The Governor-General requests that Sir James Outram will accept his most sincere thanks.

His lordship offers his hearty acknowledgments to the other General officers whose services are prominently noticed in these despatches.

To Major-General Mansfield, Chief of the Staff, of whose eminent services the Commander-in-Chief speaks with well-merited commendation.

To Major-General Sir Archdale Wilson, Bart., K.C.B., in chief command of the artillery, who, after winning lasting renown in the capture of Delhi, has borne a conspicuous part in the reduction of Lucknow.

To Major-General Sir J. Hope Grant, K.C.B., commanding the cavalry of the force, to Brigadier-General Franks, C.B., Brigadier-General Walpole, and Brigadier-General Sir Edward Lugard, K.C.B., commanding the 2nd, 3rd, and 4th Divisions of Infantry.

The Governor-General has to record his acknowledgments to Captain Sir William Peel, K.C.B., commanding the Naval Brigade of H. M.'s ship *Shannon*, and to offer his especial thanks to him for his remarkable services.

The Governor-General entirely concurs with his Excellency the Commander-in-Chief in prominently recognizing the great skill and ability of Brigadier Napier, who commanded the Engineers of her Majesty's and the East India Company's services, forming part of the force. Brigadier Napier is especially entitled to the thanks of the Governor-General, and to him, to Colonel Harness, commanding the Royal Engineers, and to the several officers under them, of both the services, his Lordship's grateful acknowledgments are offered.

The Governor-General has much satisfaction in expressing his high sense of the merits of the several officers commanding brigades and regiments.

To the commanding officers of the Royal Artillery, of the Naval Artillery and of the Bengal and Madras Artillery, the Governor-General tenders his cordial thanks.

To Major Norman, Deputy Adjutant-General of the Army, to whose superior merits and distinguished services the Commander-in-Chief bears willing testimony, a tribute in which the Governor-General concurs; to Colonel the Honourable W. L. Pakenham, C.B., Officiating Adjutant-General of her Majesty's Forces in India; to Lieutenant-Colonel Macpherson, Officiating Quartermaster-General of the Army; to Captain Seymour, Officiating Quartermaster-General of her Majesty's Forces; to Captain Bruce, Deputy Quartermaster-General, and Captain Algood, Assistant Quartermaster-General; to Lieutenant-Colonel Keith Young, Judge Advocate-General; to Captain Fitzgerald, Assistant Commissary-General, who is specially mentioned by the Commander-in-Chief; to Lieutenant P. Stewart, of Engineers, Superintendent of Electric Telegraphs; to Dr. MacAndrew, Inspector General of Hospitals, her Majesty's Forces, and to Dr. Brown, Superintending

Surgeon of the Force, the Governor-General has much satisfaction in expressing his sense of the good service they have rendered.

To the officers of the personal staff of the Commander-in-Chief, of the chief of the staff, and of general officers commanding divisions, the thanks of the Governor-General are due; and his Lordship records his acknowledgments to the officers of the staff of divisions and brigades, all of whom have zealously performed their duty.

To the officers and men of every service, soldiers, seamen and marines, composing the force by which Lucknow has been taken, the Governor-General desires to express his admiration of their conduct, and to tender to each individual the thanks of the Government of India. His Lordship will take the earliest opportunity of bringing under the favourable notice of her Majesty's Government, and of the Honourable the Court of Directors, the services rendered by the force.

In testimony of the services, the Governor-General is pleased to direct that every officer and soldier, European and native, and the officers and men of the navy, who took part in the capture of Lucknow, shall receive a donation of six months' batta.

By order of the Right Honourable the Governor-General,

R. J. H. BIRCH, *Colonel.*
Secretary to the Government of India,
Military Department, with the Governor-General.

The Right Honourable the Viscount Canning, Governor-General of India, &c., &c., &c.

Camp La Martiniere, Lucknow, 22nd March, 1858.

I have the honour to announce to your Lordship, that I transferred my head-quarters to the camp of Brigadier-General Sir Edward Lugard, K.C.B., at Buntara, on the 28th ultimo, the division which had been detached under Brigadier-General Sir J. Hope Grant, K.C.B., and that under Brigadier-General Walpole joining the next day.

Having received tolerably correct information with respect to the lines of works which had been constructed by the enemy for the defence of Lucknow, it appeared evident to me that the necessity would arise for operating from both sides of the Goomtee, when the capture of the city should be seriously entertained.

Two very important reasons conduced to show the expediency of such a course—the one being that it would become possible to enfilade many of the enemy's new works; the other, that great avenues of supply would be closed against the town, although I could not hope to invest a city having a circumference of twenty miles.

My first preparations, therefore, were made for the purpose of crossing the river. Bridges of casks had been previously constructed, and were ready in the Engineer's Park.

On the 2nd of March, I advanced on Dilkoosha with troops as per margin,* and seized that position after a skirmish in which a gun was taken from the enemy.

When the brigades of infantry began to close on the advance guard, the enemy opened several guns which were in position, in strong bastions, along the line of the canal. This fire was heavy and well sustained.

These guns commanded the plateau, and compelled me to retire the camp as far back as it was possible, but not so far as I could have wished, owing to the ravines in the rear.

The Palace of Dilkoosha was occupied as an advance picquet on the right, and the Mahomed Bagh on the left—heavy guns being placed in battery at both points to keep down the hostile fire.

During the whole of the 2nd, until these arrangements could be completed, the troops were much annoyed by the enemy's guns.

---

* DETAIL.—Head-quarters of the Division of Artillery and of the Field Artillery Brigade, under Major-General Sir A. Wilson, K.C.B., and Colonel D. Wood, C.B., Royal Horse Artillery. Lieutenant-Colonel D'Aguilar's troop, Royal Horse Artillery. Lieutenant-Colonel Tombs, C.B., and Lieutenant Bishop's troops Bengal Horse Artillery, under Lieutenant-Colonel Turner. Two 24-pounders and two 8-inch howitzers of the *Shannon's* Naval Brigade, and two companies Punjaub Sappers and Miners. The head-quarters of the Cavalry Division and the 1st Cavalry Brigade, under Brigadier-General Sir J. H. Grant, K.C.B., and Brigadier Little. II. M.'s 9th Lancers. 2nd Punjaub Irregular Cavalry. Detachment 5th Punjaub Irregular Cavalry. 1st Sikh Irregular Cavalry. The 2nd Division of Infantry, under Brigadier-General Sir E. Lugard, K.C.B., consisting of—3rd Brigade, Brigadier P. M. M. Guy: H. M.'s 34th Regiment, H. M.'s 38th Regiment, and H. M.'s 53rd Regiment;—4th Brigade, Brigadier Hon. A. Hope: 42nd Highlanders, 93rd Highlanders, and 4th Punjaub Rifles.

After that day, until an advance took place, although the shot ranged up to and sometimes into the camp, but slight loss ensued from this cause.

On the 3rd and 4th, the remainder of the siege train, together with Brigadier-General Walpole's Division, closed up on the Dilkoosha position, the right of our line resting on Bibiapore and the Goomtee, the left being towards Alumbagh.

There was an interval of about two miles between our left and Jellalabad, the right of the Alumbagh position. This interval was occupied by a regiment of Irregular Horse.* Brigadier Campbell, with a strong brigade of cavalry and horse artillery, secured the extreme left, and swept the country towards the north-west.

Three infantry regiments were withdrawn from Alumbagh, and joined the head-quarters camp.

On the 5th, General Franks, of the 4th division of infantry, came into direct communication with me. This officer had marched right across the kingdom of Oude, having signally defeated many bodies of insurgents, and kept his time with punctuality according to the orders given to him, with which your Lordship is already acquainted.

On the same day, the Goomtee was bridged near Bibiapore. Whilst the bridge was being formed the enemy showed on the left bank, causing the necessity of a disposition of troops and heavy guns. He did not, however, make a real attack.

These guns were very useful in another respect, as their practice on the Martiniere silenced much fire, which would otherwise have annoyed the picquets.

They were accordingly kept on the same ground for some days, till the advance of the troops rendered them unnecessary.

On the 6th, Sir James Outram, G.C.B., who had been withdrawn from Alumbagh, crossed to the left bank of the Goomtee with troops as per margin.† The 4th division, under Brigadier-General Franks, C B., taking the place vacated by Brigadier-General Walpole in the line.

The plan of attack which had been conceived was now developed, and Sir J. Outram was directed to push his advance up the left bank of the Goomtee, while the troops in the position of Dilkhoosha remained at rest till it should have become apparent that the first line of the enemy's works, or the rampart running along the canal and abutting on the Goomtee, had been turned.

The works may be briefly described as follows :—

---

* Hodson's.
† *Force sent across the Goomtee under Sir J. Outram.*
DETAIL.—Lieutenant-Colonel D'Aguilar's Troop, R.H.A. Major Remmington's and Captain McKinnon's Troops, Bengal H.A., under Lieutenant-Colonel P. Turner. Captains Gibbon and Middleton's Light Field Batteries, Royal Artillery and Head-quarters Field Artillery Brigade. Head-quarters Cavalry Division and of 1st Cavalry Brigade. H.M.'s 2nd D. G. (Bays). H.M.'s 9th Lancers. 2nd Punjaub Cavalry. Detachments 1st and 5th Punjaub Cavalry, under Captains Watson and Stanford. 3rd Infantry Division under Brigadier-General R. Walpole. 5th Brigade, Brigadier Douglas, C.B.; H.M.'s 23rd Fusiliers, H.M.'s 79th Highlanders, 1st Bengal Fusiliers. 6th Brigade, Brigadier Horsford, C.B.; 2nd Battalion Rifle Brigade, 3rd Battalion Rifle Brigade, 2nd Punjaub Infantry.

The series of courts and buildings called the Kaiser Bagh, considered as a citadel by the rebels, was shut in by three lines of defence towards the Goomtee, of which the line of the canal was the outer one.

The second line circled round the large buildings called the Messhouse and the Moti Mahul, and the first or interior one was the principal rampart of the Kaiser Bagh.

The rear of the enclosures of the latter being closed in by the city, through which approach would have been dangerous to an assailant.

These lines were flanked by numerous bastions, and rested at one end on the Goomtee, and at the other on the great buildings of the street called the Huzrut Gunge, all of which were strongly fortified, and flanked the street in every direction.

Extraordinary care had been expended on the defences of the houses and bastions to enfilade the street. This duty was ably performed by Sir James Outram, who pitched his camp on the 6th instant, after a skirmish of his advance guard, in front of the Chukker Walla Kotee, or Yellow-house.

On the 7th he was attacked by the enemy, who was speedily driven back.

Having reconnoitred the ground on the 8th instant, I directed Sir James Outram to arrange his batteries during the succeeding night, and to attack the enemy's position, the key of which was the Chukkur Walla Kotee, the next day or the 9th.

This was done in very good style by the troops under his command, the enemy being driven in at all points, the Yellow-house being seized, and the whole force advanced for some distance through ground affording excellent cover for the enemy.

He was then able to bring his right shoulders forward, occupying the Fyzabad Road, and to plant his batteries for the purpose of enfilading the works on the canal before alluded to.

He lost no time in doing this, other batteries of heavy guns and howitzers being constructed during the following night to play on the works and the Kaiser Bagh.

While this attack was being made by Sir James Outram, along the left bank of the Goomtee on the 9th instant, a very heavy fire was kept kept up on the Martiniere both from mortars and heavy guns, placed in position during the previous night on the Dilkhoosha Plateau.

At two P.M. the 42nd Highlanders, supported by the 93rd Highlanders, the 53rd and 90th Regiments, stormed the Martiniere under the direction of Brigadier-General Sir Edward Lugard, K.C.B., and Brigadier the Honourable Adrian Hope.

It was quickly seen that the enfilading fire on the line of the canal from the opposite side of the river had produced the expected result.

The 4th Punjaub Infantry, supported by the 42nd Highlanders, climbed up the entrenchment abutting on the Goomtee, and proceeded to sweep down the whole line of the works till they got to the neighbourhood of Banks' house, when it became necessary to close operations for the night.

Major Wylde, 4th Punjaub Rifles, distinguished himself very much on this occasion. The line of works was strongly occupied by the troops which had first entered, and by the 53rd Regiment.

On the 10th instant, Sir James Outram was engaged in strengthening his position. Sir James Hope Grant, K.C.B., being employed in patrolling towards the cantonment with the cavalry placed under Sir James Outram's orders, a system of extensive patrolling or reconnoissance having been established by my order in that direction, from the time that the first position had been taken up across the Goomtee.

At sunrise on the same day, a disposition of troops and heavy guns was made by Sir Edward Lugard for the attack of Banks' house, which was carried at noon, and secured as a strong military post.

The second part of the plan of attack against the Kaiser Bagh now came into operation, viz., to use the great blocks of houses and palaces, extending from Banks' house to the Kaiser Bagh, as our approach, instead of sapping up towards the front of the second line of works.

By these means I was enabled to turn the new works towards our own left, at the same time that they were enfiladed on the right by Sir Sir James Outram's advance.

The latter had already received orders to plant his guns with a view to raking the enemy's position, to annoy the Kaiser Bagh both with vertical and direct fire; also to attack the suburbs in the vicinity of the iron and stone bridges, shortly after daybreak, and so command the iron bridge from the left bank.

All this was carried out by Sir James Outram with the most marked success.

The enemy, however, still held tenaciously by his own end of the iron bridge on the right bank, and there was heavy cannonading from both sides, till the bridge was afterwards taken in reverse.

Sir Edward Lugard's attack on the 11th was pressed forward in like manner.

The operation had now become one of engineering character, and the most earnest endeavours were made to save the infantry from being hazarded before due preparation had been made.

The chief engineer, Brigadier Napier, placed the batteries with a view to breaching and shelling a large block of palaces called the Begum Kotee.

The latter was stormed with great gallantry by the 93rd Highlanders, supported by the 4th Punjaub Rifles, and 1,000 Goorkhas, led by Brigadier the Honourable Adrian Hope, under the direction of Brigadier-General Sir Edward Lugard, at four P.M.

The troops secured the whole block of buildings, and inflicted a very heavy loss on the enemy, the attack having been one of very desperate character.

This was the sternest struggle which occurred during the siege.

Thenceforward the chief engineer pushed his approach with the greatest judgment through the enclosures, by the aid of the sappers and of heavy guns, the troops immediately occupying the ground as he advanced, and the mortars being moved from one position to another as ground was won on which they could be placed.

The buildings to the right and the Secunder Bagh were taken in the early morning of the same day without opposition.

During the night of the 12th, Sir James Outram was reinforced with a number of heavy guns and mortars, and directed to increase his fire on the Kaiser Bagh, while at the same time mortars placed in position at the Begum's house never ceased to play on the Emmambara, the next large palace it was necessary to storm between the Begum Kotee and the Kaiser Bagh.

On Brigadier General Franks, C.B., who had relieved Sir Edward Lugard, and the 2nd division, with the 4th division, on the 12th inst., devolved the duty of attacking the Emmambara.

A column of attack was formed for that purpose by Brigadier D. Russell, on the morning of the 14th.

In the meantime, the Maha Rajah Jung Bahadoor, with a force about (9,000) nine thousand men, and with 24 field guns drawn by men, had arrived, and taken his position in our line on the 12th inst., and moved close to the canal on the 13th.

At my request, his Highness was begged by Brigadier-General McGregor, C.B., the Special Commissioner attached to him, to pass the canal and attack the suburb in his front and considerably to the left of Banks' house. To this his Highness acceded with much willingness, and his force was most advantageously employed in thus covering my left for several days, during which, from the nature of our operations, I was obliged to mass all the available strength of the British force towards the right, in the joint attack carried along both banks of the Goomtee.

The Emmambara was carried early on the 14th, and the Sikhs of the Ferozepore Regiment under Major Brasyer, pressing forward in pursuit, entered the Kaiser Bagh; the third line of the defences having been turned without a single gun being fired from them.

Supports were quickly thrown in, and all the well-known ground of former defence and attack, the Mess-house, the Tara Kotee, the Motee Mehal, and the Chutter Munzil, was rapidly occupied by the troops, while the engineers devoted their attention to securing the position towards the south and west. The day was one of long and continued exertion, and every one felt that, although much remained to be done before the final expulsion of the rebels, the most difficult part of the undertaking had been overcome.

This is not the place for a description of the various buildings successively sapped into or stormed; suffice it to say, that they formed a range of massive palaces and walled courts of vast extent, equalled perhaps, but certainly not surpassed in any capital in Europe. Every outlet had been covered by a work, and on every side were prepared barricades and loopholed parapets.

The extraordinary industry evinced by the enemy in this respect has been really unexampled. Hence the absolute necessity for holding the troops in hand, till at each successive move forward the engineers reported to me that all which could be effected by artillery and the sappers had been done before the troops were led to the assault.

The 15th instant was employed in securing what had been taken, removing powder, destroying mines, and fixing mortars for the further bombardment of the positions still held by the enemy on the line of our advance up the right bank of the Goomtee, and in the heart of the city.

Brigadier-General Sir J. Hope Grant, K.C.B., was sent out with cavalry on one side towards Seetapore to intercept fugitives, while Brigadier Campbell marched with like orders in the direction of Sundeela, on a similar duty. They returned on the 17th to their former positions.

On the 16th instant, Sir James Outram, with the 5th Brigade under Brigadier Douglas, supported by two other regiments, her Majesty's 20th and the regiment of Ferozepore, having crossed over the Goomtee by a bridge of casks opposite the Secunder Bagh, advanced according to order through the Chutter Munzil to take the Residency.

During the first movements of this operation, a movement of the enemy in retreat, across the stone bridge, became apparent.

Sir James was ordered to press forward, and he was able, almost without opposition, not only to take the iron bridge in reverse, which was my principal object, but also to advance for more than a mile and occupy the Muchhee Bhowun and great Emmambara.

In short, the city was ours.

Brigadier-General Walpole's picquets on the left bank were attacked by the retreating enemy, who was, as usual, heavily repulsed.

On the 19th, a combined movement was organized.

Sir James Outram moved forward directly on the Moosa Bagh, the last position of the enemy on the line of the Goomtee.

Sir J. Hope Grant cannonaded the latter from the left bank, while Brigadier Campbell, moving right round the western side from the Alumbagh, prevented retreat in that direction.

The rout was now complete, and great loss was inflicted on the enemy by all these columns.

On the 16th, for the last time, the enemy had shown in some strength before Alumbagh, which on that date was held by only two of our regiments.

Jung Bahadoor was requested to move to his left up the canal, and take the position in reverse from which our position at Alumbagh had been so long annoyed.

This was executed very well by his Highness, and he seized the positions, one after another, with little loss to himself.

The guns of the enemy, which the latter did not stop to take away, fell into his hands.

On the 21st, Sir Edward Lugard was directed to attack a stronghold held by the Moulvie in the heart of the city. This he occupied after a sharp contest, and it now became possible to invite the return of the inhabitants, and to rescue the city from the horrors of this prolonged contest.

Brigadier Campbell, with his cavalry, attacked the enemy when retreating from the city in consequence of Sir Edward Lugard's advance, inflicting heavy loss, and pursued him for six miles.

I beg to enclose Sir James Outram's own account of his operations, which were removed from my immediate superintendence, till he recrossed the Goomtee, prior to the attack of the 16th.

It was matter of real gratification to me to be able to entrust the trans-Goomtee operation to this very distinguished officer, and after that had been conducted to my perfect satisfaction, to bring him forward again to put the finishing stroke on the enemy, while the extended position in the town was of necessity held by the troops who had won it. My thanks are eminently due to him, and I trust he will receive them as heartily as they are offered.

I have now the pleasing task of communicating to your Lordship the name of an officer to whom not only I as commanding general, but to whom, in truth, the service at large, is under great obligation, Major-General Mansfield, the Chief of the Staff, whose labour has been unceasing, whose abilities are of the highest order, and have been of the greatest use to me during this campaign. It is impossible for me to praise this officer too highly, or to recommend him sufficiently to the protection of your Lordship and of the Government.

I desire to draw the particular attention of your Lordship to Brigadier-Generals Franks, C.B., Walpole, Sir J. Hope Grant, K.C.B., and Sir Edward Lugard, K.C.B.

Their divisions have been most admirably commanded, and they have on every occasion amply justified all my expectations.

Brigadier-Generals Walpole and Sir J. Hope Grant were employed more immediately under the direction of Sir James Outram, who speaks in the highest terms of the assistance he received from them.

Sir J. H. Grant's management of his cavalry and horse artillery is always most admirable.

As detailed above, the manner in which the attacks on the main line of operations were directed by Sir Edward Lugard and Brigadier-General Franks, reflected the greatest credit on them.

The officers in command of the cavalry brigades have proved themselves equal to their high position, and are worthy of your Lordship's favourable consideration.

Brigadier Campbell, in command of the cavalry on the left, performed his detached duty with much vigilance and judgment. His march round the city on the 19th instant, which was a running fight for the greater part of the day, was a very difficult one.

His pursuit, on the 21st, of the party which broke away after being driven by Sir Edward Lugard from Shadut Gunge, was highly effective.

Brigadier Hagart has received the marked commendation of Sir J. Hope Grant, and the brigadiers in command of infantry brigades have particularly distinguished themselves under the eyes of their divisional commanders:—

Brigadier	D. Russell	. . .	1st Brigade.
,,	P. M. M. Guy	. . .	3rd ,,
,,	Hon. A. Hope	. . .	4th ,,
,,	Douglas, C.B.	. . .	5th ,,
,,	Horsford, C.B.	. . .	6th ,,
,,	Evelegh	. . .	7th ,,

and Lieutenant-Colonel Longden (her Majesty's 10th Foot), attached to the Goorkha Brigade, by order of the Commander-in-Chief.

The head-quarters, 2nd Brigade, with the 5th Fusiliers and 78th Highlanders, under Brigadier Franklin, remained at Alumbagh in position, and were well disposed by that officer to resist the enemy's demonstration on the 16th instant.

To Major-General Sir Archdale Wilson, K.C.B., my warmest acknowledgments are due for the effective manner in which he commanded the Artillery division.

The four corps—the Naval Brigade, the Royal Artillery, the Bengal Artillery, and the Madras Artillery—worked with the greatest harmony under his happy direction as one regiment.

The merits of Sir Archdale Wilson are too widely known to gain anything by encomium from me; but I may be permitted to express my great satisfaction at having been able to avail myself of the assistance of this most distinguished officer. The effective fire of the artillery during the long operations which depended so much on the management of that arm, elicited general admiration.

The practice of the 68-pounders of the Naval Brigade was capital, while the Kaiser Bagh and other great buildings which had been stormed, showed, in a very convincing manner, how truly the shells had been directed by the Royal and Bengal Artillery.

Whenever the field artillery could be used, the troops of Horse Artillery and field batteries of Royal Artillery, the Bengal Artillery, and the Madras Artillery, did the most excellent service.

Sir Archdale Wilson expresses his great obligations to Captain Sir William Peel, K.C.B., Royal Navy, till that most gallant officer was severely wounded, and to Brigadiers Wood, C.B., Royal Horse Artillery, and Barker, C.B., Royal Artillery, respectively commanding the field and siege artillery brigades.

It would be difficult for me to give an adequate idea of the zeal and activity displayed by the Chief Engineer, Brigadier Napier, Bengal Engineers. Many of the operations depended on his proper appreciation of the obstructions to be overcome, and the means at his disposal for that purpose.

His great professional skill and thorough acquaintance with the value of his enemy, have been of the greatest service, and I recommend him most cordially to your Lordship's protection.

I am under very great obligations to him.

The officers of the general departments of the army have accompanied me during the siege, and I beg to return them my thanks. They are as follow:—

Major H. W. Norman, Deputy-Adjutant-General of the Army.

Lieutenant-Colonel W. Macpherson, Officiating Quartermaster-General of the Army.

Colonel the Honourable W. L. Pakenham, C.B., Officiating Adjutant-General, her Majesty's Forces.

Captain C. F. Seymour, 84th Regiment, Officiating Quartermaster-General, her Majesty's Forces.

Captain G. Algood, Officiating Assistant-Quartermaster-General of the Army.

Lieutenant-Colonel Keith Young, Judge-Advocate-General of the Army.

Lieutenant P. Stewart, Bengal Engineers, Superintendent of Electric Telegraphs.

Doctor Mac Andrew, Inspector-General of Hospitals, her Majesty's Forces.

Doctor Brown, the Superintending-Surgeon of the Force, has again won my sincere thanks for his admirable arrangements.

Captain Fitzgerald, Assistant-Commissary-General, who has had the disposition of the commissariat in the field, has met every want of the army. He has distinguished himself much, and is a credit to his department.

I must draw very particular attention to the services of Major Norman, Deputy-Adjutant-General, who, besides his ordinary departmental duties, has performed the very onerous one of Adjutant-General of the Army in the Field throughout the campaign; to Captain H. Bruce, Deputy-Quartermaster-General, head of the Intelligence Department; and to Captain G. Algood, Officiating-Assistant-Quartermaster-General, who performed the duties of Quartermaster-General of the Army in the Field, until the arrival of Lieutenant-Colonel Macpherson. These officers have all been most active in the performance of their duties.

To my personal Staff and that of Major-General Mansfield, my acknowledgments are due, but more particularly to my Military Secretary, Colonel Sterling, C.B., and to Captain R. G. Hope Johnstone, Bombay Army, Deputy-Assistant-Adjutant-General to the Chief of the Staff. These two officers are most indefatigable.

A list of the other members of these Staffs is appended.

Finally, I wish to draw your Lordship's attention to the conduct of the regimental officers, commissioned and non-commissioned, and to the men of the regiments.

Their conduct has been very brilliant throughout. The manner in which the 93rd Regiment flung itself into the Begum Kotee, followed by the 4th Sikhs and supported by the 42nd, was magnificent, and the subsequent attack on the Emmambara and the Kaiser Bagh reflected the greatest credit on the regimental leaders of the 4th Division, and the soldiers who followed them.

Corrected lists will be sent immediately, of the officers and soldiers who are deemed most worthy of distinction in a force in which every one has a claim.

I have, &c.,
C. CAMPBELL, <i>General</i>,
Commander-in-Chief in India.

LIST *of the* PERSONAL STAFF *of his Excellency General* SIR COLIN CAMPBELL, *G.C.B., Commander-in-Chief in India; and of Major-General* SIR W. R. MANSFIELD, *Chief of the Staff*.

Head Quarters Camp, Lucknow, 22nd March, 1858.

Colonel Sterling, C.B., unattached, Military Secretary to the Commander-in-Chief.

Captain Sir David Baird, Bt., H.M.'s 98th Regt. ⎫ A. D. C.'s to the
Lieutenant F. Alison, 72nd Highlanders ... ... ⎬ Commander-in-
Captain W. F. Forster, 18th Royal Irish ... ... ⎭ Chief.

Major J. Metcalfe, 3rd Regiment Bengal Native Infantry, Interpreter and Commandant, Head Quarters.
Lieutenant R. G. Hope Johnstone, Bombay Army, Deputy-Assistant-Adjutant-General to Chief of the Staff.
Lieutenant D. M. Murray, H. M.'s 64th Regt. ⎫ A. D. C.'s to the
Lieutenant F. R. S. Flood (severely wounded), ⎬ Chief of the
her Majesty's 53rd Regiment ... ... ⎭ Staff.
Surgeon J. Clifford, Officiating Surgeon to the Commander-in-Chief.

A. C. STERLING, *Colonel*,
Military Secretary.

MEMORANDUM *of* OPERATIONS *carried on under the Command of Major-General* SIR JAMES OUTRAM, *G.C.B., during the Siege of Lucknow.*

On the morning of the 6th instant, shortly before daybreak, I proceeded with the force named in the margin,* to cross the Goomtee River, over the two temporary bridges which had been constructed by the order of his Excellency, the whole of the cavalry being under the command of the Brigadier-General Sir James Hope Grant, K.C.B.; the infantry under that of Brigadier Walpole; the field artillery under Brigadier D. Wood, C.B.; the siege artillery, which subsequently joined me, under Lieut.-Colonel Riddell, R.A. After proceeding a short distance in a northerly direction, the enemy became visible on our left flank, and on being approached by the cavalry, they were discovered to be in considerable force, chiefly sowars. The 2nd Punjaub Cavalry then attacked on the right, while Major Smith, of the Queen's Bays, with two squadrons of his own regiment, one squadron of the 9th Lancers, and Lieut.-Colonel D'Aguilar's Troop of Horse Artillery, advanced from our left. The enemy were immediately driven back, and pursued to the banks of the river, many being cut up; but I regret to state that in this charge the gallant Major Smith was killed. Our camp was then formed on the Fyzabad road, about half a mile in advance of the village of Chinhut, on the Lucknow side. Early on the following morning, 7th March, the enemy made a smart attack on our advanced picquets, and brought out several guns under cover of ravines and clumps of trees in our front. They were, however, speedily withdrawn, on our skirmishers and horse artillery and Captain Middleton's field battery, protected by the cavalry, coming to the front and opening their fire. The artillery practice on this occasion, as on the preceding day, was admirable.

2. The following day, the 8th instant, under the instructions of his Excellency, Colonel D'Aguilar's troop of Horse Artillery and the 9th Lancers re-crossed the river to the head-quarters camp, and the siege guns named in the margin † joined me. Having decided upon an attack on the enemy's position, on the next morning, the 9th instant, I caused an entrenchment for eight 24-pounder guns and three 8-inch

---

* Already given in Commander-in-Chief's despatch.
† 24-pounder guns, 8; 8-inch howitzers, 4; 8-inch mortars, 10. Total, 22.

howitzers, to be constructed during the night. The battery was armed, and commenced its fire at daybreak with excellent effect, after which the right column of infantry, accompanied by Captain Gibbon's field battery, under Brigadier-General Walpole, covered by a cloud of skirmishers, commanded by Brigadier Horsford, C.B., and supported by the 5th Brigade under Brigadier Douglas, drove the enemy through the jungles, walls, and villages, which afforded them an excellent cover, and bringing the right shoulders forward, occupied the Fyzabad road. In the meantime, the left column of attack, composed of the 1st Bengal Fusiliers, supported by two companies of the 79th Highlanders, which had been held in readiness on the left of the battery, together with the horse artillery under Brigadier Wood, which had been formed in rear of the bridge across the Kokral, advanced, and in concert with the right column, carried the Chuker Kothee (or Yellow-house), the key of the rebel position, in gallant style, and thereby turned the strong line of entrenchment which had been constructed by the enemy on the right bank of the Goomtee. Of this success the skirmishers on the other side of the river were subsequently apprised by Lieutenant Butler, of the Bengal Fusiliers, who swam across the Goomtee, and climbing the parapet, remained in that position for a considerable time, under heavy fire of musketry, until the work was occupied. After the occupation of the Chuker Kothee, we drove the enemy rapidly through the old irregular cavalry lines, and suburbs, to the Badshah Bagh. The fortified gates of this strong-walled enclosure were blown open, and the garden occupied, where two guns were found by our troops. Three guns and a howitzer were then placed in position to enfilade the works in rear of the Martiniere. A battery of two 24-pounder guns, and two 8-inch howitzers, was placed near the river to keep down the fire from the town. A battery for five mortars was constructed during the night, and in the morning commenced playing on the Kaiser Bagh. Four heavy guns were also placed in a work thrown up by the enemy at the east entrance into the Badshah Bagh.

3. On the 10th, we were occupied in strengthening our position, the enemy being in force in the suburbs in our front, from which they made an attack in considerable numbers on a picquet held by the 79th Highlanders, but were repulsed with heavy loss. General Sir James Hope Grant occupied himself the while in patrolling the vicinity, during which operation a most valuable young officer, Major Sandford, of the 5th Punjaub Irregular Cavalry, was unfortunately killed; but the enemy suffered severely.

4. During this night, another battery was constructed at the Badshah Bagh for four 24-pounders, two 8-inch howitzers, and five 8-inch mortars, which kept up a vertical and direct fire on the defences in the interior of the Kaiser Bagh. Two more 24-pounders were also brought to bear on the Mess-house, and on the Kaiser Bagh, in compliance with the instructions of his Excellency. I made arrangements to attack the suburbs in the vicinity of the iron and stone bridges, and shortly after daylight on the 11th instant, the right column, as per margin,*

---

* 79th Highlanders; 2nd and 3rd battalion, Rifle Brigade; 1st Bengal Fusiliers; Captain Gibbon's Light Field Battery, and two 24-pounders.

formed on the Fyzabad road under the immediate command of Brigadier-General Walpole, and worked its way, covered by its skirmishers, through the town, until it reached the mosque on the old cantonment road which commands the approach to the iron bridge.

5. The left column, as per margin,* proceeded along the lower road, towards the iron bridge. These two columns were connected by a strong chain of skirmishers, which, as well as the left column, met with considerable opposition, as the enemy opened three guns on them from the opposite side of the river, and also held the ground in great strength in front of the rifle skirmishers, commanded by Brevet-Major Warren, Captains Wilmot and Thynne, and Lieutenant Grey, who all behaved most gallantly; Captain Thynne, a most promising officer, I regret to say, being mortally wounded. This column occupied the houses down to the river's bank, and the head of the iron bridge, to the right of which the two 24-pounder guns were placed in battery. The spirit and dash of the men during this critical operation were most remarkable, and merit my highest commendation. Lieutenant Moorsom, Deputy Assistant Quartermaster-General, who had been deputed by me to guide the column, was killed on the spot while reconnoitring on the opposite side of the road. I deplore sincerely the loss of this most gallant and promising young officer, whose soldier-like zeal and acquirements rendered him an ornament to his profession.

6. Having left the Bengal Fusiliers posted in the mosque on the cantonment road, I proceeded with the remainder of the right column in that direction, and shortly afterwards met Sir J. H. Grant's Cavalry and Horse Artillery, which in the meantime had been operating on the extreme right. Turning now towards the stone bridge, we surprised the camp of the rebel 15th Irregular Horse, whose standards and two guns were captured by the Rifles, the enemy flying in all directions over the plain, many being cut up by our cavalry.

7. I then penetrated to the head of the stone bridge, through the strong and dense suburbs, without encountering any material opposition. The enemy, however, were able to command it with guns, as well as with musketry from the tops of several high and strong stone houses on the opposite side of the river, and the position was, moreover, too distant, and approaches too intricate, to warrant my holding it permanently with the force at my disposal. I therefore withdrew to the mosque at the cross road, already occupied by the Bengal Fusiliers, our route being through suburbs, in which we destroyed a quantity of munitions of war, and finally we retired to camp, when the arrangements for the occupation of the iron bridge had been completed.

8. During the nights of the 12th and 13th, having been reinforced by four 18-pounder guns, two 10-inch howitzers, five 10-inch mortars, and four 5½-inch mortars, three batteries were erected, from which five 10-inch mortars, ten 8-inch mortars, four 24-pounder guns were brought to bear upon the Kaiser Bagh, on the fall of which, on the morning of the 14th, the guns and mortars were turned on the Resi-

---

* Two 24-pounder guns; three field battery guns, Royal Artillery; 23rd R. W. Fusiliers; 2nd Punjaub Infantry, under command of Lieutenant-Colonel Pratt.

dency, and the buildings to the right of the bridge. During this operation, Lieutenant Cuthbert, of the Royal Artillery, brought himself prominently to notice by extinguishing a fire in a small building in front of his battery, in a very dangerous and exposed position. The operations connected with a breastwork across the iron bridge were conducted by Lieutenant Wynne, R.E., and Sergeant Paul, who displayed great coolness and resolution in the face of a heavy and continual fire.

9. Having been ordered to join his Excellency's camp, my operations on the north side of the Goomtee were here brought to a close.

10. Our casualties during these proceedings amounted to five officers killed and nine wounded, and the loss in men, including sergeants, was twenty-one killed and one hundred and four wounded; total, twenty-six killed and one hundred and thirteen wounded. With the exception of the officers, the above statement of casualties does not include the cavalry division. General Sir J. H. Grant having been ordered off into the districts, neither his casualty list, nor his notice of his officers, has been received. From the peculiar nature of the fighting, the actual loss of the enemy is difficult to ascertain. But I cannot estimate it at less than two thousand throughout the whole operations.

11. On the 16th instant, under instructions from his Excellency, I proceeded to the Kaiser Bagh, where I found the 5th Brigade, under the command of Brigadier Douglas, C.B., comprising the 23rd Fusiliers, the 79th Highlanders, and the 1st Bengal Fusiliers, to which his Excellency had added her Majesty's 20th Regiment and the Ferozepore Regiment of Sikhs.

12. Vast numbers of the enemy having been seen crossing the stone bridge from the city, apparently with the design of attacking Brigadier-General Walpole's camp, on the north of the Goomtee, his Excellency ordered me to press our movement. I immediately ordered the advance, and took possession of the Residency with little opposition, the 23rd Fusiliers charging through the gateway, and driving the enemy before them at the point of the bayonet, the remainder of the brigade following them in reserve.

13. The enemy having been dislodged from the Residency, two companies of the 23rd, under Lieutenant-Colonel Bell, accompanied by Captain Gould Weston, who pointed out the road, pressed rapidly forward, and captured the brass gun, which was in position to sweep the iron bridge, after some opposition. In the meanwhile the Residency height was crowned by a field battery of Madras Artillery, under the command of Major Cotter, which kept up a heavy fire on the Muchhee Bhowun. This battery was subsequently withdrawn, and replaced by two 68-pounder guns of the Naval Brigade. On their arrival, the Bengal Fusiliers moved to the iron bridge, and shortly afterwards advanced, together with the Regiment of Ferozepore, and took Muchhee Bhowun and the Emmambara, the enemy precipitately retiring, and abandoning six guns. One company of the Fusiliers, under Captain Salisbury, was pushed on to the Roomidurwaza Gate, where another gun was captured. The 79th were then brought up to occupy the Emmambara, and the remainder of the Bengal Fusiliers were placed in the Muchhee Bhowun.

14. On the morning of the 17th, Brigadier Douglas caused the Hosi-

nabad mosque and the Dowlutkhana, in which two guns and a small mortar were found, to be occupied by a company of the 79th Highlanders. About one P.M., with the force named in the margin,* I moved towards the block of buildings known as Shurfoodowlah's house, having previously occupied the entrance to the Chowk with three companies of the 79th Highlanders. On arriving at the Juma Musjid, nine cart-loads of powder were found in a court-yard in the rear, which impeded our progress. I therefore directed it to be destroyed, under the supervision of the Engineers. I regret, however, to have to state that, from some accidental cause, the powder ignited.

15. Captain Clarke, R.E., and Lieutenant Brownlow, B.E., who had greatly distinguished themselves, have since died from the effects of the explosion, in whose melancholy death the service has sustained a heavy loss, which I sincerely deplore. About thirty men shared their fate, and the rest of the working party were more or less injured.

16. I then sent two companies of the 79th Highlanders, with one 8-inch howitzer, to take possession of Shurfoodowlah's house, which was occupied without any casualty, the enemy precipitately retreating, although they had made every preparation for a vigorous defence. An iron gun and a brass gun, with an ammunition waggon, together with several small guns, all in position, were captured.

17. I then reinforced the three companies of the 79th in the Chowk, with five companies of the 20th Regiment, and completed the chain of communication.

18. On the 18th, Brigadier Douglas ordered Lieutenant Gordon, commanding a picquet of the 20th, to clear the houses in his front, which he effected, much to the Brigadier's satisfaction, killing twenty-three of the enemy.

19. The stone bridge was found to be undermined, and the circumstance reported to his Excellency.

20. On the morning of the 19th, under instructions from his Excellency, I proceeded to attack the Moosa Bagh, the force named in the margin† being assembled for that purpose.

21. At about half-past six A.M., I proceeded to Gao Ghát, and found Ali Nuki Khan's house occupied by the enemy, who opened a sharp fire of musketry on the head of the column. Two companies of the 79th, led by Lieutenant Evereth, being ordered to advance, soon drove the enemy out, and took possession of it. Considerable delay here took place in consequence of having to break through a thick wall, during which time I ordered up a wing of the Bengal Fusiliers to occupy the house.

22. The troops then advanced through the suburbs without oppo-

---

* Captain Middleton's Field Battery; two 8-inch howitzers; one company Native Sappers; one wing, H.M.'s 20th Foot; one wing H.M.'s 23rd Foot; one wing H.M.'s 79th Foot; Brasyer's Sikhs.

† Two squadrons, 9th Lancers; one company, R.E.; one company, Native Sappers; one field battery (Captain Middleton's); two 18-pounders, two 8-inch howitzers, four 8-inch mortars, under Captain Carleton, B.A.; three companies, 20th Regiment; seven companies, 23rd Regiment; 79th Highlanders; 2nd Punjaub Infantry.

sition towards Moosa Bagh, which position the enemy was reported to occupy with thirteen guns and five or six thousand men.

23. On arriving on the open ground, two guns were opened on the column, and the enemy appeared in great strength on the road. I immediately ordered out skirmishers from the 79th and 23rd, and Captain Middleton's battery to the front, whose fire soon silenced that of the enemy, during which time the Lancers made a flank movement to the enemy's left, and on our advance their whole force took to flight, abandoning their guns; on finding which I sent to order back the heavy guns under escort of the three companies of the 20th Regiment, as being no longer required.

24. The two squadrons of the 9th Lancers followed up the pursuit for about four miles, when they overtook the enemy, captured six guns, and killed about a hundred of them, the rest dispersing over the country and escaping by the aid of the nullahs and broken feature of the country. The conduct of the officers and men of the 9th was most gallant, as they undauntedly charged masses of the enemy.

25. The field artillery and infantry followed in support as rapidly as possible, and captured four more guns, making in all twelve, which I believe to be the total possessed by the enemy, no trace of the reported thirteenth gun being observable.

26. I then occupied the Moosa Bagh, with the 2nd Punjaub Infantry, under Major Green, and withdrew the rest of the troops to their quarters in the city.

27. Throughout the course of these operations, which were very laborious, the cheerfulness and zeal of both officers and men were most conspicuous, and merit my warmest thanks.

28. I have to express my particular acknowledgments to Brigadier-General Walpole, who afforded me on every occasion the most cordial support, and very ably carried out the operations which fell to his share; also to Brigadier-General Sir James Hope Grant, commanding the cavalry, whose vigilance and activity in the execution of his onerous duties were unceasing.

29. Brigadier Wood, C.B., commanding the field batteries, and Lieutenant-Colonel Riddell, commanding the siege train, carried on their respective duties to my entire satisfaction. The services of Lieutenant-Colonel Turner, B.A., specially attached to the force, were of the highest value to me, and I beg to tender him my cordial acknowledgment for the same.

30. It is a source of much gratification to me to submit the names of those officers engaged in the operations on the north bank of the Goomtee, who have been honourably mentioned by Brigadier-General Walpole and their respective commanders, viz., Brigadiers Horsford, C.B., and Douglas, commanding 5th and 6th Brigades; Lieutenant-Colonel Hill, commanding 2nd Battalion, Rifle Brigade; Lieutenant-Colonel Macdonald, C.B., commanding 3rd Battalion Rifle Brigade; Captain Gibbon, R.A., who commanded the 9-pounder field battery.

31. The Brigadier-General also particularly notices the conduct of Captain Barwell, Deputy-Assistant-Adjutant-General, and Captain Carey, Deputy-Assistant-Quartermaster-General; also that of Captain Warner, A.D.C., and Lieutenant Eccles, his orderly officer.

32. The brigadiers wish to record the services of their respective staffs:—Captain Macpherson, 78th Highlanders (wounded), Brigade-Major of the 5th Brigade; Brevet-Major Mollan, Brigade-Major 6th Brigade; and Brevet-Major Ross, and Lieutenant Walker, their orderly officers.

33. Brigadier Wood, C.B., favourably mentions the conduct and professional knowledge of Lieutenant-Colonel Turner, Lieutenant-Colonel D'Aguilar, Major Yates, Brevet-Major Pennycuick, Captain Gibbon, Captain Mackinnon, Captain Remmington, and Captain Johnston; he also notices the assistance he received from Captain Frith, his Brigade-Major, and Captain Scott, in charge of the Commissariat arrangement.

34. Lieutenant-Colonel Riddell, commanding siege train, eulogizes Captains Thring, Goodenough, and Walker, R.A.; Captain Pearson, and Lieutenant Simeon, B.A.; and Lieutenants Cuthbert and Fitz Maurice, R.A.; and Major Turner and Captain Young, staff officers.

35. Major Nicholson, R.E., highly applauds the energy displayed by the officers of that department, viz., Lieutenants Malcolm, Wynne, Swetenham, and Keith, R.E.; and Lieutenants Watson, Tennant, Hovenden, and Nuthall, B.E.

36. Lieutenant-Colonel Wells records the services of Major Bruce, and Captains Provost, Duff, and Norton, of the 23rd Fusiliers.

37. I have next to notice the services of the officers engaged on the south, or the city side of the river.

38. Brigadier Napier; Captain Hutchinson, Brigade-Major; and Lieutenant Greathed, of the Engineers, afforded me on different occasions the greatest assistance by their professional advice, and I tender them my cordial thanks; they were ably seconded by Lieutenant Tulloch, and Mr. May, attached to that department.

39. Major Brasyer led his Sikhs with his usual gallantry, and I regret to add was severely wounded.

40. My thanks are also due to Captain Bennett, commanding her Majesty's 20th Regiment.

41. Captain Coles, in command of two squadrons of the 9th Lancers, did good service in pursuing the enemy when they abandoned their position in the Moosa Bagh. On this occasion the local knowledge of Captain Carey, Deputy-Assistant-Quartermaster-General of the 3rd Division, was of much use to me. Captain Dodgson, Assistant-Adjutant-General; Captain Gordon, Deputy-Judge-Advocate-General; and Ensign Hewitt, 41st Regiment Native Infantry, orderly officer, were present at the occupation of the Moosa Bagh, having joined me from Alumbagh, where they had been of much service in their respective appointments.

42. I have lastly to bring to his Excellency's consideration the services of those officers who had the good fortune to be engaged in all the operations on both sides of the river.

43. Brigadier Douglas has carried out all his instructions with signal ability and success, and deserves my cordial acknowledgments; as does Major Nicholson, R.E., who evinced the most indefatigable industry in the construction of the heavy batteries which it fell to his department to execute, and in choosing sites for which he was constantly exposed to very heavy fire.

44. Lieutenant-Colonel Wells, commanding the 23rd Fusiliers, until incapacitated by illness (on the last day's operation), when the command was assumed by Lieutenant-Colonel Pratt, who also commanded the left column of attack on the 11th instant, across the river; Lieutenant-Colonel Taylor, in command of the 79th Highlanders; Major Green, Punjaub Rifles; and Captain Cunliffe, who commanded the 1st Bengal Fusiliers, until the arrival of Captain Hume, who also deserves my thanks. Captain Middleton, commanding the Field Battery, which was actively engaged throughout.

45. Brigadier Douglas mentions with approbation, Captain Stevenson, Acting Brigade-Major; and Lieutenants Walker, 79th, and Utterton, 23rd Fusiliers, his A.D.C. and orderly officer.

46. I have the highest pleasure in acknowledging how much I am indebted to the officers of my personal staff.

47. His Excellency is already aware of the opinion I have formed of the merits and services of Colonel Berkely, her Majesty's 32nd Regiment, my military secretary; and the assistance I have derived from him throughout these operations is an additional obligation I am under to this most deserving officer.

48. Captain Chamier, A.D.C., and Lieutenant Hargood, A.D.C., (horse killed), have worked with the unremitting zeal and activity which has characterized their conduct in all the operations in which I have been engaged since I left Allahabad in September last.

49. Captain Weston, 65th Regiment Native Infantry, orderly officer, has signalized himself by the spirit and gallantry which he has displayed on several occasions, and has been of much use to me.

50. Captains Orr and Bunbury, of the Intelligence Department, have performed their duties with great ability, and Mr. Denison, Civil Service, who recently brought up despatches from the Governor-General, accompanied the forces, and was most active and zealous in rendering aid to the poor sufferers who were blown up in the explosion on the 17th instant.

51. Mr. Kavanagh, Assistant Commissioner, from his knowledge of the localities, rendered good service on several occasions.

J. OUTRAM, *Major-General,*
Commanding the 1st Div. of the Army.

N. B.—The casualties during these operations are included in the general casualty returns of the army occupied in the siege, which accompanied the Commander-in-Chief's despatch; the total loss sustained in these operations under General Outram was as follows:—

Casualties during the operations North of the Goomtee, from the 6th to 14th March (not including those of the Cavalry division under General Grant, of which no separate returns were received).

KILLED.—Officers, 5; rank and file, 21.
WOUNDED.—Officers, 9; rank and file, 104.—Total, 139.

Casualties during the operations in the City, from the 15th to 19th March.

KILLED.—Officers, 3; rank and file, 42.
WOUNDED.—Officers, 4; rank and file, 50.—Total, 99.
GRAND TOTAL.—Killed and Wounded, 238.

173

GENERAL ORDERS BY THE HONOURABLE THE PRESIDENT
OF THE COUNCIL OF INDIA IN COUNCIL.
Fort William, 27th July, 1858.
The Honourable the President of the Council of India in Council has much satisfaction in now publishing the following letters from Major-General Sir J. Outram, G.C.B., bringing to notice certain omissions in his previous* despatches:—

The Deputy Adjutant-General of the Army to the Secretary to the Government of India, Military Department, with the Governor-General.
Head Quarters, Camp, Futtehghur, the 31st May, 1858.
By desire of the Commander-in-Chief I have the honour to forward, in original, for submission to the Right Honourable the Governor-General, two letters from the Honourable Major-General Sir J. Outram, G.C.B., bringing to notice certain omissions in his previous despatches.
I have, &c.,
H. W. NORMAN, *Major*,
Deputy-Adjutant-General of the Army.

Major-General J. Outram, late Commanding 1st Division of the Army in the Field, to Major Norman, Deputy Adjutant-General of the Army.
Calcutta, 11th May, 1858.
On the — instant, I had the honour to draw the attention of the Chief of the Staff, demi-officially, to the accidental omission in my Lucknow despatches, of a service rendered me by a wing of the 1st Madras Fusiliers, and I expressed my deep regret at having thus unintentionally done injustice to a regiment which had, by its unvarying zeal, steadiness, and bravery, placed me under the deepest obligations. I regret to have now to record another omission, equally accidental, and equally unjust. I refer to Captain Gibbon's battery, which was with me throughout the whole of the operations on the left bank of the Goomtee, and was, after the night of the 8th of March, the only field battery on that side. On the 9th it was actively engaged during the whole day, and rendered most valuable service. Exposed to very heavy fire, it contributed materially to the capture of the Badshah Bagh. And on the 11th its services were put in requisition with the columns which secured the approaches to the iron bridge. The

* See G. G. O. No. 1625 of 1857.

battery suffered considerably on this occasion, having had no less than fifteen casualties, its casualties on the 9th having amounted to five.

The omission of all allusion to Captain Gibbon's battery has arisen from my having confounded him with Captain Middleton, whose battery, I find, ceased to belong to my force on the evening of the 8th March.

I sincerely hope it is not yet too late for his Excellency the Commander-in-Chief to permit a public rectification of a mistake which has very naturally hurt the feelings of a brave body of men, and is calculated to prove injurious to their commander and his subordinate officers, whose services were witnessed by Sir J. Hope Grant, as well as by myself, and are warmly eulogized by that distinguished officer.

I have, &c.,
J. OUTRAM, *Major-General.*

Major-General Outram, late Commanding 1st Division, to Major Norman, Deputy Adjutant-General of the Army.

Calcutta, 24th May, 1858.

I have the honour to request that you will do me the favour to bring to the notice of his Excellency the Commander-in-Chief, certain unintentional omissions of which I find I have been guilty in my despatches —omissions which I know have hurt the feelings, and which I fear may have proved injurious to the interests, of meritorious officers.

When, on the 25th November, I detailed for his Excellency's information, the proceedings of the Oude Field Force during the two preceding months, I ought to have stated that, in consequence of the indisposition of Major Galwey, Captain Raikes had for some time commanded the 1st Madras Fusiliers, and that he had entitled himself to my hearty thanks for the able and zealous manner in which he had acquitted himself of his duties. And the omission is the more to be regretted, as Captain Raikes' temporary accession to the command of his regiment alone prevented his conducting the operations for the admirable performance of which his junior, Captain Grant, has received his brevet majority. The fact that two of his juniors have been promoted for special services, coupled with the omission of his name in my despatches, is calculated to mislead those who were not present at Lucknow, into the belief that Captain Raikes had not merited my approbation. The very reverse of this is the case.

To Major Galwey and the Madras Fusiliers it is due to rectify a still more unpardonable omission in my despatch detailing the operations which his Excellency did me the honour to confide to my conduct during the siege and reduction of Lucknow in March last. During those operations the gallant Fusiliers, under their brave and able commander, acquitted themselves with their wonted courage and discipline A wing of the regiment, under the personal command of Major Galwey, formed part of the column detailed for the storm of

Shurfoodowlah's mansion; and they it was that actually took possession of the house.

I would also beg to submit, for his Excellency's most favourable consideration, the merits and claims of Captains Bouverie, her Majesty's 78th Regiment, and Spurgin, 1st Madras Fusiliers, who, as majors of brigade, rendered valuable assistance to Sir Henry Havelock in our advance to Lucknow, and to myself during the time we were locked up in that city. Their subsequent valuable services, while under my command at Alumbagh, have already been acknowledged in my despatch. But the zeal, gallantry, and intelligence with which they had previously served the State, in the advance to, and during our stay at, Lucknow, I had left to be described by General Havelock, who, I know, intended to render full justice to those deserving officers. There is reason to fear that the sickness which resulted in the death of that ever-to-be-lamented officer prevented the fulfilment of his purpose, and that they have in consequence suffered in professional advancement. Under this belief, I venture to hope that, in consideration of their having been under my command during the latter period of the siege of Lucknow, I may be allowed to be the means of remedying an unintentional omission on the part of my deceased and honoured friend.

I would also venture to solicit his Excellency's most favourable notice of the good services of Lieutenant Dirom, the staff officer attached to Colonel Turner, of the Horse Artillery, while serving with me across the Goomtee. Colonel Turner speaks in high terms of eulogy of Lieutenant Dirom's conduct on that occasion; and of his soldierly qualities I myself had reason to form a high opinion. The omission of Lieutenant Dirom's name in my last Lucknow despatch was purely accidental.

I have, &c.,
J. OUTRAM, *Major-General*.

The Deputy Adjutant-General of the Army to the Secretary to the Government of India Military Department.

Head Quarters, Camp, Cawnpore, 22nd Dec. 1857.

I have the honour, by desire of the Commander-in-Chief, to transmit, for the information of the Right Honourable the Governor-General in Council, copy of a letter, dated the 15th instant, No. 7, from Captain L. Barrow, commanding the Volunteer Cavalry with Major-General Sir J. Outram's force, bringing prominently to notice the names of officers who have done good service in the corps under his command; and I am to request you will have the goodness to acquaint his Lordship in Council, that Sir James Outram has been requested to inform Captain Barrow, that the merits of these officers, and more especially of Captain Barrow himself as commandant of the Volunteer Cavalry, are highly appreciated by his Excellency.

I have, &c.,
H. W. NORMAN, *Major*,
Deputy Adjutant-General of the Army.

Captain Barrow, Commanding Volunteer Cavalry, to the Chief of the Staff, 1st, or Major-General Sir James Outram's Division.

Camp, Alumbagh, 15th December, 1857.

As most of the officers of the Volunteer Cavalry have been removed by his Excellency the Commander-in-Chief, their services being otherwise required, and many others having left wounded, I trust I shall be excused for bringing prominently to notice the names of all these officers who have performed their duty well, and in an entirely new capacity.

2. The officers as per margin,* marked (*a*), served, since the force left Allahabad on the 6th July, under General Havelock, and those marked (*b*) joined at various periods of the campaign. These officers have not only performed the duties of private soldiers and non-commissioned officers, but side by side with the privates of the different regiments composing the late field force. The arduous nature of these duties is so well known to the Major-General that it only remains to bring to his notice the cheerful and exemplary manner in which the officers performed them.

3. My object in bringing forward the names at this time is, that those now with his Excellency may have their conduct as Volunteers under his notice in their nomination to other appointments, for under a somewhat new and peculiar formation, they have readily adapted themselves to all circumstances, and behaved throughout as officers should do, anxious to prove themselves good soldiers.

[The Editor has thought it advisable to insert, at this place, a series of letters addressed by Sir James Outram to the Commander-in-Chief, in which he rectified certain omissions he had made in his previous despatches. These letters, hitherto unpublished, are inserted in justice to the many gallant officers whose names were not publicly mentioned in General Orders,

---

* (*a*) Captain R. L. Thompson, 10th B. N. I.; (*a*) Captain Sheehy, H. M.'s 81st Regiment (dead); (*a*) Captain Hicks, 6th B. N. I.; (*a*) Lieut. R. Chalmers, 45th B. N. I.; (*a*) Lieut. Lynch, H. M.'s 70th Regiment; (*a*) Lieut. W. O. Swanston, 7th M. N. I.; (*a*) Lieut. Grant, 3rd M. Euro. (dead); (*b*) Lieut. Hearsey, 57th B. N. I.; (*b*) Lieut. Wild, 40th B. N. I.; (*b*) Lieut. Palliser, 63rd B. N. I.; (*a*) Lieut. W. Ramsay, 17th B. N. I.; (*b*) Lieut. Brown, 56th B. N. I. (dead); (*b*) Lieut. Birch, 1st B. L. C.; (*a*) Cornet Fergusson, 8th B. L. C.; (*b*) Cornet R. Goldsworthy, H. M.'s 17th Lancers; (*b*) Cornet W. Goldsworthy, H. M.'s 8th Hussars; (*a*) Ensign Brauder, 37th B. N. I.; (*a*) Ensign Pearson, 27th B. N. I.; (*a*) Ensign Stewart, 17th B. N. I.; (*a*) Ensign the Hon. H. H. Hare, 17th B. N. I.; (*a*) Ensign Woodgate, 11th B. N. I.

Uncovenanted.—(*b*) J. Erskine, Esq. (dead); (*a*) W. Bews, Esq.; (*a*) J. Anderson, Esq.

and who naturally felt hurt at the oversight. The chronological sequence has not been maintained in this case, as it was judged better to keep all the letters relating to the same matter together.]

Major-General Sir J. Outram, G.C.B., to the Adjutant-General of the Army, Head-Quarter Camp.

Sir, *Calcutta, 2nd May,* 1858.

I have the honour to request you will do me the favour to submit, for the favourable consideration and recommendation of his Excellency the Commander-in-Chief, this my very urgent appeal on behalf of the 1st Division of the army, which I had lately the honour to command, and which, previous to his Excellency taking the field, was denominated the Oude Field Force.

My earnest desire is, that both officers and men comprising that force, who were engaged in the first relief of Lucknow, and for two months were besieged there, encountering privations of no ordinary nature, and repelling constant and harassing attacks of the enemy, should be granted the boon of one year's service towards pension, already awarded to her Majesty's 32nd Regiment, and to the portion of her Majesty's 84th Foot who formed the original garrison there. The loss the force sustained in entering Lucknow, and during the subsequent defence of the Residency, was upwards of 80 officers and nearly 1,000 men killed and wounded; a loss fully equal to that sustained by the original garrison.

Simultaneously with the noble efforts of the garrison, under General Inglis, to maintain their post, and uphold the honour of their country, the relieving troops, under the command of Major-General Havelock, were, during the most trying months of the year, undergoing fatigues and perils, and obtaining successes, which have never been surpassed in the annals of Indian warfare. Their subsequent privations and harassing duties during the interval which elapsed before their final relief by his Excellency the Commander-in Chief, has consigned not a few to their graves, and undermined the constitution of many others.

In support of this application, I would beg respectfully to remind his Excellency that General Havelock's relieving force have already been placed on an equality with the original garrison in respect of the donation of batta.

Under these circumstances, I hope that the claims of these troops will be considered by his Excellency and Government as worthy of a similar boon to that which has been awarded to the original garrison, whom it was their good fortune to be instrumental in saving from a position of imminent peril.

I have, &c.,
J. OUTRAM, *Major-General,*
Late Commanding the Oude Field Force.

Major-General Sir J. Outram, G.C.B., to Lord Canning, Governor-General of India.

MY LORD,   *Calcutta, 2nd May,* 1858.

A year's service having been granted to the officers and non-commissioned officers and privates of her Majesty's service who formed part of the original Lucknow garrison, may I venture to express a hope that your Lordship will secure a similar recognition of their services, not only for the European officers, non-commissioned officers, and privates of the East India Company's service who formed part of that garrison, but also support the claims of the officers, non-commissioned officers, and men of both armies, who, under the late Sir Henry Havelock, effected the first relief of Lucknow in September last, to a participation in the same boon.

I hope that, in consideration of the death of Sir Henry Havelock, and the departure from India of Sir John Inglis, by whom, perhaps, this application would have been more appropriately preferred, I shall be acquitted of presumptuousness in urging the claims of the brave men with whom it was my proud privilege to be so long associated, and whom I commanded, in the Lucknow garrison, from the end of September until our final and effectual relief by his Excellency the Commander-in-Chief.

I would beg respectfully to submit to your Lordship's consideration, as the *quasi* precedent on which I base my appeal on behalf of the glorious troops whom Sir Henry Havelock led into Lucknow, the fact that you were yourself pleased to extend to the latter the six months' batta which had been previously assigned to the original garrison.

I take the liberty of enclosing to your Lordship copy of a letter I have addressed to the Adjutant-General of the army, under the impression that, as regards the royal army, the initiative rests with the Commander-in-Chief.

If it be not unwarrantably presuming on your Lordship's functions, might I venture to suggest that the civil members of the garrison, both covenanted and uncovenanted, should also receive the boon of one year's service. I limit my suggestion to one year, that being all that her Majesty's Government have seen fit to allow to the royal troops. In my own humble opinion, however, the members of the garrison might, with great justice, propriety, and the best possible future effects, have been allowed one year's service for each month of the siege. A Russian or a French garrison performing such services as those performed by the Lucknow garrison would, I feel assured, have received no less liberal a recognition of their surpassing merits. And should your Lordship feel at liberty to urge such an extension of the boon already granted, I feel assured that the people of England would cordially support and applaud your generous intervention in the matter.

I have the honour to be, &c.,

J. OUTRAM.

Major-General Sir J. Outram, G.C.B., to Major-General Mansfield, Chief of the Staff.

SIR, *Lucknow, 3rd April,* 1858.

On the I had the honour to forward, by desire of his Excellency the Commander-in-Chief, a list of officers who had been serving under my command from 26th September to the evacuation of the Residency. Amongst those therein mentioned, was Captain Olpherts, of the Bengal Artillery, who had been recommended by Major-General Sir H. Havelock for promotion to the brevet rank of major, in which recommendation I most heartily concurred. Should her Majesty be pleased to confer this rank on Captain Olpherts, I would most respectfully request his Excellency's favourable consideration to the service *since* rendered by that officer, in order that, should his Excellency the Commander-in-Chief attach as much value to them as I do, he may be included in the list of those officers deemed worthy of the honourable distinction of the companionship of the Bath.

Captain Olpherts left the Baillie Guard with his field battery in a totally inefficient state, many of his men being dead, and all his surviving horses so reduced by starvation as to be unfit for service.

In three months from that date, by dint of the most unwearying perseverance, Captain Olpherts' field battery was able to bear comparison with the generality of troops of Horse Artillery for rapidity in coming into action; and I constantly used it as such with the cavalry. On every occasion Captain Olpherts' battery rendered most essential service; and I only consider it due to this officer to bring his merits thus prominently forward to the notice of his Excellency—his gallantry being as conspicuous as his indefatigable industry.

I have, &c.,
J. OUTRAM.

Major-General Sir J. Outram, G.C.B., to the Adjutant-General of the Army, Head-Quarters, Allahabad.

SIR, *Calcutta, 18th August,* 1858.

I have the honour to forward the accompanying letter and its enclosures, from Captain Adair, her Majesty's 5th Fusiliers, for such consideration as his Excellency the Commander-in-Chief may deem it worthy of.

I can truly add, that Captain Adair, and every officer and man of her Majesty's 5th Fusiliers, nobly did their duty while under General Havelock's and my command.

I have, &c.,
J. OUTRAM.

Lieutenant-General Sir J. Outram, G.C.B., to the Adjutant-General of the Army, Head-Quarters, Allahabad.

SIR,   *Calcutta, 28th August,* 1858.

I have the honour to transmit, for the purpose of being laid before the Commander-in-Chief, a letter in original from Brigadier Stisted, commanding at Bareilly, dated 10th instant, with accompanying representation of Dr. Jee, of her Majesty's 78th Highlanders, in support of his solicitation of the Victoria Cross, which the Brigadier recommends to the favourable consideration of his Excellency. And to this I beg to add, that I believe Dr. Jee to be a most deserving officer, who, I was aware from the reports which reached me at the time, performed excellent service on the occasion referred to, of which, however, I had no personal cognizance, being myself occupied in advance, and not in command of the troops, at that time.

I have, &c.,
J. OUTRAM, *Lieut.-General,*
Late Commanding 1st *Division of the Army in the Field.*

Lieutenant-General Sir J. Outram, G.C.B., to the Adjutant-General of the Army, Head-Quarters, Allahabad.

SIR,   *Calcutta,* 31st *August,* 1858.

With reference to your letter, No. 2,314, dated 25th instant, and in reply to the call, which his Excellency the Commander-in-Chief has done me the honour to make, for my opinion as to the claim of Captain George Hutchinson, of the Bengal Engineers, to brevet promotion, it is my very gratifying duty to declare my belief that that officer deserves such promotion for his services, during the siege of Lucknow, and also, subsequently, for his services as my chief engineer at Alumbagh, which were as important perhaps as could fall to the lot of any field officer of Engineers throughout a lifetime of service. All engineering operations under his supervision were admirably executed, and invariably successful in their results; while the zeal, activity, and bravery, Captain (then Lieut.) Hutchinson displayed on all occasions, repeatedly elicited my warm commendation.

I can truly say, therefore, that I consider Captain Hutchinson well merits a majority.
I have, &c.,
J. OUTRAM, *Lieut.-General.*

Major-General Sir J. Outram, G.C.B., to Colonel Mayhew, Adjutant-General of the Army, Head-Quarters.

SIR, *Calcutta, 25th September,* 1858.

With reference to the General Order of the 2nd instant, I have the honour to transmit a roll of officers on the divisional staff of the (Oude Field Force) late 1st Division of the army in the field, entitled to Lucknow medals.

As I presume the force which joined the Lucknow garrison on the 25th December, and aided in the defence of that position for two months, is entitled to the medal for the defence, I have, you will observe, put opposite to the names of the officers belonging to that force " bars, for the first relief, and defence of Lucknow," in addition to the " bar for the capture of Lucknow," confidently hoping that his Excellency the Commander-in-Chief will support their claims to all three bars.

With reference to my recommendation rolls of the 14th February last, of officers of my division, for promotion for services during the operation of the force under my command in the months of September, October, and November, 1857, I do myself the honour again to submit a nominal roll of those named therein, who have not yet been promoted, and to solicit for the captains the brevet promotion therein named, and that the names of the subalterns (if the rules of the service admit of it) be published in orders as being registered for brevet promotion on obtaining their company; as, at present, no member of my personal staff, who served with me throughout the campaign, has in any way been noticed, excepting Sir Robert Napier; of these, one (Lieut. Hargood) is dead. And among my personal staff may be considered Captain Dawson and Lieutenant Hewitt, who served as orderly officers to my chief of the staff during the whole service.

I take this opportunity of bringing to the notice of his Excellency, the case of a most deserving officer, Captain (now Brevet Major and C.B.) Crommelin, of the Engineers, who, through the accidental omission of his name in the late Sir Henry Havelock's hurried despatches, which had the lamented General lived I am sure would have been rectified, his Excellency will perceive, has received no reward for his services under that officer, he having obtained only the promotion and distinction recommended for his subsequent services under myself; while his fellow workers under General Havelock, previous to my joining him at Cawnpore, who held positions in that General's force, not more important than that of his chief engineer, have obtained the grade of lieutenant-colonel, viz.: Lieutenant-Colonels Tytler, Olpherts, and Brasyer. During that period Captain Crommelin served on Sir Henry's staff in seven different engagements, and I know that the General assured him that his services during the retreat across the Ganges, on the 13th of August, which the arrangements made by Captain Crommelin enabled the troops to effect in half a day, and the construction of the bridge (under fire of the enemy) by which we recrossed on the 20th September, were highly appreciated by him. Yet, although these operations were certainly most remarkable efforts of engineering skill, accomplished under great personal exposure and exertion on the part of the engineer and his corps, no mention whatever was made of them in the General's brief telegraphic despatches; but I am sure Sir Henry would have done full justice to Captain Crommelin had he lived, for he expressed himself to me as very sensible of that officer's merits and grateful for his exertions. The several officers whom the General *did* mention were more immediately connected with the troops that were engaged, and they all received brevet rank in the *Gazette* that announced the rewards of the Delhi Force; and had not Captain Crommelin's name been thus accidentally omitted, he would then have received the brevet majority, which he subsequently obtained only when those officers obtained their lieutenant-colonelcy for the after services, which he in common with them had rendered at Lucknow. I respectfully but earnestly beg, therefore, to submit the claim of Captain Crommelin to a brevet lieutenant-colonelcy, to the favourable consideration of his Lordship the Commander-in-Chief.

I beg also to submit to his Excellency, the grounds on which I would recommend a similar distinction being conferred on my late Deputy Adjutant-General, Captain (now Brevet Major) Dodgson; these grounds being somewhat similar to what I have urged on behalf of Major Crommelin, viz.:—the non-recognition of previous services at Benares, under General Neill, prior to his being placed on my staff and sharing in General

Havelock's campaign in Oude, for which only, and his subsequent services under myself, he has now been rewarded by a brevet majority.

Major Dodgson was major of brigade at Benares, when the native infantry at that station mutinied in June last year, when he was wounded. His services on that occasion were such as to elicit the commendation and public thanks of General Neill, and also of Mr. Tucker, the then commissioner at Benares. And had they been communicated to Government at the time, which the confusion then prevailing may have prevented, I presume he would, for those services, have obtained a brevet majority, in which case his after services in Oude would have been rewarded with the lieutenant-colonelcy which I now solicit for him, in the conscientious belief that he well deserves it, for the zeal, ability, and devotion to his duty which he has ever displayed.

I have, &c.,
J. OUTRAM, *Lieut.-General*,
Late Comdg. 1st Div. of the Army in the Field.

Lieutenant-General Sir J. Outram, G.C.B., to Colonel Mayhew, Adjutant-General of the Army, Head-Quarters.

SIR, 29th September, 1858.

With reference to my letter, dated 25th instant, I have the honour to hand up for submission to his Lordship the Commander-in-Chief, in substitution for the nominal roll of those officers named in my recommendation roll of the 14th February, but who have not yet been promoted, an amended list which I have just received from Major Dodgson, late deputy adjutant-general of the 1st division. And I beg to offer my apologies for having previously furnished an incomplete list, owing to my not having all the requisite documents with me to refer to.

Captain Dodgson has, at the same time, furnished me with a copy of General Havelock's recommendation roll, dated the 14th October, 1857, from which I perceive, that although Captain Crommelin was not named in that General's despatch, he was recommended by him for the brevet majority and C.B., which he has obtained, and also that Captain Dodgson was recommended by General Havelock for the brevet majority which he has obtained. It is, therefore, the services of those officers under myself which have not been recognized; and I beg most respectfully to solicit his Lordship's favourable consideration of the recommendation I submitted on their behalf on the 14th February last, for the additional step in rank, which has been granted to their comrades, as mentioned in my last.

The list I now submit reminds me of Captains Barrow, MacBean, and Spurgin, whose cases I omitted to notice in my letter of the 25th instant, which inadvertence I very much blame myself for, especially my forgetfulness of Captain Barrow; for to no officer in my force was I more indebted, or had I a higher opinion of, and who is in exactly the same position as that I therein described Captain Crommelin to be; he having served with General Havelock from the first, in command of the volunteer cavalry, and was present at, and actively engaged in, every action. He, like Captain Crommelin, obtained the brevet majority and C.B., for which he was recommended by General Havelock, but has not obtained the additional "step in rank" for which I recommended him for his subsequent services, under myself, in the garrison of Lucknow, and at the Alumbagh. Captain MacBean, the able and indefatigable commissary to whom the 1st Division was so greatly indebted for supplying the force at the Alumbagh, has only received the promotion recommended by General Havelock for his previous services; and Captain Spurgin has only received the brevet majority recommended by General Havelock, as brigade-major of his 1st Brigade, although the brigade-major of his 2nd Brigade, Captain Bouverie, has obtained his lieutenant-colonelcy, these officers having been in the same position, and having performed the same duties, and being recommended in exactly the same terms, by General Havelock and myself. On behalf also of Major Barrow, Major MacBean, and Major Spurgin, I therefore respectfully solicit his Excellency's support to my recommendation of the 14th February.

In the medal roll which accompanied my letter of the 25th instant, the name of a civil officer, Mr. George Couper, was inserted by mistake, which I beg you will erase, I having submitted that gentleman's and other civil officers' names to his Lordship the Governor-General.

I have, &c.,
J. OUTRAM.

Lieutenant-General Sir J. Outram, G.C.B., to Captain Hutchinson, Military Secretary to Chief Commissioner, Lucknow.

SIR, Calcutta, 9th October, 1858.

In reply to your letter, dated 2nd instant, forwarding an application from Captain Alexander Orr, for local promotion on behalf of himself and his brother Captain Adolphus Orr, and communicating the Chief Commissioner's wish that I would give my opinion on their cases, I have the honour to inform you, that I have already twice brought Captain Alexander Orr's services to the notice of his Lordship the Commander-in-Chief, with my earnest recommendation for his obtaining a brevet majority, he having served zealously, and ably, as the head of my intelligence department, from the date of our advance from Allahabad, in the beginning of September, 1857, until the capture of Lucknow, in March, 1858.

As Captain Adolphus Orr served only in a subordinate capacity in the intelligence department, during the time I held the Alumbagh, and throughout the operations against the city in March, I do not consider him entitled to the same distinction as his brother, while serving under me. And as none of the other officers commanding posts in the garrison have, so far as I know, received brevet promotion, I should not consider Captain Adolphus Orr entitled to any distinction not conferred on others for that service, such as Captain Evans, &c. If, however, other officers of the garrison have received brevet promotion for commanding posts, I consider that Captain Orr also would be entitled to the same, provided similar mention is made of him in General Inglis's despatch to what is made of others who have been promoted.

I have, &c.,

J. OUTRAM, *Lieut.-General.*

Lieutenant-General Sir J. Outram, G.C.B., to Colonel Mayhew, Adjutant-General of the Army, Head-Quarters, viâ Allahabad.

SIR, *Calcutta, 16th November,* 1858.

I regret extremely to find that, through inadvertence, an officer's name was omitted in the recommendatory list of officers which I submitted for the favourable consideration of his Excellency the Commander-in-Chief in February last, and in which I had always supposed it had been included, until I received, by last mail from England, a letter from the officer in question, pointing out that he had not received the promotion which had been accorded to other officers similarly situated with himself on the general staff of the division under my command at the Alumbagh.

The officer I allude to, is Captain Gould Read Weston, of the 65th Bengal Native Infantry, a most deserving officer, who commanded one of the posts in the Lucknow Residency throughout the siege, and afterwards served with me at the Alumbagh, where he displayed a zeal and alacrity on all occasions which certainly entitled him to be included in my first recommendation roll, and as he certainly would have been but for the oversight for which I have expressed my regret.

But he was included in the list subsequently furnished after the capture of Lucknow; and was favourably noticed in the memorandum which I submitted to his Excellency on that occasion.

Under these circumstances, I beg you will do me the favour to submit my recommendation of this officer for a brevet majority to the generous consideration of his Lordship the Commander-in-Chief, with my respectful apology for now intruding a recommendation so long after the event; but which, in honour and justice, I could not avoid, feeling as I do that through my own negligence I have unwittingly been the cause of the claims of a deserving officer being so long passed over.

I have, &c.,
J. OUTRAM, *Lieut.-General.*

Colonel Seaton, Commanding 1st Madras Fusiliers, to Lieutenant-General Sir J. Outram, G.C.B.

MY DEAR GENERAL, 17th *November*, 1858.

May I bring to your notice one officer of my regiment—Lieutenant Thomas Butler. I hear so much of this young lad's gallantry, that I firmly believe there are few who would not rejoice to see him in possession of the Victoria Cross. I have made him write the enclosed memorandum. The modesty with which he puts his interview down on paper, is quite characteristic of the little fellow. I hear you said more to him :—

Conversation between Major-General Sir James Outram, G.C.B., and Lieutenant T. A. Butler, 1st Bengal Fusiliers, at Lucknow, on the 16th March, 1858.

Q. Is your name Butler?

A. Yes, Sir.

Q. Are you the officer who swam the Goomtee the other day (9th March, 1858)?

A. Yes, Sir.

Sir J. O. Well, Sir, it was a most gallant thing, and I have spoken to Sir Colin Campbell on the subject, and you may depend upon it you will not be forgotten.

Reply of Sir J. Outram.

MY DEAR COLONEL,

The above memorandum furnished to you by Lieutenant Butler, correctly gives the *substance* of what passed between that officer and myself on the occasion referred to. But my impression is, that I must have expressed myself more strongly, for I regarded what he had done as one of the most daring feats achieved by any individual throughout the campaign. I mentioned the circumstance to Lord Clyde, who was, I believe, as much struck with it as I was myself. I also noticed it in my "memorandum" which was published with the Chief's despatch.

I, myself, would have recommended Butler for the Victoria Cross had I not thought that, to do so, would be irregular, the act being performed when we were under the Chief's immediate command. But I had hoped that my notice of it in my "memorandum" would secure the cross for him; and can only conclude that it escaped his Excellency's recollection. I still hope, therefore, that if you brought it to his Lordship's notice, he may be induced to obtain the Cross for that gallant young soldier.

Very sincerely yours,
J. OUTRAM.

Lieutenant-General Sir J. Outram, G.C.B., to Lieutenant Colonel Mayhew, Adjutant-General of the Army, Head-Quarters.

SIR,   *Calcutta, 27th December,* 1858.

With reference to your letter, dated 4th ultimo, to the Government of India in the military department, which only lately came under my observation, I observe that my letter to your address of the 29th September last was therewith handed up to the Governor-General by the Commander-in-Chief's order, with a commentary on the recommendatory list, which I had transmitted with that letter for his Excellency's consideration.

But my letter of the 29th September referred to a previous one, which I had addressed to you on the 25th September, without which his Lordship the Governor-General could not fully appreciate the grounds on which I advanced certain of my recommendations.

I beg, therefore, that you will do me the favour to obtain the Commander-in-Chief's sanction for laying my letter of the 25th September also before the Governor-General.

In the commentary appended to your letter of the 4th November, I observe that it is stated that the cases of Captains Clerk and Rich, of the Military Train, are "not known to the Chief of the Staff."

The correspondence, or communications, regarding those officers, passed between Colonel Berkely and Major Norman, I believe, to which circumstance I attribute the Chief of the Staff not being cognizant of those cases; but I can have no doubt that his Excellency the Commander-in-Chief was cognizant of them; for I understood, at the time, that his Lordship approved of the names of two officers of the Military Train being submitted with recommendation for promotion, in the same manner as the names of two officers of each of the European infantry regiments of the 1st Division had been submitted by order of the Commander-in-Chief, conveyed through Major Norman. And, with the utmost respect, I beg leave to appeal to his Excellency for confirmation of this fact; for, to the best of my recollection, his Lordship did me the honour to express to me, personally, his approval of my recommendation of Captain Clerk, if not also of Captain Rich.

With reference to the remark in your commentary respecting the "subalterns" recommended by me, I beg to submit, that, in my previous letter of the 25th September, I solicited merely that "their names (if the rules of the service admit of it) be published in orders, as being registered for brevet promotion, on obtaining their company," a course which, I believe, had been followed on previous occasions. And in justice to

Lieutenant Hewitt, and to myself, as having recommended that officer, who you remark "is simply an officer of less than two years' standing," as also to the late Captain Dawson, I beg to refer to the eulogy of those officers contained in Brigadier-General (then Colonel) Sir R. Napier's report, dated the 5th October last, transmitted with my despatch, dated the 25th November.

I am, &c.,

J. OUTRAM, *Lieut.-General.*

Lieut.-General Sir J. Outram, G.C.B., to Major Norman, Officiating General of the Army.

SIR,   *Calcutta,* 17*th May,* 1859.

I have the honour to acknowledge your letter, dated 7th instant, forwarding copy of a despatch from the Right Honourable Secretary of State for India, dated 16th February last, communicating observations on the list of recommendations made by me for further promotions and honours on account of services performed by several officers recently under my command, which, by desire of his Excellency the Commander-in-Chief, I am requested to return with such remarks as I may have to offer either with reference to the cases particularized by you, or any other points upon which the documents touch.

I beg most respectfully to observe, that had it not been for the unfortunate omission, when handing up my letter of 29th September, to transmit therewith a previous communication, therein referred to, which I had had the honour to tender to the Adjutant-General, under date the 24th idem, and without which I considered that "the grounds on which I had advanced certain of my recommendations could not be fully appreciated," this reference would, I believe, have been unnecessary, as I therein had submitted the requisite explanations. And as that document was subsequently forwarded to the Governor-General by order of his Excellency, in continuation of the letter of the 4th November, to which the Right Honourable the Secretary of State's communication is a reply, I presume that it has been transmitted to his Lordship (together with my letter, dated the 27th December last, bringing the omission to notice) with yours of the 2nd March in reply, and your letter to the Secretary to the Government of India, dated the 3rd March, conveying his Excellency the Commander-in-Chief's animadversions on the representations which, in my letter of the 24th September, I had submitted, of what I conceived to be the inequality that had occurred in the distribution of rewards to the officers enumerated in the list which accompanied that letter (and in the subsequently amended list transmitted with my letter, dated the 29th September). I do not, therefore, now—in deference to the decision which his Excellency pronounced in rejection of these claims—presume to recapitulate my arguments in their support: and I confine myself accordingly to barely enumerating some of the individuals who, according to my conviction, have not been adequately rewarded, in comparison, at least, with others employed on the same service who had obtained greater rewards, as shown in my letter dated the 24th September; their relative positions being practically as follow:

Major Barrow, Major Dodgson, and Major MacBean,* have received only the rewards to which they

---

* In the memorandum which accompanied Colonel Mayhew's letter of the 4th November, it is stated that Major MacBean had not been *in charge* of the commissariat since the first relief of Lucknow, which is a mistake, that officer having continued in charge of the commissariat of the 1st Division while we held the Alumbagh.

were recommended by the late Sir Henry Havelock, but no recognition of their subsequent services under myself after our junction with the Lucknow garrison on the 25th September, 1857, and at the Alumbagh, nor of Major Dodgson's previous services, under General Neill at Benares; whereas their comrades, Lieutenant-Colonels Olpherts and Brasyer, obtained the brevet rank of lieutenant-colonel and C.B., in addition to the brevet majority, which they had all acquired in common.

Major Crommelin has received only the rewards which I know were designed for him by General Havelock, for his services while under his own command, and no further recognition of his subsequent services under me during the two months we were besieged with the Lucknow garrison.

All these six officers got their majorities early in 1858 (Olpherts on the 19th January, the others on the 24th March), but shortly afterwards Lieutenant-Colonels Olpherts and Brasyer were advanced to the higher rank they now hold (Olpherts on the 24th March, 1858, Brasyer on the 20th July, 1858), while the others remain majors.

I was not aware, until informed by your letter, now under reply, that Lieutenant-Colonel Bouverie had obtained his majority, for services in Persia; that fact removes the inequality which I had supposed existed between his case and that of Major Spurgin.

Lieutenants Hutchinson, Innes, and James, have since obtained brevet majorities on obtaining their companies.

My explanation regarding Captains Clerk and Rich, of the Military Train (whose names appeared in my list as recommended for majority), submitted in my letter to your address dated the 27th December last, elicited from you, in your letter to the Secretary to the

Government of India, dated the 2nd March, the reasons why Captain Rich had not been recommended by his Excellency the Commander-in-Chief, while no mention was made of Captain Clerk; but I have since observed his name in the *Gazette* as promoted to major.

Lieutenants Thomas, Russell, Limond, Johnson, and Garden, and local Captain Alexander Orr, have not, I believe, obtained any promotion; but I rejoice to observe it stated in Lord Stanley's letter, that the claims of the last-mentioned deserving officer are under consideration.

It appears that Lieutenant Hudson, of H. M.'s 64th Regiment, was erroneously designated "captain" in my list, as I observed, in the memorandum which accompanied Colonel Mayhew's letter of the 4th November, that that officer had subsequently obtained his company.

Surgeons Scott and Ogilvie have, I understand, obtained the companionship of the Bath, but not, I believe, the step in rank which I recommended.

Lieutenant Fraser is dead.

The above are all the names contained in my list, with the exception of personal staff, my aides-de-camp, Lieutenants Chamier and Sitwell, have received no reward (a third aide-de-camp, Lieutenant Hargood, died before the list was submitted). The only recognition I had suggested for these officers—they being subalterns—was, "that their names (if the rules of the service admit of it) be published in orders as being registered for brevet promotion, on obtaining their company," and the same to Captain Dawson (since died of his wounds), and Lieutenant Hewitt, orderly officers to Colonel Napier, my then chief of the staff. With reference to the latter it is observed in your memorandum of the 4th November, that "Lieutenant Hewitt is simply an officer of less than two years' standing; he was simply orderly officer to Colonel Napier," on which I would beg to remark, that his being so young in the army renders, in my judgment, the zeal and devotion with which he performed the arduous and frequently dangerous duties he was exposed to, in attendance on Colonel Napier (to which that officer bears warm testimony), the more conspicuous and praiseworthy, while the short period of his service renders it very improbable that he can reap the reward I had suggested for many years, as it can be obtained only when promoted to captain by regular rise in a seniority service.

Having been called upon to offer these remarks on the cases contained in my recommendation roll, I beg to remind you of my subsequent letter to the Adjutant-General, dated the 16th November last, bringing to notice the fact, for which I expressed my extreme regret, that I had unwittingly omitted the name of Captain Gould Weston, of the 65th Bengal Native Infantry, which I solicited might be inserted in the roll with my recommendation to a brevet majority. A copy of that letter is appended, to which I have received no reply. And I have since had to reproach myself for another omission in my list, of which I was not aware until I received a letter of remonstrance from the neglected officer, Captain Hicks, of the 22nd Native Infantry, dated the 3rd instant, which I beg leave to submit in original, for the consideration of Lord Clyde, with my earnest recommendation of a brevet majority for him also; for I am bound to testify to the strict correctness of the modest statement of his services contained in this letter.

On receiving Captain Hicks's most just remonstrance, I was much distressed by the supposition that the door was now closed to my bringing forward further claims, and on expressing my inability now to take the initiative in his behalf, I suggested to him the only course I thought still left, viz. : to submit a memorial to the Commander-in-Chief, which I hoped his Excellency would allow me the opportunity of supporting, by referring the memorial to me for my report. But the opening now given to me will, I hope, be deemed by his Lordship to warrant my thus bringing forward Captain Hicks's case also, and recommending it to his favourable consideration.

I have, &c.,

J. OUTRAM, *Lieut.-General.*

Lieutenant-General Sir J. Outram, G.C.B., to the Adjutant-General of the Army, Head-Quarters, Allahabad.

SIR,   *Calcutta, 16th August,* 1858.

Under the impression that, when called upon last February* to submit the names of the officers who had served under me, from the 26th September, 1857 (the date of my assuming command at Lucknow), until the 17th November, when relieved by his Excellency the Commander-in-Chief, whom I believe deserving of commendation or reward, I was expected to notice those only who had served under me at Lucknow, I confined myself, therefore, in the reply which I then submitted, to the mention of members of that garrison alone. I am now informed, however, that his Excellency's intention was, that I should submit the names of those who served under me, within the limits of my then command, and as those limits included Cawnpore at that time, I hope, if not too late, I may now be permitted to rectify my mistake in omitting to mention the services of an officer to whom I was indebted for maintaining my communications with Cawnpore—con-

---

* As these documents are with Captain Dodgson, my late Deputy Adjutant-General, I am unable to give the precise dates.

veying my orders to the officer commanding there—and, as the medium of my correspondence with Government and Head-Quarters, Major (then Captain) Herbert Bruce, of the 2nd Bombay European Regiment; which services, though repeatedly and gratefully acknowledged in my letters addressed to himself, I regret to think I may not officially have brought to the notice either of his Excellency or of Government.

The important duties of a civil nature which Major Bruce performed at Cawnpore are well known to Government. But they may strictly be regarded as military services; for martial law then prevailed throughout the Cawnpore districts, and Major Bruce administered a military government under the direct orders of the successive generals commanding, *i. e.*, Brigadier-General Neill, Major-General Havelock, and myself. And to his exertions are to be attributed the tranquillity that prevailed during the whole period we were beleaguered in Lucknow; the maintenance of communication between Cawnpore and Alumbagh, through the police posts which Captain Bruce established; and, in a great measure, the supplies which were from time to time thrown into the Alumbagh, by which that important post was preserved.

The military aid which Major Bruce at the same time afforded to Brigadier Wilson, commanding at Cawnpore, and in the intelligence department, through which communication was maintained with me, were most important.

I trust, therefore, I may be pardoned for now submitting these services for the consideration of his Excellency the Commander-in-Chief, and such notice as he may deem them deserving of.

I have, &c.,
J. OUTRAM, *Lieut.-General.*

Lieutenant-General Sir J. Outram, G.C.B., to L. Bouring, Esq., Private Secretary to the Governor-General.

SIR, *Calcutta*, 29*th September*, 1858.

The military authorities having called for rolls of all officers of the Staff who served under me at Lucknow, entitled to the Lucknow medal, I have accordingly furnished such a roll of the military officers to the Adjutant-General of the army. But there were civil officers likewise attached to my staff whose names I beg you will do me the favour to submit to the Right Honourable the Governor-General, with the expression of my hope that his Lordship will consider them to be entitled, in addition to the medal, to the bars specified opposite to their names, viz. :—

Mr. W. J. Money, my late private secretary, for medal and three bars, viz.: one for first relief, one for defence, and one for capture of Lucknow.

Mr. G. Couper, late secretary to the Oude Commissioner, medal and two bars, viz.: one for defence, and one for capture of Lucknow.

I take this opportunity of begging respectfully to submit to his Lordship's consideration the great claim which I consider Mr. Couper may justly be deemed to possess, to some higher and personal distinction, for his services, not only in the garrison during the siege, of which such honourable mention was made in General Inglis's despatch, but, also, for his subsequent services under myself while holding the Alumbagh, and during the operations for the capture of the city, throughout which period he attended me in the field, and officiated as aide-de-camp. But my official obligations to Mr. Couper were not confined to services of this nature: still more important services were rendered by this gentleman, and he displayed a devotion to his duty seldom equalled, if ever surpassed, by a civil functionary, in sacrificing family and personal considerations to remain with the Alumbagh force, on my representing that the public interests required his presence. On this subject I did myself the honour to address Mr. Secretary Edmonstone on the 24th March last; and for convenience of reference I annex an extract from that letter, to which I beg to refer his Lordship.

For these services, and his self-devotion, I think Mr. Couper is well entitled to the honour of a civil companionship of the Bath, for which I feel myself bound to solicit his Lordship's recommendation.

I have, &c.,
J. OUTRAM, *Lieut.-General.*

Extract Para. 7 of Letter to Mr. Edmonstone.
Dated Lucknow, 24th March, 1858.

7th. Mr. Couper, my official secretary, has already been brought to his Lordship's notice in the military despatches of Sir John Inglis and myself. But I should be guilty of great ingratitude did I not avail myself of the present opportunity again to solicit his Lordship's favourable recognition of this zealous and able officer. On the final relief of Lucknow by the Commander-in-Chief, the state of Mr. Couper's health rendered a change of climate most desirable, and he had strong and valid reasons, personal and domestic, for wishing to return to England. But when I represented to him that his local knowledge and official experience rendered his continued presence with the Alumbagh force of great importance, he promptly and cheerfully consented to sacrifice his interests and feelings to the public good; and I do not hesitate to say, that by this act of self-denial he has placed the State under very great obligations. To myself he has, indeed, been an invaluable assistant; and I acknowledge, with gratitude, the aid, information, and counsel, he has rendered me.

(True extract.)
J. OUTRAM, *Lieut.-General.*

GENERAL ORDERS BY THE RIGHT HONOURABLE THE GOVERNOR-GENERAL.

Allahabad, 15th May, 1858.

The Right Hon. the Governor-General directs the publication of the two following despatches from the Honourable the Court of Directors, with the greatest satisfaction.

It will be seen that the Honourable Court fully approve and support the recommendation in respect of prize, which the Governor-General in Council has made in favour of the gallant troops composing the field force by which Delhi was captured.

It will also be seen that in respect of batta, the grant of six months' batta which has been already awarded by the Governor-General in Council, and beyond which the authority of the Government of India does not extend, has been increased by the Honourable Court to a grant of batta for twelve months, in favour of the Delhi Field Force and of the original garrison of Lucknow.

The Honourable Court have further ordered a donation of six months' batta to be given to all those belonging to, or accompanying, the force under Major-General Sir H. Havelock, which entered the Residency on the 25th of September last.

R. J. H. BIRCH, *Colonel,*
Secy. to the Govt. of India, Mily. Dept.,
with the Govr. Genl.

Our Governor-General of India in Council.

London, 31st March, 1857.

1. The whole of these documents* have been published in the *London Gazette*. The perusal of them has excited throughout the British dominions, and we may add, throughout the civilized world, sentiments of enthusiastic admiration for the undaunted courage and the still higher qualities of indomitable resolution, fidelity, and endurance of long-continued danger, trial, and privation, displayed by the comparatively small body of troops and volunteers, which so successfully defended the Residency; for the distinguished gallantry of the forces under the late lamented Sir Henry Havelock, and the Commander-in-Chief, by which they were successively relieved; for the generous and soldierlike feeling which prompted Major-General Sir J. Outram, on joining Sir H. Havelock's force, to abstain from assuming the position due to his superior rank, and to leave in the hands of that officer the completion of the service he had so triumphantly begun; for the eminent services of Sir J. Outram, after a junction had been effected with the garrison of the Residency, on the 25th September, until the arrival of the relieving force under his Excellency Sir C. Campbell; and pre-eminently consummate skill manifested by General Sir Colin Campbell, in withdrawing without loss the noble garrison, and all protected by them, to a place of safety.

2. It affords us the highest gratification to communicate to you our cordial approval of the measures adopted by you, in recognition of the heroism of the defenders of Lucknow, viz.:—

I. "Every officer and soldier, European and native, who has formed part of the Residency between the 29th June and the 25th September last, shall receive six months' batta.

II. "Every civilian in the covenanted service of the East India Company, who has taken part in the defence of the Residency, within the above-named date, shall receive six months' batta, at a rate calculated according to the military rank with which his standing corresponds.

III. "Every uncovenanted civil officer or volunteer, who has taken a like part, shall receive six months' batta, at a rate to be fixed according to the functions and position which may have been assigned to him.

IV. "Every native commissioned and non-commissioned officer and soldier who has formed part of the garrison shall receive the order of merit, with the increase of pay attached thereto, and shall be permitted to count three years of additional service.

V. "The soldiers of the 13th, 48th, and 71st Regiments N. I., who have been part of the garrison, shall be formed into a regiment of the line to be called the 'Regiment of Lucknow.'"

3. We have now to announce to you our resolution to grant an

---

* Reply to letter, dated 11th December, 1857, No. 324. Government forwards a narrative of the defence of the Residency at Lucknow, and copies of the despatches announcing the relief of the garrison.

additional donation of six months' full batta, to all those engaged in the defence of the Residency between the 29th June and 25th September, 1857, and a donation of six months' batta to all those belonging to, or accompanying the force under the command of Major-General Sir H. Havelock, which entered the Residency on the 25th September, and was engaged in its defence from that time till the 22nd of November, 1857.

We are, &c.,

Ross D. MANGLES,
F. CURRIE,
And Eight Others.

GENERAL ORDERS BY HIS EXCELLENCY THE COMMANDER-IN-CHIEF.

Head-Quarters, Camp Bareilly, 11th May, 1858.

The Commander-in-Chief has received the most gracious commands of her Majesty the Queen to communicate to the army the expression of the deep interest felt by the Queen in the exertions of the troops and the successful progress of the campaign.

Sir Colin Campbell has delayed giving execution to the Royal command, until he was able to announce to the army that the last great stronghold of rebellion had fallen before the persevering efforts of the troops of her Majesty and the Honourable East India Company.

It is impossible for the Commander-in-Chief to express adequately his sense of the high honour done to him in having been chosen by the Queen to convey her Majesty's most gracious acknowledgment to the army, in the ranks of which he has passed his life.

The Commander-in-Chief ventures to quote the very words of the Queen:—

"That so many gallant and brave and distinguished men, beginning with one whose name will ever be remembered with pride, Brigadier-General Havelock, should have died and fallen, is a great grief to the Queen. To all European, as well as native troops, who have fought so nobly and so gallantly, and amongst whom the Queen is rejoiced to see the 93rd, the Queen wishes Sir Colin to convey the expression of her great admiration and gratitude."

By order of his Excellency the Commander-in-Chief,

W. MAYHEW, *Lieutenant-Colonel*,
Adjutant-General of the Army.

PART III.

CORRESPONDENCE.

LUCKNOW.

CORRESPONDENCE

Relating to the Military Operations for the Rescue of the Garrison in Lucknow, from the middle of August, 1857, when Sir James Outram assumed command at Dinapore, until its final Relief by Sir Colin Campbell on the 17th November, 1857.

Sir James Outram to the Governor-General.

Dinapore, 19th August, 1857.

ON the evening of the 15th instant we anchored off Bhaugulpore, where I landed to inspect the defensive preparations of Mr. Yule, the Commissioner, which I found to be everything I could desire, eighty men of H.M.'s 5th Regiment occupying a Mahomedan tomb on an elevated position, impregnable by any enemy not furnished with artillery, and which thoroughly commands and protects the Commissioner's house and public offices. Mr. Yule had kindly given up a portion of his house as an hospital for the Europeans, among whom cholera had broken out. Three had died; others were suffering; but the disease had taken a milder form, and I trust will have entirely ceased by this time. At midnight, Mr. Yule came on board to inform me that the 5th Irregular Cavalry, stationed at Bhaugulpore, had mounted and fled with their arms three hours before, though the circumstance was only just reported to him. It appears that as our steamer and flat exhibited only some twenty soldiers, they imagined that a stronger body was concealed for the purpose of surprising and disarming them during the night, and this caused the panic through which they fled.

Half of their native officers remained; the troopers molested no one, and left all their property behind them. Before our departure, shortly after daybreak on the 10th, Mr. Yule reported having ascertained that the cavalry had taken the direction of Bowsee, 36 miles from Bhaugulpore, where the head-quarters of the 32nd N. I. are situated. Up to this moment we have learnt nothing further of their proceedings, or whether they induced the 32nd Regiment to follow their example; but the flight of the sowars having been reported by telegraph to Monghyr and Dinapore, created, as we found on our arrival at these towns, a very unnecessary alarm.

Mr. Tucker had withdrawn his detachment of Europeans (fifty men of the 5th Fusiliers) into the fort, some three miles in circumference, all the gates of which, except one, he had closed up, and the town was left without any protection.

Fifty European soldiers would be no real protection to so extensive a place; but their mere appearance in the town gave a sense of security to the people; and taking them away to shut them up in the fort had of course the very contrary effect. I therefore wrote to Mr. Tucker, remonstrating against the measure (copy enclosed), and caused corresponding instructions to be conveyed officially to the officer commanding. I also directed the officer commanding at Bhaugulpore to send up to Monghyr thirty of his Europeans; the remainder of his detachment being quite sufficient for that place in addition to the hill rangers. Both places have now as much European protection as can possibly be afforded, and quite as much as is needed to give confidence. On arrival near Patna, the night before last, I learnt that the panic had extended to Dinapore, and that the 90th Regiment, which had passed up the river four days before, had been recalled. I immediately despatched an express to prohibit the return of the regiment; but unfortunately it did not reach in time to stop the return vessels, which came back yesterday evening, and, I regret to say, with cholera on board (a doctor had died). This has necessitated landing the men, in order to cleanse and purify the vessels, which cannot be ready for their reception before to-morrow evening.

The delay thus caused in the advance of this regiment, and the disease likely to be engendered by long confinement on board crowded boats during the present extreme heat, are the more provoking as there is in reality not the slightest cause for alarm here. So satisfied am I on this subject (after the precautions I have ordered to be carried out, the mountain train guns being placed at the Opium Godowns in such positions as to effectually protect them, and at the same time overawe the town, &c.), that I have ordered a detachment of 100 men of the 90th Regiment, which had been kept back here, to join the regiment. And I would send away another 100 men of the 5th Fusiliers, who also have been detained here, were they not required for the town duties, which could not safely be entrusted to the * * Regiment under the * * * * * exasperated feelings it displays towards natives of all classes just now,

* * * * * *

* * * * * *

in revenge for the slaughter of their comrades at Arrah.

I purpose taking on two guns of the battery here (leaving the mountain train for service in Behar if necessary hereafter, for which I intended it), and also Major Eyre's battery, to Benares, where I propose, if practicable, to organize a column to advance to Lucknow, through Jaunpore, between the Syc and Goomtee rivers;—the only course now left by which we can hope to relieve our garrison in Lucknow; General Havelock having again retired from the attempt, and recrossed the Ganges to Cawnpore, being unable, I imagine, to cross the Syc in the face of the enemy, the Bunnee bridge having been destroyed. In addition to the Artillery above mentioned, I can only have the 5th Fusiliers and 90th Regiments, so weakened by detachments as to amount together to less than 1,000 men— some of the Ghoorkas perhaps, and the Madras Regiment now on its way up the river. But I hope to arrange with General Havelock—after effecting a junction with such troops as he can forward from Cawnpore —to cross the Ganges about Futtehpore, and pass the Syc near Roy Bareilly. I would there prepare rafts (on inflated skins) by which these reinforcements would cross the Syc. We should then be in sufficient strength, I trust, to force our way to Lucknow.

All my arrangements here will be completed by to-morrow, and no time shall be lost in pushing up to Benares, whence I hope to send back most of the steamers and flats now here, and above. Aware as I am how urgently these vessels are required at Calcutta, I am very much vexed that such great and unnecessary delays should have interposed, by detentions here, at Dinapore, and other places; and your Lordship may rely on my preventing any further delay that can possibly be avoided.

213

To G. F. Edmonstone, Esq., Secretary to Government.
Dinapore, 20*th August*, 1857.

I have the honour to transmit for the information of the Right Honourable the Governor-General in Council, copy of a memorandum received from Commissioner Samuells, explaining his views of the state of Behar, and the measures necessary for its pacification, with copy of my reply of this date.

(Enclosure.)
MEMORANDUM *by Mr. Samuells for General Sir James Outram.*

Patna, 18*th August*, 1857.

There are three objects in this division for which it appears necessary to provide. The first is, the security of the city of Patna, including the opium Godown; the second, clearing the district of Arrah of the rebel bands which now infest it, and re-opening the communication between Benares and the Soane; and, thirdly, the protection of the district of Gyah, which is at present open to the incursion of the rebel troops from Ramghur. The first of these objects seems to be, in a great measure, secured. The only *desiderata* appear to be a small detachment of Europeans in the Godown, the improvement of its defences, and the construction of a fortified post in the civil station of Patna, which would at once protect that portion of the city in the vicinity of the station, and serve as a place of security for the residents in the event of any sudden *émeute*.

The second of these objects, the pacification of the Arrah district, is of very great importance. On the speedy attainment of this object the opium crop in that district depends, which is worth to Government, as I am informed, not less than half a million sterling. While Arrah remains also disturbed, the districts in its immediate neighbourhood will continue in an inflammable state, and the communication between Calcutta and Benares—whether by dâk or telegraph—interrupted. Were a small force, similar to that now under Major Eyre, to be posted at Sasseram, it would, with the aid of the detachment at Buxar, be able, it is presumed, to preserve the peace of the district; to keep the Trunk Road free; and to prevent the Ramghur and Bhaugulpore mutineers from crossing the Soane at Dehree.

The Madras Column, which is about to move up the Trunk Road, may, when it reaches Sasseram, perform the same service as Major Eyre's detachment, or any similar detachment, from this side, in keeping the road and district free of insurgents, but it is to be considered that they will not be able to head mutineers, who will have a long start of them, and that the latter, by occupying the ghâts on the Soane, may render it impossible for the column to cross without the co-operation of a force on the Arrah side.

Gyah, it is obvious, is in a dangerous position, if the rebel troops from Ramghur should move upon it, the small party now there being quite inadequate for its protection. If the ghâts on the Soane are unoccupied, and the road towards Benares open, it is not at all improbable that they may avail themselves of the trunk road as far as they can, and plunder the district of Gyah until the approach of the column which is moving up the trunk road, and which cannot reach Gyah for the next three weeks, forces them to decamp. It would thus seem that the safety of Gyah and Shergotty would be, in a great measure, secured by a small force at Sasseram. For the rebels, finding the trunk road closed, would naturally take the hill road by Lohardugga.

These are, in a concise form, the considerations which occur to me on the subject of the defence of this division. It is, of course, for the military authorities to consider whether the force at their disposal, or the pressing need of troops in other quarters, will admit of the arrangements which I have suggested being carried out, or whether better arrangements cannot be made for the attainment of the objects which I have specified.

E. A. SAMUELLS, *Commissioner*.

(Enclosure.)

Colonel Napier, Military Secretary to Sir James Outram, to E. A. Samuells, Esquire, Commissioner of Patna.

Dinapore, 20th August, 1857.

I am directed by Major-General Sir James Outram, K.C.B., commanding the Dinapore and Cawnpore divisions, to acknowledge the receipt of your memorandum, on the protective measure for Behar, which I laid before him.

The first point of the memorandum, the security of the city of Patna, has been provided for in the following manner:—

The Opium Godown is being fortified in a temporary but substantial manner, by Captain Harris, an experienced engineer officer, and armed with six mountain train guns. In addition to its present garrison of 70 Sikhs, and a small party of Najeebs, it has a detachment of 80 of H.M.'s Fusiliers, which, with two 9-pounder guns, is posted at the civil station.

During the Mohurrum these detachments will be doubled, from the cantonment of Dinapore, or still further increased should the Commissioner think it necessary.

Sir James Outram considers these arrangements amply sufficient for the present security of Patna. Regarding the remaining points of your memorandum, the pacification of Arrah, and its results as affecting the opium crop, he deems them less urgent than the vital interests at stake higher up the country, to forward which every European soldier not absolutely necessary for the protection of Dinapore and Patna must be sent on. The rebels in the Arrah district have been defeated and dispersed. With Gyah and Arrah reoccupied, those districts must be held by the detachment now there,* and such police and local means as the civil authorities can organize: and the principal zemindars should be held strictly responsible for the peace of the claquas under their influence.

Major Eyre's battery is most urgently called for in advance, and under no circumstances can it be longer detained at Arrah. Should Koer Singh reappear in force, the column approaching by the trunk road must be called upon to act against him if absolutely necessary.

The Madras Regiment now coming up the river may be employed under circumstances of extreme urgency, but, in addition to the demand for its presence in advance, it is of the utmost importance that its upward-progress should not be interrupted, if it can possibly be avoided. For it is of the greatest moment that the vessels it occupied should be speedily released to return to Calcutta, after landing the regiment at Benares.

The Commander-in-Chief (Sir Colin Campbell) to Sir J. Outram.

(Telegraphic.)   18th August, 1857.

It is hoped that Eyre's signal success at Jugdespore will restore tranquillity in the Dinapore division, and enable you to send on the 5th and 90th Regiments to their original destination, Allahabad; or at least one of those regiments. If one must be retained in Behar, keep the 5th, and send on the 90th the moment you can spare it. The flats and steamers they now have should take on the regiments to Allahabad. Give notice to the officer commanding at Allahabad as soon as you despatch the troops, in order that every preparation may be made for their reception.

The wing of the 37th Regiment was sent up expressly for the purpose of relieving the detachments belonging to the regiments of Havelock's force as far as practicable; it is very desirable that this arrangement

---

* Arrah: 150 Sikhs, Lieutenant Robertson, Lieutenant Powis; Gyah: 43 men H. M.'s 54th, 3 officers, 150 Sikhs, and head-quarters, under Captain Rattray.

should still be carried out, and those detachments pushed on rapidly to Cawnpore, to join their regimental head-quarters.

Havelock's force is composed of portions of the 64th, 78th, 84th, and 1st Madras Fusiliers. Your returns will show you where the detachments belonging to them are posted in the Dinapore and Cawnpore divisions. Bear in mind the extreme importance of maintaining a strong garrison in Allahabad; 500 Europeans, at least, are required.

A column of troops will start from Raneegunge to-morrow or the next day, and march along the great trunk road to Benares, and thence on to Allahabad. The officer in command has been directed to report to you daily, and attend to any instructions you may send him.

The column consists of—

Wing of 53rd Foot.
Madras Field Battery, 6 guns.
27th Regiment Madras Native Infantry.

Possibly this column may be moved on Hazareebaugh, to re-establish order there; but its detention will be very short, and a report will be made to you.

P.S.—It is an exceeding satisfaction to me to have your assistance, and to find you in your present position.

Sir J. Outram to the Commander-in-Chief.

(Telegraphic.) *Dinapore*, 20*th August*, 1857.

Received at Dinapore, on the evening of the 20th August, by letter from Monghyr, dated yesterday, the purport of a message from your Excellency, read by a gentleman at the telegraph station, five miles from

Monghyr, which he thus communicated. Last message which should have arrived at Patna not yet received. Beg to refer to letter I yesterday addressed to Governor-General, stating manner in which I purpose relieving Lucknow (not prudent to entrust to telegraph), which would necessitate disembarking 5th and 90th Regiments at Benares, instead of Allahabad. If not approved, your Excellency's orders by telegraph may reach me at Benares by the time those regiments can get there. Had already telegraphed to-day, urging despatch of wing of the 27th to relieve the detachments of regiments at Berhampore, Bhaugulpore, Monghyr, Patna, and Buxar, which cannot rejoin their head-quarters until so relieved. Will see that the garrison of Allahabad is up to the strength your Excellency mentioned.

The Commander-in-Chief to Sir J. Outram.

(Telegraphic.)   20*th August*, 1857.

Information from General Havelock, of yesterday's date, made it appear expedient to send this forenoon the following instructions to the officer commanding the detachment on board the steam-vessel *Benares* at Mirzapore.

P.S.—I was not aware that the 90th Regiment had passed Dinapore when I sent the message.

The Commander-in-Chief to the Officer commanding Her Majesty's 5th Regiment, on board the Steamer " Benares."

            Calcutta, 20*th August*, 1857, 11 *a. m.*

If you should not have received instructions from

General Outram as to the future movements of the detachment of her Majesty's 5th Regiment under your command, you are to order the steamer with her Majesty's detachment to proceed with all possible despatch to Allahabad.

Sir J. Outram to E. A. Samuells, Esq.

Dinapore, 20th August, 1857.

As I am resolved to make my way to Lucknow from Benares, through Jaunpore, passing up between the Goomtee and the Sye, and thus turn the latter obstacle, which Havelock was, I understand, unable to cross owing to the bridge being destroyed,* I must collect all the few Europeans that can be rendered available, and shall be obliged, therefore, to withdraw the 100 men of the 90th left at Buxar, which town must hold its own until the Madras Regiment comes up (due in a week at furthest, I should think), on which you can make requisition for a company to be landed as the steamer passes that place—should you not be able to afford a portion of the 150 Sikhs at Arrah for the protection of Buxar. I enclose an order to the officer commanding the Madras Regiment, to obey any requisition you may make on him.

When I reach Buxar, I shall ascertain if one company will suffice; should I find that more be necessary, I will leave an order with Cowper accordingly. Please don't let out my proposed plan of advance on Lucknow, it being an object to make it believed I purpose taking the Fyzabad route.

---

* Such was our information at that time, but it was afterwards ascertained that the Bunnee Bridge had not been destroyed.

Sir J. Outram to Henry Tucker, Esq., Commissioner of Benares.

Dinapore, 20th August.

I thank you for your suggestions for the relief of the Lucknow garrison. From the reports prevailing here, it would appear scarcely possible they can hold out for the length of time that would be occupied by my advance by either of the routes you recommend; but it is my determination to make the attempt if their position is still maintained. I had intended to push on yesterday, but to my extreme vexation, on my arrival at Patna the day before yesterday, I learnt that orders had been sent to recall the 90th four days after it had left this. I instantly sent off an express, directing it to proceed to Benares without delay, but unfortunately my message was met by the vessels on their way down, when only an hour's sail from here. And as they required coal, and cholera had broken out, they were obliged to come down, and arrived the night before last. It was found necessary to land the men for twenty-four hours, in order to fumigate and cleanse the vessels. They re-embark this evening, and no further delays will be allowed in their upward progress. Grant and I also embark to-night, and will join you as soon as possible. For reasons which I will explain when we meet, I prefer the land route (through Jaunpore to Lucknow) to that of the Gogra, independent of the consideration of the detention of the steamers which would be caused by the latter operation, they being urgently required to bring troops, &c., from Calcutta.

My idea is, to form a column at Jaunpore, consisting of portions of the 90th and 5th Fusiliers, and any other European troops that may be available, the Ghoorkas, Eyre's troop, and two guns from this battery which I shall take up with me. With this column, I would make my way up between the Syc and Goomtee till about opposite Pertabghur or Roy Bareilly, where I would prepare skin rafts to enable such portion of Havelock's force as can be spared from Cawnpore (to be dropped down in steamers, and landed at the nearest point to the place fixed on for crossing the Syc) to effect a junction with me there. I should then have little difficulty in forcing my way to Lucknow.

I have no accounts as to Havelock's proceedings on his last advance, or why he again retired, or of the state and proceedings of the garrison. Pray send every intelligence you may have on these points to meet me at Buxar, which they tell me is three or four days' steaming from hence. Also let me know if the troops retained at Mirzapore (or what portion of them) may now be withdrawn, to add to our Jaunpore column.

In the meantime, I beg you will cause the necessary commissariat preparations to be made for the troops which will proceed from Benares to Jaunpore. (All will go from Benares in the first instance, I presume, where the 90th, 5th, and all other Europeans had best land.) Ample carriage, camp equipage, and supplies, should be ready at Benares, as also supplies at Jaunpore.

As many skins (mussucks) as procurable should be got, and bamboos, poles, &c., for preparing rafts. Pray telegraph to Havelock, in my name, to keep up every appearance of preparation to recross the Ganges, as if meditating another advance on Lucknow—but in reality to keep the enemy in that direction, who otherwise would move down to oppose our advance from Jaunpore. Better say nothing to Havelock at present of my intention to call for his co-operation (from *below* Cawnpore), lest it might get wind through the telegraph. There will be time enough to arrange this when I join you at Benares.

If the Ghoorkas have already gone to Allahabad, they can, when the time comes, be sent over to the same point where Havelock crosses to effect his junction with me across the Sye. It would be as well for you to let Havelock know that you had recommended me to go up the Gogra and relieve Lucknow from Fyzabad, without telling him I had decided on taking the other route, thus leading the telegraph people to suppose I am to come that way, and I hope this may ooze out at Cawnpore, and so lead the enemy to expect and prepare for us at Fyzabad, which would have the good effect of obliging those rebels to remain there (who otherwise might move down upon our districts), besides putting them on a false scent calculated to facilitate my operations.

Sir J. Outram to the Secretary to the Government of India.

(Telegraphic.)   *Dinapore, 20th August,* 1857.

I recommend that all spare medical officers in Calcutta or the lower provinces may be sent to Allahabad for field service, with orders to call at Dinapore and Benares for instructions in case of any urgent demand for their services.

The Secretary to the Government of India to Sir J. Outram.

(Telegraphic.)   *Calcutta, 24th August,* 1857, 5 *p.m.*

We have been collecting some medical officers at the Presidency to accompany detachments of troops going upwards; does this arrangement answer the purpose you have in view?

The Commander-in-Chief to Sir James Outram.

(Telegraphic.)   22nd *August*, 1857, 11.45 *p.m.*

I am rejoiced to hear of your arrival at Dinapore.

The force under General Havelock is reduced by casualties on service, and by cholera, which has been and still rages in his camp, to 700 men in the field, exclusive of detachments which guard the entrenchment, and keep open the communication with Allahabad. He is threatened by a force of some 5,000 men, with twenty or thirty guns, from Gwalior, besides the Oude force. He says, he "is ready to fight anything, but the above "are great odds, and a battle lost here would do the "interest of the State infinite damage: I solicit rein- "forcements." His applications for assistance have been frequent, and, deeming his situation to demand immediate aid, I ordered the 90th Regiment to be sent to him with all possible speed, as also the detachment of the 5th Regiment, which was on board the *Benares* steamer, if it could be spared. Pray send the 90th Regiment at once to his aid. I will write to you to-morrow.

The Commander-in-Chief to Sir James Outram.

(Telegraphic.)   *Calcutta*, 23rd *Aug.* 1857, 11.15 *a.m.*

Since my telegram to you of 11.45 last night (August 22nd), urging the immediate despatch to Allahabad and Cawnpore of the 90th Regiment, and, if possible, also of the detachment of the 5th Regiment on board the *Benares* steamer, I have received two fresh telegrams from General Havelock, pressing for reinforcements. He states, unless immediate reinforcements are promised by telegraph, he must at once abandon Cawnpore, and fall back on Allahabad.

His loss by cholera was six men daily, and he had lost two officers on the 20th by the same disease. His sick in hospital were 331, principally for cholera and wounds. The Gwalior force, rated at 5,000 men, with thirty guns, had crossed the Jumna.

I will send you by post, copies of all his recent telegrams, addressed to the Commander-in-Chief. This includes those to General Grant, as well as to myself.

I believe the troops, not only in the Dinapore but also in the Cawnpore division, have been placed under your orders, and you should therefore be acquainted with all that has recently taken place in the neighbourhood of Cawnpore.

Brigadier-General Havelock to the Commander-in-Chief.

(Telegraphic.) *Cawnpore, 23rd Aug.* 1857, 5 *p.m.*

I forward to you a copy of a letter this day received from Colonel Inglis, 32nd Regiment, commanding at the Residency, Lucknow:—

"My dear General, *Lucknow, August* 16*th*, 1857.

"A note from Colonel Tytler to Mr. Gubbins reached last night, dated Mungulwar, 4th instant, the latter part of which is as follows:—

" 'You must aid us in every way, even to cutting your way out, if we can't force our way in. We have only a small force.'

"This has caused me much uneasiness, as it is quite impossible, with my weak and shattered force, that I can leave my defences. You must bear in mind how I am hampered, that I have upwards of 120 sick and wounded, and at least 220 women, and about 230 children, and no carriage of any description, besides sacrificing twenty-three lakhs of treasure and about thirty guns of sorts. In consequence of the news received, I shall soon put this force on half rations. Our provisions will last us then till about the 10th of September. If you hope to save this force no time must be lost in pushing forward. We are daily being attacked by the enemy, who are within a few yards of our defences. Their mines have already weakened our post, and I have every reason to believe they are carrying on others. Their 18-pounders are within 150 yards of some of our batteries, and from their position, and our inability to form working parties, we cannot reply to them, and therefore the damage is very great. My strength now in Europeans is

350, and 300 Natives, and the men dreadfully harassed, and, owing to part of the Residency having been brought down by round shot, many are without shelter. If our native force, who are losing confidence, leave us, I do not know how the defences are to be manned. Did you receive a letter and plan from me? Kindly answer this question.

"Yours truly,
"J. INGLIS."

Mr. H. Tucker, Civil Commissioner at Benares, informed me that it is the intention of Sir J. Outram to ascend the Gogra, and relieve Lucknow by Fyzabad, and that Sir James desires my co-operation by making a demonstration of recrossing the Ganges; even to do more by striving to regain my strong position of Mungulwar, or more nearly approaching Lucknow; but I must have fresh troops to enable me to do either of these.

The Commander-in-Chief to Sir J. Outram.

Calcutta, 24th August, 1857.

I am extremely happy, and deem myself most fortunate, to find myself associated with you on service, and to have the advantage of your able assistance in carrying on the duty on which we are now engaged.

I send you, herewith, the different telegraphs received from General Havelock since my arrival; they will make you fully acquainted with his operations in Oude; his reasons for recrossing the Ganges; his subsequent operations in the neighbourhood of Cawnpore, with account of his loss by sickness and casualties in the field; his present numbers, and their condition as to health and efficiency.

I have been favoured by the Governor-General with a perusal of yours to his Lordship of the 19th instant, in which you propose to collect a force of about 1,000 infantry and eight guns at Benares, with a view to march to the relief of our garrison in Lucknow, by the most direct route from thence, and that the force under General Havelock at Cawnpore should co-operate with you in this movement, by crossing the Ganges at Futtchpore, and the Sye subsequently (with your assistance) at Roy Bareilly, and forming a junction with you beyond that place.

General Havelock states, in his telegraph of the 20th instant, that his force is reduced to 700 men in the field, exclusive of the detachments required to guard his entrenchments and keep open his communication with Allahabad, and so inadequate does he consider his force to be for the defence of his post, that he states in his telegraph dated August 21st, 12.30 P.M., that, if not assured of reinforcements by return of telegraph, he will retire to Allahabad. Hope of co-operation from General Havelock (by a force equal to accomplish the movement you propose, by crossing the Ganges at Futtchpore) is not to be entertained. The march from Benares, by the most direct route, to Lucknow, is a long one — some 150 miles — and the population through which you would have to pass, hostile. Its great recommendation I presume to be that you (by that route) turn, or, rather, come in rear of, the many nullahs which, I am told, interpose between Cawnpore and Lucknow, and this would be an important advantage. But if the force you propose to collect at Benares were to be moved by the river to Cawnpore, and united with Havelock's reduced numbers, do you think it would be equal to force its way over the numerous nullahs, necessarily full of water at this season, which are to be found on the road from the latter place to Lucknow? By this route all incumbrances, such as sick, &c., would be left at the different stations or posts along the road, and the troops, being conveyed by steam, would suffer less than if obliged to march, and Havelock's anxiety about his post would be removed.

In offering these remarks or suggestions to you, who are acquainted with the country, people, and difficulties attending the movements you propose, it is not with any view to fetter your judgment and perfect freedom of action, but I mention these as they occur to me in writing to you, and I think I may venture to say, that the measures you may deem most advisable to pursue, will receive the approval of the Governor-General. I hope to have the pleasure of hearing from you.

The Commander-in-Chief to Sir J. Outram.

(Telegraphic.)   *Calcutta*, 24*th Aug.* 1857, 12 *p.m.*

I have written to you by the post of this evening, forwarding copies of all telegraphs received from General Havelock, with my replies to this date.

The Governor-General showed me your letter to him on the movement you proposed to make from Benares, and of the object of that movement; General Havelock to co-operate with you by crossing at Futtehpore, and subsequently the Sye, near to Roy Bareilly.* . . . .

Since writing the above, the following despatch has come in from Havelock :—

(Enclosure.)

Brigadier-General Havelock to the Governor-General of India in Council and the Commander-in-Chief.

(Telegraphic.)   *Cawnpore*, 24*th August*, 1857, 12 *a.m.*

I am thankful for the effort you made to reinforce me. I will communicate with Sir James Outram, and have telegraphed to Benares to learn where he is. I am leaving Lieutenant-Colonel O'Brien 650 infantry in Allahabad, but as he will have Captain Peel's Naval Brigade and powerful guns for the defence, it would be advantageous to me if I

---

* Recapitulation of the previous letter of this date.

could be authorized to send him back the thirty invalid artillery, and receive in exchange the 3rd Company 5th Battalion now at Allahabad, which would enable me to equip and work my heavy guns. With the reinforcements promised, I could resume the initiative, and march to Lucknow, if the place should not unfortunately have fallen before the reinforcements arrive.

The Governor-General of India to Sir J. Outram.

(Telegraphic.) 25th *August*, 1857.

Upon well considering the plan proposed in your letter of the 19th, it seems open to these objections:—

The road to Lucknow by Jaunpore is bad; it lies through a country in insurrection; there would be great difficulty in keeping communications open in your rear; there would be no safe places at which to leave the sick and wounded; supplies must be uncertain; the march will be 150 miles, and will not be eased or expedited by carriage or water conveyance.

The road by Allahabad and Cawnpore is much longer; but none of these objections apply to it. It will bring you into junction with General Havelock's force, which, considering the small strength of each force, seems very necessary; and if the Gwalior regiments advance, you will have them in front. But the road by Jaunpore may have advantages of which I am not aware; and I am confident that your deliberate judgment will decide for the best.

It is not probable that the relief of the Lucknow garrison will be facilitated by the abandonment of Cawnpore; but, if this should be the case, do not hesitate to abandon it. The political importance of it, and the cost of recovering it, are not to be weighed against the relief of Lucknow.

Accounts from Lucknow to the 16th were received last night. There are 350 Europeans and 300 natives; but they have 120 sick, and 450 women and children, and no carriage; they cannot therefore cut their way out. They are hard pressed; but a reduction to half rations will enable them to hold out till the 10th of next month.

Endeavour to communicate with Colonel Inglis, and tell him that he is not to care for the treasure if it should be an incumbrance, but that he may use it in any way for the release of the garrison.

The detachment of the 29th Regiment cannot be sent from Calcutta; but more than 400 men of the 90th and 5th will be despatched to Benares by bullock train, at the rate of 80 a day, beginning from Friday next: each batch will be eleven days on the road.

I wish you to communicate with Mr. Frederick Gubbins at Benares, respecting Rajah Maun Sing; he will be able to give you the latest information of the Rajah's proceedings.

I am told that Rajah Maun Sing is gone to Lucknow on business of his own. If his influence there should enable him to obtain by any means the unmolested retirement of the garrison from the Residency, and its safe passage to your camp, or to any place of security, any reward may be paid for this, both to Maun Sing and to those who may help him, which shall not be inconsistent with the sovereign authority of the British Government in Oude.

Sir J. Outram to the Commander-in-Chief.

(Telegraphic.) *Ghazeepore, 25th Aug.* 1857, 10 *p.m.*

Received your message of the 22nd instant this evening.

In accordance with these orders, the 90th Regiment complete (minus three companies coming from Calcutta), and such portion of the 5th as I have collected, will be sent on by steamer to Allahabad, and thence pushed on by quickest means practicable. This prevents my carrying out my intended advance to the relief of Lucknow from Jaunpore or Roy Bareilly, as proposed in my letter to the Governor-General from Dinapore dated 20th instant, no other European troops being available; but the necessity for reinforcing General Havelock seems imperative.

By a letter from Cawnpore, dated the 19th instant, I learn that General Havelock's moveable column consists of 1,100 Europeans and 250 Sikhs, exclusive of 300 Europeans holding Cawnpore under General Neill.

The 90th, the detachment of the 5th, and Eyre's battery, left Buxar yesterday in three steamers and three flats, and I hope may overtake me at Benares the day after to-morrow.

I have relieved the half of Eyre's battery, left here, by two guns from the battery at Dinapore.

Sir J. Outram to the Commander-in-Chief.

(Telegraphic.)   *Ghazeepore, 25th August,* 1857.

Since my message of this morning, I have received your message of the 23rd, stating that, if not assured of speedy relief, General Havelock will have to fall back on Allahabad; I shall send express to Benares desiring my message to be sent to General Havelock, informing him when he may expect the 90th and the 5th, and any other troops that may now be available at Allahabad.

Sir J. Outram to Henry Tucker, Esquire, Commissioner, Benares.

Ghazeepore, 25th August, 1857.

Imperative orders have reached me here by telegraph to send on the 90th to Cawnpore, where all troops that can be spared are needed to enable Havelock to hold that place; consequently my intended advance on Lucknow *viâ* Jaunpore is out of the question for the present. Pray transmit the accompanying telegram as soon as possible to Calcutta. And also telegraph in my name to Havelock, informing him that the 90th and 5th will be here to-day, en route to Allahabad; that the steamers will get up as quick as they can; and that those troops, and any others that may be available, shall be pushed on from Allahabad by the quickest possible means. Also tell him of any other Europeans that may be on their way to join him—as those relieved from Mirzapore, I presume.

I trust to be with you to-morrow evening.

P.S.—Tell Havelock that of course I have given up the intended advance direct on Lucknow for the present, as all available Europeans will be sent to him. Also say, I beg to congratulate him on his brilliant successes against the enemy.

Sir J. Outram to Lord Dunkellin, Military Secretary to the Governor-General.

Ghazeepore, 25th August, 1857.

The enclosed notes, which I received last night from Cawnpore and Benares, give a more favourable view of our positions at Cawnpore and Lucknow than we had been led to apprehend. And I do hope the Lucknow garrison may be able to hold out till we obtain such further reinforcements as may enable me to advance to their relief through Jaunpore and Roy Bareilly, as I informed the Governor-General I contemplated.

That expedition cannot be carried out for the present, as all European troops must be pushed on to reinforce

Havelock. I write in great haste, as we are just about to start for Benares.

I trust my telegrams hence, in reply to those of the Commander-in-Chief of 22nd and 23rd, showing that his orders would be carried out as soon as possible, have been duly received.

The Commander-in-Chief to Sir J. Outram, at Benares.

(Telegraphic.) 26th *August*, 1857, 7.30 *p.m.*

General Havelock wishes to have the 3rd Company 5th Battalion of Artillery, now in garrison at Allahabad, sent to him at Cawnpore, in exchange for the 30 invalid artillery-men now in his camp. If you approve of this, give the necessary orders by telegraph to the officer commanding at Allahabad, to forward them to him by the first opportunity, and to tell off a special party of infantry to assist in working the guns in the meantime. Kindly inform General Havelock of your decision on this point.

Captain Peel, R.N., with his sailors, left this for Allahabad by river on the 20th instant.

Sir J. Outram to the Commander-in-Chief.

(Telegraphic.) Benares, 28th *Aug.* 1857, 5 *p.m.*

May Captain Peel's brigade occupy Allahabad for the present, as proposed by General Havelock, thus releasing infantry, so much required just now? As the Marine Brigade could not be provided with infantry escort beyond Allahabad, until General Havelock returns from Lucknow, Captain Peel's brigade could not be more usefully employed.

Sir J. Outram to the Secretary to the Government in India.

(Telegraphic.)   *Benares, 28th Aug.* 1857, 2 *p.m.*

When were the horses for Major Eyre's battery despatched? Were they sent by the trunk road, or by river?

Sir J. Outram to the Commander-in-Chief.

(Telegraphic.)   *Benares, 29th August,* 5.30 *p.m.*

The Collector of Mirzapore reports that there is only a small supply of coals at Mirzapore; that the rebels from Arrah have passed by Segowlee, and destroyed the coal there. No more to be got thence at present. Very little coal remains at Benares. More coals should be sent up immediately.

Sir J. Outram to the Commander-in-Chief.

(Telegraphic.)   *Benares, 29th Aug.* 1857, 5.30 *p.m.*

Major Cotter, commanding Madras battery at Benares, reports that the sergeant-turners, artificers, and drivers, were detained at Dum Dum. I recommend that they may be sent to him as soon as possible.

The Commander-in-Chief to Sir J. Outram, or the Officer commanding at Benares.

(Telegraphic.)

Eighty men of the 9th Regiment were sent off to Raneegunge yesterday, to be forwarded by bullock train and horse dâk to Benares. A like number will be despatched every day, until the whole detachment of the 5th, 64th, and 90th Regiments, now at Chinsurah, have been exhausted. The total strength of these detachments is 582 men. The officer commanding at Allahabad to forward this despatch by telegraph to Cawnpore, if General Outram is not at Allahabad. General Outram is requested to give directions as to the disposal of these several detachments, after their arrival at Benares.

Sir J. Outram to the Commissioner of Goruckpore.

Benares, 29th August.

Thanks for your letters of 22nd and 25th instant, the first received on my arrival here yesterday, and the latter just now (one P.M.)

The enclosed from Chester, received this morning, gives a very different view of affairs at Lucknow from what you gather from the intercepted correspondence. I trust, however, the report that the garrison were negotiating for terms which the so-styled King scorns to grant, has no foundation in truth, being set about probably by the enemy.*

My proposed advance to Lucknow through Jaunpore has been knocked on the head by Havelock's urgent call for reinforcements, without being assured of which (he telegraphed to Government on the 21st) he would fall back on Allahabad, and the consequent orders of the Commander-in-Chief, which I have received by telegraph to send on to him the 90th and 5th. Those being the only European troops I had for my intended expedition, of course *that* cannot now be carried out; and you will gather what I now propose doing from the enclosed copy

---

* As will be afterwards seen, the reports of a king having been thus early proclaimed at Lucknow were erroneous. No such measure was adopted, and no regular government attempted to be established, until after General Havelock's force had been fairly shut up in Lucknow, under circumstances which the rebels believed must ensure the speedy destruction, by famine, of it, and of the original garrison. Then only did the entire population of Oude believe that it would be impossible to restore the British Raj in that province; and then only did the majority of the Oude chiefs and landed proprietors give in their adhesion to the rebels.—ED.

of a telegram I yesterday flashed up to Havelock. Under these circumstances, as I cannot move through Jaunpore, whence the aid of the Goorkhas would have been available, the latter cannot better be employed for the present than in maintaining Jaunpore and Azimghur, and if possible recovering Goruckpore; but I fear *that* is too much to hope for.

No greater service could be rendered by them to the British Government, and no higher proofs of our confidence in them could be given, than thus placing two of our richest districts under their protection.

I have ordered four 9-pounders complete, with ample store of ammunition, to be landed, and made over to the Goorkha commander. They are in a steamer which left Ghazeepore the day after us, and ought to be here to-day.

I leave to-morrow for Allahabad, where I hope again to hear from you. I can only write this hasty note to-day, being much interrupted.

P.S.—At Colonel Strachey's suggestion, I have also ordered two 12-pounder howitzers to be landed for you.

Sir J. Outram to the Commander-in-Chief.

Benares, 29*th August*, 1857.

I was honoured yesterday by the receipt of your Excellency's letter dated 24th instant, and beg to thank you for the very kindly and cordial greeting with which it commences, and which I very gratefully appreciate.

The objections your Excellency urges against the advance from Benares on Lucknow direct are well grounded. Still I am satisfied I might penetrate into the city by that route without much difficulty; the chief objection I see to it being the length of the route. It is indispensable, however, that General Havelock should

be reinforced under the circumstances he represents; and as this necessitates my sending him all the Europeans I possess, of course my proposed expedition must be given up, and I still hope they may reach Cawnpore in time to enable General Havelock to relieve Lucknow in accordance with his message to your Excellency of the 25th instant, wherein he says that—"with the re-
"inforcements promised, I shall resume the initiative,
"and march to Lucknow, if the place should not unfortu-
"nately have fallen before the reinforcements arrive."
I repeat so much of his message, lest it may have miscarried between this and Calcutta. I send for your Excellency's information the copy of a message I sent by yesterday's telegraph to General Havelock; also a copy of one I addressed to yourself from Ghazeepore, in case it may not have reached. Very gloomy reports of the state of affairs at Lucknow have prevailed for a day or two past; but I trust the rumour is an invention of the enemy, viz., that the garrison wishes to negotiate, and that the so-styled King scorns to give any terms. It is just what the rebels would propagate. The enclosed copy of a letter I have just received from Mr. Wingfield speaks of letters he has intercepted from Lucknow, of fifteen days back, which by no means evince such confidence on the part of the besiegers. I have arranged to give the Goorkhas four 9-pounders and two 12-pounder howitzers, in the trust that they will hold Jaunpore and Azimghur. The best service they can render us at present is to hold the Oude frontier.

(Enclosure to the above.)

Telegram from Sir James Outram to General Havelock.

Benares, 28th August, 1858.

I arrived here this morning, and have seen your messages to the Commander-in-Chief of the 23rd and 24th, and to myself of the 20th instant. I expect the 90th and 5th to-morrow, and shall push on at once to Allahabad with them, and with all Europeans that can be spared from Chunar and Mirzapore. The stream is strong against us, but I hope we may be at Allahabad by the 2nd or 3rd, and leave by forced marches for Cawnpore by the 5th. My force, including officers, will consist of 90th Regiment 765, 5th Fusiliers 437, 3rd Company 5th Battalion of Artillery 66. Total 1,268, besides what I pick up at Mirzapore and Chunar. This reinforcement will, I trust, enable you to relieve Lucknow. The details of 64th, 78th, and 84th Regiments, and Madras Fusiliers, now at Allahabad (493 officers and men), will also be sent on when the Marine Brigade arrives there. I shall join you with the reinforcements, but to you shall be left the glory of relieving Lucknow, for which you have already so nobly struggled. I shall accompany you only in my civil capacity as Commissioner, placing my military services at your disposal should you please to make use of me —serving under you as volunteer. Encourage the Lucknow garrison to hold on. Spare no cost in effecting communication with Colonel Inglis. If he *does* negotiate, which God forbid, really influential hostages should be secured. His treasure might be judiciously employed in obtaining supplies, *cost* being no consideration, and in exciting discord in the enemy's camp, &c. He has 23 lakhs, the outlay of which will not be grudged by Government. Proclaim at Cawnpore, and cause it to be made known to the leaders of the enemy's forces at Lucknow, that, for every Christian woman or child maltreated at Lucknow, an Oude noble shall be hanged. If you could afford a sufficient detachment to hold its ground on the Lucknow bank of the river opposite Cawnpore, it would have a beneficial effect in distracting the enemy's attention from the Lucknow garrison, besides facilitating the passage of the river when the time arrives.

Reply to the above.—(Enclosure.)

Brigadier-General Havelock to Major-General Sir James Outram.

Cawnpore, Saturday, 29th August, 4 p.m.

Received your telegram of 28th instant, at 5.45 P.M.

The reinforcements announced will reduce the relief of Lucknow almost to a certainty, if the garrison can hold out till their arrival. I have written to Colonel Inglis to defend himself to extremity, and propose, as soon as the 1st detachment reaches me, to recross to the left bank and resume my strong position of Mungulwar, on which I will mount heavy guns. The Sirdars of Oude have already been warned, in a proclamation, of the vengeance that will be taken for any injury done to the women and children in Lucknow.

The Commander-in-Chief to Sir J. Outram.

(Telegraphic.)   Calcutta, 30th Aug. 1857, 1 p.m.

By all means employ Captain Peel's Naval Brigade as a garrison for Allahabad, when it arrives. I have heard that the vessel Captain Peel was in grounded at Berhampore, and I fear he has not yet got beyond that point.

The Commander-in-Chief to Sir J. Outram.

(Telegraphic.)   Calcutta, 31st Aug. 1857.

General Outram is informed that the 17th Madras Native Infantry, under orders for Dinapore, were at Monghyr on the 27th August, and would probably reach Dinapore about the 30th August. He is requested to dispose of this corps as he may think necessary. The want of coals, reported in his telegram of yesterday's date, has been made known to Government and to the proper authority.

The Secretary to the Government of India to Sir J. Outram.

(Telegraphic.)   Calcutta, 31st Aug. 1857.

Your message of the 28th instant received. The remount horses for Major Eyre's battery, in charge of Captain Smyth, of Artillery, proceeded, on the 28th instant, with the moveable column commanded by Colonel Fisher, from Raneegunge, towards Benares and Allahabad.

Sir J. Outram to the Commander-in-Chief.

(Telegraphic.)   Mirzapore, 31st Aug. 1857, 1.31 p.m.

I fear, from the underwritten message from Colonel O'Brien, that there is a deficiency of Enfield rifle ammunition at Allahabad, and request that an ample supply may be sent up, without delay, to that station. Be most careful that the greatest possible amount of Enfield ammunition is brought. I am quite dependent on those below for the supply of this ammunition.

Sir J. Outram to the Commander-in-Chief.

(Telegraphic.) *Mirzapore*, 31*st Aug.* 1857.

Information has been received through Mr. Hamilton, Opium Agent, Ghazeepore, that Mahomed Hossain, the Oude Chuckladar, is occupying the Collector's bungalow, and his followers, numbering some five or six thousand, are located in the town of Goruckpore. The Mussulman population went to pay respects with nuzzurs. The Chuckladar above-mentioned had taken regular possession of revenue and police establishment, &c. The special object which General Outram has in view prevents his detaching any force to recover Goruckpore, or to prevent the disorder from spreading to Chupra or Sarun districts. If the Supreme Government can send any native force to act in those districts, two hundred Europeans of the 10th Regiment might join them from Dinapore, with two guns. His Excellency the Commander-in-Chief might think it advisable to telegraph to Dinapore to detach two hundred Europeans and two guns from Dinapore, to occupy Chupra. The Mohurrum will have terminated. Should the Shekawattee battalion be considered available, it might be steamed up from Calcutta, and joined to the detachment of Europeans from Dinapore, for preserving north-western frontiers of Bengal from further encroachments. This suggestion is respectfully submitted to his Excellency.

R. NAPIER, *Colonel*,
Military Secretary.

The Commander-in-Chief to Sir J. Outram.

(Telegraphic.)   *Calcutta, 5th Sept.* 1857.

With reference to your telegram of the 31st August, proposing to collect at Chupra a detachment 10th Regiment and the Shekawattee battalion, it has been proposed, in lieu of the Shekawattee battalion, which it is not considered advisable to move, that the 17th Madras Native Infantry, now on its way up the river, should be stopped at Dinapore, and that 300 of her Majesty's 10th Regiment, and two of the 9-pounder guns, should be held in readiness to move along with the Madras Native Infantry, towards Segowlee, on the arrival at that place of 1,000 Goorkhas.

2. The whole to form one body at Segowlee, for the same object which you proposed to attain by placing a force at Chupra. Segowlee, however, appears to me very distant from any support. Do you approve of this? and how would it affect your arrangements?

3. With reference to your telegram on the supply of rifle ammunition, arrangements have been made to send up the river immediately to Allahabad $4\frac{1}{2}$ lakhs (4,50,000 rounds).

Sir J. Outram to the Commander-in-Chief.

(Telegraphic.)   *Allahabad, 5th Sept.* 1857.

Prior to the receipt of your Excellency's message of this date, regarding arrangements for Chupra, I had telegraphed to Colonel Gordon, and written to the Lieutenant-Governor as follows: " The column consisting of "her Majesty's 53rd Regiment, the 27th Madras Native "Infantry, and troop of Horse Artillery, now marching "up the trunk road, were at Bagoda on the 2nd Sep-

"tember. When the column reaches Benares, Colonel
"Gordon is authorized to employ it in communication
"with the Lieutenant-Governor, on any expedition for
"restoring the tranquillity of the Central Provinces."
As the 17th Madras Native Infantry must now be close
to Benares, it would be a pity to send it down to Chupra,
where the detachment of her Majesty's 10th Regiment,
from Dinapore, will answer for the present; and Benares
appears to be the most convenient position to operate
generally.

*Sir J. Outram to Mr. Hamilton, Opium Agent,
Ghazeepore.*

Below Allahabad, 1st *Sept.* 1857.

Your letter of 30th ultimo reached me yesterday at
Mirzapore, whence I despatched a telegram to the
Commander-in-Chief, of which I enclose a copy.* Be
so kind as to send it on to the authorities at Dinapore,
and to Mr. Samuells, to prepare them for the orders
likely to be sent to them.

Mr. Tucker, at Mirzapore, informs me that Koer
Sing is supposed to be at a place some 24 miles from
Mirzapore, with 3,000 or 4,000 followers; his object not
known. I suppose he is trying to make off into Oude.
I could not delay the troops now following up the river
by sending any to hunt after Koer Sing, which most
likely would prove but a wild goose chase. My object
is to push them on to Cawnpore without delay, and
thence to Lucknow. The Goorkhas will, I trust, suffice
for Azimghur, and possibly may yet be induced to occupy
Goruckpore.

---

* Already given under date 31st August.

Sir J. Outram to Military Secretary to the Governor-General.

Allahabad, 2nd September, 1857.

You may glean from the enclosed some information worth communicating to the Governor-General. I have no time to prepare a synopsis, and all my staff are employed. General Neill's account of our gallant allies the sweepers, headed by the hangman, will amuse his Lordship. Another letter from Cawnpore dated 31st, from a good source. Captain Barrow says, "*Lucknow is all right, and in good spirits. We shall meet opposition on the road; but if we take lots of heavy guns, they won't stand long.*" I have just received the Governor-General's message of the 31st, instructing me to denounce vengeance for any maltreatment our people may suffer at the hands of the rebels. My message to General Havelock of the 28th ultimo will show that I had in some measure anticipated his Lordship's instructions. I may perhaps issue a more ship-shape proclamation when I reach Cawnpore.

See how I am denounced for my supposed shortcomings in the accompanying anonymous missive. The Governor-General is aware that I was as much vexed at the detention of the troops as the writer could be.

Sir J. Outram to Mr. Secretary Edmonstone.

Allahabad, 2nd Septemler, 1857.

I am disappointed at no notice having been taken of the letter I addressed to you before leaving Calcutta, on Persian affairs; but I can easily imagine that other and more important matters occupy the attention of Government for the present.

I hear from Cawnpore to-day that Lucknow is all

right, and in good spirits. I have little doubt we shall be in time to relieve them. The 90th will be here to-day I trust, and I hope to join Havelock on the 9th.

General Neill reports yesterday that Mr. Probyn, of Futtehghur, wife and children, and Mr. Edwards, Collector of Budaon, have been sent in safe and well, by Hurdée Bux, of Dhurrenepore.

Sir J. Outram to Martin Gubbins, Esquire, Lucknow.

Allahabad, 2nd September, 1857.

I arrived here last night with, and am followed by reinforcements, all of which will be here in the course of to-day or to-morrow, and I hope I shall be with General Havelock on the 9th or 10th at farthest, when no time will be lost in pushing on to Lucknow.

The rebels have given out that you are negotiating for terms, which I know to be a lie; for what terms could be relied on after the Cawnpore atrocities? Do not scruple to expend the Government treasure in securing supplies, or in any other manner calculated to benefit the garrison. No expenditure on this account would be grudged by Government. I have proclaimed that for every defenceless Christian, man, woman, or child, maltreated by the rebels in Oude, a noble shall be hanged. But you will not allow any such to get into their hands. How I long to greet you all; please God I shall do so before many days have passed.

Sir J. Outram to General Havelock.

Allahabad, 2nd September, 1857.

I arrived at this place late last night with a detachment of the 90th; but the rest of the troops, which sailed from Benares on the same day, have not yet come in sight. I trust, however, they will be here to-day; and, if so, we shall be off to join you on the 4th or 5th at latest. I was unable to bring away more troops from Chunar or Mirzapore, as Koer Sing and his rebels are hovering in that neighbourhood; so only the 90th and 5th, which I mentioned, will be with me; but I shall bring on Eyre's battery instead of the 3rd Company 5th Battalion from this place. You could not have a more efficient battery, only unfortunately its horses have not yet joined. I shall take on, however, bullocks for two batteries. I hope you have prepared skins, bamboos, and ropes, for crossing the nullahs on our way to Lucknow; for I suppose all the bridges will be broken down.

The Officer commanding at Allahabad to the Commander-in-Chief.

(Telegraphic.) *Allahabad, 2nd Sept.* 1857, 11.15 *a.m.*

Major-General Outram and ninety men of the 90th Foot arrived at Allahabad on the evening of the 1st September.

I beg to report having sent the *Jumna* steamer up the Jumna, to look after the party of the Dinapore mutineers, whom I referred to in my telegram of the 20th ultimo. It is reported that these mutineers intend crossing the Jumna, and making for the trunk road, not far from Cawnpore. This report requires confirmation.

Sir J. Outram to the Commander-in-Chief.

(Telegraphic.) *Allahabad, 2nd Sept.* 1857, 5.48 *a.m.*

In message of the 31st August, regarding Enfield ammunition, I was guided by Colonel O'Brien's message. That officer subsequently received a supply of

Enfield cartridges; and anxiety on that head is removed, as regards our present supply. Ample provision will, doubtless, be made by your Excellency for future demands here.

Sir J. Outram to Mr. Mangles, Chairman of the Court of Directors.

Allahabad, 3rd *Sept.* 1857.

I arrived here on the evening of the 1st instant, and had hoped to be overtaken yesterday by the troops which were to follow in two hours after I sailed from Benares on the morning of the 3rd; but they have not yet (8 A.M.) made their appearance. I hope they will arrive in the course of the day; and in the meantime everything is prepared for their onward march. I trust I shall join Havelock at Cawnpore by the 10th or 11th, and that then no time will be lost in forcing our way to Lucknow, and relieving the garrison, as I confidently rely on doing.

We have no direct accounts thence, but I am pretty sure they are not in such stress as represented—even to the length, it is said, of negotiating for terms!!—reports set about by the rebels, no doubt. Indeed, an officer likely to be well informed writes from Cawnpore on the 31st ultimo, "Lucknow is all right and in good spirits." The amount of reinforcements I am taking on to General Havelock, and his confidence that they will suffice, you will gather from the enclosed copies of telegraph messages which have lately passed between us. In coming up the river I have made every disposition the means at my command permitted for the security of the principal stations bordering thereon; and I trust they will suffice so far; but of course I could not provide military means for ridding the districts of the gaol-birds and budmashes let loose on the country by the blundering of the authorities at Dinapore. I, however, suggested to the civil authorities to augment their police, and to impress on the zemindars, &c., that *they* would be held responsible for keeping the peace within their own limits. By such means Behar and Tirhoot ought to be kept tolerably quiet, until troops can be released from their more pressing duties in advance. The abandonment of Goruckpore by the Goorkhas was a sad mistake, and has encouraged an invasion in that quarter from Oude, which would never otherwise have been attempted. I trust, however, that the evil will not spread farther in that direction, and that the Goorkhas may yet be induced to resume their position at Goruckpore for the present, in addition to Azimghur and Jaunpore, which they are now holding with great advantage—securing those districts from incursions from Oude. I trust my next will be from Lucknow, and my object in writing this hasty note, which I am told will be in time for the mail, is to relieve you from the anxiety which the critical position of those at Lucknow must naturally inspire. I rely on their holding out till we can advance, and in that case that we shall succeed.

Sir J. Outram to Mr. Secretary Edmonstone.

Allahabad, 3rd Sept. 1857.

I have the honour to transmit, for the information of the Right Honourable the Governor-General in Council, translation of a letter which I have addressed to each of the following Rajahs:—

  Rajah Maun Sing, of Shahgunge,
  Rajah Madoo Sing, of Ramnuggur,
  Baboo Roostun Sahah, of Deyrah,—

which I trust will meet with his Lordship's approval. All the above-named Rajahs have displayed a friendly spirit in protecting British interests.

(Translation referred to above.)

I have heard of your having during the late mutiny at Fyzabad, &c. &c., saved the lives of several British officers, their wives, and children. With this conduct on your part I have been much pleased; and I cannot but feel convinced that you will by your future conduct continue to prove your fidelity to the British Government. Rest assured that the British Government is ready to reward its faithful subjects, and that I shall have much pleasure in bringing to its notice any act on your part, during the present disturbances, which may tend to prove that you are a sincere well-wisher to the State.

It cannot be hidden from you that the British Government will soon quell this rebellion. Troops in great numbers are on their way from Europe, and will shortly arrive, before whose overwhelming power the cowardly rebels will be annihilated. But, although the British Government will punish with the utmost rigour those who have dared to rebel against the State, it will always have pleasure in rewarding those of its subjects who, notwithstanding the evil examples by which they are surrounded, hesitate not to show their staunch fidelity to the British Government, and amongst such I hope to reckon yourself.

I am now on my way to Cawnpore and Lucknow, and shall be happy to receive any communication from you expressive of your readiness to obey the orders I may think it necessary to send you.

Sir J. Outram to the Lieutenant-Governor, Central Provinces.

Allahabad, 4th September, 1857.

* * * I go on to-morrow night. I trust we shall all be at Cawnpore by the 11th; and as I have requested Havelock to have everything prepared for crossing the river, I hope little delay will occur in our advance on Lucknow. The *Jumna* went up the Ganges the day before yesterday to cut off the mutineers said to be contemplating crossing at Royapore. She returned yesterday, the mutineers having (it is supposed) gone on to cross higher up at a point which the steamer could not reach.

The telegraphic communication with Cawnpore has been interrupted for the last two days. But this is supposed to be merely accidental, as the dâks come in regularly, and Havelock's sick and wounded arrived yesterday without having encountered any obstacle on the way. I have every confidence in our making our way to Lucknow in ample time to save the garrison.

I enclose translations of letters I have addressed to Maun Sing and others who protected our people, which I hope you will approve, as well as of my denunciation against such as may maltreat man, woman, or child. Excuse a hasty chit.

General Havelock to Sir James Outram.

Cawnpore, 4th September, 1857.

I had this morning the pleasure of receiving yours of the 2nd instant, from Allahabad.

As you are so soon to be here, it is needless I should say much of the state of affairs. The cholera has almost left us; and my soldiers have benefited much by the repose I have been enabled to give them here. When we get up the 5th and 90th, I trust an advance on Lucknow will not be a difficult operation; but I consider that it can only be undertaken with the view of the relief of the gallant and enduring garrison. The reconquest of the province would require a full division of British troops.

By my latest accounts from Lucknow, the garrison was holding its own. They had repulsed the last attack with great slaughter, and their foes were said to be much discouraged. They had provisions also, and I entertain great hopes we shall yet be able to get them out of their scrape. But it is most desirable to increase the force here as much as possible; for, as soon as we move towards Lucknow, our foes will organize some menacing movement on Cawnpore to disturb our attention.

It would be advisable that some three lakhs of rupees should be sent us with the troops, as we are in want of money. Three or four assistant-surgeons also *urgently* required. I telegraphed to Colonel Otter to send up shafts for my elephant guns, of a pattern they have at Allahabad, and which is better than that we have here. I should like to have them as speedily as possible; also two 8-inch howitzers, to complete the heavy guns I am equipping for the field. About the last I wrote to Colonel O'Brien. It would be well—indeed, most desirable—if the winter clothing of all the troops here should be sent up immediately.

By my latest accounts, the Bunnee Bridge was untouched. But, at all events, Captain Crommelin will carry on with us bamboos, ropes, &c., and some canal boats on hackeries, which he thinks will suffice to cross the nullahs.

The enemy are in force at Mungulwar; but Oonao and Busseerut-gunge, where I beat them before, as well as Nuwabgunge, are said to be unoccupied.

Sir J. Outram to Henry Tucker, Esq., Commissioner, Benares.

Allahabad, 5th September.

I return the enclosed with thanks. * * *

Unless the Goorkhas can be induced to recover Goruckpore, I do not see how else the Nazim, now in possession there, is to be kicked out, for no troops can be spared; not at least until the Madrassees, now coming up the trunk road, reach Benares. *They* might be available for that duty, perhaps. They were at Bagoda on the 2nd, and were to halt there one day for baggage. I shall send Colonel Gordon authority to make use of that brigade should the Lieutenant-Governor think the recovery of Goruckpore the most important duty on which it can be occupied.

Sir J. Outram to the Commander-in-Chief.
Allahabad, 5th September, 1857.

On the day before yesterday, the steamer and flat conveying Major Eyre's battery and portion of 5th Fusiliers arrived. All day yesterday was occupied in landing and putting together the guns; and at 2 A.M. this morning, a detachment, consisting of 611 infantry (*i.e.* 420 5th Fusiliers, 178 64th, and 13 of 84th), with Major Eyre's battery (72), marched towards Cawnpore, taking with them two 8-inch howitzers, which General Havelock had applied for, two lakhs of treasure, engineer tools and stores, &c. &c. Yesterday the *Mirzapore* arrived with H.M.'s 90th Regiment, with which I march to-night, 679 strong (leaving 68 sick); and I expect a company of the 78th from Benares (89 strong), which also I propose taking on. This will give General Havelock a reinforcement of 1,377 infantry and a field battery; ample, with what he has, to effect our objects at Lucknow, of which garrison we receive favourable reports, ensuring their being able to hold out till we arrive. My detachments will, I hope, join Havelock on the 11th and 12th; and no time, I trust, will be lost in crossing the river and pushing on to Lucknow, as I have requested General Havelock to have everything prepared in the meantime.

In order to reinforce General Havelock to as nearly the strength he called for as I can, I am obliged to weaken this garrison for the present somewhat below the 500 men at which it was ordered to be maintained. Thus:—

Effective European bayonets and artillery	239
Convalescents	100
Seamen (Europeans)	20
In Camp—Sikhs	100

But the first detachment of 500 European troops, which left Calcutta on the 28th ultimo, will be here on the evening of the 11th instant. And, after that, successive detachments will arrive daily. Thus the garrison will be at the reduced strength above mentioned only five days. Mr. Chester, the Commissioner, apprehends no danger whatever; he knows of no insurgents likely to appear in this quarter; and he is satisfied that the mere appearance of troops pressing forward, as they are now doing, would of itself prevent any hostile attempt.

Under these circumstances, I trust your Excellency will approve my arrangements.

The Madras regiment coming up the river must be now at or very near Benares, where it will remain in garrison for the present. And I have authorized Colonel Gordon, commanding at Benares, to make use also of the Madras brigade coming up the trunk road in recovering Goruckpore, or any other measure the Lieutenant-Governor may consider of primary necessity, which will not occupy it at any distance beyond easy recall, if necessary.

The Naval Brigade will soon be here, and I am anxious to submit for your Excellency's consideration, whether it would not be best, for the present at least, to employ it in garrisoning Allahabad; thereby releasing some 600 or 800 infantry, which by that time would be available here—consisting of detachments of the various regiments in advance.

The enclosed copy of a letter from the Commissary of Ordnance will show your Excellency that we can hardly possibly provide the means of transporting 68-pounders by land, independent of the objection that their transport would cut up and greatly destroy the trunk road.

I communicated to your Excellency that I had furnished Colonel Gordon, at Benares, with a requisition for two of the 68-pounders to be landed there (where they would be most usefully placed in position on the new works), subject, of course, to your Excellency's approval.

Sir J. Outram to General Havelock.

Allahabad, 5th September, 1857.

It took till late last night to get Eyre's battery all landed, and his guns remounted; but they were all ready to march at three this morning, when the following detachment, under Major Simmons, of the 5th Fusiliers, started for Mooftee, a distance of thirteen miles (the first regular march), with orders to push on by the following stages:—

2nd march	Kussia	15½ miles	7th September.
3rd ,,	Kulonghon	22½ ,,	8th ,,
4th ,,	Futtehpore	24½ ,,	9th ,,
5th ,,	Aong	23½ ,,	10th ,,
6th ,,	Cawnpore	28 ,,	11th ,,

where Eyre would be on the morning of the 11th, unless he should find his men knocking up (foot-sore), in which case he would report to you, and you would order him to lighten his marches or otherwise, as you thought proper, influenced, as your orders doubtless would be, by the state of the Lucknow garrison, which, if you are certain it can hold out, may admit of more leisurely movement. To-night I follow with the 90th, taking the same marches, so as to join you on the 12th. And I hope by that time you will be pretty well prepared for crossing the river. Simmons's detachment consists of,—

Eyre's battery (provided with double bullock establishment)	72 men.
5th Fusiliers	420 ,,
64th Regiment	178 ,,
84th Regiment	13 ,,
Total	683 ,,

I myself take on the 90th (678 rank and file), and I expect a company of the 78th from Benares (87 rank and file) to accompany us; giving a total of 1,448 men, with which, and what you already have, you can, I am sure, effect your great object, and thus, in addition to the triumphs you have already achieved, add the crowning glory of rescuing our beleaguered countrymen at Lucknow.

I accompany you in my capacity of Commissioner, but I shall be too glad to serve under you as volunteer, and I trust you will not scruple to give me work.

Kind regards to your son. The sick and wounded (who arrived the day before yesterday) speak of him as a perfect hero.

P.S.—I am bringing you as many bullock mussucks for rafts as I can get. Simmons has two lakhs of rupees for you; also two 8-inch mortars, 9-pounders, and Enfield rifle ammunition.

Sir J. Outram to Lieutenant-Governor, Central Provinces.

Allahabad, 5th September, 1857.

* * * In my message of to-day to Colonel Gordon I limited somewhat the operations of the Madras column, by restricting them to such as "would not remove it too far beyond reach of recall in case of its being required for operations with the column advanced towards the North-West Provinces;" but, on further consideration, it appears to me that no operations in the North-West Provinces can be of more importance than restoring order in the districts bordering on Bengal. And as we must look to European troops chiefly for carrying out our objects west of Allahabad, the Madras troops could not be more beneficially occupied than in the districts eastward of that point. I think, therefore, we may best promote the public interests by devoting the whole of the Madras troops to that duty.

I shall therefore so far modify my message to Colonel Gordon, as to omit the proviso above quoted; and pray tell him to expunge all the message of to-day except the previous portion, viz., " the column consisting of her Majesty's 53rd, the 27th Madras Native Infantry, and troop of Madras Horse Artillery, now marching up the trunk road, were at Bagoda on the 2nd September. When the column reaches Benares, Colonel Gordon is authorized to employ it, in communication with the Lieutenant-Governor, on any expedition for restoring the tranquillity of the Central Provinces."

In addition to his garrison, Colonel Gordon has also Major Cotter's battery and the other Madras regiment. He will thus have a respectable force, in conjunction with the Goorkhas, to carry out your wishes.

Sir J. Outram to General Havelock, Camp, Mooftee.

Ke Poonwa, 6th September.

I arrived here with the 90th this evening, and to-day the other column is a march in advance at Kussia. The 90th having been cooped up on board ship and in river boats for five months past, is quite unequal to double marches, I find, a very large proportion being knocked up by this first march of fourteen miles. And certainly, if they have to undergo the forced (double) marches I proposed, but few of them would be fit for work when we reach Cawnpore. As, therefore, we have such favourable accounts of the Lucknow garrison (there can be no doubt, I think, of their ability to hold out as long as need be), and it being of importance you should receive your reinforcements in an efficient state, I propose, unless I hear from you that quicker movement is indispensable, or at least desirable, to pursue the ordinary ten marches to Cawnpore, which will delay this detachment's arrival at Cawnpore till the 15th, instead of the 11th, as I proposed, Major Simmons's column being with you the previous day. Pray let me hear from you if this will do. Should you think our earlier presence necessary, I will endeavour to push on quicker, though confident that many will be disabled by longer marches who otherwise would reach you in an efficient state.

Sir J. Outram to General Havelock.

Camp, 6th September.

Since I wrote to you just now, it has occurred to me to suggest that we should take tents, if possible, for the Europeans, for exposure in September in Oude is more deadly than at any other season. We have a good many elephants with us, and I have just sent back an order to Allahabad for *all* that can be spared to be sent after us. They are the best " carriage ;" but we may also be able to get carts across the river ; if so, there is no reason why we should not carry every requisite with us to secure the comfort of the troops, for the Lucknow garrison appears to be so secure, as to allow of our advancing as leisurely as we please. Pray tell me whether you think it will be possible to cross over sufficient carriage to provide tents, &c., for the Europeans on the march to Lucknow.

Sir J. Outram to Major Simmons, Camp, Mooftee.

Ke Poonwa, 6th September.

From the way the first march of fourteen miles has told on the 90th, it is very evident that they will be unequal to double marches for some time to come. Cooped up as they have been five months on shipboard and in river boats, of course they more easily knock up than old hands. And as the accounts we have of late received of the state of the garrison at Lucknow render it very certain they can hold out a much longer time than would be required by us to get to them leisurely, I have written to Havelock that we shall proceed by regular marches, instead of the double stages I had proposed, unless we should learn from him that a more rapid advance is necessary.

Unless, therefore, you should receive any requisition from Havelock to push on by forced marches, I request you will take the following stages instead of those I previously put down; viz., from your present camp (Kussia) to Synee (11 miles)—Kulonghon ($11\frac{1}{2}$)—Thurriaroon (13)—Futtehpore ($11\frac{1}{2}$)—Malwa ($11\frac{1}{2}$)—Aong (13)—Maharajpore (14)—Cawnpore (14); or as near to those (the usual) stages as convenient to you.

Let me hear occasionally how you get on, by the dâk which passes through our camps.

General Havelock to Sir James Outram.

Cawnpore, 6th September, 1857.

I had the pleasure this morning of receiving yours of the 5th instant, and in the hope that this may perhaps find you still at Allahabad, I write to say I fear it will not, in the present state of the weather, be possible for either column to make the marches you have designated without the certainty of throwing a great number of men into hospital, and rendering inevitable a halt to refresh after arrival here. I do not think, in the present heats, they will be able to accomplish more than fifteen miles daily. I have telegraphed Colonel O'Brien to this effect, requesting him to send the substance of my telegram on to Major Simmons by mounted express.

The guns I require are 8-inch howitzers, *not* mortars, with which last I am supplied. I hope the howitzers can be sent on with your column, and I should wish to have 800 Enfield rifles by the same opportunity. The two last will be welcome. Our commissariat is making large purchases here. My latest accounts give me reason to hope that Colonel Inglis will be able to hold out until we arrive, since from some cause the siege is not pressed with the same ardour as before.

If you would prefer a bungalow to being under canvas whilst here, I will tell Colonel Tytler to select a good one for you, as they have not all been destroyed during the late troubles.

Hoping soon to see you, I remain, &c.

P.S.—There are in the Fort of Asota, fourteen miles nearly due south of Futtehpore, some English refugees from Banda, who write for help, and whom it would be desirable to assist if it would not peril the success of our main enterprise at Lucknow.

The Officer Commanding at Allahabad to the Commander-in-Chief.

(Telegraphic.) *Allahabad, 6th September,* 1857, 5 P.M.

* * * * The troops sent from this, under General Outram's orders, reduce the strength of this garrison to 10 officers and 235 effective European soldiers. There are, however, the following supplementary aids speedily to be had :—convalescents from the sick sent from Cawnpore; those left by the troops proceeding up country ; and the armed steamer *Jumna*. General Outram has further ordered the detachment of the 90th coming from Raneegunge to be detained here until further orders. A detailed report will be sent by post tomorrow.

The Commander-in-Chief to Sir J. Outram.

Calcutta, 5th September, 1857.

I have been much bothered with fever for some days, and this, with the amount of detail work to be got through daily, has prevented me writing.

I have had the pleasure to receive your letter of the 29th ultimo, with copies of one telegram to Havelock, dated 28th, and one to myself of the 25th ultimo. I showed these papers to the Governor-General, and he expressed himself in the warmest terms of admiration of your truly handsome and generous proposal to Havelock, to accompany him in his movement upon Lucknow in your capacity as Commissioner, and as a volunteer. God grant you may succeed.

I have sent you four and a half lakhs of rifle ammunition, all of that kind made up in Calcutta. We have materiel in store for four lakhs, but none made up, and our means only enable us to make up about 80,000 weekly. Lord Canning has begged that a supply may be sent to us, by the overland route, in sufficient quantity to meet our wants until a supply can arrive by sailing ship round the Cape.

The column under Colonel Fisher, Madras Infantry, has been

retarded in its march by the heavy rains, the difficulty of getting his baggage and supplies over the rivers, and his cattle getting sickly. A detachment of the Military Train Corps has arrived here from China; it is now formed into a body of mounted men, to act as cavalry, the strength of the detachment about 185, 120 of whom have served in the cavalry. They are to be mounted with horses of the 8th Madras Light Cavalry, which have been sent here, the men of the corps having refused to embark for Bengal. I hope to have this nice detachment, mounted on these horses, armed and suitably equipped, and in movement from Rancegunge within a week from the present date, accompanied by two guns of Madras Horse Artillery, and a company of Madras Sappers.

The Government are afraid of moving the Shekawattee regiment from their present position.

I should be glad to hear your opinion as to the proposed employment of the 17th Madras Infantry, with a detachment of 300 men of her Majesty's 10th, and two guns from Dinapore, in the direction of Segowlee. Proposals may be made here, but the disposal and employment of the troops under your orders must be ordered and arranged by yourself. The Governor-General is anxious, like yourself, about that district; and I will beg you to have the kindness to give the directions you may think most advisable for carrying out his wishes for affording it protection.

We expect, in eight or ten days, two companies from China of the Royal Artillery. I shall endeavour to get them to Allahabad, where are two or three 9-pounder batteries, complete as to gun and carriages, but not, I believe, with extra waggons.

Kind regards to Havelock and Napier.

Sir J. Outram to the Commander-in-Chief.

Camp, Kussia, 7th September.

I informed your Excellency that I purposed pushing on to Cawnpore in six marches, instead of the usual ten; but the 90th suffered so much in their first (the usual) march of about fourteen miles yesterday, as you will observe from the enclosed note from the superintending surgeon (and I regret to say two men died of apoplexy last night—three in all), that I was obliged to resolve on making the regular stages, and accordingly informed General Havelock so yesterday. *All* the reinforcements will therefore only be assembled at Cawnpore on the 15th instead of the 11th instant as I had proposed.

This delay is of the less consequence, as we are well assured the Lucknow garrison is quite able to hold its own until we get there, however leisurely we may advance. They have gained great successes over the enemy of late, and replenished their provisions; and their assailants are tiring out, getting dispirited, and going off to their homes in great numbers.

Our first march from Allahabad yesterday was by moonlight. We arrived at our ground before daylight, and the men were kept to their tents all day; so the sun had nothing to do with the apoplectic cases above alluded to. The air was peculiarly heavy both night and day, but we had a drenching shower during our march this morning, which has cleared the atmosphere, and we certainly have benefited by the change. Though to-day's march was longer than yesterday's, the men stood it better. The colonel reports:—"The men who fell out to-day averaged twelve per company, but many afterwards joined, and limped along." The remaining marches are shorter.

Sir J. Outram to General Havelock.

Camp, Kussia, 7th September.

* * * The company of the 78th, which was at Benares, overtook us here by bullock train.

With reference to the allusion in your note received yesterday to the "reconquest" of Oude, I should have informed you, but thought you knew, that our present object is merely to withdraw the garrison, after forming a provisional government of influential inhabitants to maintain the city on behalf of the British Government, until we can conveniently reoccupy it. *But say nothing of this*, as it is an object to make believe that we shall hold the city with British troops, until we have effected our arrangement.

[On the 25th August, Brigadier Inglis forwarded to General Havelock a duplicate of the urgent letter he had addressed to him on the 16th, fearing lest the original might have miscarried. As a further protection against accidents he, at the same time, sent a copy to Lieutenant-Colonel O'Brien, which that officer lost no time in telegraphing to Calcutta. A portion of Brigadier Inglis's letter has already been given in General Havelock's telegram of the 23rd August (*vide antea*, p. 224). But as the General's telegram does not communicate the Brigadier's entire letter as telegraphed by Lieutenant-Colonel O'Brien, the whole of the latter officer's telegram is here reproduced.]

Lieutenant-Colonel O'Brien to the Governor-General and the Commander-in-Chief.

(Telegraphic.) *Allahabad, 9th September,* 1857, 5.10 P.M.

Lucknow, 25th August, from Colonel Inglis, commanding at Lucknow :—

"Lest my letter of the 16th of August should have miscarried, I send herewith a duplicate of its contents; viz., 'A note from Colonel Tytler to Mr. Gubbins reached last night, dated Mungulwar, the 4th instant, the latter paragraph of which is as follows:—" You must aid us in every way, even to cutting your way out, if we cannot force our way in. We have only a small force."'

"This has caused me much uneasiness, as it is quite impossible, with my weak and shattered force, that I can leave my defences. You must bear in mind how I am hampered; that I have upwards of 120 sick and wounded, and at the least 22 women and 130 children, and no carriage of any kind, and besides sacrificing twenty-three lakhs of treasure, and about thirty guns of sorts. In consequence of the news, I shall soon put the force on half rations. Our provisions will last us till the 10th September. If you hope to save this force, no time must be lost in pushing forward. We are daily attacked by the enemy, who are within a few yards of our defences; their mines have already weakened our post, and I have every reason to believe they are carrying on others; their 18-pounders are within 150 yards off. Some of their batteries are in position, and from our inability to form working parties, we cannot reply to them. The damage done hourly is very great. My strength is now in Europeans 350, and about 300 natives, and the men dreadfully harassed; and owing to part of the Residency having been brought down by round shot, many are without shelter. Our native force, having been assured, on Colonel Tytler's authority, of your near approach some twenty days ago, are naturally losing confidence; and if they leave us, I do not see how the defences are to be manned. Since the above was written, the enemy have sprung another mine, which has given us a great deal of trouble, and has caused us some loss.

"I trust that you will lose no time in coming to our assistance, regardless of the statements contained in any letters from Mr. Gubbins. Military men are unanimous regarding our case. We have had no letter from you of a later date than the 4th; and since the 18th the enemy have most alarming reports, too, of the disaffection and plots of our troops inside, who are wavering in their fidelity, owing to your return across the Ganges."—J. INGLIS, *Colonel Commanding at Lucknow, to General Havelock, commanding relieving force.*

The cossid reported to Lieutenant-Colonel O'Brien that he was detained in Lucknow, nine days after he left the Baillie Guard, on suspicion; that the garrison was fighting well up to the 4th September, the day he left Lucknow; that Rajah Maun Sing, who had gone to Lucknow, had returned to his place, Shahgunge, near Fyzabad; that the Rajah had not acted against the garrison; and that a man from camp was making percussion caps for the rebels. But this does not seem possible; if any caps were attempted to be made, they must be a wretched imitation.

General Havelock to Sir J. Outram.

Cawnpore, 8*th September,* 1857.

I send by express the latest intelligence from Colonel Inglis. His danger appears to be pressing, and would be an argument for your coming on rapidly; but it is vain so to press the troops as to render them all inefficient on arrival here, or kill numbers of them. To create a diversion in favour of Inglis is of the utmost importance. Your assurances to Maun Sing that Sir Henry Lawrence's promise would be fulfilled, might decide him to act against the rebels, and I could get it conveyed to him by messengers if you thought proper to send it me written small. The enemy are increasing their force in men and guns on the opposite bank; but I will make every preparation for passing, and on your joining me think I could well turn them out of their position at Mungulwar, and we might then advance at a good pace towards Lucknow.

The telegraph wire between this and Allahabad is again cut.

(Enclosure.)

Colonel Inglis to General Havelock.

Lucknow, 1*st September.*

Your letter of the 24th has duly reached me, in reply to mine of the 16th ultimo.* I regret your inability to advance at present to our

* " This night (August 28) we learnt, by a letter from General Havelock, dated Cawnpore, the 24th instant, that we had no hope of being relieved for another twenty-five days."—*The Defence of Lucknow,* by A Staff Officer: Smith, Elder and Co., London, 1858.

relief, but in consequence of your letter I have reduced the rations, and with this arrangement, and our great diminution in numbers from casualties, I trust to be able to hold out from the 20th to 25th instant. Some stores we have been out of for the last fifteen days, and many others will be expended before the above date. I must be frank, and tell you that my force is daily diminishing from the enemy's musketry fire, and our defences grow weaker daily. Should the enemy make any determined efforts to storm this place, I shall find it difficult to repulse them, owing to my paucity in numbers, and the weak and harassed state of my force. Our loss since the commencement of hostilities here has been, in Europeans alone, upwards of 300. We are continually harassed in countermining the enemy, who have above twenty guns in position—many of them heavy ones.

Any advance of yours towards this place will act beneficially in our favour, and greatly inspirit the native part of my garrison, who hitherto have behaved like faithful and good soldiers.

If you can possibly give me any intelligence of your intended advance pray do so by letter. Give the bearer the pass-word "Agra," and ask him to give it to me in person. Oblige by forwarding a copy of this letter to the Governor-General.

I have prohibited the civil authorities from corresponding with your camp.

P.S.—Copy of this sent to the commanding officer at Allahabad for information and guidance, with the further remark that Maun Sing, who was promised a jagheer of two lakhs, conditionally on his affording no assistance to the rebels, is reported to be still holding aloof; and it is by no means impossible [illegible] that if he is assured [illegible] to the relief [illegible] that Sir Henry Lawrence's promise shall be confirmed by Government, he may be induced to afford us active help. His followers are estimated at 6,000 in number.

Sir J. Outram to the Commander-in-Chief.

(Telegraphic.)

Camp, Kulonghon, 9th September, 1857.

General Havelock has sent me a note, received by him from Colonel Inglis, yesterday, dated Lucknow, 1st September, in which he says he is hard pressed, and calculates that his provisions will only last till the 28th. But the favourable reports received at Cawnpore, on the 6th, through sources considered reliable, lead to the hope that the garrison had really had the success reported after the date of Colonel Inglis's letter; for the sowars of Cawnpore receive communications from friends in the city of Lucknow in as many hours as a cossid might take days in passing out of the closely watched garrison, and, secretly, through the intermediate country. The successes I referred to were telegraphed direct to your Excellency by General Havelock. I have no doubt we shall force our way to Lucknow by the 28th; but, if delayed, our then near approach will, I trust, encourage the garrison to hold out; if not, perhaps their friends in the city will secretly supply their wants. We are getting on better, as the 90th grow more accustomed to their shore legs. Try to expedite the march of the 12th Cavalry, to overtake us, as much as you can.

Sir J. Outram to General Havelock.

Camp, Kulonghon, 9th September.

I received your express of yesterday, with copy of Colonel Inglis's note from Lucknow, 1st September, at midnight.

I agree with you that to press on quicker than by the ordinary marches would disable too many soldiers. As it is, the 90th sick list was forty yesterday (and, as I told you, three died the day before), besides seventy we left at Allahabad. Simmons informs me he has lost two men. If, however, you can have the bridge for crossing the river prepared, and have established your position on the opposite side before we join you on the 15th, no time will be lost, as we should cross at once. Simmons's column, being at Cawnpore on the 14th, would be all over by the morning of the 15th; and *we* should be the same by next morning. Thus we should reach Lucknow before the time specified by Colonel Inglis expires; though I trust he could hold out longer. The mere fact of your crossing the river would, as Colonel

Inglis says, give some relief to his garrison by drawing out the main force of the rebels to oppose our advance. I enclose a letter for Maun Sing, transmitting copy of a previous one I wrote to him from Allahabad, which I hope you will be able to send to Colonel Inglis, to whom you will doubtless give every encouragement to hold out.

I yesterday had your note of the 6th instant, in which you express your wish that I should take on to you 800 Enfield rifles. When I got this note we were three marches from Allahabad, and Colonel O'Brien has not the means to afford an escort to send them after us. I regret I was not made aware of this want when at Allahabad.

It is two 8-inch *howitzers*, not mortars, we are bringing to you. I shall look after the refugees said to be at Assota from next camp.

Sir J. Outram to the Commander-in-Chief.
Camp, Kulonghon, 9th September.

I beg to enclose for your Excellency's information copies of a note I received last night from General Havelock, and of its enclosure from Colonel Inglis, commanding at Lucknow; also my reply of this morning to General Havelock. Native accounts from sources relied on at Cawnpore represent the position of the Lucknow garrison more favourably, and that their assailants are much dispirited by the springing of a mine which destroyed a house (and some 200 of its rebel inmates) that domineered over the Residency, disabling at the same time the two big guns which had most annoyed us. I hope this may be true, and that the occurrence took place after Colonel Inglis wrote; for though his letter had occupied eight days in being brought by stealth to Cawnpore, as many hours would not be employed by natives of the city in communicating with friends at Cawnpore. The report is, also, that the garrison had secured provisions.

At any rate I trust we shall force our way to Lucknow by the 28th, the limit Colonel Inglis specifies. Certainly so if General Havelock effect the passage of the river by the time we arrive at Cawnpore—a measure of no great difficulty, I think—with the artillery at his command, and some hundreds of European troops, to establish a position on the opposite bank, even *if* the enemy contest the passage, which I hardly expect. The following is the purport of the letter to Maun Sing which I forwarded to General Havelock. May I beg that your Excellency will communicate it to the Governor-General, as my official report through the Secretary (passing under flying seal through Mr. Grant's hands) will not reach so soon.

(Enclosure.)

To Rajah Maun Sing.

"I sent you a friendly letter by cossid from Allahabad, dated 2nd instant. In case that letter may not have reached you, I herewith forward a copy. Since it was written, I have been informed that Sir Henry Lawrence had made promises to you of high reward for your good faith to the British Government. As Sir Henry Lawrence is no more, and I am his successor as Chief Commissioner in Oude, I write to you my solemn pledge, as representative of the British Government, that whatever promises were made by Sir Henry Lawrence shall be fully recognized and strictly fulfilled by the British Government. I am on my way to Lucknow accompanied by a powerful army, with which I shall annihilate the rebels now beleaguering the British at that place; and I shall arrive there in a few days. But in the meantime I rely on your aiding the garrison by such means as may be in your power. If you cannot do so openly, at least prevent any of your troops joining the rebels; because, if they do, you will forfeit your claims on the British Government, and I shall have to treat *you* also as an enemy."

General Neill to Sir J. Outram.

Cawnpore, 9th September, 1857.

. . . . . Mr. Edwards informs me that the men-servants of Missur Byjinath, a banker of great wealth and much influence at Bareilly, have come to him to-day from their master. They describe the hostility, between Hindoos and Mahomedans, as very bitter. The former have taken up arms, and, in one fight, killed several hundreds of Khan Bahadur Khan's men, who are an ill-armed rabble. There are no regular troops in the province. Mr. Edwards says—in which I agree with him—that, if the Hindoos were encouraged by our people in authority, they would, doubtless, adopt more energetic measures for ridding themselves of their oppressors.

Captain Gowan and five other officers, who are in hiding with the Kearee Thakoor, offer to organize the Thakoor's troops, if they are authorized to draw money from bankers for this purpose, and receive some guarantee from here. I agree with Mr. Edwards that the present is a favourable opportunity for communicating with Captain Gowan and Byjinath, and that Government might be induced to authorize a sum up to 50,000 rupees being placed at Captain Gowan's disposal for the purpose mentioned. Indeed, so impressed am I with the very great advantage to our Government, of fostering and promoting bad blood between the two races, besides encouraging our friends and well-wishers, that, had I been in supreme command here, and you had not been appointed, I would have taken upon myself at once to have given the authority for the money, and asked for the sanction of Government afterwards. However, the matter is now in better hands, and will, no doubt, receive your every consideration.

I feel perfectly assured when you get up here, and into Oude, you will be able to effect a vast change for us in encouraging the well-disposed. I have heard nothing to-day, whether the General crosses before you come up, or when. I hope, however, all will be ready to start by the time the troops you are bringing reach this, or very soon afterwards. The sooner Lucknow is relieved, the sooner we shall be in a position to attack and dispose of others.

Sir J. Outram to General Havelock.

Camp, Kurreda, 10th September, 1857.

I ordered Simmons's column to halt at this ground, where I joined him this morning. My object was, to detach a couple of guns and 150 infantry against the Oude zemindars who have crossed over and commenced plundering, to the number of 400 men and two guns. We have got what appears good information of their whereabouts, fifteen miles nearly due north, and close to the river. As Major Eyre commands the party, he will succeed, if any one can, in discomfiting the scoundrels. A squadron of the 12th Irregulars, under Captain Johnson and your nephew, is to-day at our yesterday's encamping ground, and will rendezvous with Eyre to-night at a village equidistant from that place and this camp, and some four or five miles from the enemy's position.

The Europeans (100 of the 5th Fusiliers, and 50 of the 64th) will be all mounted on elephants, and I leave bullock train waggons here to bring them up after us, when they return from the dour. So they will not be exposed to much fatigue, and will overtake us before we reach Cawnpore.

To-morrow we all, with the above exception, march on together, and shall be with you on the date assigned for my last detachment, viz., 15th, though Simmons's column will not now reach you on the previous day as originally intended. It appears that there are no Christians detained at Assota, and the Cutwal of Futtehpore, who is now in camp, thus writes in explanation of the mistake :—

"I have been honoured with your Purwana, in the matter of there being three Christians at Assota. The case is this, they were neither Christians nor Europeans. Three men—Kulka, Sookareedun, and Aranjun—have been made prisoners by the Rajah of Assota, on the charge of murder: their relations said they would rescue them; they were, by order of the Cawnpore magistrate, sent to Cawnpore on the 4th instant."

Macnaghten has, however, sent to the Ranee of Assota to make sure.

If you have secured a position on the opposite side of the river, with preparation for crossing us over the moment we arrive, I should hope there can be no doubt you will be in time to relieve the Lucknow garrison, even if their utmost limit *is* the 28th.

Sir J. Outram to General Neill.
Camp, Kurreeon, 10*th September.*

I am in your debt two letters — the last, dated yesterday, and this instant received. I can only hastily thank you for them, as the dâk is waiting; but I am anxious no delay should occur in carrying out the measure you suggest, of opening communication with Captain Gowan, and authorizing him to draw money on Byjinath or other bankers for the purpose of organizing the Kearee Thakoor's troops as you propose. I will take upon myself to give authority to Captain Gowan to draw to the amount of 50,000 rupees to that end; and I beg you will give the requisite sanction on behalf of Government on my responsibility.

I do hope Havelock will be in possession of the opposite bank, with the means of crossing, by the time we arrive on the 15th, so that not a moment may be lost in our advance to Lucknow.

I have overtaken Major Simmons's column here, with a view to detach a party from it to disperse some Oude zemindaree rabble, who, with two guns, have crossed to this side, and are plundering in the Doab. But this makes only the difference, that we shall *all* reach Cawnpore on the 15th, instead of half of us on the previous day.

Sir J. Outram to Colonel O'Brien.
Camp, Thurriaroon, 11*th Sept.* 1857.

I received an express last night from Armstrong, stating that 700 men and four guns had crossed from

Oude, and were about to attack his post. I had heard of these fellows (about half the strength reported by Armstrong) having crossed the river at a point 15 miles due north of Khaga (on the Grand Trunk Road), their object being supposed to be the plunder of Hutgam Koss and Khaga; not likely they would attack any post where no plunder and only bullets were to be met. As it is of importance to disperse this body at once, I yesterday despatched against them a party of 150 Europeans (mounted on elephants) and two guns, under Major Eyre; and in the evening he was joined at Hutgam Koss by thirty of the 12th Irregulars, under Captain Johnson, from our yesterday's camp, where they had arrived in the morning. As the rebels could not have been above five miles from the point of rendezvous, I trust Eyre may have surprised and given a good account of them. If not, he is doubtless now following them up. This has necessarily detained us a day.

Simmons's column went on to Futtehpore this morning, taking on the company of the 78th; and I follow with the Europeans to-morrow. Eyre will overtake us by the time we reach Cawnpore. The 90th will be the better for this halt, their sick amounting to fifty-two. But though the Oude people may now be driven back, they would probably return shortly after this force passes on; or the Dinapore and Rewah rebels may cross the Jumna with a view to plunder the Doab and interrupt our communications. It is absolutely necessary, therefore, that a post be established between Allahabad and Cawnpore, sufficiently strong to detach against any parties of rebels crossing either the Jumna or Ganges. Futtehpore offers the most convenient position, and I beg, therefore, you will cause preparations to be made for passing on to that place all the men of the 90th and

64th (except their sick) now coming up from Benares, either by bullock train or marching, as you think most advisable. But the first detachment (which is to reach Allahabad to-morrow) should be despatched by bullock train *at once*, to take charge of the tents, which I shall leave there, for upwards of 500 Europeans, intended for the accommodation of the Futtehpore force when all are assembled there.

Even that small detachment, magnified as it will be by rumour, will suffice to keep the Oude rebels dispersed by Eyre from again venturing to come across the Ganges; and long before they learn the real force of the detachment, it will have been reinforced by further details. This post would, moreover, tranquillize the Futtehpore district, which is becoming utterly disorganized from the absence of any European supervision, if an experienced civil functionary could be sent to assume charge of it.

I beg you will inform Mr. Chester how absolutely indispensable it is that he *should* depute the most experienced magistrate he has. Reduced as the civil duties at Allahabad now are, surely one of the several civilians he has with him may be spared without much inconvenience; but, convenient or not, such great interests are involved in preserving the tranquillity of the Futtehpore district at present, that I trust Mr. Chester will not grudge any inconvenience that may be caused him, by assuming for the present the control of Futtehpore, through such officers as he may depute to manage it. I shall urge on the Lieutenant-Governor the expediency of attaching Futtehpore to Allahabad with this view.

Until relieved by the first detachment of Europeans, the havildar's party of Sikhs, who came in charge of the dooly bearers and bheestees, will remain at Futtehpore in charge of the tents. You will, I trust, send an experienced officer of our army to aid the senior officer who may be in command of the Queen's detachment at Futtehpore, until you can assume the command there yourself when relieved by Colonel Otter. The garrison and convalescents now at Allahabad must suffice until the Naval Brigade arrives; and they should be ample while a force of 500 Europeans are passing through to be established so near as Futtehpore. These detachments, so frequently passing up from Benares to Allahabad, should suffice to preserve the communication between *those* places; and I trust the Goorkhas are by this time in occupation of Jaunpore, which will effectually shut out the Oude rebels from that quarter.

Mr. Sherer, now at Cawnpore, belongs I believe to Futtehpore, and I may find, perhaps, that he can now be spared to return there, and place himself under Mr. Chester's orders. But I hope Mr. Chester will not rely on this, as possibly he may be too necessary at Cawnpore just now to be spared immediately; and at any rate an experienced civilian should come up with the first detachment, and remain till Mr. Sherer arrives; if not, to continue there with Mr. Sherer. It may be convenient to have a telegraph station at Futtehpore, if it can be managed.

Sir J. Outram to the Commander-in-Chief.

Camp, Thurriaroon, 11th September, 1857.

I last night received your Excellency's letter dated 5th instant, from which I much regret to learn that you have been unwell. Your Excellency's illness at this time would, indeed, be a national calamity. I trust the telegraph message I sent from Allahabad will have relieved your anxiety regarding the rifle ammunition, a considerable supply having arrived subsequent to Colonel O'Brien's report of the deficiency. With what you mention as being sent in addition, we shall have an ample supply for some time to come.

The 185 cavalry organized from the waggon train will be invaluable. General Havelock has only about seventy volunteer cavalry, to whom I have about a dozen to add, besides a troop of the 12th Irregulars (under Captain Johnson), who being Affghans may, I think, be depended on. This comprises our whole cavalry force on this side Agra.

With regard to the proposed measure of employing the Madras 17th Regiment, with 300 of her Majesty's 10th, and two guns from Dinapore, I should have thought it excellent had I not supposed that the 17th Regiment was, by the time I received your Excellency's message on the subject, close to Benares, which induced me to reply—" As the 17th Madras Regiment must now be close to Benares, it would be a pity to send it down to Chupra, where the detachment of the 10th Regiment from Dinapore will answer for the present; and Benares appears to be the most convenient position from whence to operate generally." This was assuming that your Excellency might have sent orders to Dinapore direct, to detach the 200 of her Majesty's 10th and two guns for the protection of Chupra, as I had suggested on the 31st August, in consequence of Mr. Hamilton's information.

As the only means of communicating with Dinapore by telegraph is *viâ* Calcutta, I thought *that* the quickest and the surest mode of ensuring your Excellency's and the Governor-General's views, on learning the fall of Goruckpore, being at once carried out. And I at the same time sent by post to Mr. Hamilton, and through him to Mr. Samuells, copy of my telegraph message to your Excellency, with authority to make requisition accordingly in anticipation of the expected orders from Calcutta. These I, however, concluded would long precede the receipt of my communication by letter. As I have heard nothing further from Mr. Hamilton, I trust his apprehensions of disturbances in the neighbourhood of Chupra have proved unfounded. Probably the Sikh detachment stationed at Allygunge Sewan, 30 miles north of Chupra, may have sufficed. It subsequently appeared that the Madras regiment did not reach Dinapore till the 31st August, as I learnt only yesterday by a report from Colonel Guy, dated 18th instant. And he purposed passing it up without delay; but though it takes long to steam up from Dinapore to Benares, the regiment would occupy little more than one day in steamer from Benares to Chupra, or but three days in river boats.

Should it, therefore, still appear preferable to your Excellency to operate on Goruckpore from Chupra, direct your orders by telegraph to Colonel Gordon to despatch the 17th Madras Regiment, and also three or more of Colonel Cotter's horse artillery guns from Benares (in preference to the foot battery guns from Dinapore, the former being perhaps more available than the latter); and your orders to Dinapore to send the detachment of her Majesty's 10th to Chupra, with instructions how to act, would reach in a few hours and be carried out immediately; whereas it would take many days, with more uncertain communication, to convey my orders from hence. I have directed Colonel Gordon to prepare the 17th Regiment, and two of Colonel Cotter's guns, to be in readiness to despatch to Chupra, in the event of such order being issued by your Excellency. If a steamer and flat should be at Benares, he is told to retain them till your orders are received;

otherwise, to have the requisite river boats ready. I
shall request Colonel O'Brien to telegraph to the above
effect to your Excellency, and also to Colonel Gordon
at Benares, to have the 17th Madras Regiment and
half of Colonel Cotter's battery in readiness for immediate despatch to Chupra, in the probability that
orders to that effect may arrive direct from your Excellency. As my letter will reach Colonel O'Brien at
Allahabad during the night, I trust the message will
reach Calcutta to-morrow.

My own idea was, that operations on a more general
scale for rescuing Goruckpore and re-establishing our
authority in the North-Eastern Provinces, would best
be conducted from Benares—the present seat of the
Government and in immediate communication with the
Lieutenant-Governor; and that those operations had
best be undertaken on the arrival of the brigade now
coming up the trunk road. And the Lieutenant-
Governor quite concurred in my views, as your Excellency will observe from the following quotations from
our correspondence on the subject. I relied on the
influence of the Lieutenant-Governor to secure all the
requisites for the troops crossing the rivers between
Benares and Goruckpore; and I thought it might be
of advantage thus to cut off the retreat of the rebels to
Oude, by taking the more northerly route to Goruckpore.

With this view I deemed it preferable to await the
arrival of all the Madras troops at Benares. I must
confess, however, that I am inclined to alter my opinion
on further reflecting on the little influence our Government now possesses beyond a few miles from Benares;
that the Lieutenant-Governor consequently may not be
able to secure that ready assistance in boats, supplies,
&c., which our troops have heretofore been accustomed

to look for in passing through the country; that the rivers we have to pass between Benares and Goruckpore may not be so speedily crossed as is desirable; and that, therefore, the movement direct from Chupra may produce more immediate results than the more tardy operations of the Madras column after its arrival at Benares. The latter may, however, co-operate very effectually by taking the northern route to Goruckpore, while the Chupra column operates from the opposite quarter. The annexed papers marked A, are extracts from my correspondence with Mr. Grant to which I refer above.

As the simplest mode of informing your Excellency of our proceedings and prospects, I beg to enclose copies of my correspondence with General Havelock and Colonel O'Brien during the past two days. In my yesterday's letter to General Havelock (B), I express my intention to march with *all* the troops to Futtehpore to-day. Afterwards, on reflecting that *all* the reinforcements could not cross the river in one day after our joining General Havelock (even if he has prepared his bridge and occupied the opposite bank before our arrival, which he does not appear to contemplate), I considered that no time would be lost by giving the 90th Regiment a day's halt, whereas the repose would be of great advantage to the sick and footsore, of whom the former were reported to-day 44, the latter 23. I thought it as well, too, to keep within supporting distance of Major Eyre's detachment, of whose proceedings since he left us yesterday I have yet had no report, but I hope to hear from him before this letter is despatched.

P.S.—I enclose a note just received from Cawnpore giving the latest news from Lucknow.

2nd P.S.   3 P.M.—Colonel Eyre's official report of the entire success of his expedition has just arrived, and is being copied to forward to your Excellency officially. With his despatch Major Eyre wrote me privately as follows:—" I hope the enclosed despatch will please you. Your note reached me just as our morning work was done. If I can find a tolerable road to Futtehpore from this direct, I propose taking that route, as it will do good. The blowing up of the boat has singed some poor fellows terribly, but they had a wondrous-escape. The boats were full of dead men, and at least 200 must have been shot in the river, so we have given them a good lesson."

3rd P.S.—The Thanadar here has just paid me a visit. He assures me this invasion was to have been followed by a general rising in these parts.

Sir J. Outram to Colonel O'Brien, Commanding at Allahabad.

Camp, Thurriaroon, 11th September, 1857.

Oblige me by telegraphing in my name to the Commander-in-Chief, as follows:—

" Received your Excellency's letter, dated 5th instant. I had myself considered that it would be most effectual to operate on Goruckpore from Benares, when Colonel Fischer's Brigade, coming by the Grand Trunk Road, should arrive there; and, assuming also, that the 17th Madras Regiment, coming up the river, was already close to Benares. The facilities for advancing on Goruckpore, direct from Chupra, would, however, be greater, as avoiding the rivers which intervene between Benares and Goruckpore—if the Madras regiment, half a battery of artillery, and 200 (or 300 might, perhaps, be spared) of her Majesty's 10th Regiment be deemed sufficient. In that case, as the Madras

17th Regiment must be at Benares by this time, it and half Major Cotter's Horse Artillery might be despatched from Benares to Chupra; *there* to be joined by the detachment of her Majesty's 10th Regiment, either by steamer or river boats. If the former is available, little more than one day would be occupied in the passage; if river boats, three days. As my orders to Dinapore, by telegraph, can only be sent through Calcutta, and would take many days to reach by post, your Excellency's orders and instructions, if sent direct to Dinapore, would ensure their being rapidly and correctly carried out."

And the following message to Colonel Gordon:—

"It is not improbable you will receive orders from the Commander-in-Chief direct, to despatch an expedition to Goruckpore through Chupra. If any steamer and flat be available, keep them till you hear from the Commander-in-Chief; if not, prepare river boats for the following troops, to be held in readiness for immediate despatch. The 17th Madras Regiment, and three guns of Major Cotton's battery, with tents complete; for which bullocks would be provided at Chupra."

Pardon this shamefully blotched letter. I have not time to re-write it. I have not yet ($11\frac{1}{4}$ A.M.) had any report from Major Eyre of the result of his tour after the Oude rebels.

P.S.—Since this was written, I have received Eyre's report of the entire success of his expedition, and the destruction of the Oude invaders, as you will see from his official despatch, which I have ordered to be sent through you under a flying seal, and the purport of which please telegraph to the Commander-in-Chief.

General Havelock to Sir J. Outram.

Cawnpore, 11*th September,* 1857.

I wrote you yesterday by express regarding the Oude zemindar, of whom I learn by your letter of the 10th, this morning received, that you had already heard.

* * * * * *

Time presses; but I regret to say I cannot find a place well fitted for crossing to the opposite bank. The islands directly opposite are too swampy for occupation. I could easily throw a bridge direct to them; but to remain on them, or get out of them, would not be easy, as there are muddy channels between them, fordable perhaps, but not under the fire of a numerous enemy who warily watches the whole bank. Under these circumstances I would suggest for your consideration, whether it might not be feasible for you to cross to the left bank lower down—say at Nudjufghur Ghat below Sirsood: I could send you down the steamer and as many boats as she could tow, and though this might attract the enemy's attention, you might anticipate him, and get your men and a battery across. Then, if it were previously ascertained that there is no impassable obstacle on the route, you might march up and turn the enemy's entrenchments whilst we crossed by the bridge thrown direct over to the islands. You would in this case, however, have to leave on the trunk road troops sufficient to convoy the stores of various kinds coming up for us. Pass as we will some risk must be incurred, so the above idea may be worthy of consideration.

P.S.—Since writing the above, it appears certain that the enemy have troops and guns at each of the several points to which we could cross, excepting on the swampy island directly in our front. So it remains to be considered whether we should avoid the evils of separation of force involved in the plan above suggested—crossing below at Nudjufghur Ghat. Probably the safest plan after all would be to effect the passage to the island.

Sir James Outram to General Havelock.

Camp, Futtehpore, 11*th September,* 1857.

After despatching my last, I decided on halting the 90th, instead of bringing on all the troops here yesterday, because it would benefit the sick; because possibly the Oude rebels might have been reinforced, and Eyre might require support; and because, as (even had the bridge been ready for our crossing on arrival at Cawnpore) all could not have got over on that day, no time would be lost by reserving the 90th for the following day.

Yesterday I received Eyre's report of his complete success, copy of which I send you. The rear companies of the 90th and 84th, some 500 men (coming up by Palkee Gharree to Benares, and by bullock train to Allahabad), I have ordered to be assembled here, and to occupy this place until further orders; that is, until we return from Lucknow, as they could not join us in time to accompany us there. The first party will be here in two or three days. The lesson Eyre has given the Oude rebels will prevent their return in the interim; the mere news of European troops being stationed here will prevent any further attempts; and thus our communication between Allahabad and Cawnpore will be uninterrupted during our absence in Oude. I met on the march this morning your express of yesterday.

*　　　*　　　*　　　*　　　*

Under the circumstances you represent, I quite agree with you in thinking our surest and best plan is that which you suggest, viz., for me to cross the Ganges some miles below Cawnpore, march up the opposite bank, and turn the enemy's intrenchments, while you cross by the bridge thrown directly over to the islands. Nudjufghur Ghat appears in the map to be about twenty miles below the enemy's works in your front. This I think too far. For we should attack him the same day we cross; whereas, after landing twenty miles below, we should have to bivouac midway for a night, thus affording ample time (twenty-four hours) for the enemy to bring up his detachments from a distance, and so interpose his whole force when we advance next morning, while we are still out of reach of co-operation with you.

My idea is, that we should cross within six or eight miles at farthest. And we could have sufficient force on the opposite bank in time to protect the landing of the remainder, even if the enemy should early discover my movement, and come down to obstruct it, if the following plan is carried out, in which I see no difficulty.

Simmons's column will be at Maharajpore on the 14th, where he would halt, and I close up with him next day, 15th.

On that day a couple of intelligent officers (or four would be better—two to come to me, and two to return to you) would examine and make inquiries regarding the river for six to ten miles down, to find out the best place for crossing, if this had not been previously done. Deep water on both sides, to facilitate embarking and landing, should, if possible, be selected. If not to be had, the most favourable that can be found in other respects. If available, a grove of trees near the landing place, or a mile or two above it towards the enemy's position, to afford us shelter during the few hours we may remain before advancing to the attack.

Having chosen the spot, one of the officers to come to my camp to guide us to the place, so that we may arrive there by daybreak the next morning, the other to return to you, to guide the steamer to the same spot and at the same time.

Two hundred riflemen from your force, or as many as the steamer can carry, to be brought in the steamer, accompanied by an engineer officer acquainted with the position of the enemy's works. These 200 men would but fill the place of the 64th men and sick 90th, who would escort our baggage and stores to Cawnpore.

If the steamer, with boats in tow, drops down during the night without steaming, but with steam up, ready to do so if necessary to prevent grounding, it may escape the enemy's observation. I wish the party of riflemen to be in her, to ensure their securing our landing, even if the enemy should be on the alert and follow the boats. On arriving near the crossing place, the steamer would cast off the boats on our side, and then, without stopping, steam over to the opposite bank to land the riflemen. The soldiers would form in extended order a hundred yards or so from the top of the bank, and so be ready to check any body of the enemy who might make their appearance, while the steamer comes back to us, and at once embarks a couple of guns, and as many more men as she can carry. These we should have ready to put on board. This reinforcement would render us sufficiently strong to defy the enemy, while the remainder of the troops were crossing, who in the meantime would have got on board the boats ready for the steamer to tow over at leisure.

All being on the Oude side, we would then move to the nearest tope of trees, and there breakfast and wait until the hour appointed for advancing to turn the enemy's entrenchments.

Our advance would be timed so as to open our attack at the time previously arranged for your opening your guns upon the enemy's works from the island, your bridge of boats having been prepared so far the previous day or that morning. Our mode of co-operation then, such as may have been arranged between us.

Having driven the enemy from his position, and followed him up as far as is advisable, your bridge would be completed during the night, and next day our baggage and stores would be brought over.

Of course it would be necessary to carry with us two days' cooked provisions.

Let me know if you approve of this plan, or what alterations you would wish to be made. If you approve, tell me at what hour of the day we cross you would wish us to advance to the attack.

The Governor-General of India in Council to Sir J. Outram.

(Telegraphic.) Calcutta, 12th September, 1857.

I have received, this morning, Brigadier Inglis's letter of the 1st of September.

Maun Sing may be assured that if he continues to give the Governor-General effective proof of his fidelity and good-will, his position in Oude will be at least as good as it was before the British Government assumed the administration of the country; whilst the proprietors in Oude, who have deserted the Government, will lose their possessions.

The same assurance may be given to any other chiefs, who will be rewarded in proportion to the support which they may afford.

Whatever promises may have been made to Maun Sing, or to others, by Sir Henry Lawrence, are confirmed, and shall be fully redeemed. None, however, have been reported to me.

I send the above message to Mr. Grant, as well as to yourself. He will endeavour to convey the assurance to Maun Sing, by a sure route, in case your communication with Oude should be interrupted.

I hope you will be able to send a reply to Brigadier Inglis, and inform him of the exertions which have been made for the relief of his brave little band, and of the anxious sympathy which is felt for them.

General Neill to Sir J. Outram.

Cawnpore, 13th September, 1857.

Early on the morning of the 11th I had the pleasure of receiving yours of the previous day, and lost no time with Mr. Edwards in carrying out your instructions. I wrote to Captain Gowan as follows :—

"In consequence of representations made by you through Mr. Edwards, Collector of Budaon, of your being able, if assisted with money, to organize the troops of the Thakoors where you are, and to get them to assist Government in acting against the rebels, I, on being made acquainted with them, wrote to General Sir J. Outram, commanding the forces in the Central Provinces, suggesting to him that you should be assisted to the amount of 50,000 rupees for that end, and Mr. Edwards has to-day communicated with the native bankers at Bareilly to assist you with sums of money to that extent, as you may require them. I must add that no time is to be lost in organizing these troops, and making an impression against the enemy in any place you can."

I also quoted the order by Government as to the rewards for sepoys brought to any military authority, as also those for horses, &c., the property of Government, brought in, and requested him to give them circulation and publicity as extensively as he could. Also to communicate my letter to the officer commanding at Nynee Tal, and to request his co-operation in every way for the good of the service, and energetic and vigorous movements against the enemy.*

Sir J. Outram to Colonel O'Brien.

Camp, Malwa, 13th September, 1857.

In reply to your letter of yesterday, on the subject of the sepoys of the 67th Native Infantry, who are in your neighbourhood on leave from Mr. Colvin, and whose petition you forward, and to your proposal to employ them and others similarly situated, to the number of 200 men, as convoys and posts on the Grand Trunk Road, I have to say, that I not only agree with you in considering it would be highly advantageous to have such a body as you propose organizing under your orders at Futtehpore; but that, as additional security for our communications between Allahabad and Cawnpore is urgently required, I take upon myself to authorize your entertaining such men to the extent of two hundred.

Your proposal to place Mr. Glyn at their head, I shall submit to Government with my recommendation.

You will of course satisfy yourself by the most care-

---

* The following letter addressed to Mr. Secretary Edmonstone on the 1st December, 1857, shows the futility of this attempt:—
"With reference to the Chief Commissioner's letter to his Lordship the Governor-General, dated 14th September last, in which he stated that he had authorized the sum of 50,000 rupees to be expended in an attempt to raise the Hindoo population of Bareilly against the Mahomedan rebels, I am directed to submit the accompanying extract of a letter from Captain Gowan, dated 14th ultimo, from which his Lordship in Council will perceive that the attempt was quite unsuccessful, and has been abandoned without the expenditure of any portion of the amount in question."

(Extract.)

"I have been quite unsuccessful in my attempt to induce the Thakoors round about here to collect together any number of men. I had been led to suppose that they were inclined to render effectual aid to Government, but find it does not go beyond professions of good-will for the present, and boastings of what they would do if they were backed by a well-appointed European force, which force could do very well without them, and would only be hampered by their presence. I have consequently not spent any money whatever, or drawn any cheques upon Government for any purpose."

ful scrutiny, that every man you entertain had really, as represented, departed on leave from Agra before any excesses were perpetrated by the mutineers there, and that he has not since been concerned in any act of violence or disloyalty.

Rolls should be kept of every one you entertain, with the grounds on which you form your judgment as to his innocence registered opposite to the name of each individual, copy of which is to be furnished to Government. I purpose recommending to Government the establishment of an office at Futtehpore, under your supervision, for receiving and registering such evidence, oral or written, as may be brought forward by native officers or men belonging to mutinied regiments who are desirous of proving their innocence of any complicity in the mutiny, or showing that they exerted themselves to prevent their comrades from mutinying and to preserve their officers from violence, in order that every such case may be submitted for the consideration of Government. But, until you receive orders on the subject, you will take no steps in the matter.

The pay of the men entertained for the service above stated to be what they would be entitled to in their regiment.

Flint lock, *not percussion*, muskets should be supplied to them.

It is essential that civil authority should be established in these districts. Mr. Chester will accompany you to Futtehpore in the first instance, to whom you will of course afford cordial support.

I have proposed to the Commander-in-Chief that the Naval Brigade shall garrison Allahabad Fort, and in that case I can withdraw the infantry and foot artillery company now there, to be added to your force at Futtehpore.

Commander-in-Chief to Sir J. Outram.

(Telegraphic.) *Calcutta, 13th September.*

To the regret of the Commander-in-Chief, his Excellency has to inform Sir James Outram, that the columns which were marching to his support have in two cases been divided and diverted from their original purpose, at the instance of the civil authority. Of Colonel Fisher's column one half has been directed on Dorunda, and the remainder will reach Shergotty about the day after to-morrow, when it will probably be pushed to Sasseram with a view of punishing the mutineers of the 5th Irregular Cavalry. The route of Madras 17th Native Infantry has also been altered—one wing having gone to Allygunge, and the other to Mirzapore with two of Major Cotter's guns. Upon the arrival of Lieutenant-Colonel Langdon at Dinapore, his Excellency will send forward two hundred men of the 10th Foot to reinforce you. His Excellency's efforts are interfered with at every moment by the requisition of the civil authorities. A column is being now organized under the command of Colonel Berkeley, her Majesty's 32nd Regiment, which will be completed at Ranceguuge by the 23rd instant, consisting of the following detachments:—Major Robertson's Cavalry corps, numbering in all ranks two hundred and thirty-seven ; two Madras Horse Artillery guns, a company of Madras Sappers, and a company of her Majesty's 53rd Foot. The cavalry corps but just put together, and little thought of, promises to be very efficient : it will proceed to join you as soon as possible. The 53rd Regiment will be concentrated at Benares eventually. A company of her Majesty's Royal Engineers has arrived, as well as two companies of Artillery. The former will be pushed up by bullock train to Allahabad, where their services are much required for the defences ; and the artillery, by similar conveyance to Benares, where they will receive their guns and horses. You are requested not to send for either her Majesty's Engineers or the Madras Sappers, if you can possibly do without them for the present. As there is so much of importance to be done at Allahabad, it is most desirable that they should not be used for mere infantry purposes. Head-quarters and three hundred and fifty men of her Majesty's 23rd Foot have arrived, and will take their duty in the fort, thus releasing the head-quarters of the 53rd Foot. The Commander-in-Chief will request the Governor-General to send the necessary orders to Captain Peel as desired in your letter, dated Camp, Futtehpore, 10th September. All the naval detachments are under the immediate command of the Governor-General. Will you, for the future, send all the telegraphic communications regarding your numbers, the state of the force under your command, and your wishes, to Major-General Mansfield, Chief of the Staff; other correspondence to be maintained in the channels heretofore employed. I should be much obliged by your communicating this injunction to Brigadier Havelock.

Sir J. Outram to the Lieutenant-Governor, Central Provinces.

Camp, Malwa, 14th September.

I send under a flying seal for your perusal, and that you may let the Governor-General know your sentiments on the subject therein mooted (should you please to do so), a letter I have addressed to his Lordship. Only pray don't delay its transmission, if you purpose remarking upon it, but pass it on with a note to say you will forward your comments hereafter. It is high time measures should be taken to show that we do not purpose war to the knife, and extermination, against *all Hindoos* because they *are* Hindoos, or against *all sepoys* because they *are* sepoys.

We were detained a day by the necessity of detaching a party against a body of Oude invaders, whom we utterly destroyed; and this I trust will deter others from coming over.

My advanced column will be in Cawnpore to-morrow, and I, with the remainder, next day.

I trust it will not be many days after ere we reach Lucknow, where, so far as we know, the garrison appears to be holding out manfully.

Sir J. Outram to the Governor-General.

Camp, Malwa, 14th September, 1857.

It is my painful duty to bring to your Lordship's notice the very disorganized state of the Allahabad, Futtehpore, and Cawnpore districts,—comprising the whole country between the Ganges and Jumna rivers, from Allahabad to Cawnpore,—which appear, so far as I can learn, to be almost without any civil government beyond the immediate influence of the garrisons of

Allahabad and Cawnpore. Futtehpore, indeed—the central district—I may say, is utterly uncontrolled.

No civil functionary, I am told, has visited those districts beyond the immediate vicinity of the military stations since Futtehpore was sacked; and over the Futtehpore district there appears to have been no supervision beyond that of some subordinates, aided by a few wretched burkundazes, whom the zemindars defy, attacking and plundering one another with impunity, for no one attempts to enforce the law. Some zemindars have been engaging armed followers, with the avowed intention of raising the standard of rebellion as soon as aid from Oude should arrive, which has been promised. Every native functionary who has waited on me, as I marched through these districts, assured me that the spirit of disaffection is strong among the more powerful zemindars, and would explode, so soon as the invaders from Oude appeared, in a general insurrection.

The passage of my troops into Oude was the time appointed, as thus my communications would have been cut off, and I must (they thought) return to reopen them, when I should have had too much occupation here to admit of further attempts to relieve Lucknow. Fortunately, they commenced too soon. The advance guard of the invaders, 300 men and four guns, crossed over before I had passed beyond reach, and paid the penalty of their rashness, being utterly destroyed by Major Eyre. This severe example will, I trust, deter others from repeating the attempt. And the precaution I have taken of forming a camp at Futtehpore will, I believe, secure the tranquillity of the province during our absence in Oude. But, above all, the presence there of so able and energetic an officer as Mr. Commissioner Chester, who, on my requesting him to send an experienced magistrate, has determined to go himself, will, I trust, soon re-establish order, supported as he will be by a strong body of European troops.

I beg to refer your Lordship to the accompanying correspondence for further explanation of the measures I have adopted, and which I hope may meet approval.

As a supplementary means of securing our communications by the trunk road, I have authorized Colonel O'Brien, the officer who is to command at Futtchpore, to organize a small body (200) of certain well-disposed sepoys of the Agra disbanded regiments, who went on leave, duly provided with certificates, on the faith of Mr. Colvin's proclamation, and have not since or previously been implicated in any disloyal act.

For further information as to the class of men to be engaged, and the terms of their employment, I transmit copies of correspondence with Colonel O'Brien on the subject, confidently trusting that the measure will meet with your Lordship's approbation.

The time has now arrived, I conceive, for your Lordship to decide how the native soldiers who have committed no overt act of mutiny or rebellion, and are not implicated in any deed of atrocity, should be dealt with. Among such, I may mention those who were peaceably disarmed at Agra, and went to their homes on the faith of Mr. Colvin's proclamation, before the announcement of its withdrawal by Government; those who allowed themselves to be disarmed, and have since remained with their regiments doing duty without arms; and, above all, the very few regiments still stanch to us, who have retained their arms.

Unless these men receive an assurance that they will remain in our service, with the present pay and privileges, their minds will naturally be imbued with doubts as to their future fate, rendering them yet liable to seduction; while, in the other case, their fidelity may be assured, and we certainly cannot entirely dispense with the services of these men. The most favourable time for the promulgation of such a determination on your Lordship's part, would be the announcement of the fall of Delhi and the awful retribution that must then be taken on the mutineers congregated in that city. But if that event, so long delayed, be deferred much longer, the opportunity for taking advantage of the favourable reaction will pass away, and thus no opening for mercy would be available to any of the classes now composing the Bengal native army. Has not the time arrived, my Lord, for a proclamation announcing that, as more than four months have elapsed since the outbreak of the rebellion, the Government is satisfied that those regiments which have so long withstood the menaces and temptations with which their disaffected comrades have assailed them, have thus proved themselves stanch and trustworthy servants of the Government, which, therefore, deems it but just to remove any apprehensions they may entertain as to the future, by assuring them of its continued favour? They will be retained in the service, with all the privileges and advantages hitherto enjoyed, and be rewarded for their fidelity, especially those regiments which have served under arms through the crisis, by sharing in the extensive promotions to be announced on the reorganization of the native army. It may also be added that Government has made this announcement at the moment when all India is convinced of the speedy re-establishment of the Government's power, which four months' rebellious conflagration could not shake, and when the legions of England are about to pour into the country.

But I humbly conceive the Government should go further: it should express its conviction that thousands of the sepoys unhappily belonging to the regiments that fell away from their duty, were the unwilling victims of a powerful majority, whom they were helpless to oppose, and were no party to the violence and crimes of their comrades; to avoid participation in which, they retired peacefully to their homes, and in many cases proved their devotion by saving the lives of their officers. The Government, acting upon this conviction, and being desirous not to confound the innocent with the guilty, has, therefore, empowered a committee of officers to assemble at ——, who will investigate and report on the cases of those officers and men who appear before them to establish their innocence. After the evidence produced has been considered and recorded, their cases will be submitted for the consideration of Government.

Should some such course be decided on, Futtehpore would be a convenient place for holding one of the committees, and Colonel O'Brien well qualified to preside over it.

I entreat your Lordship's pardon for intruding these suggestions; but I am convinced there are many sepoys in a similar position to those whose petition is attached to enclosure B, and that others possess documents from their officers, acknowledging their devotion to them in extremity, to whom it would be just and politic to give employment. I am also aware that the belief is gaining ground that Hindoos are to be entirely excluded from our service, and that those still remaining in it will be expelled, and such a belief, by depriving them of all hope, is calculated to keep alive among that class the flame of insurrection which might otherwise be speedily extinguished. Hence, I feel I should be unworthy of the confidence with which your Lordship honours me, were I not frankly to inform you of these facts.

Believing that the interests of the State cannot be

better advanced in the rebellious districts, at present beyond our control, than by inciting a portion of the people to espouse the cause of our Government, I have sanctioned a measure calculated to raise the Hindoo population of Bareilly against the Mahomedan rebels who have usurped the Government of that province. Your Lordship will understand the nature of the measure I allude to on perusing the accompaniment (C).* I do not advocate that measure on the ground avowed by General Neill in this correspondence, *i.e.* the "policy of promoting bad blood between the two races" (Hindoo and Mahomedan); but I think, as he does, that it is our policy to "encourage our friends and well-wishers," by the example of our Hindoo subjects seeking to retrieve the past by now fighting in our cause; and that the outlay of 50,000 rupees, of which I have authorized the disbursal, in anticipation of your Lordship's sanction, will be well bestowed in promoting that object, besides securing the recovery of the officers alluded to as concealed in Bareilly.

Sir J. Outram to General Havelock.

Camp, Aong, 14th September, 1857.

A second post has come from Cawnpore since you ought to have been in possession of a letter I wrote to you from Futtehpore on the 12th, though I received next day the reply to a note I sent Bruce by the same post that took—or ought to have taken—my letter to yourself. I am afraid, therefore, my letter may have been put, by mistake, into the mail for Allahabad, instead of in that for Cawnpore. Lest this should be the case, I now send you by express the duplicate of

---

* Appendix C. From General Neill, 9th September. To General Neill, 10th September. From General Neill, 13th September.

that portion of my letter, in reply to your proposition that I should cross some miles below Cawnpore, move up the opposite bank, and take the enemy's works in reverse, which you will see I think highly of. In reply to a request I made to Bruce for information regarding the opposite bank, he says, "From this point" (the islands where you last crossed) " the Oude bank is low, swampy, and intersected by numerous small channels, to a distance of eight or nine miles, below which the man did not go." I trust you will approve of the mode in which I purpose carrying out the movement you suggested—and, in that case, I beg you will ascertain and let me know to what distance *inland* the swamps and channels on the Oude side extend;—consequently what length of détour I should have to make round them to the enemy's position, supposing I cross eight or nine miles down;—the point of crossing depends on the information the officers bring me whom I have requested you to send to-morrow to reconnoitre the bank and then to come to my camp at Maharajpore.

As it is of the utmost importance I should receive your answer to-night, I send this express, and beg you will despatch your reply in the same way.

Sir J. Outram to General Havelock.

Camp, Aong, 14*th September*, 1857.

I have just received your express of to-day, replying to mine of the 12th, for which I was anxiously looking.

* * * * * *

As little or no opposition to your crossing is now expected, the détour I proposed to make at the opposite bank to take the enemy's works in reverse, may be unnecessary; and as the Oude side is said to be a swamp, it is as well to avoid the attempt to operate that way, as no pressing necessity warrants the risk. I shall, therefore, as you advise, join you at Cawnpore. Simmons's column will be with you to-morrow morning, and I, with the remainder, next morning. I only hope you may have the bridge ready to cross over without further delay, for the renewed activity of the enemy at Lucknow in mining, makes me feel anxious about the garrison holding out many days longer. I don't know whether I replied to your note mentioning the organization you propose for your force. As I purpose deputing to you the command, until the great object for which you have so long fought is attained, of course I shall leave you unfettered in your arrangements; but I would suggest for your consideration whether, instead of calling your two columns *wings*, you should not constitute each a brigade, with a brigade-major to each brigadier, and with a field hospital to each brigade. The latter, I think, would be especially advantageous, and I have a field hospital ready for your second brigade if you desire it. Perhaps, in your position, *your* forming these brigades might be questioned; but I will take upon myself the responsibility of doing so, if you wish it.

I propose, on joining you, to issue an order nominating the divisional force to be placed at your command for service in Oude, stating why I waive the command, and accompany you in my civil capacity, until the relief of the garrison has been effected; when my functions, civil and military, will commence. Hoping this will meet your views, believe me, &c.

Sir J. Outram to the Commander-in-Chief.
Camp, Maharajpore, 15th September, 1857.

I have prepared the accompanying extracts from my correspondence with General Havelock of the last three or four days, that your Excellency may thus learn what our plans and prospects are.

Had the enemy determined to hold the works they were supposed to have prepared to oppose our crossing at Cawnpore, the movement I had intended, by which I should have taken those works in reverse, would have been decisive.

As it now appears that they have no intention of attempting to oppose us there, that movement, of course, is unnecessary; and we shall all cross at Cawnpore. Major Simmons's column reaches that place to-day. I shall go on this evening; and the troops now with me will be there to-morrow morning.

If General Havelock has, as I hope, commenced his boat bridge to-day, all will, I trust, be over by the evening of the 18th; and five days more will see us at Lucknow, unless more formidable obstructions are prepared on the road than I have reason to expect. As yet none of the bridges have been destroyed.

In this correspondence your Excellency will observe that General Havelock proposes to form his force into two wings of three regiments each; but it appears to me that in the form of two brigades, with brigade staff, it would work better, especially with a field hospital to each; and I hope your Excellency will approve my so constituting the force while employed in Oude. The brigades to be broken up on recrossing to Cawnpore, for such new formation as you probably will have in the meantime directed for the force which I presume will then be pushed on to Agra.

My only apprehension is of the failure of the Commissariat department to supply the vast demand for carriage, &c., that will be required for the troops soon expected from England. And this apprehension, your Excellency will observe from the enclosed extract, is shared by the Lieutenant-Governor.

I have to-day addressed you officially on the subject, suggesting the steps which I think should be adopted. If a *permanent* cart-carriage department, on a very extensive scale, could be organized at Raneegunge, with thousands of bullocks well fed and maintained, as the property of Government, our carriage difficulty would be overcome; for the carts and cattle, being Government property, would accompany the troops through Benares and Allahabad to their destination, wherever it might be, instead of being relieved, as at present, every second or third stage, by bullocks pressed from the villages, in such wretched condition as ensure their breaking down on the road; and further delays to replace. As the troops from England will all have to come up the trunk road, the river being no longer available, this mode of transport is a serious consideration.

Sir J. Outram to Colonel Inglis, Commanding at Lucknow.

Cawnpore, 16th September, 1857.

All the troops have now come up—the bridge getting ready, and no time will be lost. Cannot of course fix the exact day. My only apprehension is, lest, when you hear us engaged on the opposite of, or in, the town, forcing our way to you, your garrison, in its eagerness to aid us by a sortie, should be tempted to go far from your works, so that too few European soldiers might be left to guard your defences. In the probability of this occurring, it is not unlikely the enemy may have a strong body concealed near you, ready to make a rush upon your works in the expectation that they may be left weakly guarded, as their last chance of getting at you.

If a small and compact body can with safety be spared to penetrate a short way in the direction in which we are engaged, it might have a beneficial effect by opening a fusilade towards the rear of our opponents. Even though the latter may not be within reach, the mere sound of firing in their rear would compel the enemy to run lest they should be caught between two fires. It may be ten days yet before we reach you if much opposed on the road; but depend on our coming.

With heartfelt wishes for the welfare of my numerous friends with you, believe me, &c.

Sir J. Outram to the Commander-in-Chief.
Cawnpore, 16*th September*, 1857.

I joined General Havelock here last night, and have to-day issued an order of which I enclose a copy in the hope it may meet your Excellency's approval, particularly as to the organization of the division I have placed under General Havelock's command, of two brigades of infantry and one of artillery.

As a special and peculiar case, I thought myself called upon to take upon myself the responsibility of forming the force into brigades; not merely because so large a body of troops—or rather a force composed of so many different regiments—can be more effectively handled in the field under such formation; but particularly with a view to maintain strict discipline during the time the troops may occupy the city, for which General Havelock will certainly require the aid of his brigadiers and their staff, in addition to the commanders of regiments, to whom alone he would otherwise have had to look.

Unless I receive your Excellency's order to break up

the division when it recrosses the Ganges to Cawnpore, this division so formed might be well adapted for immediate movement on Agra, after completing the regiments by closing up the detachments belonging to them from Futtehpore, should in the meantime another regiment have come up to occupy that position.

I have just (5½ P.M.) returned from the bridge, which I regret to find is only half completed to the island, beyond which there are two small creeks to cross, where fascines must be laid over the mud. I fear, therefore, it will be the evening of the 19th ere we have all got over, instead of the 18th, as the engineers had led me to expect.

From what we can learn from Lucknow, it would appear that the besiegers have slackened in their attacks lately, the sepoys tiring of the work, and going off to their homes in great numbers. But I do not think our sources of information are much to be relied on. My only anxiety is lest they should be more successful in mining, which they appear to have taken to of late. Unless seriously damaged by such means, there need be no fear that the garrison cannot hold out till we reach them.

Sir J. Outram to the Governor-General.

(Telegraphic.)   *Cawnpore,* 17*th September,* 6½ A.M.

If I find that a brigade of three regiments can securely hold Lucknow by being placed in an invulnerable position, commanding the city and its resources, shall Lucknow be retained? If that place is abandoned, a larger body of troops will be expended in watching Oude than in holding Lucknow, in securing the communication from Benares to Allahabad, and along the line of the Ganges to Furruckabad. The moral effect of abandoning Lucknow will be very serious, as turning against us the many well-disposed chiefs in Oude and Rohilcund who are now watching the turn of affairs, and would regard the loss of Lucknow as the forerunner of the extinction of our rule. Such a blow to our prestige may extend its influence to Nepaul, and will be felt all over India. The civil government of the city may be maintained without interfering with the province for the present.

Sir J. Outram to the Governor-General.
Cawnpore, 17th September, 1857.

The information I have obtained from all sources, at Benares, Allahabad, and this place, as well as during my progress through the country, establishes the fact satisfactorily in my mind that there is a large and influential class in Oude and Rohilcund among the more powerful, and most of the middle class, of chiefs and zemindars, who really desire the re-establishment of our rule; while others well disposed to us have only been induced to turn against us because they believe that our Raj is gone. I am so deeply impressed, therefore, with the impolicy of abandoning Lucknow at this crisis, that I write to implore your Lordship to reconsider the resolution of your Government which at present binds me to that course.

The entire abandonment of Lucknow after withdrawing the present beleaguered garrison, will, I am convinced, be very seriously detrimental to our interests, and will be regarded by the classes above referred to as the first step towards the extinction of our rule in India—certainly as resigning Oude for ever. They would then of course be compelled to make common cause against us; and far more troops would be required to secure the communication from Benares to Allahabad, and along the line of the Ganges to Furruckabad, than would be requisite to hold Lucknow;—irrespective of the consideration of the cost we shall hereafter be put to in retaking that city. Whereas the occupation of Lucknow will encourage the well-affected or peaceably disposed to keep their followers from joining our enemies, and the ill disposed would do so in self-defence; while our open foes would have to keep the field in the vicinity of the city, to hold our garrison in check, to guard against sallies, though not daring to assail the garrison in its commanding position. And thus the hostile elements in Oude would be in a great measure, if not entirely, paralyzed so far as regards offensive operations in our districts beyond the frontier of Oude.

I am satisfied that three regiments of European infantry can be placed in such commanding positions in Lucknow, having secure communication with each other, as would effectually command, not merely the submission, but also the resources, of the whole city. I have no doubt that the aid of the neighbouring chiefs can be secured for maintaining the communication between Lucknow and Cawnpore without the aid of European detachments stationed on the road. And, under General Neill's able command, aided by such civil functionaries as I would place at his disposal for the management of the city, I am convinced that our position there can be maintained with credit and with little opposition.

After selecting the troops to be left with General Neill at Lucknow, the remainder would escort the liberated garrison to this place. And then a very efficient force would remain to despatch to Agra or elsewhere. I have to-day telegraphed the substance of these propositions to your Lordship, and beg that orders may be sent me by telegraph through Captain Bruce, cantonment magistrate at Cawnpore, who will secure their reaching me, to the effect—"Do as you propose," or "withdraw," as your Lordship may be pleased to decide.

I have not dwelt on the very obvious advantage to accrue from our districts bordering in Oude, through which our troops have to pass, being secured from molestation or disturbance; in ensuring the resources of those provinces for the supply of our advancing armies; nor, on what must be equally apparent to your Lordship, the severe blow to our prestige the abandonment of Lucknow would be, extending its evil influence probably to Nepaul, and certain to be severely felt throughout India.*

---

* It is to be recollected that, when the above was written, no rebel government had been organized in Oude, and that the city was dominccred over by the mutineer soldiery, who had been joined by only a few of the chiefs. The principal chiefs and landholders still evaded joining in hostilities against us, and watched the turn of events. Had we succeeded in permanently expelling the sepoy mutineers from Lucknow, when General Havelock's force joined the garrison on the 25th September, there would have been a reaction in the city in our favour; for all the middle and higher classes were anxious for our protection, and longed to be relieved from the tyranny and exactions under which they had suffered during the previous three months of sepoy domination. About 2 P.M. the sepoys began to leave the city, accompanied by "armed men" and "large bodies of Irregular Cavalry." It is a fact that, on the night of the 25th, the sepoys *entirely* evacuated the city. Next morning, none but the city budmashes, the palace retainers, and Maun Sing's followers, remained to oppose us; and, had the whole of General Havelock's force been then united, the entire city would then have been completely under our control, and could have been held by our troops occupying those commanding positions they have occupied since the recapture of the city. For the majority of the inhabitants, *and all the more wealthy of them*, were equally interested with ourselves in preventing the return of the sepoys; and thus, the general defection throughout Oude, which took place when it was found that General Havelock's force were fairly shut up in Lucknow, would have been, in a great measure, averted. Instead, however, of waiting in the Chutter Munzil, where we had a safe position until joined by the rear guard—covering its advance by opening a heavy fire on those guns at the Kaiser Bagh from which it afterwards suffered so severely—and opening a safe communication with the Residency through the deserted palaces, the troops, unfortunately, left the rear guard to its own resources, and pushed on through the streets. The consequence was that the rear guard—one-third of the entire force—was cut off for two nights and a day, and suffered most severely ere it effected a junction on the morning of the 27th September; and, besides its heavy loss in killed, whose bodies could not be brought in, those who had been wounded in the earlier part of the day and had been sent to the rear—

It is rumoured that the rebels propose to negotiate for the peaceable surrender of the garrison if we will not advance to the city, a proposition which of course cannot be received.

Mr. Secretary Beadon to the Secretary to the Government of Bengal.

(Extract.) *Calcutta, 17th September, 1857.*

I am directed by the Right Honourable the Governor-General in Council to acknowledge the receipt of your letter, No. 1,673, dated the 12th instant, forwarding a correspondence with the Commissioner of the Patna Division, relative to the state of the division, and the means taken for its protection.

2. I am desired to state, that his Lordship in Council regrets the detention of the detachment of the 17th Regiment Madras Native Infantry by the Commissioner.

3. His Lordship in Council considers that the circumstances under which Mr. Samuells detained these troops were not of the extreme urgency contemplated by Sir James Outram, in Colonel Napier's letter of the 20th August; and no authority but that of the Supreme Government, or of the General in command, is sufficient to warrant the diversion of troops from their destination at the present time. . . .

Sir J. Outram to the Military Secretary to the Governor-General.

Cawnpore, 17th September, 1857.

Lest the newspapers should misrepresent the fact of a body of troops, which Havelock had put in orders to

---

amounting to seventy-seven—fell into the enemy's hands, and were murdered. These losses, added to those sustained in advancing through the streets from the Chutter Munzil to the Residency, encouraged the remaining rebels, who despatched the heads of our slain (with exaggerated reports of the slaughter) after the flying sepoys, and thus induced them to return; and as, after its heavy losses, the relieving force was too weak to withdraw the garrison, the rebels, believing that the garrison commissariat had been almost exhausted before General Havelock's arrival, made sure of the entire and early destruction of the aggregate force by famine. Then it was—*and only then*—the conviction became general that British rule could not be re-established in Oude. Then was the boy-king proclaimed—a regular government was established; and all those chiefs, who had heretofore wavered or held aloof, were induced to embrace the rebel cause. Had the reaction in the city taken place—which, but for the abandonment of the rear guard, would certainly have taken place—we could, with the force proposed in this letter, have held the positions in Lucknow which we now hold, and all the advantages which the letter contemplates would have resulted.—(See *Letter to Sir Colin Campbell, in his Despatches.*)

cross the river yesterday morning, having been countermanded after my arrival the evening before, as an interference on my part involving delay in our advance, I beg you will have the kindness to explain to Lord Canning and Sir Colin Campbell what are the real facts of the case.

On my arrival here on the evening of the 15th, General Havelock informed me that he purposed commencing to construct the boat bridge next morning, and that he had ordered troops and guns to be passed over in boats before daybreak, to occupy the sandy hillocks on the opposite side, and thus prevent obstruction to the bridge operation. On ascertaining from the General that his 24-pounders, planted on this side, had been proved to range as far as the position the enemy would occupy, if they wished to annoy us, and that he had not prepared to send any tents,—the soldiers being intended to hold the post during the two days it was supposed the construction of the bridge, &c., would occupy, without shelter from the dews at night or sun by day,—I represented that such exposure at this season, and in the midst of a swamp, would entail greater loss than an engagement with the enemy. And I recommended that no troops should be sent across, at least until the bridge was completed, to the island, where there was little chance of the enemy coming near enough to molest the work under the fire of our guns; adding that, if they did, it would be time enough then to send troops to repel them; and that, so soon as the bridge to the island was nearly ready, a detachment with guns could occupy the island to protect the workmen employed in making the road over the opposite muddy creek with fascines and planking, strongly urging that tents should be provided for this party. To this General Havelock consented, and, indeed, it had been his original plan, but was overruled by the engineers. Accordingly, the troops were countermanded, and the bridge is being constructed without their aid. It will be completed to-day. The detachment marches over to the island this afternoon, provided with tents; and I trust that the creeks will be bridged to-morrow, and that all the troops, &c., will have crossed by next evening at furthest. However that may be, not one hour's delay to the actual advance of the army has been caused by the countermand of the detachment which had been ordered to cross yesterday, and much suffering has been avoided.

The reports from Lucknow are that the attack is very slack—scarcely any firing. My only fear is that mining may be going on.

Sir J. Outram to the Lieutenant-Governor, Central Provinces.

Cawnpore, 17*th September,* 1857.

I have only time to answer you very hastily about Futtehpore. Of course, I cannot pledge myself always to retain Europeans at Futtehpore, under the changes and exigencies that are constantly liable to arise in times like these. But there must always be a military post there of some sort, to secure our communications. Unless, however, your civil officers avail themselves of the opportunity to recover their authority over that district, now that the crops are ripening, they will do little good, and it will be a long time ere they redeem the evil which will be suffered from any delay that may occur in looking after Futtehpore.

As I have not time to write to Mr. Chester to-day (being in all the bustle of preparation for crossing into Oude, and clearing off correspondence in the interim), I will send this note open through him to forward to you.

I am glad you have opened communication with Maun Sing. I wish you would persuade him to join me at Lucknow, where I have some idea of establishing a native government, to hold the capital in our name until we resume our authority there. But I see infinite evils from abandoning Lucknow, and I have urged the Governor-General to allow of its being held, as it can be, by a strong brigade (three European regiments), so located as to be unassailable themselves, while they command the whole city and its resources. A far larger force would be tied up in watching Oude, and protecting our communications from Benares to Furruckabad than would hold Lucknow; and the latter course would prevent any serious attempt of the enemy beyond the Oude frontier.

If you are *perfectly secure* of the good faith of the Nepaulese, they might perhaps be trusted with two more guns. But it is a great risk; and if guns are given, much ammunition should not go with them. On your responsibility the guns will be given, on your making official requisition on Colonel Gordon to that effect; but I must confess I would rather not trust them with more.

We received, and passed on to you by telegraph yesterday, the news of poor Colvin's death. I suppose anxiety of mind must have been greatly the cause—poor man!

P.S.—Since this was written, I have learnt that only one 9-pounder battery was landed at Benares, instead of two, as I had been informed. In this case, I don't think any 9-pounder guns can be spared from the Raj Ghât works; and I have, by to-day's telegraph, replied to you to this effect, and that Colonel Gordon is directed to furnish two 12-pounder howitzers from the first steamer that passed up.

Sir J. Outram to the Governor-General.

Cawnpore, 18*th September,* 1857.

With reference to the letters which I addressed to your Lordship on the 14th instant and yesterday, I beg to forward the statements of three gentlemen of the Civil Service, now here, with which I was yesterday favoured on my requesting they would frankly state to me, for submission privately to your Lordship, the impressions they have formed, under the peculiarly favourable opportunities afforded by their personal intercourse with the classes now in revolt. I may especially refer to those of Messrs. Edward and Probyn, who lately were sent in by the Hindoo Chief Hurdoo Bux, a powerful talookdar of Oude, by whom they had been protected since the outbreak, and during their stay with him the motives and feelings which influenced the disaffected were freely disclosed. I will not presume to offer any opinion on the policy of the course which has heretofore been adopted, and to which these gentlemen attribute the disaffection of the landed gentry; but the perusal of these documents may possibly induce your Lordship to favour me with instructions as to the demeanour I am to adopt towards, and the communications I may make to, influential persons of that class with whom I may hold intercourse in Oude; especially as regards the suggestions made by Mr. Edwards of the measures which he considers (and I quite concur in his conviction) would not fail to cause the leading men to support us—certainly to abstain from all opposition.

Your Lordship's orders, if telegraphed to Captain Bruce, Superintendent of Police, would be conveyed by him to me, probably while I am still at Lucknow.

I enclose for your Lordship's information extracts from a letter I have received from my wife at Agra, which, though dated 4th instant, only reached me to-day, having gone on to Allahabad.

Telegraphic messages on the subject of assurances to the Gwalior Maharaj were, however, I am told, transmitted to your Lordship some days ago, before Mr. Colvin's death.

I regret to say, bridging the Ganges has proved a more tedious work than I was led to expect. Instead of being completed in one day, as the engineer officers hoped, this is the third since its commencement; and it cannot be completed till the evening, if then. If it is, the troops and baggage, &c., will all be over by to-morrow evening.

P.S.—I enclose translation of a Purwana I have addressed to a zemindar of Oude, at the suggestion of General Havelock, who had opened communication with that chief; and I hope we may succeed in eventually effecting, through him, the capture of the notorious Nana.

(Enclosure.)

Copy of a Purwana despatched by Major-General Outram, G.C.B., Chief Commissioner of Oude, to Nurput Sing, son of Jussa Sing, Talookdar residing at Futtehpore-Chourasse, in Oude.

Dated Cawnpore, 17th September, 1857.

I have been informed that the traitor " Nana Sahib " is residing with you. You must be aware of the consequences of harbouring such characters. On the other hand, if you secure him and make him over to me, on my crossing the river, I, Major-General Outram, Chief Commissioner of Oude, do solemnly promise, that not only shall you receive the reward offered by the British Government for the capture of this criminal, *i.e.* a sum of 50,000 rupees, but that full indemnity shall be granted to you for the past, and all your lands secured to you. Should it be ascertained that the late Sir Henry Lawrence had promised to you a still greater reward than the one offered by Government, you have my assurance that it shall be given to you.

I cannot but feel assured that you will not so far neglect your duty to the British Government, and at the same time mar your own interests, as to screen and withhold a notorious and proclaimed offender—a disgrace to his own kindred, and an object of horror to all.

The Governor-General to Sir James Outram.

(Telegraphic.)   *Calcutta*, 18*th September*.

Lucknow may be retained if you can hold it securely and without depending upon early reinforcements ; but the one paramount object is the rescue of the garrison, and whatever will most surely conduce to this will be best. If the safety of the garrison can be more thoroughly secured by retiring, pray do not hesitate to do so. We will recover our prestige before long. As to reinforcements, the China regiments are very slow in arriving. The head-quarters of the 23rd Regiment (350 strong) arrived to-day, but it is not known where the rest are. Therefore you must not count upon any addition to your Europeans at present.

Sir J. Outram to the Governor-General.

Camp, left bank of the Ganges,
opposite Cawnpore, 20*th Sept.* 1857.

I have the pleasure to forward extracts from a letter I have to-day received from Captain Patrick Orr, dated 13th instant, from Mutowlie, the residence of a rajah in Oude, under whose protection Captain Orr, three other gentlemen, two ladies, and two children, have remained since the outbreak. And also a note from Lieutenant Barnes, writing from the same place, who mentions that there are nine males and three ladies under the protection of another chief, at a place called Muttcara, in Oude.

These complete a list of ten chieftains of Oude who have proved their fidelity to Government by protecting our subjects. And to these two chiefs I have addressed letters, of one of which I annex a translation for your Lordship's information and, I hope, approval, as ensuring, I think, the preservation of their guests until I can send for them from Lucknow.

I also transmit the translation of a proclamation which will be printed to-day at Cawnpore, and extensively circulated in Oude to-morrow.

Under any circumstances, such an intimation would, I trust, meet your Lordship's approval, as opening the door to those who are not irretrievably committed beyond the pale of mercy; but it is particularly called for at this juncture, to counteract the effect of the strenuous endeavours now being exerted at Lucknow by the rebel leaders, to draw all classes to their cause by representing that all who have in any way borne arms against the British are equally certain to meet the fate we award to the mutineers who fall into our hands; consequently that nothing is left for them but war to the death against the English.

P.S.—Since the above was written, we have received information that a gentleman, his wife, and child (lately born) are protected by another chief, Jhan Sing, zemindar of Brahmpore, twelve miles north of Beeugurmhow, in Oude.

In every case where the zemindars have afforded such protection, they have resisted all the wiles and threats of the rebel leaders to induce them to give up their guests.

Sir J. Outram to Colonel Inglis, Commanding at Lucknow.

Alum Bágh, 24th September, 1857.

The army halts here to-day, to recruit after three days' exposure to incessant rain, also to clear some obstacles in our front. To-morrow it will advance, but it may be late in the day ere it reaches you; don't risk any sally from your post that might expose your position to assault or surprise.

Sir J. Outram to Captain Bruce.

Lucknow Residency, 26th Sept. 1857.

I hope you received my letter of day before yesterday,* telling you of our victory on the previous day at Alum Bâgh over hosts of the enemy, and seizure of guns as usual.

Telegraph to the Governor-General from me as follows :—

"Yesterday General Havelock's force, numbering about 2,000 men of all arms, the remainder being left in charge of the sick, wounded, and baggage, occupying the Alum Bâgh, forced their way into the city under serious opposition. After crossing the Char Bâgh bridge, the troops skirted the city to the right, thus avoiding the enemy's defensive works prepared through the entire length of the main street leading directly to the Residency. Still much opposition had to be encountered ere we attained the Residency in the evening, just in time, apparently; for now that we have examined the outside of the defences, we find that two mines had been run far under the garrison's chief works, ready for loading, which, if sprung, must have placed the garrison at their mercy. Our loss is severe; not yet correctly ascertained, but estimated at from four to five hundred killed and wounded.

"Among the former, General Neill, Lieutenant Weld, 40th; Major Cooper, of Artillery; Lieutenant Webster, 78th Regiment; Captain Pakenham, 84th; Lieutenant Bateman, 64th; and Lieutenant Warren, 12th Irregular Cavalry. Among the latter, Colonel Campbell, H.M.'s 90th Foot; Lieutenant Havelock, Deputy Assistant Adjutant-General; Major Tytler, Deputy Quartermaster-General, and many others.

---

* Miscarried—intercepted by the enemy.

"To-day the troops are occupied in taking the batteries bearing on the garrison, which have been held till now, and continued occasionally to fire on the Residency. Since our junction with the garrison last night, many thousands of the enemy have deserted the city, and the late king's son and his court have fled to Fyzabad."

P.S.—Pray inform Lady Outram that I am all right. Lest any report should reach her that I am wounded, tell her that it is really *the merest trifle*—only a flesh wound in the right arm, which, though got early in the day, never incapacitated me for a moment. During the remainder of the day I remained on horseback, and scarcely feel it to-day. Don't mention anything about my wound in the telegraph to the Governor-General. John Anderson, the Fayrers, Gubbins, and Ogilvies, Banks's and Ommaney's widows, Mrs. Hayes, and the Conners and their families, in whom she is so interested, are all well. I send lists of the survivors in the garrison, which should be telegraphed first, and afterwards the other list of the dead should be given.

Sir J. Outram to Major McIntyre, Commanding at Alum Bágh.

Lucknow Residency, 28th September, 1857.

I have been unable to get any despatches forwarded to you since we reached the garrison on the evening of the 25th, owing to the bands of rebels swarming in our rear. As our men have had much to do on this side of the city, I am unable yet to detach troops to reopen our communications, and it may still be two or three days before I can do so. In the mean time, should you be assailed, you will be able to hold your own. The only damage they can do you is by firing long shots into the garden, but I trust the four guns left with you will soon silence such fire. If elephants, camels, &c., should be killed in the garden, have them dragged out by the draught bullocks to such distance as will prevent your air being tainted.

We have lost a good many men, but hold some of the palaces near the Residency, where we have good shelter.

The Commander-in-Chief to Sir James Outram.

(Extracts.) *Calcutta, 28th September, 1857.*

Pray accept my hearty congratulations on the brilliant manner in which you opened your campaign in Oude, and the success which attended your operations up to the 22nd. This is the date of the last intelligence we have of your movements. The Governor-General is much pleased, and joy was in every countenance when the news was made known to the public of your having reached within fourteen miles of Lucknow. I have received your many very full and interesting communications, which I immediately on receipt made known to the Governor-General.

My occupation here since my arrival has been one of attention to details, which have been thrown upon me in consequence of the absence of the staff. I hope, however, to have been of some use in pressing forward reinforcements, most of which have been made known to you by telegraph. A company of Engineers (Royal) left this on the 26th by bullock train, and the first company of the 93rd Highlanders left this morning. Two companies of Artillery under Colonel Crawford left this on the 25th instant, by steam vessel, for Benares, to take over the guns of the two batteries at Raj Ghât. Horses for these batteries are on their way to Benares with Colonel Fisher's column, and fifty-seven gunners and drivers from the Cape of Good Hope leave to-morrow by steamer to join Captain Maude's field battery, now with Havelock.

I last night had some conversation with the Governor-General about your position in Oude, and I certainly am of opinion, and I believe his Lordship agrees with me, that the force now with you is not more than sufficient for your occupation of Lucknow with due regard to its security, and the freedom of action of the force in the neighbourhood, and to the maintenance of its communications with Cawnpore. The chain of posts of Allahabad, Futtehpore, and Cawnpore, should be strongly maintained. I have been using every effort to push forward troops for the purpose of reinforcing these several posts, and I have been vexed and disappointed to see them diverted to other duties than the one for which I intended them.

I may mention to you in confidence that I intend myself to get to Cawnpore as soon as I can, and put myself in the centre of the troops. No advance will take place there without me, even if it be made with only a single regiment. With the communication open to Delhi, Agra, and the Punjab, it is absolutely necessary for me to get into the right place for directing the movements of the army, and restore something like connection to them. I have three officers coming here immediately, Lugard, Generals Wyndham and Dupuis. Any one of these would do to put in command at the Presidency, for the purpose of pushing the troops up as they arrive. . . . . My work here, therefore, which has been tiresome enough, is done.

I want a really sound, experienced officer to be placed at Benares, or Dinapore, who would be under your command, and who, maintaining an active correspondence with you and Government, would undertake that which I have been superintending myself during the past month, viz., the guard of the trunk road, and the districts on either side of the Ganges. This duty requires the greatest discretion and firmness, experience of the country, of the civil authorities, and of the mode of doing business of the last named. An officer fresh from England might get into trouble and impede the action of Government. I have therefore thought of Havelock, with the rank of Major-General, so soon as it can be got for him, if his Royal Highness approves of my suggestions in his favour, which I have already made. Neill, under you, at Lucknow, with another brigadier, will I hope be a sufficient staff for you, at all events for the present.

The Saugor and Nerbudda territories are in an unsatisfactory state, and we shall have to think of them also, I fear, as it will be impossible to hope for aid in that direction, either from Bombay or Madras, till the jungle fever season is past. This will not be, we are informed, for some months to come.

I took the liberty of attracting attention in orders to the manner in which you supported Havelock by pressing forwards the reinforcements, as it had been brought to my notice that the newspapers of Bombay had attacked you on this score, and I thought it best at once to demolish their false statements in justice to you.

(N.B.—This letter did not reach Sir J. Outram until after the Lucknow garrison was relieved by Sir Colin Campbell on the 17th November.)

The Chief of the Staff, Calcutta, to Sir J. Outram.

(Telegraphic.) *Calcutta, 28th September,* 1857.

Your despatch of the 17th September, addressed to the Deputy Adjutant-General, has been received. I am to inform you, by his Excellency's desire, that Captain Peel is still in the river between Dinapore and Benares, and that his arrival at Allahabad can only be looked for as a distant contingency. This, of course, falsifies your calculation with regard to the strength of the garrison of that place, and renders the retention of Captain Moir's company of artillery necessary for its security.

Two complete companies of Royal Artillery have left by steamer for Benares, where they will find guns, equipment, and horses. As soon as they are organized in batteries, they will close on Allahabad.

The first party of the 93rd Foot left Chinsurah, by bullock train, this morning, *en route* to the same place. The stream of men will now be continuous till at least two battalions have been despatched. They will be equipped for field service at Allahabad.

Another company of artillery arrived from the Cape, a few days ago, with drivers, but without guns. This company will be despatched from Raneegunge, by bullock train, after a few companies of the 93rd have been forwarded, and will take up guns at Allahabad.

A detachment of fifty-five men leaves by steam this day, to join Captain Maude's battery, which is under the command of Brigadier-General Havelock.

The Adjutant-General will address you at greater length upon this subject, in answer to your despatch of the 17th.

Sir J. Outram to the Commander-in-Chief.

(Telegraphic.)   *Lucknow*, 2*nd October*, 1857.

The insurgents are too strong to admit of withdrawing from this garrison. The sick, wounded, women and children, amount to upwards of 1,000. The force will retire, therefore, after making arrangements for the safety of the garrison, by strengthening it with all but four of our guns, and leaving 90th Regiment; then destroying all the enemy's works; exploding all the six mines which have been found since our access to the interior, and so disturbing the ground in front of each work as to render future mining a difficulty, and demolishing the houses in the neighbourhood which command the entrenchments. The remainder of our force, reduced by casualties, will make its way back to Cawnpore, and will leave two or three days hence. Two additional brigades, with powerful field artillery, would be required to withdraw the garrison, or reduce the city. I hope these brigades may be speedily assembled at Cawnpore.

The Officer Commanding at Allahabad to the Chief of the Staff, Calcutta.

(Telegraphic.)   *Allahabad*, 3*rd October*, 1857, 11.30 A.M.

When I telegraphed to you, Major Barnston, thirteen officers, and 296 men, were at Futtehpore; ninety-five men more proceed to join, and ought to reach Futtehpore on the 6th. I have since heard that Major Barnston and 150 men have been withdrawn by the officer commanding at Cawnpore, who states he has to send a company to Lucknow. On this, I cautioned the officer commanding at Cawnpore not to meddle with the Futtehpore post, except under Commander-in-Chief's or General Outram's orders. I don't know on what authority he withdrew the men from Futtehpore. One railway engine runs for forty miles on the Cawnpore road. Things are not sufficiently advanced to send two guns and their escort and battery, &c. Oude rebels concentrating at Futpore, twenty miles north-east off, this day, are said to have several guns (not good ones), and a very large number of men. I repeat my request, that I may be permitted to take the 64th Company, in preference to odds and ends of regiments in advance. I should like to have 300 Europeans, but if they can't be spared for general purposes, it can't be helped. Please answer quickly.

The Chief of the Staff, Calcutta, to the Officer Commanding at Cawnpore.

(Telegraphic.) *Calcutta, 3rd October,* 1857, 11.30 P.M.

I have just received a report that Major Barnston, with 140 men of the 90th Foot, has been ordered up to Cawnpore from Futtehpore, thereby seriously weakening the latter post beyond Sir James Outram's original intention. You are to let me know by telegraph, for the information of his Excellency, by whose authority the movement has been made.

The Chief of the Staff to Lieutenant-Colonel O'Brien, Allahabad.

(Telegraphic.) *Calcutta, 1st October,* 1857.

Captain Peel will join the garrison of Allahabad, with his first party, in two or three days, by the river. His Excellency desires you to recollect that that officer is under the orders of the Governor-General only.

Although the strength of the garrison at Allahabad will be increased, his Excellency desires that you are to entertain no thought of making detachments without express orders from him or Sir James Outram.

Equip and provide with bullocks and ammunition as many 9-pounder guns as Captain Moir can sufficiently man—say three or four—and send them under him, when organized, to Futtehpore, after the arrival of the Naval Brigade. Retain, as escort for Captain Moir's battery, the company of the 64th Foot just reaching you from Benares, and send them on together.

Inform Major Barnston and Sir James Outram of this arrangement. In the absence of Sir James Outram, let Major Barnston apply to me for orders by telegraph before undertaking anything beyond the mere defence of his post.

Captain Bruce to Colonel Lord Dunkellin.

Cawnpore, 5th October, 1857.

I lose no time in enclosing for the Governor-General's perusal a letter I have this moment received from Sir James Outram.

I have already, as directed, telegraphed to his Lordship, and also to his Excellency the Commander-in-Chief, the respective messages; and my letter to you of yesterday's date will have informed his Lordship the Governor-General of the departure early that morning of two guns and about 270 Europeans, of all ranks, under the command of Major Bingham, her Majesty's 64th Foot, convoying the required Commissariat stores. I have done all that General Outram has directed. Colonel Wilson has perused the enclosure, and has sent requisitions to Benares and Allahabad for troops; he has ordered also that 150 men, of all ranks, be detained by the officer commanding at Futtehpore, and the remainder (about 100 men) pushed up here immediately, all in excess of the 150 being moved forward, without delay, as they arrive.

We have now about 250 Europeans, of all ranks, fit for duty here, and the 100 men ordered from Futtehpore may be looked for the day after to-morrow.

I understand there are also two detachments on the way up between this and Allahabad; these will, of course, come on here.

The country upon the Oude side as far as Busseerutgunge is quite free from mutineers, and these districts are undisturbed, except by a few petty refractory zemindars and occasional marauding parties.

P.S.—I hope I need hardly add how rejoiced I should have been had Sir James Outram's letter reached in time for me to have proceeded in so honourable a command.

Sir J. Outram to Captain Bruce.

Lucknow, 2nd October, 1857.

Oblige me by conveying the following message to Brigadier Wilson :—

"I request you to prepare a detachment of not less than 300 Europeans and two guns, to advance to the relief of the retiring column; send rockets with the detachment to give us notice of its position when we are supposed to be in the vicinity. An experienced officer to command; I wish you could be spared for this command; if so, and you wish it, tell the Brigadier I wish it should be so arranged.

"Draw from Futtehpore, Allahabad, and Benares,

all men that can be spared to be sent to Cawnpore with all practicable despatch.

"Request the authorities at Agra to make known to the General at Delhi the urgent necessity there is for reinforcements being pushed on to Cawnpore as speedily as possible, without which the Lucknow garrison cannot be withdrawn.

"Delhi having fallen, it is to be hoped, at least, one strong brigade may be spared from there, and another may be completed by the troops from the eastward.

"Telegraph to the Commander-in-Chief that the insurgents are too strong to admit of withdrawing, besides this garrison, the sick, wounded, women, and children, amounting to upwards of 1,000.

"The force will retire, therefore, after making every disposition for the safety of the garrison by strengthening it with all but four of our guns, and leaving the 90th Regiment there, destroying all the enemy's works, exploding all the six mines which have been found since our access to the exterior, and to disturbing the ground in front of each work so as to render future mining very difficult, and demolishing the houses in the neighbourhood which commanded the entrenchment.

"The remainder of our force, reduced by casualties, will make its way back to Cawnpore, leaving two or three days hence.

"Two additional brigades, with powerful field artillery, will be required to withdraw the garrison or reduce the city.

"I hope the brigades will be speedily assembled at Cawnpore by troops from Delhi and the eastward. In the mean time this reduced force will be strengthened by its detachments still in the rear, and may, when completed, form a strong brigade. Telegraph to the Governor-General: ' My hopes of a reaction in the city.

are disappointed; the insurgent sepoys have inspired such terror among all classes, and maintain so strict a watch beyond our picquets, that we have not been able to communicate with one single inhabitant of Lucknow since our arrival. Nothing but a strong demonstration of our power will be of any avail."

The Chief of the Staff to the Officer Commanding at Cawnpore.

(Telegraphic.) *Calcutta, 4th October,* 1857.

Send in a statement to me of your strength by telegraph daily, with remarks on the communication between you and Lucknow, and the country generally. In the absence of directions from General Outram, apply for his Excellency's orders, through me, by telegraph, on every subject requiring instant direction. If Sir James Outram has not given orders personally affecting Major Barnston, of her Majesty's 10th Regiment, his Excellency desires that that officer may be sent back to Futtehpore, without his company, to take permanent command of that post. I see in your statement of the 28th September, that you have no cattle at all. Is this correct?

Captain Peel, R.N., to the Chief of the Staff, Calcutta.

(Telegraphic.) *Allahabad, 6th October,* 1857, 8 A.M.

An express from General Outram received: all troops that can be spared from the garrison to be sent immediately to Cawnpore. Colonel O'Brien will do so; his own expedition is stopped.

The Officer Commanding at Cawnpore to the Chief of the Staff, Calcutta.

(Telegraphic.) *Cawnpore, 6th October,* 11 A.M.

In answer to your message of the 3rd instant, Major Barnston had my orders only to send up 150 men, with due proportion of officers. Finding on its arrival here he had himself come up, I immediately ordered him back to resume his command; he left this accordingly the same night. General Outram left instructions to bring up troops from Futtehpore in the event of their being required; and as I had to send forward a large detachment of 252 infantry, two 9-pounders, with one sergeant, one naik, six gunners (European), and six trained Sikhs, I found it necessary to bring up the detachment (90th) to Cawnpore.

Captain Bruce to the Governor-General of India in Council.

(Telegraphic.) *Cawnpore, 7th October*, 1857, 11 P.M.

General Outram, dated 6th instant, orders me to inform your Lordship that there are alterations in the position of his force since the message of the 2nd instant, and he urgently requires more troops to enable him to move the position of his force.

Sir J. Outram to Captain Sibley, Alum Bâgh.

Lucknow Residency, 6th October.

I received your note of yesterday last night. I did not carry out my intention of moving out to you last night, and you must not now expect us; for all our force is required to aid this garrison. You must prepare, therefore, to hold your own, by strengthening your position and husbanding your garrison. Lest the reinforcement called for from Cawnpore may be unable to force its way, should it meet with opposition, as you are said to have caught some villagers in your last foray, I hope you may be able, through them, to open communication with the people and induce them to bring in supplies, for which *no cost should be spared.* I authorize McIntyre and yourself to *expend any amount of the public cash with you on this account.* Don't grudge *any cost* to induce the villagers to bring in supplies—not if 500 per cent. is charged. When once a commencement is effected, others also will be tempted to supply you.

Be careful in not attempting forays beyond reach of your guns. It is most dangerous to weaken your position for ever so short a time; and you might fall into an ambuscade.

Occupy the mosque in front of your gate by a small picket of Rifles, night and day; for if seized by the enemy they might harass you much thence. Burn all huts and cover within gunshot of your post. If you can spare time and followers to work, erect an earthen banquette inside your wall—at least at the most exposed spots, if not all round—and some flanking defences round your towers, or in front of your curtains.

Sir J. Outram to Captain Bruce, Cawnpore.
Lucknow Residency, 6th October, 1857.

I send duplicate of my letter of the 2nd instant. I have been obliged to abandon the intention of withdrawing any portion of this force for the present. The obstacles to communicating *between the Residency and Alum Bágh* being too formidable to be overcome with less than our whole force; even were it in a condition to be withdrawn.

I must rely, therefore, on support from Cawnpore for the Alum Bâgh detachment, and I hope the reinforcement which I formerly requested might be sent there, of not less than 300 Europeans and two guns, has been despatched to their aid, with such supply of provisions (chiefly atta and rice) as they can without difficulty escort on camels.

I believe the entire strength of the enemy is *here*, and that they have little force beyond the Char Bâgh; but it is possible they may have cavalry on the look out to obstruct communication with Cawnpore, or perhaps zemindaree matchlock men, at Bunnee or Busseerutgunge. It may be advisable, therefore, to take the old road should there be any reason to apprehend obstruction on the new road, according to the information the commanding officer may receive, who I hope may be yourself if you can be spared from Cawnpore, for it is essential that the commander should be a good officer.

If the detachment has not yet gone, it should be made as much stronger as can possibly be afforded from Cawnpore, in proportion to the additional troops expected from Futtehpore and Allahabad, leaving the garrison at its original strength, unless you should have ground for apprehending any attack on Cawnpore. Convey from me this official message to Brigadier Wilson :—

" If not already despatched, I request you will increase the detachment ordered to Alum Bâgh to whatever additional strength the reinforcements expected from Futtehpore and Allahabad could afford above the required garrison of your fort."

Alum Bâgh, thus reinforced, should be gradually strengthened by additional troops as they can be afforded, and supplied from Cawnpore. Telegraph to the Commander-in-Chief from me the substance of the above, and that " it will be impossible to withdraw this garrison without the support of a force of two strong brigades, which should be advanced as early as possible to Alum Bâgh, whence they would concert operations with us." Also to the Governor-General, that " there is no alteration in our position since my message of 2nd October."

Alum Bâgh is not on the road map, but it is situated about a mile from Char Bâgh Bridge, close to " Fákeer Shahgeekee Tánda," and I suppose there would be no difficulty in diverging from the old road so as to get into the new, anywhere between Bunnee and Alum Bâgh.

Sir J. Outram to Major McIntyre, Alum Bâgh.
Lucknow Residency, 7th October, 1857.

I enclose duplicate of letter I sent Sibley yesterday. You must not rely on reinforcements reaching you for some time, as they may consider the detachment I called for too weak, perhaps, and wait till they can send stronger. So husband your supplies as much as possible —Europeans three-fourths and natives half rations.

Bhowanee Deen, the bearer, a pensioned zemindar, will do his best to procure you supplies, but *arrange with him* to introduce what he gets in such way as to make it appear that *you looted his carts* on passing near your post. Otherwise you would get no second supply. He might be instructed to bring his carts into the vicinity of the Alum Bâgh, when you would creep out and rush upon him with a cheer, and pretend to plunder, taking him and the banians with him (to whom the grain belongs) prisoners, and, when out of observation, paying them most liberally, in hard cash, from the public treasury, five rupees for every rupee's worth of supplies, and, sending them off again with the carts *after dark*, with instructions to repeat the experiment. It is obviously necessary to manage it so that our friends must appear victims.

Sir J. Outram to Captain Bruce, Cawnpore.

Lucknow Residency, 7*th October*, 1857.

I send duplicate of a letter I despatched to you yesterday, enclosing copy of a previous one of 2nd instant. Our whole force is now besieged by the enemy, who have increased in number and audacity, which leads me to think the Delhi mutineers must now be here. Our position is more untenable than that of the previous garrison, because we are obliged to occupy the neighbouring palaces outside the entrenchment to accommodate the Europeans, which positions the enemy are able to mine from cover of neighbouring buildings. Still no communication with the town, and little prospect of procuring provisions; the neighbouring streets, into which we have made sorties at much cost of life, containing nothing. We have grain, and gun bullocks, and horses, on which we may subsist a month I hope,* but nothing else. No hospital stores, and but little medicine. Make this known to the Governor-General and Commander-in-Chief. I trust to support from Cawnpore for the safety of the Alum Bâgh detachment. It could not be withdrawn to Cawnpore with all its sick, wounded, 200 elephants, camels, and waggons, without being greatly reinforced; and such reinforcement would enable it to hold on where it is, in its fortified post, greatly to our advantage. The moral effect of maintaining troops there, and gradually reinforcing that post, must tell in our favour ere long; and, sooner or later, I hope to transfer there some of the troops now here, thus avoiding the necessity of retaining the exposed accommodation which is now required to contain them all.

But supplies must be sent with every strong escort you can prepare. So far as we can learn, the enemy have no troops beyond the Char Bâgh; but it may be prudent, perhaps, to take the old road, to avoid Busserutgunge and Bunnee, lest opposition might be met there from zemindaree followers, until troops can be furnished to occupy both those places, with a wing of infantry and two guns each, which would secure the whole road for the safe convoy of provisions hereafter for the Alum Bâgh post. I hope the first detachment may find the road sufficiently clear to admit of sending back, from Alum Bâgh to Cawnpore, the elephants and camels, under escort of 100 riflemen mounted on their backs. This should be done *on the night of the day the reinforcement*

---

* Such was the representation of our commissaries at this time:—we afterwards found that they had much underrated their store of grain.

reaches Alum Bágh; the escort back being taken from the Europeans now there, who (the animals being fresh) should make their way to Cawnpore (forty-five miles) almost without a halt.

I omitted to mention, that in capturing the palaces on the 26th, we secured the children of the ex-king's brother, styled the *General,* who is in England (*i. e.* an only son, an adopted son, and a daughter), who are prisoners. I regret to say our loss in killed, wounded, and missing, since we crossed the Ganges has been very heavy—246 killed, and 700 wounded and missing. Among the former sixteen officers.

The Chief of the Staff to the Officer Commanding at Cawnpore.

(Telegraphic.) *Calcutta, 6th October,* 1857.

The Commander-in-Chief finds it necessary that Major Barnston should get to his regiment. He will, therefore, proceed to Lucknow, instead of, as directed yesterday, to Futtehpore. Two lakhs and a half of ammunition, and about 250 Europeans, have been ordered to Cawnpore from Allahabad. Communicate this to General Outram.

The Chief of the Staff to Major Barnston, Futtehpore.

(Telegraphic.) *Calcutta, 7th October,* 1857.

His Excellency having been under the impression that the party of her Majesty's 10th Regiment, lately under your command, was going on to Lucknow immediately, changed his mind respecting you, and directed that you should accompany it; but as it now appears that such was not the case, other troops having gone forward, you are to remain at Futtehpore, and command the latter post. If the detachment of her Majesty's 90th Regiment, now at Cawnpore, leaves for Oude, you must get to it. His Excellency has ordered two guns, equipped with bullocks, to be sent from Allahabad to Futtehpore. Communicate the last order respecting yourself to Colonel Wilson by telegraph. Inform me by telegraph what precautions have been taken for strengthening the post at Futtehpore, and whether, in your opinion, two 9-pounder guns are enough for it; also, what provisions are laid in.

Procure grain, sheep, and beef for 500 men for two months. Lose no time.

Colonel Wilson to the Chief of the Staff.

(Telegraphic.)　　　　　Cawnpore, 8th October, 1857, 4 P.M.

A messenger, with a letter from General Outram written in Greek character, arrived late last night; it was directed to Captain Bruce, superintendent of police, and contains the below written order to me :—

"SIR,　　　　　　　　　　　　　　"Lucknow, 6th October.

"If not already despatched, I request you will increase the detachment ordered to Alum Bâgh, to whatever additional strength the reinforcements expected from Futtehpore and Allahabad could provide above the original strength of your post."

Another part of Sir James Outram's letter states the impossibility of withdrawing his force without the support of two strong brigades; likewise that his communication with his rear at Alum Bâgh, four miles distant, is not preserved. Again, that the Alum Bâgh detachment should be gradually reinforced from Cawnpore as troops come in; that the whole strength of the enemy is in his vicinity and Residency, but that it is probable that cavalry may be detached to his rear, to occupy Bunnee and Busseerutgunge, &c. It were needless for me to dilate on the perilous position General Outram's force is in. The Chief of the Staff will observe that his communication with his depôt at Alum Bâgh, only four miles distant, is closed; between this and Alum Bâgh communication is precarious and uncertain; the roads and adjacent pathways are zealously guarded. A cossid may perchance carry a letter through from here safely, but to my knowledge none have.

I would request his Excellency's commands regarding the way reinforcements are to be forwarded when they do arrive. I am strongly against hazarding and jeoparding small detachments of 400 or 500 men; such driblets, under existing circumstances, would run the chance of being destroyed in detail, and, even if they effect a junction, would be of no use for the General's main object. I would not myself forward a reinforcement of less than 1,500 European bayonets, and six guns, and then only if a second reinforcement of similar strength could follow them in ten days. I most sincerely trust none of the mutinous brigades, let loose by the fall of Delhi, will retire through Rohilcund, viâ Anoopshuhur or Ramghal, and join the Lucknow rebels. The Gwalior rebels threatened us with a visit, but I do not anticipate any likelihood of their doing so. It appears to me quite evident that in Oude the aspect of affairs has extended far beyond that of mutiny with sepoys, as revolt has plainly spread through the whole province.

Sir J. Outram to Major McIntyre.

Alum Bâgh, Lucknow Residency, 8th October.

I have received your note of yesterday, announcing the arrival of the convoy under Major Brigham. It is now most necessary to send back the elephants and camels, which, if the road is clear, might, unladen, make their way to Cawnpore in one forced march, if started off after dark under guidance of an intelligent officer who knows the fords of the Bunnee River. They should keep a sharp look out in passing Bunnee and Busseerutgunge, making a détour should there be any appearance of opposition; which, however, could hardly be prepared if they moved rapidly on, and strict precautions are taken to prevent traitors in your post sending notice of your intention, by preventing a soul getting outside your walls from the moment your preparations begin. But they must be well guarded, for the capture of our elephants would be an irreparable loss to us. One hundred riflemen at least should escort them, half of whom might be mounted on the elephants —the animals to be kept well together—as many Europeans as can be spared, who understand the native language (such as conductors, &c.), to be sent with the party, to prevent misunderstanding between the soldiers and the Mahouts (elephant drivers), and to guard against the latter taking their animals off the road on any pretext, lest they should walk off with them to the enemy.

I hope the old pensioner who took my yesterday's note to you, may concert with you a plan whereby to supply what is required for your natives.

In the meantime, if you cannot seize cattle in the field without exposing your men to risk of being cut off by cavalry, kill your cart bullocks (and sheep if you have them) for their subsistence, and supply something from your European stores to those natives whose caste will not allow them to eat meat.

P.S.—What news from Delhi and Gwalior? In telling you to send an escort with the elephants, I take it for granted that, with the reinforcements which reached you on the 6th, you are now upwards of 500 strong.

Sir J. Outram to Major McIntyre.

Alum Bágh, Lucknow, 8th October, 1857.

I was horrified to learn by your note of the 29th that your followers are out of supplies, for I had understood that the whole force had been provided for fifteen days. Of course you have killed some of your bullocks for the Mahomedan and low-caste followers. And I give you full authority to slaughter as many cattle as are required for that purpose, and for the Europeans, and I trust you have given a portion of your European supplies, such as flour, &c., to the Hindoos who cannot eat meat (sufficient to give them half rations). For of European supplies you have half of what was intended for 3,000 men, eight days only having been supplied to our force. Thus, as you have only about 400 Europeans, the remaining half should last them sixty days on full rations (minus what you give the followers). But of course, seeing such necessity for economy, you will have issued half or three-quarter rations; for the part of this force which will return to escort you to Cawnpore must also be provided. As most of the carts will have to be abandoned, you need have no scruple about killing as many bullocks as necessary. Your elephants, &c., can be foraged from the paddy fields under the walls and trees within range of your guns. If threatened by the enemy, a rifleman or two on the back of each elephant sent for forage, ought to suffice to protect them. But they should not go beyond range of your guns, and your men should guard against treachery on the part of the Mahouts, who might take the animals into the enemy's hands under pretence of their running away. I cannot yet say positively when you may expect the returning troops, but hope it will not be long. Be vigilant : the enemy are round you, and may try to get into your enclosure, unless a sharp look out is kept from your towers and the roof of the house. Should elephants or camels die in the enclosure, the carcase should be yoked to bullocks and taken out sufficiently far to prevent them tainting the air. Send answer by bearer.

Sir J. Outram to Major McIntyre.

Alum Bâgh, Lucknow Residency,
9th October, 1857.

On questioning the cossid who brought your note of the 7th, he tells me the detachment which brought the supplies from Cawnpore was sent back with the empty carts. Surely this is not the case, for you cannot have relinquished a reinforcement so necessary to your safety, at least without referring to me. Nor would you have sent them back without availing yourself of the opportunity for returning the elephants and camels, which are so necessary for our future supplies (as for the carts, you will of course make firewood of them, and feed your people, &c., with the bullocks). I trust, therefore, the cossid's report is not true, and that you will have carried out my instructions sent yesterday, in the understanding that you had retained the reinforcement. I trust the old pensioner I sent to you on the 6th to secure supplies from the villagers has joined you.

Sir J. Outram to Captain Bruce, Cawnpore.

Lucknow Residency, 9*th October,* 1857.

Lest my letter of the 7th miscarried, I now send duplicate. I therein contemplated sooner or later forcing our way back to Alum Bágh with the surplus troops not required to garrison these entrenchments— a measure imperative if practicable, as there appears now no hope of obtaining further supplies, and for our whole force now here our grain alone and gun bullocks may possibly be eked out for a month; and but little else for twenty days. No expenditure of cash is of any avail, for we have no means of communicating with any of the townspeople.

Unless we can move off a portion of the force to Alum Bágh, therefore, such is the utmost length of our tether; but I grieve to say I am not now certain of effecting even this. All the bridges between us and Alum Bágh are destroyed, so that we could not take guns, and without artillery we should suffer greatly in forcing our way against the masses of the enemy prepared and watching for us on every road, and increasing every day; Maun Sing being with the rebels, and exerting his influence to raise the whole country against us, besides rebel troops arrived from Delhi it is said. But it is of the utmost importance that the Alum Bágh post should be maintained, which we may yet force our way to. And it is well able to maintain itself now that it has been reinforced, I am happy to say, by 350 men and two guns, under Major Brigham, and with good store of European supplies. On hearing of this reinforcement, I sent orders to the commanding officer to despatch the elephants and camels after dark, escorted by 100 riflemen mounted on the animals, which, being unladen and travelling rapidly all night, should reach Cawnpore without a halt. The carts of course could not return at present. The followers must be supported, until supplies for them come from Cawnpore, on slaughtered cattle; those sharing the European supply whose caste cannot eat meat, unless—as they are in the open country, and there are friendly zemindars in that neighbourhood—they obtain something from the villages. The detachment at Alum Bágh, minus 100 sent back, will now amount to 500 rank and file, besides about 100 convalescent sick and wounded capable of bearing arms, who with their six guns (counting the two which came with Major Brigham) may, until reinforced, confidently defy the enemy, who are not likely, however, to assail a fortified position, exposed as they would be to our guns.

Sir J. Outram to Captain Sibley.

Alum Bágh, Lucknow Residency,
11th October, 1857.

I received yours of last night, and am glad to learn that you are so strong. I shall be anxious till I learn the safe arrival of the elephants at Cawnpore; but if due precautions were taken to prevent information outside of your intention to start them off, I trust they would have got beyond reach of pursuit before their departure was known to the enemy. If they started soon after dark, they would be past Oonao by morning, and then comparatively safe. But I wish I had not encumbered them with camels, which cannot go so fast as elephants.

In reply to your questions,—

(1.) The Provost Marshal will inflict fifty lashes on any man caught in the act of plundering our own stores. If not *caught* in the act, but convicted, he will receive fifty lashes under sentence of court-martial.

(2.) The troops should be warned that the commanding officer has received my orders to direct the Provost Marshal to hang on the spot the next man found thus offending, and that the order will be carried out without fail. The Jemadar and Mahout found communicating with the enemy should be tried by court-martial for rebellion, and, if found guilty, hanged.

Do not relax in strengthening your position, which must be held until Greathed's column of the army from Delhi (3,000 strong of all arms, with eighteen guns), now on its way to Cawnpore, joins you. In addition to the ramp inside the wall, loopholes and a redoubt outside each corner bastion, you should make a ditch outside all round, commencing with the most exposed places, of course.

A traverse also should be constructed, connecting the mosque with your square.

Give your working parties the same as we allow here, paid daily from the public treasury. European and native soldiers and camp followers, for ordinary work in the trenches, one rupee for four hours' work, or more or less in proportion to the time of work. Officers commanding working parties (not on staff pay) will receive field engineers' allowances. Surround your corner towers with a rampart of sandbags.

Sir J. Outram to Captain Bruce, Cawnpore.

Lucknow Residency, 11*th October,* 1857.

In your note of the 5th you acknowledge mine of the 2nd, but make no mention of previous ones, so I fear you have not received that of the 26th. I therefore send list (in a quill) of the survivors of the garrison.

I also send duplicate of my last letter to you of the 9th. As the detachment reached Alum Bágh without opposition, I am now glad you were not sent with it, for your absence just now from Cawnpore would be more injurious to our interests than your presence at Alum Bágh could do any good. There they have merely to remain on the defensive, trusting to your exertions at Cawnpore to supply them. I hope you will be able to induce some of the Oude zemindars with whom you have influence, to take supplies to Alum Bâgh, giving them an order on the treasure-chest there, for payment *in cash*, at whatever rate you may fix for the amount delivered. Of course no price should be grudged—500 per cent. would be cheap payment—until other zemindars are induced to come forward. Promise them *cash* payment *on delivery*, at that, or any rate you may think proper. I trust the column from Delhi with Greathed will be urged to come on to Cawnpore as quickly as possible, and from thence be pushed on to Alum Bâgh, where its presence alone will suffice, most probably,[*] to disperse the armed mob which now commands the city, for they would not risk attack from opposite quarters, and at any rate, when at Alum Bâgh, it could open communication and concert measures with us, which it could not do from Cawnpore. Indeed I am pretty confident that the arrival of a brigade at Alum Bâgh would at once break up the confederate malcontents here, and enable the well affected to obtain with our aid the control of the city, when all our requisitions for supplies and carriage for removing sick, wounded, and women and children, would be complied with. But even if this result be not accomplished by the mere arrival of the Delhi force at Alum Bâgh, and should it not of itself be sufficient with our aid to force through the city, it would certainly be able to bring

---

[*] At this time we were led to hope, by Maun Sing's cunning overtures, that he was about to abandon the enemy's cause, in which case his example would have been followed by all the principal zemindars, who composed the chief strength of the enemy, against the remainder of whom I hoped our well-wishers in the city would have been able to make head, when encouraged to do so by the approach of the relieving force. It afterwards proved, however, that Maun Sing was deceiving us; and he strenuously opposed us to the last, and it was he alone who prevented the breaking-up of the coalition hostile to us; consequently the friendly-disposed dared not to move in our favour.

supplies to the Dilkoosha, and thence, by a concerted movement, enable us to meet and bring them here. In the meantime the present force at Alum Bâgh (700 effective soldiers and 6 guns) can hold that position *certainly*, if only supplies for its followers be provided; and *on no account should it be now withdrawn*. Its presence is our greatest security, and the moral effect of its withdrawal would possibly be our destruction. Urge the speedy advance of the Delhi column, therefore, in my name, and telegraph the substance of the above from me to the Commander-in-Chief.

I believe the elephants and camels were despatched to you last night from Alum Bâgh, under instructions which I trust would secure an unobserved departure after dark, and, by rapidly pushing on all night, enable them to reach you in the course of the day. But I am anxious to hear of their safe arrival. I directed that they should be escorted by at least 100 riflemen, half mounted on the elephants. I am anxious about the supply of food for the native followers there, as only supplies for the Europeans were sent. These the higher caste followers—who cannot eat meat—must share; and the others must be fed on slaughtered cart bullocks till supplied. By the strictest scrutiny it is ascertained* that at our present rate (three-quarters rations for Europeans, and half for natives) our grain, allowing it to be all good, will last only till the 6th of November; our meat not so long. Rice will be out in four days. Unless, therefore, the Delhi troops come speedily to our aid, we must starve.

Promulgate the news of the approach of the Delhi force as publicly as possible.

Urge Greathed to push on with all possible despatch.

---

* So reported by the commissary. Afterwards more grain was ascertained, and the estimate of meat was found to be underrated. It was subsequently calculated that, on further reduced rations, we could carry on till the end of November.

The Chief of the Staff to Colonel Wilson, Cawnpore.

(Telegraphic.) *Calcutta, 10th October,* 1857.

Do not send any small detachment from Cawnpore to Lucknow. It is not safe.

By the 23rd instant, the 93rd Foot will be at Allahabad; by the 2nd of November, her Majesty's 23rd, and a wing of her Majesty's 53rd. Send my message, by cossid, to General Outram, to inform him of this. Her Majesty's 82nd has arrived in the river. Captain Christopher, of the Commissariat, has been ordered to Cawnpore from Allahabad. Direct all your attention to commissariat, ordnance stores of every sort, and the collection of carriage.

The Chief of the Staff to Colonel Wilson.

(Telegraphic.) *Calcutta,* October, 1857.

With regard to the arrival of the convoy from Alum Bâgh, what intelligence did it bring, and is the road through Oude to that place to be considered safe ? What does the commissariat officer of the party report ? Answer by telegraph.

Colonel Wilson to the Chief of the Staff.

(Telegraphic.) *Cawnpore, 12th October,* 1857, 2 P.M.

Convoy of unladen elephants and camels, with escort, arrived last night from Alum Bâgh; detachments previously giving emergent indents from officer commanding there, for hospital clothes, medical comforts and stores, as all the camp-followers, servants and baggage were left at Alum Bâgh; food for natives urgently demanded; 130 sick and wounded men there, greatly in want of bedding and linen. Escort were not molested by rebels, but the animals had to ford the river, Bunnee bridge being destroyed. Officers of escort could furnish no information of General Outram's force, but state that frequent firings were heard from Lucknow day and night; a quill cossid arrived occasionally. I have had no communication from General Outram since my last report was sent. I have stated my opinion already about sending small detachments. I do not see how these supplies can be sent; it is only putting more men in peril. The Nana is supposed to cross the river to-day or to-morrow at Futtehpore Chowrasse. He has about 400 cavalry. Report states he goes to meet Gwalior Contingent marching down. Please to send orders quickly about my sending supplies.

Captain Bruce to the Governor-General in Council.

(Telegraphic.) *Cawnpore, 12th October,* 1857.

Letter of 9th from Alum Bâgh reports incessant firing at Lucknow, with occasional salvos of artillery. Cannot communicate with General Outram yet. The road between Cawnpore and Alum Bâgh is infested by thieves near the latter place.

Sir J. Outram to General Havelock.
12th October, 1857.

It is my pleasing duty to recommend to you, as deserving the high distinction of the Victoria Cross, two officers, of whose heroic gallantry, on the 25th ultimo, I was an admiring witness; but who, having on that occasion been under your command, can only through yourself receive the reward they so justly merit. The officers I refer to are Captain Maude, of the Royal Artillery, and Lieutenant Havelock, Assistant Adjutant-General. The former of these, as you are aware, with his bullock battery, supported by a small party of the 5th Fusiliers, formed the advance guard when the troops moved on from the Alum Bâgh. The enemy had on that occasion flanked his road under cover of long high grass, and a murderous fire was poured on the column from a double-storied house full of musketeers, and from loopholed walls of the large surrounding gardens; from two guns that raked the road from the right flank, and from another that commanded his front. But steadily and cheerily Captain Maude pushed on with his brave men, and, in the face of this desperate opposition, brought them through, though not without the loss of nearly one-third of his artillery force. This was no reckless or fool-hardy daring, but the calm heroism of a true soldier, who fully appreciated the importance, the difficulties, and the dangers of the task he had undertaken.

But for his nerve and coolness on this trying occasion, the army could not have advanced, and I shall be glad to learn that you agree with me in considering that he has fully and honourably earned a right to the Cross which our gracious Sovereign has instituted as a reward " For Valour."

Not less deserving of this proud distinction, in my opinion, is Lieutenant Havelock; and I trust I may, without giving offence, beg you, as my friend and comrade, as well as my official colleague, not to allow the name of this gallant young officer to militate against his just claims. Under the tremendous fire of guns and musketry, which the enemy directed across the Char Bágh bridge, Lieutenant Havelock, with the Madras Fusiliers, stormed the bridge, took the guns, and cleared the street sufficiently to allow of the troops in rear closing up. I cannot conceive a more daring act than this forcing of the bridge; and the officers who led the Fusiliers on that occasion, in my opinion, *most richly deserve promotion;* but, hazardous as was their position, they—being on foot, and, therefore, not readily distinguished from their men—risked little comparatively with Lieutenant Havelock, the only officer on horseback, who cheered the men on, and became the target of the enemy's musketry. I shall feel truly delighted to learn that you accept my recommendation of this brave officer; and I shall deeply regret having divested myself of the command during the advance on Lucknow, if (from what I must regard as a morbidly sensitive delicacy) you withhold from Lieutenant Havelock, because he is your relative, the reward to which, as a soldier, he has so unmistakably established a just claim.

General Havelock to Sir J. Outram.

Lucknow, 13th October, 1857.

It will afford me the highest pleasure to attend to your recommendation for the Victoria Cross in favour of Captain Maude, Royal Artillery, and Lieutenant Havelock, Deputy Assistant Adjutant-General.

All that you have so forcibly narrated of the conduct of the former at the Char Bágh entirely corresponds with my own observation of his distinguished gallantry from the day our first shot was fired at Futtehpore up to this period.

It must of course afford me peculiar satisfaction that the behaviour of my son in action has attracted your attention, and I feel that when his merits are thus pointed out to me, I ought not to deprive him of that reward from any consideration of his near relation to me. From my hand I well know that he never would have consented to receive the Cross; if the observation that he had deserved it had originated with myself. As it comes spontaneously from you, every such scruple may be laid aside, and the value of the decoration will be much enhanced to him, by its being virtually awarded by an unprejudiced judge, as well as by one, I trust you will permit me to add, whose proved gallantry and devotion to the service peculiarly fit him to judge of these qualities in another.

Sir J. Outram to Captain Bruce, Cawnpore.

Lucknow Residency, 13*th October*, 1857.

I received the night before last yours of the 8th, conveying the gratifying information that the Delhi force moving down the Doab would be near Futtehghur at that date, and that you had forwarded direct to its commander my urgent request that he should push on to Cawnpore with all practicable despatch. I beg you will now make the following communication to him from me:

"It is most urgent that you should move to our support as early as practicable. In forcing our way from the Alum Bâgh to the Residency with 2,300 men, our casualties were so heavy that our sick, wounded, and women and children, numbering upwards of 1,000, cannot be removed until we are greatly reinforced, nor could we obtain carriage for them while our communication with the well affected in the city is cut off by the rebels, who still domineer over it, and surround our position. Neither can we obtain supplies; our condition in respect to which Captain Bruce will inform you of. Being unable to remove the garrison, our whole force is required to support it; and the enemy, having destroyed the bridges between this and our Alum Bâgh post, five miles off, we cannot communicate with it. For, without artillery (which could not cross the canal), we could not overcome the intervening obstacles without heavier loss than we can now afford. At Alum Bâgh we have our carriage and supplies, 600 European infantry, besides convalescents, six guns of our own, and some others taken from the enemy, in a well-fortified walled enclosure, with open country around, quite safe against attack, and a secure plank for your force if encamped there. Two more infantry regiments, with guns, I hope, will probably be there, with further supplies, before you arrive, and the whole will be an available addition to your force, minus a small guard to hold the place when you move, as probably you would soon do, to the Dilkoosha. When there, we could open more direct communication, and concert combined movements. But all this can be arranged after you arrive at Alum Bâgh, which I hope you will do as early as possible; for the mere presence of your force there will probably cause the dispersion of the party which now enthrals the city; so far, at least, as to enable us to obtain supplies. Alum Bâgh is forty-five miles, or three easy marches, on good road from the Cawnpore bridge; and a day's halt at Cawnpore would, I hope, suffice to replenish your supplies, bringing on with you for a few days only, and leaving the rest to follow; for, as your force advances, the communication with Cawnpore will not be obstructed.* At Alum Bâgh you will soon be reinforced by H. M.'s 93rd and 23rd Regiments, which commenced leaving Raneegunge by bullock train on the 28th. Also, two or more troops of Horse Artillery are on the way up. But their junction should be awaited at *Alum Bâgh*, not Cawnpore. There the assemblage of forces would have no effect; whereas, at Alum Bâgh,

---

* At this time we knew nothing of the advance of the Gwalior rebels, and relied much on Captain Bruce's exertions to establish intermediate police thannahs.

not merely would your presence in such close vicinity be favourable to our communication with friends in the city, but would encourage many of the neighbouring landholders who are in our favour to come forward. Moreover, by pushing on to Alum Bâgh, you would be far ahead of the main body of the Delhi rebels, who, on learning that you are there, would be deterred from coming to Lucknow.

When I urged your (Bruce) being sent in command of the party to Alum Bâgh, I meant the *first* party, which I thought might be opposed. But as that met no opposition, and all that is now required at Alum Bâgh is merely to hold a position not likely to be attacked, there would be little worthy of your doing with any subsequent detachment; and as your services are invaluable at Cawnpore, I would not take you thence merely to command the escort now required to bring provisions for the followers there, the supply of which has hitherto been so strangely neglected. It is most urgent that they should be supplied to the utmost extent that suitable escort can be provided. As all your camels and elephants may be required for the Delhi force, these supplies might come in carts, which could go back to you empty with comparatively small escort. I don't think the Cawnpore garrison should be less than 350 effective Europeans, and that of Futtehpore 150. Beyond this you enumerate parties of only 80, 90, and 150, as immediately expected. If so, you could hardly afford to send more than 200 or 250 Europeans in addition to the return escort of 100 which took back the elephants. I am most anxious to learn that they reached you safe.

Urge Greathed to come on to Alum Bâgh with all possible despatch.

Should orders from Calcutta direct the organization

of the reinforcements for Lucknow at Cawnpore, represent how imperative I consider it that they should be assembled at Alum Bâgh instead; and that *there* they can be supported from Cawnpore with perfect safety. Small detachments maintained at Busseerutgunge, Nuwabgunge, and Bunnee, will amply secure the communication. On no account send any of your Mehter police into Oude. Their presence would confirm the belief so industriously circulated by our enemies here, that we purpose forcibly to destroy *caste*. If your party at Busseerutgunge is so composed, pray relieve them by Sikhs, or others. Your police cavalry would be most useful at Alum Bâgh, and I hope will accompany the bazaar supplies. With their assistance commissariat agents might perhaps communicate with distant villages and purchase supplies.

Telegraph to Allahabad to expedite the advance of the two regiments coming by bullock train. A large quantity of powder should be sent with the Delhi column for explosive purposes; also a few $4\frac{2}{5}$ mortars, and entrenching tools. Communicate all the above to Brigadier Wilson from me, as if sent direct to himself.

I send copy of a proclamation issued some days ago. I appoint you commandant of the depôt, to receive and organize all who produce the certificates referred to in the proclamation, who engage on the understanding that they will have to stand the consequences if hereafter proved to have joined in acts of rebellion, &c.

Telegraph the substance to Government, and ask if others who received similar leave to their homes, under Mr. Colvin's proclamation, are to be similarly embodied, or how.

(Enclosure.)
Proclamation dated 4th October, 1857.

"All those sepoys and sowars of the 13th, 48th, and 71st Regiments, and 7th Light Cavalry, who were sent to their homes on *compulsory furlough*, in June last, are hereby called upon to proceed to Cawnpore, where a depôt of their regiments will be formed for their reception.

"All those sepoys of the above regiments who availed themselves of their furlough in the usual manner, and have since taken no part in the rebellion, are also directed to join the depôts of their regiments at Cawnpore."

Sir J. Outram to Captain Sibley, Alum Bâgh.

Lucknow Residency, 14th *October*, 1857.

The accompanying packet is for the Officer commanding the Delhi column, which will, I hope, ere long reach Alum Bâgh.

I send duplicate of my last to you of 11th instant. In future, always tell me the dates of the communications you receive from me, and let me know the dates of those you have already received.

Oblige me by telling my servant John to pay whatever may be required for food for my servants.

(Enclosure to above.)
Sir J. Outram to the Officer Commanding the Troops advancing to the Relief of Lucknow.

I now send a sketch of the ground intervening between Alum Bâgh and this position,* and beg to suggest the following mode of operations, by which you may effect a junction with us with the least difficulty.

From Alum Bâgh, passing round the southern face of the enclosure, and between the villages of Hushtunggee and Poorwah, and proceeding almost due east for about three miles, over a level country of grass land and cultivation—with a shallow jheel to cross shortly after leaving Alum Bâgh, probably not more than ankle deep now, and no obstacle to guns—you will arrive opposite the village of Jamcitha, on your left. Slanting past this for about a mile to north-west, you arrive at the Dilkoosha Palace; nothing but the park wall (about eight feet high) intervening, which can be broken down anywhere by a couple of pioneers. The palace having large windows in European style, is not

---

* See the plan at the end of this volume.

likely to be defended. But if so, a few cannon shot would soon empty it. Indeed, I anticipate little or no opposition to your occupation of Dilkoosha Palace and park, or of the neighbouring Martiniere, or of the Beebeapore II, should you think it necessary, the enemy's troops being chiefly on this side of the canal. The union-jack hoisted at the top of the palace, and a royal salute from your guns to draw our attention to it (should you have had no previous firing), would inform us of your arrival. And our union-jack, which we would then hoist over the Chutter Munzil (distant two and a half or three miles), will show you that we *are* informed.

At the Dilkoosha you have an open plain for encampment of nearly a mile, before the palace, and between it and the town a deep canal, the bridges over which are broken down. By encamping with your front to the canal, and your guns on your front and flanks, you would keep down any fire which the enemy could bring against you from the town side; for they have only seven or eight guns in different positions on this side of the Goomtee, guarding the different egresses towards the Dilkoosha from our position. These guns are of different calibre, and so badly found in carriages that the enemy would have some difficulty in moving them away to turn against you; but if they *did* remove them for that purpose, it would facilitate our dash out to meet you on your advance to this side of the canal; where, however, they are not likely to stand when they find you prepared to cross the canal, exposed as they then would be to attack from front and rear.

Under cover of your guns, you will have no difficulty in sloping passages for your artillery down *your* side into the canal, and up *our* side, during the first night, ready to pass over early next morning.

Further delay, I think, would be impolitic, as it would give the enemy time to bring guns from distant places.*

Lest messengers should miscarry, your signal for intending to cross the canal in the morning might be three guns, followed by three rockets, the night before, after reconnaissance had satisfied you of the feasibility of preparing the slope during the night.

The banks of the canal are from twenty to twenty-five feet deep; there is little or no water, and sandy bottom. You would, of course, leave parties in occupation of the Dilkoosha Palace; and also, after passing the canal, in some of the principal buildings commanding your line of communication.

But we should meet you half way with a pretty strong column of Europeans and guns;† and we would then arrange together the

---

* The Commander-in-Chief's force was obliged to halt a day, after occupying the Dilkoosha and Martiniere, and the enemy *did* take forward guns. The resistance he met with was far more serious than had been anticipated, owing to Mann Sing's deceit.

† This was written on the 14th October. By the 17th November, when the Commander-in-Chief came, the Lucknow troops had exhausted their gun bullocks, the last being killed for food on that very day; they were, consequently, without the means of moving out half way. They, however, advanced their guns by manual labour, and thus enabled themselves to storm the enemy's works which interposed between their advance posts and the Mess-house the day

mode of maintaining the communication between your camp on the canal (or Dilkoosha) and our entrenchment.

You would perhaps halt two or three days at Alum Bâgh, and might continue to give us notice of the day of your advance. Of course, all the troops at Alum Bâgh will be under your command, and a small guard (including the convalescents) will suffice to maintain that place; thus placing 500 or 600 Europeans at your disposal, besides guns.

Sir J. Outram to Brigadier Wilson, Cawnpore.

Lucknow, 15th October, 1857.

In case Bruce may have been detached by you to Alum Bâgh, I address you direct, instead of as hitherto through him, that he might turn the Greek letters into English for you. But I trust there are others with you who can do so. Pray write your notes to me in the same character. Herewith I send duplicate of a letter I forwarded through Bruce to the officer commanding the Delhi column, which (if the former miscarried) pray communicate to him in the most expeditious manner possible. Also please attend to my instructions respecting the sepoys who return from leave —referred to in the accompanying proclamation—and forward the messages to the Governor-General and Commander-in-Chief, if not already gone. If Bruce is not with you, appoint any other officer most competent to superintend the depôt of returned sepoys. I enclose a sketch of the ground between Alum Bâgh and this place, for the officer who commands the relieving force.

Date your notes, and tell me the dates of those you receive from me. Please show this to Bruce, if still with you. It is most urgent that the Alum Bâgh post

---

before the junction. They then opened their guns on the Mess-house and Motee Mehal, and their fire, in conjunction with that of Sir Colin Campbell's artillery from the opposite side, compelled the enemy to vacate those strong positions.— (See *Despatches of General Havelock, Colonel Napier, Brigadier Eyre, &c., relating to these operations.*)

should be furnished with bazaar supplies for followers, which I trust will have been forwarded under suitable escort before this reaches you. Gun and musketry powder, 5½ and 8 inch shells, 24-pounder shot, good fuzes, with proportion of stores and Enfield ammunition, are most required, and should be sent with the relieving column.

Mark what I wrote to you, through Bruce, of the necessity of the Delhi column coming on to Alum Bâgh as soon as possible, and inform the Commander-in-Chief of what I say on the subject. I hear there is a letter for me from his Excellency at Alum Bâgh, marked "private," which there has been no means of sending to me. Please, in your telegraph to the Commander-in-Chief, tell him this.

Sir J. Outram to Captain Sibley, Alum Bâgh.
Lucknow Residency, 16th October, 1857.

A camp follower who has made his way from Alum Bâgh informs me that you charge the poor followers one rupee a seer for atta! I directed that the Mahomedan and meat-eating castes should be furnished with meat, by slaughtering the cart bullocks necessary to supply them, and that the castes who cannot eat meat should be furnished from the European supplies, until bazaar supplies arrived from Cawnpore; but this did not warrant your charging famine prices for the articles so supplied, or charging one fraction beyond the price they cost at Cawnpore; so I trust I am misinformed.

I learn from Bruce that the strange omission to furnish bazaar supplies with Major Brigham's detachment, is owing to your having *specified* as required, only "rum, tea, sugar, and tobacco." This is the more strange, indeed, as you had written to me on the 29th, "Not a seer of atta in camp for the followers; they and the cattle in great want of food." Yet, notwithstanding this, no intimation of their wants was made to Cawnpore, and consequently the convoy brought nothing for the followers. *You*, therefore, are answerable for the lamentable straits to which the poor fellows are subjected.

Bruce also writes on the 21st—" I wish Sibley would not change my men. The note you mention having been sent by a return cossid, came in by one of Sibley's people, and has taken just nine days *en route*." This is an allusion to a note I wrote from Alum Bâgh on the 24th. How it came into your hands I know not.

P.S.—Did you keep the note sent you for the officer commanding the Delhi column—as of course I intended you should do—or did you send it with the other enclosure to Bruce?

Sir J. Outram to Captain Bruce, Cawnpore.
Lucknow Residency, 16*th October*, 1857.

Circumstances cause me to suspect that Munsoof Ali has been tampering with our cossids. My letter of the 6th, which you acknowledge on the 8th, was sent by one of Thomson's men, Bissas Sing; but instead of *his* returning with your reply, it was brought on the 11th by a cunning little chap (name I forget), late naib nazir of Durriabad, with whom, my suspicion not having been then excited, I sent you a long letter on the 13th. As Bissas Sing has not returned, it appears to me too probable that Munsoof Ali must have got hold of him, taken his quill, and, after copying the contents, perhaps forwarded it to you, and got your reply, which, after reading, he sent on to me; thus obtaining for his emissary a thorough insight into the state of this garrison, and getting a sight also of my reply to yours, which of course he will have sent on that he may see your answer in the same way.

Unfortunately, you write always in *English*, which Munsoof Ali knows as well as you or I. Mine, luckily, have always been in Greek character, which it is to be hoped he cannot read. But if he learns what is said on one side, he must have a tolerable guess as to what is written on both. Your letters to me (those dated 7th and 8th) which came together, mentioned the intention to despatch a party with the bazaar supplies for Alum Bâgh—400 Europeans with two guns. Your messenger, the naib nazir, left with my reply on the night of the 13th; *and on the 14th troops marched hence in the direction of Cawnpore* (the Nana with them, it is said), probably to enable Munsoof Ali to intercept the expected convoy.

I know not if the convoy has started, or if this will be in time to put you on your guard. As possibly my letter of the 13th may not be delivered, I send duplicate. Write your letters in Greek characters. Tell me the dates of all you have received from me, and all you have despatched. Of course Brigadier Wilson will open this, should you have accompanied the convoy; and I beg he will kindly carry out what I have requested you to do. I hear Munsoof Ali is disposed to serve us, and keep open the communication with Lucknow, if assured by me of future protection; this you may grant him in my name, as well as immunity for the past, if he should desire to open negotiations with you. If the Nana has actually gone in that direction, possibly he may be induced to earn the reward for that villain's capture.

P.S.—The name of Lieutenant Wild, 40th Native Infantry, was entered by mistake among those mentioned to you as killed, in my letter of 26th ultimo.

345

Sir J. Outram to Brigadier Wilson.
16*th October,* 6 P.M.

The commissary has just informed me that after the strictest scrutiny, he finds that our atta and bullocks (we have nothing else) will last only till 18th proximo, on half rations for natives, and three-quarters for Europeans.

No possibility of our obtaining any supplies unless previously relieved. The Delhi column must push on to Alum Bâgh. Spare no cost in sending express to Greathed, urging his immediate advance, and let there be no delay in bringing troops up from Allahabad.

Enclosures, mentioned in the accompanying to Bruce of this morning, will be forwarded to-morrow, being too bulky for a quill.

Colonel Wilson to the Chief of the Staff.
(Telegraphic.) *Cawnpore,* 15*th October,* 1857, 3.15 P.M.

As already telegraphed on the 12th instant, the officer commanding the convoy brought no intelligence further than that occasionally a cossid, with difficulty, made his way from the Baillie Guard to Alum Bâgh; that they heard constant firing, and that they were not molested on their road here. As far as Alum Bâgh, with a strong detachment and guns, I consider the road safe. I beg to refer you to my message of the 12th instant, more particularly as we have not had any communication from Lucknow since, which fact is daily telegraphed to you.

Captain Bruce to the Governor-General of India and the Commander-in-Chief.
(Telegraphic.) *Cawnpore,* 15*th October,* 1857.

Letter from General Outram, dated Lucknow, 13th. He desires me to urge strongly the imperative necessity for supplies, to the utmost extent that our escorts from this can guard. Represents how imperative he considers it that reinforcements for Lucknow be organized at Alum Bâgh, not at Cawnpore, where the assembly of forces would have no effect at Lucknow; whereas, concentration at Alum Bâgh would favour communication with friends in the city, and encourage loyal zemindars to come forward. Reinforcements at Alum Bâgh can be supplied from

Cawnpore with perfect safety; the road so far open, that native police posts, as far as Nuwabgunge, are unmolested, and detachments at Busseerutgunge, Nuwabgunge, and Bunnee, will amply secure the communication. Alum Bâgh is a well-fortified wall inclosure, with open country around.

The Chief of the Staff to Colonel Wilson, Cawnpore.

(Telegraphic.) *Calcutta*, 16th October, 1857.

If you believe that the road to Lucknow is not more obstructed than when the last detachment marched on, send a party to the relief of Alum Bâgh, made up to 500 rank and file, with four guns; the whole being under the command of Major Barnston, with Captain Bruce as staff officer.

Having thrown in provisions, which should be sufficient for a month at the very least, including a due supply of atta for the use of the native troops, this party should return, if possible, bringing back unladen elephants and camels, as otherwise they would eat up all the food they take. Send some police sowars with it, if you have any, as scouts, and impress upon Major Barnston the necessity of taking every precaution when returning. He must bring back his guns.

If, on due reflection, Major Barnston thinks it absolutely necessary to reinforce Alum Bâgh with a company of Europeans, he must do so; but his Excellency is of opinion that, if such a step can be avoided, it would be much better for the garrison on account of supplies, as well as for the safety of the returning column.

Colonel Wilson to the Chief of the Staff.

(Telegraphic.) *Cawnpore*, 16th October, 1857, 8.50 A.M.

Captain Bruce read to me Sir James Outram's letter, dated 13th, upon which the telegraphic message was forwarded, as despatched last night to the Governor-General and Commander-in-Chief. I have the party and provisions all ready, and only await the Commander-in-Chief's orders to despatch them.

Captain Bruce, for Major-General Sir J. Outram, to the Governor-General of India in Council.

(Telegraphic.) *Cawnpore*, 16th October, 1857, 11 A.M.

General Outram has issued proclamation to those men of the 7th Light Cavalry, 13th Regiment Native Infantry, 48th Regiment Native Infantry, and 71st Regiment Native Infantry, who were granted furlough by the Chief Commissioner in Oude in June, as well as those who went as usual on leave previous to June, to repair to the officer commanding at Cawnpore for duty, upon the understanding that, if they afterwards proved to have joined in rebellion, they must stand the consequence. General Outram orders me to organize this depôt, and has desired me to ask your Lordship if others, who received similar leave under Mr. Colvin's orders, are to be similarly embodied, or not.

The Governor-General of India in Council to Major-General Sir J. Outram.

(Telegraphic.) *Calcutta, 17th October, 1857.*

The furlough men who received leave from Sir Henry Lawrence in June, or before that time, and who have been summoned to Cawnpore by Sir James Outram's proclamation, may be received there; but arms must not be put into their hands at present.

It is not likely that the proclamation can have penetrated to any distance from Lucknow; if it has not done so, those who act upon it will have been amongst the insurgents, and must not be too readily trusted.

Do not receive any other furlough men at Cawnpore.

Sir J. Outram to Brigadier Wilson, Cawnpore.

Lucknow Residency, 17th October, 1857.

I send duplicates of letters addressed to you and Bruce on the 13th, 15th, and 16th, and beg your particular attention to the postscript of the last, and that you will communicate it to the Commander-in-Chief by telegraph. I have only to-day to add the suggestion, that, as the troops of artillery despatched from Calcutta by the river have no chance of being in time, Captain Moir's battery should be drawn from Allahabad where the Naval Brigade will surely suffice for the present.

Sir J. Outram to Brigadier Wilson, Cawnpore.

Lucknow Residency, 18th October, 1857.

Your note to Napier, dated 11th instant, reached me last night, and disappointed me much, as conveying nothing but the Commander-in-Chief's message of the 8th, whereas Government should not have been put to the expense of such highly-paid cossids, without your availing yourself of the opportunity to inform us of the progress of the force expected from Delhi, which it is so necessary I should be acquainted with. As the note now received is marked *duplicate*, it appears that Government has been put to the expense of double cossids for this brief message—four times the bulk of which could have been inserted in the quill.

The Commander-in-Chief, when he interdicted small detachments to Lucknow, could not have been informed of the urgent necessity there is to convey provisions, not to *Lucknow*, but to *Alum Bágh*, which you so strangely neglected to furnish with bazaar supplies for the camp followers, at the same time that you sent supplies for the Europeans.

His Excellency could not have been made aware that a detachment of 230 men and two guns had already escorted carts thither; that 100 riflemen had taken back the elephants, &c. to you without opposition; and that, *when you wrote*, the road was clear. He could not have been informed that the followers at Alum Bágh would absolutely starve if not supplied; and that the escort intended, of 400 Europeans with two guns, and Bruce's cavalry, were not likely to meet with any opposition which they could not overcome, even if the enemy *should* have troops on the road. But, knowing the urgency of the demand for bazaar supplies at Alum Bágh, you of course must have informed the Commander-in-Chief of all this by telegraph, in reply to his message of the 8th. I informed you that troops (infantry, no guns that I can ascertain) were supposed to have gone towards Cawnpore on the 14th; but of this you knew nothing when you received the Commander-in-Chief's message. And as your cossid saw nothing of these troops, it is likely that they were on their way to Bithoor or elsewhere, and not to occupy the road to

Lucknow; and Bruce would have given you timely information if they were in such strength on the road as to oppose your convoy.

It does not appear that you gave Bruce information of the despatch of this cossid; or surely—as head of the intelligence department to whom I look for information —he would have acquainted me with the progress of the Delhi column. I request that no Government cossid be sent henceforth without due notice to Captain Bruce; and to him you should look for supplying the cossids.

I enclose duplicate of what I wrote you yesterday, also of letters to Bruce and yourself of 13th, 15th, and 19th. Such portions of them as should be communicated to the Commander-in-Chief, you will, of course, telegraph, if not already sent.

P.S.—Did you get the letters of instruction for the officer commanding the Delhi column, and the map which accompanied it? Have you telegraphed to the Governor-General the substance of such portions of my letters as may be important?

The Chief of the Staff to Colonel Wilson, Cawnpore.

(Telegraphic.)   *Calcutta*, 17th *October*, 1857.

Inform Sir James Outram, by cossid—your communication being made in Greek characters—of Major Barnston's advance, and that Sir James Outram's letter of the 13th instant has been laid before the Commander-in-Chief. Much as the Commander-in-Chief may desire to meet Sir James Outram's wishes, he is obliged, from want of means, to declare the impossibility of carrying out Sir James's plan.

2. There are no troops to form a line of posts across the Province of Oude, and there is no other available carriage than that now sent.

3. Even one brigade cannot be formed at Cawnpore, putting, for the present, Alum Bágh out of the question, before the 10th of November at the earliest.

4. Let Major Barnston, after arrival at Alum Bágh, wait there three or four days to rest his people and cattle, and communicate, if possible, with Sir James Outram; and let the latter understand that the only means of supplying Alum Bágh, at the disposal of his Excellency,

is to allow of the return of Major Barnston, with his camels and elephants, to Cawnpore, with a view to the subsequent march of a similar but stronger column, with a like object.

5. Tell him that every possible effort is being made to close the new arrivals up to Cawnpore; and his Excellency has a confident hope that the gradual, but never-ceasing, concentration at that place will have a beneficial influence on the minds of the leaders by whom Sir James is now blockaded.

6. Instruct Major Barnston, when he commences his retreat, to start in the middle of the night, and march at least twenty miles, so as to effect the passage of the nullah at Bunnee in the first stage. He will be able to do this by using his elephants and camels freely.

7. Let him leave his weakly men and bad marchers to reinforce Alum Bâgh.

8. He is also to communicate his Excellency's orders to the officer commanding at Alum Bâgh, that the latter is personally to superintend the stores, and economize the delivery as much as possible.

9. Let Major Barnston take a lakh of Enfield rifle ammunition with him, if possible; also let Sir James Outram know that the Commander-in-Chief will write fully by post.

The Chief of the Staff to Colonel Wilson, Cawnpore.

(Telegraphic.) *Calcutta,* 17*th October,* 1857.

Instruct Major Barnston to take advantage of his elephants, on his return from Alum Bâgh, to bring back such sick men as are able to travel.

Captain Peel, R.N., to the Chief of the Staff.

(Telegraphic.) *Allahabad,* 17*th October,* 1857, 4 P.M.

I received by telegraph from Cawnpore an order from General Outram of the 15th instant from Lucknow, to expedite as much as possible, the two regiments coming up. He does not specify what regiments.

Colonel Wilson to the Chief of the Staff.

(Telegraphic.) *Cawnpore,* 17*th October,* 1857, 10.10 P.M.

Having made all my arrangements to send off 500 infantry, with four guns, 9-pounders, under the command of Major Barnston, with Captain Bruce as staff officer, to march this night at 2 o'clock, the Commissariat were not ready. Captain Bruce informs me, at 7 o'clock this evening, that the Delhi fugitives had reached Bithoor. They had been obliged to divide in consequence of scarcity of food. Each division marched one ahead of the other. The first would probably reach Sheorajpore to-morrow, and so on. The Nana is in communication, and is trying to induce them to join him at Bithoor, where his valuables are buried. Such being the case, I move out with 600 infantry and six guns (five 9-pounders, one 24-pounder howitzer) at 1 A.M. to-morrow morning, the 18th. No elephants will carry near the party, so that I hope to be able to give a good account of our enemies. This will probably prevent a number of guns and men being brought into Oude, which might obstruct the movements of our relief parties, and I sincerely trust that the Commander-in-Chief will approve of the steps I have taken, and of my great wish to thwart, and, if possible, to seize on, the murderous rebel Nana. The moment I return I will then carry out the Commander-in-Chief's views of sending the supplies to Alum Bâgh, which will be all ready to-morrow evening.

Major Stirling to the Chief of the Staff.

(Telegraphic.) *Cawnpore, 19th October*, 1857, 11.10 A.M.

The following, received from Captain Bruce, dated Sheorajpore, 18th October, 7 P.M. :—

"We reached at half-past 3 o'clock; drove the enemy right out of the place, which was strong, with hardly any resistance, and followed them up two miles, and continued for a mile and a half farther, with a few sowars; but they could not be overtaken. I suspect their almost nominal opposition was to cover their flight. Our casualties seven or eight. No guns taken, but some ordnance stores."

The Governor-General of India in Council to the Officer Commanding at Cawnpore.

(Telegraphic.) *Fort William, 19th October*, 1857.

You are requested to forward the following message to Colonel Fraser, Chief Commissioner at Agra, with the utmost expedition :—

" The presence of Lieutenant-Colonel Greathed's column is urgently required in Oude; therefore, do not let him be detained at or near Agra an hour longer than is necessary. Allow him to exchange some of his sickly and weak European Infantry for some of your fresh men, if he desires it. Let Lieutenant-Colonel Greathed know that his cavalry is especially needed.

"The reinforcement of General Outram at Lucknow is the object which most presses, and you are requested to do everything in your power to hasten the accomplishment of this by Lieutenant-Colonel Greathed."

The Chief of the Staff to Colonel Wilson, Cawnpore.

(Telegraphic.) *Calcutta, 20th October*, 1857.

Increase the party going to Alum Bâgh to 700 rank and file. Let 200 remain at Alum Bâgh to reinforce the garrison, and 500 return with the unladen elephants and camels.

Captain Bruce, for Major-General Sir J. Outram, to the Governor-General and Commander-in-Chief.

(Telegraphic.)　　　　Cawnpore, 20th October, 1857, 10 A.M.

A letter, dated 7th October, from General Outram, desires me to inform you that the force at Lucknow, now besieged by the enemy, has grain, gun-bullocks, and horses, upon which they can subsist for another month; but they have no hospital comforts, and little medicine. Repeats, that maintaining troops at Alum Bágh, and gradually reinforcing that post, must tell favourably ere long; adds that a wing of infantry and two guns at Busseerutgunge and Bunnee would secure the whole road for safe convoy of provisions to Alum Bágh. The loss in killed, wounded, and missing, since the force crossed the Ganges, has been very heavy, 256 killed, and 700 wounded and missing; out of the former, sixteen officers.

Colonel Wilson to the Chief of the Staff.

(Telegraphic.)　　　　Cawnpore, 20th October, 1857, 12.2 P.M.

The party for Alum Bágh will leave, if possible, to-morrow morning. Captain Bruce cannot just now be spared; his Excellency, perhaps, is not aware that the Intelligence Department, by General Outram's wish, is entirely in his hands, as also most of the magisterial and police work of the whole district. Intelligence is of the greatest importance, now that the country is covered with Delhi fugitives. Captain Moir, an experienced Bengal Artillery officer, is the party, and, if necessary, Mr. Ranson, of the Civil Service, can accompany, as both these gentlemen know the language well. Sir James Outram, in a subsequent letter to Captain Bruce, wishes him not to leave Cawnpore.

Captain Bruce, for Major-General Sir J. Outram, to the Governor-General of India in Council.

(Telegraphic.)　　　　Cawnpore, 21st October, 1857, 5 P.M.

Rajah Maun Sing has written to me, with enclosure for General Outram: the purport of these is as follows :—

Says he never intended to go to Lucknow at all, had not the rance of the late Rajah of Buktwar Sing been seized there by the rebels; he went with Mr. Gubbins' (of Benares) sanction to rescue her; he could not get away until all the rebels opposed the British at Alum Bágh ; he seized this opportunity of rescuing her, making every arrangement to move back twenty coss from Lucknow. He swears, on oath, up to this time he did not connect himself with the rebels. It was willed his name now should be connected with the rebels, and himself fall under displeasure of Government thus. He suddenly heard the rebels were defeated, and the British, attacking the place, were about to disgrace his Majesty's harem. He at once marched to protect it, for he had eaten the King's salt. If the General views with justice his actions, he will see that he did not join the rebels. He protected the British authorities in his district, and could not keep himself aloof from protecting the King's honour. Now he was ready to obey all Government orders, and, if his vakeel's life be spared, he will submit the whole facts; he hopes the General will let him know his design, that he may carry it out.

To this letter I sent the following reply :—" I have received your letter, and enclosure for General Outram. The British do no injury to helpless women and children, however humble their rank, and you ought to have known that those of the King would not have been dishonoured. I have written to-day to General Outram, who is now in the Lucknow Residency; and in the meantime, if you are really friendly to the British Government, you are desired at once to withdraw all your men from Lucknow, and communicate with the Chief Commissioner. I have sent to tell your vakeel that if he likes to come in and see me, he will meet with no injury."

The vakeel has since come, and, having expressed his master's willingness to comply with the terms of my letter, departed for Lucknow.

Sir J. Outram to Captain Sibley, Alum Bágh.

Lucknow Residency, 20th October, 1857.

From your note of 17th, it would appear that you could not have received mine of 16th instant; of which I send copy.

The price you put on meat and biscuit is much too high for poor camp followers. An anna a seer is the utmost that should be charged; but the allowance, of course, to be limited in accordance with your means.

I received no reference from you on the subject of "sentry sleeping on his post." Consult the Articles of War, and act accordingly.

I hope your defensive works are progressing. Work on perseveringly.

The packet for "the officer commanding the Delhi column" was directed to *Alum Bágh*, and intended to await him *there;* the other duplicate of letters to Bruce I meant to go on. But as you sent them by one of Bruce's own men, it is to be hoped the packet has not fallen into the enemy's hands. We hear that the Delhi column was three marches from Cawnpore on the 17th.

Sir J. Outram to Captain Bruce, Cawnpore.

Lucknow Residency, 21*st October*, 1857.

Yours, dated the 17th, was brought to me on the 19th by Canojee Lall, Naib Nazir of Durriabad, against whom I expressed suspicion in my letter of the 16th. This is now quite removed by the expedition with which he brought your letter, with which he left Cawnpore on the morning of the 18th; and, by the fact that the latter evidently had not been tampered with.

In that letter, you alluded to one despatched on the previous day by Bussarut Ali Khan, Sheristadar of the Chief Commissioner's office at Lucknow, which I have not received. In it probably you may have informed me of the progress of the Delhi column; for you make no allusion to it in your note of the 17th—a great disappointment, containing as that does nothing but the substance of Maun Sing's letter. Your paper was not nearly filled; surely you might have told us something of the progress of the troops expected from both sides. Your messenger tells me that a force was prepared to cross the river, with convoy, for Alum Bâgh, on the morning he left; but that, during the night, information having arrived that a large body of rebels (including Gwalior mutineers) was approaching Cawnpore, the troops had suddenly been sent off in their direction, instead of crossing the river. As my letter from you prior to this of the 17th was dated the 11th, I knew nothing of this intended movement, of which intermediate letters, not received, may have been intended to inform me. I sent (in a separate quill) a despatch from General Havelock, which please telegraph to Calcutta, with this copy of one from myself to the Commander-in-Chief, which oblige me by copying and expressing.

Your letter of the 8th was brought by Canojee Lall on the 10th. I have received nothing else from you before this of the 17th, which I now acknowledge, and only one from Wilson of the 11th.

As Canojee Lall took mine of the 13th to you, I presume you have received it, though you do not say so. I have sent the following despatches to you or Wilson; let me know which of them have been received: 26th, 29th, September 2nd, 5th, 6th, 7th, 9th, 11th, 13th, 14th, 15th, 16th, 17th, 18th. I am particularly anxious to know whether those of the 14th and 15th were received. The former, sent through Alum Bâgh, and addressed to the officer commanding the Delhi column, I intended to await his arrival at Alum Bâgh; but Sibley stupidly sent it on to Cawnpore by one of your men. The latter, directed to Brigadier Wilson, was sent direct. They contained plans of the ground between Alum Bâgh and this place, with suggestions as to mode of co-operation; and I should not wish the enemy to have got hold of them, though written in the Greek character.

P.S.—I send duplicate of my letter to Wilson of the 16th. Our food, *upon a very reduced allowance indeed*, may possibly last till 20th November, but we should have no bullocks left to move the guns.

I trust you inform Lady Outram that I am well every time you hear from me. Tell her I cannot write to her, because, as our expensive cossids can only carry a *quill*, private communications have been forbidden to others, and I cannot, in honour, take advantage to write privately myself.

I send a list of killed and wounded in our force since we left Cawnpore up to the present time.

Sir J. Outram to Captain Sibley, Alum Bágh.
Lucknow Residency, 22nd October, 1857.

The bearer of this is sent to inquire the particulars of the heavy fire heard in your direction to-day.

Send all the particulars. We hope it is a convoy which should have left Cawnpore some days ago. Kindly tell my servant John to look after the servants of my staff and their horses. Colonel Napier's khansama has the key of his desk, whence John might take some money if required.

Send me all you know from Cawnpore of the approach of troops from Delhi and Calcutta, and of the enemy's movements towards Cawnpore. Have you made earthen flanking defences outside your towers at the angles?

How have you managed to feed your bullocks, and in what condition are they?

The Commander-in-Chief to Captain Bruce, Cawnpore.

(Telegraphic.) *22nd October,* 1857.

Send my best regards, by cossid, to General Outram. Tell him I have never ceased my exertions to press every available soldier up to his support. My presence here has enabled me to ensure the execution of orders necessary to this effect. I believe, in consequence, that, after making due deduction for sickness, I shall have 2,500 British Infantry by the 7th of November, together with Cavalry of the Military Train, two companies of Sappers, and a small detail of Artillery, at Cawnpore and Alum Bágh together.

The Governor-General has written to desire that Colonel Greathed's column may be directed on Cawnpore, but for the present I have no power over that force. I trust it may arrive.

My intention is to throw forward to Alum Bágh about 1,500 men of the above force, as soon as practicable; the remainder of the force indicated will close up on Alum Bágh as it arrives at Cawnpore.

Of course, much must depend upon the collection of carriage and supplies. No effort is being left untried to ensure a sufficiency of both.

Communicate this confidentially to Colonel Wilson.

Sir J. Outram to Captain Sibley, Alum Bágh.
Lucknow Residency, 26*th October*, 1857.

I last night received information from Cawnpore that a convoy left for Alum Bágh on the 22nd, escorted by 500 infantry, 50 cavalry, and 4 guns, and that the escort is ordered to return after waiting three or four days for my orders.

If Major McIntyre, Major Bingham, and yourself are of opinion that any additional men are required to hold your position, you may retain such portion of the escort which has now arrived, as may be safely spared from the force required to take back the empty carts, camels, and elephants now at Alum Bágh. The remainder of the escort, with its four guns, to return to Cawnpore with all such carts, camels, and elephants. The bullock-train vans, or a portion of them, also to be sent back, unless their bullocks are fit for your service, in which case the bullocks should be retained at Alum Bágh, and well fed, to replace the gun bullocks which have been consumed for food. As the Delhi column will have plenty of cavalry, the fifty cavalry which accompanied the convoy would be best employed at Alum Bágh in guarding the gun bullocks when out grazing, &c., provided you have grain for the horses.

I was much vexed to learn that the enemy carried off some of your elephants the other day; for I had supposed *all* elephants and camels had been sent back to Cawnpore, as I had directed, and as your letter of 10th instant had led me to believe. I can only suppose that you retained the *gun* elephants, as I did not *specify* them. But in desiring that "the elephants" should be sent back, without making *any reservation*, I of course meant that *all* should be sent, and had hoped they were so. I now desire that all that are left may go with the return convoy.

Such of the sick and wounded as are not likely to be soon fit for duty, but are capable of bearing the journey to Cawnpore, should be sent back with the convoy, together with such troops as may be necessary.

When the Delhi column arrives (expected at Cawnpore by the end of the month), you should recommend pitching their camp on the Cawnpore side of your post, facing towards Jellalabad, with rear to the road, and their left on your garden wall. There they would not be exposed to fire from the enemy's guns, which obliged us to change our position.

I send you a list of the deaths in this garrison prior to our arrival, as that formerly sent may have miscarried. Take the opportunity of the return column to send it to Captain Bruce, at Cawnpore, to be telegraphed to Government.

Sir J. Outram to Captain Bruce, Cawnpore.

Lucknow Residency, 26th October.

Yours of 13th and Brigadier Wilson's of 21st were brought *together* last night by the old pensioner, Bhowanee Deen; and last night I also received yours of the 20th, brought by one of Thomson's men, who delivered mine of the 15th to Wilson.

Your letter of the 17th, sent by Bussarut Ali, Sherishtadar of the Chief Commissioner's office, Lucknow, has not been received, nor have I heard anything of Mr. Bussarut Ali. As you have not told me what letters you have received, nor on what dates you have despatched letters, I know not what may have miscarried.

As this will be taken to you by the return escort from Alum Bâgh, I take the opportunity of sending a list of the deaths in this garrison before we joined; also, in another quill, a despatch from Havelock, which please telegraph to the Commander-in-Chief.

I hope you received his and my despatches of 30th, sent by the Naib Nazir of Durriabad on the 21st. Maun Sing's sincerity is very doubtful; nothing has yet come of it.

As no private letters can be sent at present from hence, telegraph to Allan Deffell to write to my mother, Mrs. Outram, 16, Abbyn Place, Edinburgh, that I have *entirely recovered* from my trifling wound, and am perfectly well.

Sir J. Outram to Captain Bruce, Cawnpore.

Lucknow Residency, 28th October, 1857.

I received last night, by the hands of Canojee Lall, your letters of the 24th and 25th, with duplicate of that of 16th (neither original nor Bussarut have come).

Canojee has certainly proved himself most zealous and able, has richly earned reward, and shall assuredly obtain it. Having such faith in him, I purpose sending a plan and further instructions to the officer commanding the relieving force by him to-night, if ready in time.

If not ready to send by him, I hope it may safely reach Alum Bâgh by other means, there to await the arrival of Colonel Grant, or whoever may be in command of the force. I shall not detain Canojee beyond to-night, being anxious to prevent the force being hurried from Cawnpore to Alum Bâgh. The latter post, having now been amply supplied with food, and sufficiently strengthened to defy attack, is no longer a source of anxiety; and however desirable it may be to support me here, I cannot but feel that *it is still more important that the Gwalior rebels (said to be preparing to cross into the Doab) should be first disposed of.* I would therefore urge on Brigadier Wilson, to whom I beg you will communicate this as if addressed to himself, that I consider that the Delhi column, strengthened to the utmost by all other troops that can be spared from Cawnpore, should in the first instance be employed against the Gwalior rebels, should they attempt to cross into the Doab, or be tangible to assault elsewhere within reasonable distance. We can manage to screw on, if absolutely necessary, till near the end of November on further reduced rations. Only the longer we remain the less physical strength we shall have to aid our friends when they do advance, and the fewer guns shall we be able to move out in co-operation.

But it is so obviously to the advantage of the State that the Gwalior rebels should be first effectually destroyed, that our relief should be a secondary consideration. I trust, therefore, that Brigadier Wilson will furnish Colonel Grant with every possible aid to effect that object before sending him here. Pray tell the Brigadier that it is suspected the enemy obtain supplies of shot and shell from the Cawnpore magazine—stolen thence, and sold by blackguards who have access to where they are lying outside without any guard over them. So I am told. Ask him from me, with my salaam, to take such measures as will render pilfering ordnance stores impossible.

It is hard that your good service at Cawnpore should debar you from military duty with your regiment. Still, you are too zealous a servant of Government to grudge the sacrifice, if your presence there is indispensably necessary. I should hope, however, that the magistrate could make arrangements for the temporary performance of your civil duties, and the Brigadier supply an efficient officer to conduct those you perform of a military nature, during the period your regiment may be employed at Lucknow. If, therefore, Government has not positively interdicted your departure from Cawnpore, I beg you will express to Brigadier Wilson and Mr. Sherer my hope that they will oblige me by effecting such arrangements for the temporary performance of your duties, as may admit of your taking command of your regiment for a time.

Telegraph the substance of the above to the Commander-in-Chief, so much as relates to the advisability of taking measures to guard against the invasion of the Doab by the Gwalior mutineers.

Sir J. Outram to Major McIntyre, Alum Bâgh.

Lucknow Residency, 30th October, 1857.

I am glad to hear you are well again. I enclose duplicate of a letter I wrote to Cawnpore on the 28th, which will account to you for the delay in the advance of the relieving force—if they *should* be delayed.

I am so anxious that the accompaniment to this may reach safely, that I beg you will, on its receipt, hoist a flag on the most conspicuous tower on the top of the Alum Bâgh house, and keep it flying all day, that we may be sure of seeing it. I beg you will get friends to prepare English versions, written out clear, of the letter and its enclosure which I have addressed to the officer commanding the relieving force (and which you will find in the cossid's *stick*), that he may not be confused by the cramped hand and Greek character in which they are written. I have promised the bearer 200 rupees if he deliver this safe. Of course, keep the documents till the arrival of the relieving force. We must not risk them by sending them to Cawnpore.

Can you send us any home newspaper of last mail, or

late Calcutta papers noticing our proceedings? I would not risk *letters;* but they sometimes manage to bring *papers*, &c., concealed in bundles of grass.

I wrote you on the 26th, but as the bearer has not returned, I send duplicate. If you have any opportunity of writing to Cawnpore before the relieving column leaves, urge that persons be sent with it who are *well acquainted with the Martinière.*

(Enclosure to the above.)

To the Officer Commanding the Relieving Force.

[Along with the following important and deeply interesting letter, Sir James Outram forwarded a plan of the ground intervening between the Alum Bâgh and the Residency, together with minute descriptions of every position and building capable of being held by the enemy. The plan was based on the surveys made by the late Captain Morrison prior to the outbreak, the only surveys that had been made of Lucknow. The copy of this plan, which will be found at the end of the volume, should be consulted in the perusal of the following letter. It is Plan No. I.]

My communication of the 14th instant informed you I consider your first operation should be the occupation of the "Dil Khoosha" house and park, by a direct movement to that place from the Alum Bâgh. The Fort of Jellalabad, which is situated a mile or a mile and a half to the right of that route, is said to be occupied by the enemy, with two guns; but it is too distant to interrupt that line of communication, and it is not likely to be maintained after the Dil Khoosha, in addition to Alum Bâgh, has been occupied in its rear. I think it hardly worth while, therefore, to waste time against that place, which at the commencement of the outbreak was little capable of defence, and is not likely since to have been repaired or stored sufficiently to admit of its retention. The guns now there appear to have been sent merely to interrupt the forage parties from Alum Bágh. (A description of Jellalabad, as it was just before the outbreak, is appended.) Yet it will be prudent, in afterwards communicating with Alum Bágh, to afford strong escort until it is known whether or not Jellalabad is evacuated.

The direct advance from Alum Bágh *viâ* Char Bágh, and the main street marked (1) (1) (1) on the plan, should *not* be attempted, very formidable opposition being prepared on the other side of the Char Bágh bridge, the bridge itself being destroyed, and the passage strongly fortified; besides which there are two miles of street to pass through, in which every means of obstruction have been prepared, the houses loopholed, and guns in position at various points, with ditches, mines, and other obstacles. For the same reason I would deprecate any attempt to force the street which runs from the junction of the Dil Khoosha and Martinière roads to the Kaiser Bágh, marked (2) (2) (2).

At Dil Khoosha, it is stated, there are at present only some Rajwarra matchlockmen, with cavalry at Beebeeapore village perhaps, and at the Martinière; but these are almost certain to decamp when you approach, and may perhaps suffer considerably ere they get across the canal, if followed up sharply by cavalry and horse artillery. Two guns were said to be at Dil Khoosha some days ago, probably those now at Jellalabad. If still there, they would have to be abandoned ere they could be crossed over the canal, if followed up.

It is possible that some of the so-called Regular Infantry may be sent over to the Dil Khoosha when they hear of your approach. If so, they will but add to their own confusion and panic flight when you attack, for never by any chance do they stand in the open. Two regiments of infantry and one of cavalry, sent out to oppose Major Barston's convoy, fled at his approach without firing a shot; and on every occasion where whole hosts of them were opposed to ourselves it was just the same. The Dil Khoosha palace cannot be maintained under fire of our artillery, having large windows on every side. If any force of the enemy is assembled there, they must suffer awfully from your guns in escaping across the canal. Or should they fly to the Martinière, they will be in a similar predicament when you follow them up.

On seeing the Dil Khoosha occupied by your troops, the enemy would most probably evacuate the Martinière. After lodging your baggage in the garden to the rear of, and commanded by, the Dil Khoosha house (and surrounded by walls without houses, something like Alum Bâgh, and easily defensible), you would proceed against the Martinière through the road marked (3) (3) (3). But it would be well, ere getting within musket range of the building, to throw a few shells and round shot into it, in case it should be occupied by the enemy, whose fire from the terraced roof might cause much loss ere you get near enough to rush up and blow open doors for entry. It would be well for you to have some one with you well acquainted with the Martinière building. And it may be a matter for your consideration whether it would not be better, if the place appears strongly fortified, to mask it by encamping your troops between the road (3) (3) and the canal, contenting yourself by bombarding the Martinière during the day and night, which will almost ensure its evacuation before morning. The mound marked (4)* would be a favourable site for

---

* Sir J. Outram afterwards availed himself of this mound to plant a 24-pounder battery of the Shannon Brigade, which effectually kept down the enemy's fire opened on the rear division under his command, when he finally retired to the Alum Bâgh.

a 24-pounder battery, which would command the opposite bank of the canal, where you purpose effecting your passage to protect the sappers in making a road for your guns.

It is possible the bridge leading to the Martinière may not be destroyed, and that you may prefer advancing over it. But, on reconnoitring, you will, I believe, find places where the cannal may be crossed without much difficulty farther down, towards (6), which would enable you to turn any defensive works the enemy may prepare on the main road (2) (2) (2). If you cross the bridge, therefore, I would recommend your turning to the right after passing it, and making your way through the mud huts (indicated by the brown colour on the plan) until you get into the road running from (6) to (W) (W) (W)—W denotes some deserted and destroyed infantry lines,—leaving the houses, marked D D D, on your left, and thus making your way into the road (7) (7), which passes the open front of the enclosure in which the barracks are situated. Should the barrack buildings be occupied (they were precipitately abandoned when we advanced from the same quarter), it may be prudent to throw a few shot and shell ere the infantry advances to the attack. Having large doors, open on both sides, as is customary in European barracks in India, I anticipate little difficulty in your effecting an entry. Staircases lead to the terrace roof from the interior of the centre room. The terrace is considerably raised above, and therefore commands, the houses of the Huzrutgunge, and a few rifles placed there could keep down any musketry fire from thence (Huzrutgunge), which alone could disturb the party left in occupation of the barracks when you advance farther. But it would be necessary to throw up a parapet of sand-bags, or screens of shutters, to protect the riflemen on the roof, as it has no parapet. The south wall of the enclosure is, however, sufficiently high to afford some protection against direct fire.

Should you cross by the bridge, your whole force would, I presume, come that way. And your next operation, after leaving an adequate guard for the barracks (say 300 or 400 infantry, some cavalry, and a couple of guns; or, probably, you might secure a gun, or two guns, which the enemy are said to have there), would be to proceed by the road (7) (7) to the Secundra Bâgh (G), which, if held, could easily be breached by 24- or 18-pounders—the wall being only about $2\frac{1}{2}$ feet thick—*vide* enclosed description.* It is said to be occupied by Maun Sing, with some 200 or 300 Rajwarras and two guns; the former are pretty sure to bolt when your guns open upon the place, and two or three shells are thrown into it.

If you cross the canal at (6), the main body of your force should proceed by the road from (6) to (W). A regiment and portion of artillery might, perhaps, make their way by the road which leads direct to the Secundra Bâgh (8) (8); but as it is not well defined, it may be more prudent to keep all together till you occupy the barracks.†

Should you have met with opposition, or been delayed much in crossing the canal, the day will be pretty far advanced ere you have occupied the barracks and

---

* The Commander-in-Chief's force met with serious opposition at the Secundra Bâgh, owing to their having approached it by a cross-road from the rear, whence their breaching guns could not be brought up until the troops had been exposed for some time to a heavy fire. Had they come by the broad pucka road leading from the barracks, as suggested, their heavy guns could have opened upon the place while the infantry remained out of musketry fire. A practicable breach would then have been made, or the shelling would have driven the enemy out. As it was, however, the occupants, greatly more numerous than reported, had no means of egress, *and were destroyed to a man;* but our own troops also suffered severely in taking the place.

† Neither the roads (7) (7) or (8) (8) were followed by Sir Colin Campbell's force, which was taken by a more circuitous and intricate road than either, and suffered greatly before its guns could be brought to the front.

Secundra Bâgh. These might be the limit of your operation that day—encamping your force between, and a little in advance of, those two points, with its right rear on Secundra Bâgh, and the barracks on its left rear—thus obtaining a tolerably open plain to encamp on, with almost clear space in front, from which your guns would play upon the buildings which still intervene between your camp and our position, namely, the Shah Nujjif (H), Motee Mahal (K), Mess-house (M), and Tara Kottee (N), which, if held, might be bombarded from both our positions prior to commencing combined operations next morning. You would then decide on the garrisons to occupy the barracks and Secundra Bâgh, to maintain communication with Dil Khoosha, where your baggage would, I trust, be secure in the garden, protected by 200 men occupying the house, and a couple of guns. About the same strength (with convalescents) would suffice for Alum Bâgh, aided by the enemy's guns we have there. And, perhaps, two of our own guns, supported by 100 riflemen, would hold the Martinière, with a small body of cavalry to command the plain down to the canal. A strong picquet also should be placed in the nearest huts to the road by which you cross the canal. You would, perhaps, occupy the houses D D also, as further security for your communications.* Another point to which you should turn your attention while delayed in breaching the Secundra Bâgh is the destruction of the bridge of boats some few hundred yards thence.† If a troop of horse artillery and cavalry are sent off rapidly to any point commanding the boats, many men would be destroyed with

---

* All this was carried out, with the exception that the barracks and the houses D D were refused in the *advance* to the Secundra Bâgh, and had, therefore, to be taken afterwards, and (it is believed) at a greater loss than had they been assailed in the first instance.

† The enemy's leaders themselves caused the bridge to be broken up to prevent the flight of their followers.

the boats that would be sunk by your guns; and the destruction of the boats will prevent the enemy's force on the other side of the Goomtee coming over to molest you at night.

The signal that you are crossing the canal will be my notice to spring certain mines, and storm the posts now held by the enemy in my immediate front (9) (9); and once in possession of these, I shall open my guns on the buildings above mentioned, and endeavour, also, to silence the fire of the Kaiser Bâgh, which commands the open space betwen us, to favour our junction next morning* when our united batteries could be turned upon the Kaiser Bâgh. And they would, I hope, in a day or two, effect its capture, which is necessary to ensure the entire submission of the city.

It only remains to suggest a code of signals by which we may understand your movements.

(1.) A salvo of four or more guns, fired three times at five minutes' interval, at 2 P.M. on the day you reach Alum Bâgh, to let us know you have arrived there. (2.) A similar signal to be fired at 2 P.M., on the day before you advance to the Dil Khoosha house. (3.) On occupying the Dil Khoosha, display a regimental colour from the roof. (4.) Also the same on obtaining the Martinière, which we will answer by a colour on the top of the Chutter Munzil (10).

As it may occupy a longer time than I anticipate to make your arrangements at Dil Khoosha, and to cut your road for guns to cross the canal, &c., on the evening before you cross the canal, hoist two colours on the

---

* This was done. Sir James Outram's troops stormed and took the buildings (9) (9) on the day Sir Colin took the Secundra Bâgh. Sir James then opened his batteries on the Mess-house, Kaiser Bâgh, &c., exactly as here proposed, until the junction was effected; and the Kaiser Bâgh could have soon after been taken, had it not been determined to withdraw our forces for a time.—(*See the Despatches of General Havelock, Brigadier Eyre, Colonel Napier, &c., in reference to these operations.*)

top of the Dil Khoosha, one above the other, that we may be prepared to spring our mines when you advance next morning.

You will, I suppose, leave all heavy baggage at Alum Bâgh, bringing only light carts, elephants, camels, and pony or bullock carriages, to the Dil Khoosha. But I beg you will bring the kits of the European troops here; for the cold weather is coming on, and they have neither great coats nor bedding.

When you advance from the Dil Khoosha, I hope you will be able to bring on with you a few days' supply of rum, tobacco, and tea, for the Europeans (who have been so long without these luxuries), and *gram for our horses*. Other supplies, which are less pressing, we can obtain when an escort can go back to the Dil Khoosha for more. Those which I have specified could come with you on elephants or camels, to be pushed on to the garrison the moment we effect a junction. We cannot rely on the resources of the city being opened to us until we secure the Kaiser Bâgh, which may occupy some days. Until then, we must rely on sharing your supplies.

I think it most probable the enemy will abandon his positions between the Dil Khoosha and this place, when you cross the canal, in dread of being caught between two fires.*

In that case our junction will be effected on the same day you cross the canal; but it will be equally necessary to occupy the intermediate positions I have indicated, in order to secure our communication with the Dil Khoosha. The enemy's bridge of boats must be destroyed to prevent their getting to your rear.

So far as we learn, the enemy have, between the Dil

---

* This they probably would have done, had not their egress from Secundra Bâgh been cut off by approaching it from the rear.

Khoosha and this place, one gun in a "morcha," at the junction of the Dil Khoosha and Martinière roads, two guns at the barracks, and two guns at the Secundra Bâgh, which are all that could be brought within a day or two to oppose your passage across the canal. Other guns are directed against this position from the Kaiser Bâgh, and at (9) (9), but they are not likely to be withdrawn for other work; and there are four or five heavy guns on the other side of the Goomtee which it would take some time to get over; and they are not likely to be removed, as they play upon our position: these will be cut off when you destroy the bridge of boats.

If you delay crossing the canal more than a day after occupying the Dil Khoosha, two or three other guns may perhaps be brought, which now guard the main street leading from the Char Bâgh; but they have great difficulty in moving their guns, as they are so badly mounted.

I would recommend your bringing on the 24-pounders and 8-inch howitzers from Alum Bâgh, and at least two of the 9-pounders now there. (If the enemy's captured guns will suffice for the defence of that post, bring all ours.) Also plenty of ammunition, for the big guns especially; powder for explosive purposes; and mining-tools. I send descriptions of all the buildings that may be occupied by the enemy between us and the Dil Khoosha.

[The reproduction of these descriptions has been deemed superfluous.]

Sir J. Outram to Major McIntyre, Alum Bâgh.

Lucknow Residency, 31*st October,* 1857.

The flag at the top of your house proclaims, I presume, that you received my despatches concealed in a bamboo stick, which I sent off during the night.

I hope you found the plan as well as the despatches, by splitting up the whole of the bamboo. But it is now reported that there are *two* flags shown by you—one above the other—which I can only interpret as indicating that the relieving force has already reached you. This is just possible, as the Delhi column was expected at Cawnpore on the 26th (my last communication from that place was dated the 25th). If so, it is sooner than I expected, supposing as I did that it would be detained to oppose the Gwalior rebels; and sooner than I now wish; for certain mines that I am preparing cannot be ready for a week or ten days; and I require to explode these ere I can move out to co-operate with the relieving column.

The delay is desirable, also, to increase the strength of the column as much as possible by the additional European troops closing daily up to Cawnpore.

The stronger the column is the better able it will be to afford garrisons for Alum Bâgh, Dil Khoosha, and Martinière, ere it reaches the canal; and to furnish the various detachments afterwards required to maintain the positions necessary to secure our communications with the Dil Khoosha after its junction with us. At the lowest computation these drafts will diminish the strength of the column by at least 1,200 infantry, besides cavalry and guns; and could more men be spared, it might be prudent perhaps to garrison the Dil Khoosha (having to protect the baggage and stores, &c.) by more than the 200 men and two guns, and cavalry, as I have suggested.

If, therefore, the column has arrived at Alum Bâgh, I would beg the commanding officer to wait there till further orders, and more troops join him from Cawnpore; where you should send copy of this express to Brigadier Wilson, with my request that he pushes on to Alum Bâgh all further troops as they arrive, or such detachments as can conveniently be spared beyond the 350 required for his own garrison, *if he is not seriously threatened from any quarter.* As the column would be detained so long at Alum Bâgh, it might be advantageously occupied in driving the enemy from Jellalabad, which I should think might be done by the mere appearance of a strong detachment before the place, and throwing a few shells into it. And I trust no tedious siege operations would, under any circumstances, be required.

The column, when it does advance, should be well supplied with ammunition, especially for the large guns, and shot and shell; for we may have a good deal of bombardment work after our junction; also abundance of powder for explosive purposes. All food supplies should be brought on to the Dil Khoosha—except what may be required for the Alum Bâgh garrison—to save us from the necessity of detaching escorts.

We cannot calculate on obtaining anything from the city for some days after the column joins, as perhaps the place I indicated in my yesterday's letter may have to be got hold of first.* But your *heavy* carts had perhaps better be left at Alum Bâgh, as there is no made road to the Dil Khoosha.

If there is a long string of baggage, the rear-guard should be strong, even though the enemy are not likely to venture an attack in the open country between Alum Bâgh and Dil Khoosha.

Please send our private carriage, kit, and servants with the column.

Should the column not have arrived, oblige me by forwarding copy of this to Brigadier Wilson, with a

---

* The Kaiser Bâgh.

request that he will consider it addressed to himself, *i. e.* so far as Cawnpore arrangements are concerned.

I enclose a plan for telegraphic communication; your share of which Sibley will, I hope, be able to construct, as I know he is a great mechanic. Ours will, I hope, be ready in a couple of days, and you will be able to make it out from the top of your house. A second set of apparatus should be got ready to send with the relieving column, for the purpose of being placed on the top of the Martinière.

The evening before the day on which we purpose telegraphing to you, a bonfire will be lit on the highest point of our position (the Residency roof), to enable you to know exactly our whereabouts. A similar illumination on the top of the Alum Bágh will be proof to us that our signal has succeeded.

We shall signal at twelve, noon, of each day, the time best suited; for the enemy annoy us least at this hour, and our signallers consequently will incur less danger.

Even should our signals fail from your being too far from us, still do not delay in having two sets of telegraphic apparatus prepared; for so soon as we establish one set of apparatus at the Martinière, and yours also is ready, the signals will be carried on without difficulty.

The Private Secretary to the Governor-General to the Officer Commanding at Cawnpore.

(Telegraphic.) *Fort William*, 1*st November*, 1857.

The Governor-General wishes to know whether you have received any intelligence of a sortie having been lately made from the Residency at Lucknow into the town, in which many officers were killed and wounded. If so, the Governor-General requests that you will communicate the particulars to him by telegraph.

You are also requested to keep the Governor-General informed of any news which may reach you from Lucknow, and if Captain Bruce has left Cawnpore: his Lordship will thank you to take measures for the speedy transmission to Calcutta of any messages which may be addressed to the Governor-General by Sir James Outram or others.

Brigadier Wilson to the Private Secretary to the Governor-General of India.

(Telegraphic.) *Cawnpore*, 1st *November*, 1857, 10.45 A.M.

By cossid from Alum Bâgh, 30th October, Major McIntyre writes as follows :—" Communication with General Outram very uncertain and at long intervals. All well at Alum Bâgh. This morning, 440 European Infantry and 100 Naval Brigade marched from Cawnpore to join Brigadier Grant's force, which is halted one mile and a half beyond Bunnee Bridge, by order of the Commander-in-Chief." I have had no fresh communication with General Outram since my last telegram of the 2nd instant.

The Governor-General of India in Council to the Officer Commanding at Cawnpore.

(Telegraphic.) *Fort William*, 1st *November*, 1857.

I request that you will take the first opportunity that presents itself of conveying to Brigadier-General Havelock my hearty congratulations upon his being raised by the Queen to the honour of Knight Commander of the Bath, and to the rank of Major-General. I beg you to say that it is a very great pleasure to me to make this announcement to him, and that I most cordially wish him a long enjoyment of these well-earned distinctions.

Sir J. Outram to Major McIntyre, Alum Bâgh.

Lucknow Residency, 7th November.

I wrote a long letter to you on the 31st, which, as I see no telegraph yet prepared on the top of the house, I presume has miscarried.

As I have since heard from Cawnpore the probable date of arrival of the relieving column, I will only recapitulate what I said about the telegraph, and I send a fresh code of signals in supersession of that previously furnished (if it *should* happen to have turned up), and repeat my general directions as follows.

[*Recapitulation of previous letter.*]

The hour for signalizing will be from twelve to one, at noon, next day; and every succeeding day there should be a look out at that hour. As we can distinctly see your house, and as no signal pole has yet been erected by you, I concluded that my letter has miscarried.

When your pole is up, I shall light my beacon the night we see it, and have our telegraph ready for noon, next day. Should there be difficulty in making out the signals at this distance, at all events the telegraph will be of service after the intermediate one is erected at the Martinière.

I have requested the officer commanding the relieving force to light a beacon fire on the top of the Alum Bâgh at 8 P.M., on the evening before advancing to Dil Khoosha. To prevent mistakes, a salvo of four or more guns should be fired *twice*. I have requested him to fire a similar salvo three times (five minutes interval) at 2 P.M. on the day of his arrival at Alum Bâgh.

You ask me to write in the English character; so would the enemy wish me to do. As the only security against their understanding what we write in case our letters fall into their hands, the Greek character *must* be used.

When the force advances from Alum Bâgh, pray oblige me by obtaining permission for my servant John to bring on my carriage and kit, also for the servants and kit of Colonel Napier and the officers of my staff.

The Commander-in-Chief to the Governor-General of India in Council.

(Telegraphic.) *Cawnpore, 9th November,* 1857.

I beg to inform your Lordship that I am now starting to join the troops in Oude.

Major-General Windham to the Governor-General of India in Council.

(Telegraphic.) *Cawnpore, 12th November, 1857, 11.30 A.M.*

Since the Commander-in-Chief's departure on the 9th, I have forwarded troops of all arms to him, amounting to about 1,300 men. Three companies of the 82nd went on to Alum Bagh this morning. To-morrow morning three companies of the 23rd, the Military Train, and Lieutenant-Colonel Crawford's Artillery, will start for the same place. All troops now going there go in two days. As yet I have heard of nothing beyond a harmless cannonade having taken place at Alum Bagh. Brigadier Carthew I expect, with his Madrassees, to-morrow. I shall forward them to Bunnee if no information reach me of the advance in force of the Gwalior Contingent. Captain Bruce has already sent you a message as to their whereabouts this morning. Should they cross in force at Calpee, I shall retain the Madras brigade for the defence of this place. I have rather more than 500 Europeans here, and about 50 horses, and all daily strengthening the works. As soon as anything of the least importance reaches me from Lucknow, your Lordship shall receive it. The Gwalior Contingent Artillery is said to consist of eight heavy guns and thirty light ones. 1,200 of their men and three light guns are certainly at Calpee.

Captain Bruce, for Major-General Sir J. Outram, to the Governor-General of India in Council.

(Telegraphic.) *Cawnpore, 12th November, 1857.*

The Commander-in-Chief marched with his force to Alum Bagh this morning. There was some innocent firing at that post yesterday. His Excellency had been able to communicate with General Outram. Gwalior rebels are not yet reported to have reached the Jumna. The Nana's followers have crossed the Ganges into the Doab; he himself still in Oude.

Major-General Windham to the Governor-General of India in Council.

(Telegraphic.) *Cawnpore, 13th November, 1857, 7 A.M.*

The Commander-in-Chief was to have advanced to Alum Bagh yesterday, and begins operations in earnest to-day: every man and all the stores here expected will have joined him by to-morrow. The Gwalior Contingent had certainly 20 guns and above 3,000 men, at Calpee, on the 11th: this we had from two different sowars yesterday. In fact, another division had entered Calpee.

Major-General Windham to the Governor-General of India in Council.

(Telegraphic.) *Cawnpore*, 14*th November*, 1857, 8 P.M.
News from Commander-in-Chief's camp at Alum Bâgh, 9 A.M., the 13th. After several skirmishes in the day, ending in the capture of two guns, the Fort of Jellalabad was taken and blown up. The Commander-in-Chief communicated with Sir J. Outram by means of a semaphore, and will probably occupy the Dil Khoosha to-day. The country people round Lucknow are hostile.

Captain Bruce to the Governor-General of India in Council.

(Telegraphic.) *Cawnpore*, 16*th November*, 1857, 11 A.M.
The Commander-in-Chief occupied the Dil Khoosha and the Martinière after a running fight of two hours yesterday, at noon. The enemy came forward to attack at 3 P.M.; after a struggle of an hour he was beaten back, repulsed heavily. An advanced picquet having cleared some villages across the canal, we took post there for the night. Our loss was very trifling:—Lieutenant Mayne, Horse Artillery, Quartermaster-General's Department, and Lieutenant Wheatcroft, Carabineers, killed.

The Governor-General of India in Council to Brigadier Campbell, Allahabad.

(Telegraphic.) *Calcutta*, 17*th November*, 1857.
Pray endeavour to send the following message to the Commander-in-Chief:—
"I have received your letter of the 10th. I earnestly hope it may be possible to avoid a total abandonment of Oude, and to retain a safe position at some point between Lucknow and the Ganges. A complete withdrawal will do us much mischief.
"I write to-day."

The Governor-General of India in Council to the Commander-in-Chief.

(Telegraphic.) *Calcutta*, 21*st November*, 1857.
I congratulate you, my dear Sir Colin, with all my heart, on this great and joyful success.
Pray let me know how your wound is, and do not put yourself in the way of another.
You have effectually inspired your 93rd. I fear their whole loss must be very great.

The Commander-in-Chief to the Governor-General of India in Council.

(Telegraphic.) *Camp, Lucknow, 20th November, 1857, 6 P.M.*

The garrison of Lucknow has been removed, and I am now engaged in carrying the women and wounded to the rear. I propose to move the whole force to an open position outside the town, without further loss of life. Sir James Outram, on the contrary, desires that an attack on the Kaiser Bâgh should be made, and then to continue to hold the position in the town. He thinks that two strong brigades of 600 men would suffice to hold the town after the Kaiser Bâgh had fallen. But I am of opinion that at least the same force would be necessary to preserve the communication now mentioned by me to the Alum Bâgh, and constantly under the fire of the enemy—that is to say, four strong brigades would be required, unless it is wished that the garrison should be again besieged.

I have always been of opinion that the position taken up by the lamented Sir Henry Lawrence was a false one; and after becoming acquainted with the ground, and worked my troops upon it to relieve the garrison, that opinion is confirmed. I therefore submit, that to commit another garrison in this immense city is to repeat a military error, and I cannot consent to it.

I conceive that a strong moveable division outside the town, with field and heavy artillery in a good military position, is the real manner of holding the city of Lucknow in check, according to our practice with the other great city of India. Such a division would aid in subduing the country hereafter, and its position would be quite sufficient evidence of our intention not to abandon the province of Oude.

Such are the general grounds for my opinion. The more special ones are—the want of means, particularly infantry; field and musket ammunition for prolonged operations, owing to circumstances beyond my control; and the state of our communications in the North-West Provinces. The first of these is, of course, unanswerable; the second appears to me an insuperable objection to the leaving of more troops in Oude than such a division as I have mentioned, as evidence of the intentions of Government.

In the meantime I await the instructions of your Lordship in the position I have taken up.

Owing to the expression of opinion by the political authority in the country, I have delayed further movement till I shall receive your Lordship's reply.

The Governor-General of India in Council to the Commander-in-Chief.

(Telegraphic.) *Calcutta, 21st November, 1857, 3 P.M.*

I have received your message of yesterday. The one step to be avoided is, a total withdrawal of the British forces from Oude.

Your proposal to leave a strong moveable division, with heavy artillery, outside the city, and so to hold the city in check, will answer every purpose of policy.

Major-General Windham to the Governor-General of India in Council.

(Telegraphic.)   Cawnpore, 23rd November, 1857, 4 P.M.

Not a word from Lucknow for three days. One-half the Gwalior Contingent has crossed, and eighteen guns. The force at Shewalee has moved towards Akberpore. Captain Bruce's police were attacked at Bunnee the day before yesterday ; 74 killed. I sent Lieutenant-Colonel Fischer, and 400 of the 27th Madras Native Infantry, and two 9-pounders, this morning at 3 A.M., to hold the place for the future. The police having absconded after the convoy of 300 Europeans I had sent, under command of Fischer, of her Majesty's 53rd, had passed to Alum Bâgh with ammunition.

The Commander-in-Chief to the Governor-General of India in Council.

(Telegraphic.)   Lucknow, 23rd November, 1857.

Last night I caused the garrison of Lucknow to execute its retreat from the Residency, covered by the relieving force, which then fell back on Dil Khoosha, in the presence of the whole force of Oude. The women, wounded, and State prisoners, and King's treasure, and twenty-three lakhs of rupees, with all the guns worth taking away, are in my camp: a great many guns were destroyed before the Residency was given up, those that were worth bringing having been transported with much labour and made available for our own purpose. The State prisoners were brought with us.

Major-General Windham to the Governor-General of India in Council.

(Telegraphic.)   Cawnpore, 27th November, 1857, 10 A.M.

All going on well at Alum Bâgh. General Havelock died two days ago.

Captain Bruce to the Governor-General of India in Council.

(Telegraphic.)   Cawnpore, 27th November, 1857, 10 A.M.

I am desired by the Commander-in-Chief to transmit the following to your Lordship, dated Alum Bâgh, 24th November :—

"I have arrived here with all the long convoy attendant upon the rescued garrison. I propose to march the day after to-morrow for Bunnee, leaving Sir James Outram with a division, which will be complete in all details except carriage."

The Governor-General of India in Council to Brigadier Inglis, Cawnpore.

(Telegraphic.) *Calcutta, 3rd December, 1857.*

I have heard of your arrival at Cawnpore with the greatest pleasure, and I beg you and your gallant band to accept my hearty congratulations. I thank you for your admirable report of the 27th September, and for your letter. The report will be gazetted in time for the English mail. I shall be glad if a return of casualties can arrive before that, but the publication of the report shall not be delayed.

Be sure that justice shall be done by me to your truly heroic companions and to yourself.

Captain Bruce to the Governor-General of India in Council.

(Telegraphic.) *Cawnpore, 5th December, 1857, 7 P.M.*

The following has only just reached me, and, although his Excellency is now in camp, the information has not been previously communicated; therefore, I forward it to your Lordship.

From the Commander-in-Chief to the Governor-General, Camp, near Alum Bágh, 26th November, 1857 :—

"I march to-morrow for Bunnee, with all the wounded, &c. I leave Sir James Outram in possession, with a force, including the post of Alum Bágh and Bunnee, of 4,000 men, with twenty-two guns, of which four are heavy, besides ten mortars, namely, six 8-inch and four 5½-inch. If it is completed with a month's supplies and ammunition of every description (and I have denuded my moveable columns of tents to supply his troops, which will be in a standing camp), I think his position a good one; but I learn from him that he would rather have it farther back, near the Ganges. Sir James will probably address your Lordship on the subject. I beg only to report that your Lordship's instructions have been carried out to the letter."

Here terminates the correspondence, &c., relative to the relief of Lucknow. On the extrication of the garrison, in November, 1857, Sir Colin Campbell redistributed his army, which then consisted of three different elements : the European and native force which had served under Sir John Inglis ; the force with which Generals Havelock and Outram effected the first relief in September; and that with which Sir Colin Campbell succeeded in effecting the second relief in November. With the main body of the redistributed army, he escorted the women and children, with the original garrison and the sick and wounded, to Cawnpore, leaving Sir James Outram to hold the armed hordes of Lucknow in check, until circumstances admitted of his undertaking the recapture of that city.

Sir James Outram was engaged in the execution of this very delicate and difficult duty from the 25th November, 1857, till the beginning of March, 1858, during which period he had to conduct a copious correspondence; but this, having reference to his duties, present and prospective, in his capacity of Chief Commissioner of Oude, he has not felt himself at liberty to print, though portions of it have already been published by authority of Parliament.

The active part he took in the operations which resulted in the final capture of Lucknow, is sufficiently elucidated in the despatches which immediately precede the correspondence. On the fall of Lucknow, there devolved on him the difficult and important duty of re-establishing order in that city, obtaining the confidence and securing the return of its peaceable inhabitants, and extemporizing a civil government for the province. But, for reasons which the parliamentary papers have made known, and which it is unnecessary to allude to in this place, he begged to be speedily relieved of his duties as Chief Commissioner of Oude, and to be permitted to proceed to Calcutta to occupy that seat in the Supreme Council of India, to which, some months previously, he had been provisionally appointed by the Court of Directors. On the 3rd April, therefore, he handed over his office to Mr. (now Sir Robert) Montgomery, and left Lucknow amidst the affectionate and tearful farewells of the whole army.

Were the editor at liberty to consult his own wishes, he would in this place reproduce some of the affecting descriptions of Sir James's departure from Lucknow that appeared in the Indian newspapers of that day; but, knowing that this would not be approved by Sir James himself, he abstains from doing so. The same consideration has prevented him from giving insertion in this volume to the very touching testimonials of the devotion with which Sir James was regarded by the regiments which served under him both in Persia and India, contained in a correspondence which has been submitted to the editor, and which it would doubtless gratify these regiments to have printed.

The same considerations, however, do not prohibit the reproduction of those public notifications of the approbation of Sir James Outram's conduct by his Sovereign, by Parliament, by the late East India Company, and by the city of London; these, having been published, are now matters of history; and the omission of them would be unjust to those recipients of the volume to whose devoted attachment and zealous services Sir James Outram has so often declared himself indebted for the honours and rewards which have crowned a life devoted to the service of his country in war and diplomacy.

APPENDICES.

APPENDIX A.

The GOVERNOR-GENERAL *to* MAJOR-GENERAL OUTRAM, *transmitting the Resolution passed by the House of Commons on the 8th February*, 1858. *Similar letters forwarding also the Resolutions of the House of Lords, the Hon. the Court of Directors of the East India Company, and the Court of Proprietors.*

SIR, *Allahabad*, 11*th May*, 1858.

It affords me the highest satisfaction to be made the channel of communicating to you the copy of a Resolution passed by the House of Commons on the 8th February, 1858, conveying to you, among other distinguished officers, the thanks of the House, for the eminent skill, courage, and perseverance with which you have contributed to the achievement of many and important triumphs over the numerous bodies of mutineers and others who have defied the authority and opposed the troops of the British Government in India.

It would ill become me to add anything beyond the expression of my cordial congratulations to the honourable testimony of approbation which your valuable services have received at the hands of the House of Commons.

I have the honour to be, &c.,
CANNING.

To Major-General Sir James Outram, G.C.B.

HOUSE OF LORDS.—*February* 8, 1858.

RESOLVED, *Nemine Dissentiente, by the Lords Spiritual and Temporal in Parliament assembled:*

That the thanks of this House be given to His Excellency General Sir Colin Campbell, G.C.B., Commander-in-Chief in India; Major-General Sir James Outram, G.C.B.; Major-General Sir Archdale Wilson, Baronet, K.C.B.; and Major-General John Eardley Wilmot Inglis, K.C.B.; for the eminent skill, courage, and perseverance displayed by them in the achievement of so many and such important triumphs over numerous bodies of the mutineers.

ORDERED *by the Lords Spiritual and Temporal in Parliament assembled:*
THAT the said Resolutions be transmitted by the Lord Chancellor to the Governor-General of India, and that His Lordship be requested to communicate the same to the several Governors, Commissioners, and Officers referred to therein.

JOHN GEORGE SHAW LEFEVRE, *Clerk Parliamentorum.*

March 16, 1858.

RESOLVED, *Nemine Dissentiente, by the Lords Spiritual and Temporal in Parliament assembled :*—That a copy of Resolution II., dated 8th February, shall be presented to His Excellency General Sir Colin Campbell, G.C.B., Major-General Sir James Outram, G.C.B., Major-General Sir A. Wilson, Baronet, K.C.B., and Major-General Sir J. E. W. Inglis, K.C.B.

HOUSE OF COMMONS.—*February* 8, 1858.

RESOLVED, *Nemine Contradicente:*—That the thanks of this House be given to His Excellency General Sir Colin Campbell, G.C.B., Commander-in-Chief in India; Major-General Sir James Outram, G.C.B.; Major-General Sir Archdale Wilson, Baronet, K.C.B.; and Major-General John Eardley Wilmot Inglis, K.C.B.; for the eminent skill, courage, and perseverance displayed by them in the achievement of so many and such important triumphs over numerous bodies of the mutineers.

ORDERED,—That the said Resolutions be transmitted by Mr. Speaker to the Governor-General of India, and that His Lordship be requested to communicate the same to the several officers referred to therein.

DENIS LE MARCHANT, *Cl. Dom. Com.*

AT A COURT OF DIRECTORS, HELD ON WEDNESDAY, THE 10TH FEBRUARY, 1858.

RESOLVED, *Nemine Contradicente:*—That the thanks of this Court be given to His Excellency General Sir Colin Campbell, G.C.B., Commander-in-Chief in India; Major-General Sir James Outram, G.C.B.; Major-General Sir Archdale Wilson,

Bart., K.C.B.; and Major-General Sir John Eardley Wilmot Inglis, K.C.B.; for the eminent skill, courage, and perseverance, displayed by them in the achievement of so many and such important triumphs over numerous bodies of the mutineers.

AT A GENERAL COURT OF THE EAST INDIA COMPANY, HELD ON WEDNESDAY, THE 17TH FEBRUARY, 1858.

RESOLVED,—That the thanks of this Court be given to His Excellency General Sir Colin Campbell, G.C.B., Commander-in-Chief in India; Major-General Sir James Outram, G.C.B.; Major-General Sir Archdale Wilson, Bart., K.C.B.; Major-General Sir John Eardley Wilmot Inglis, K.C.B.; and Captain Sir William Peel, R.N., K.C.B.; for the eminent skill, courage, and perseverance displayed by them in the achievement of so many and such important triumphs over numerous bodies of the mutineers.

We are, &c.,
ROSS D. MANGLES, F. CURRIE, and nine others.
London, 24th February, 1858.

GOVERNOR-GENERAL.—GAZETTE EXTRAORDINARY.

Allahabad, 15th May, 1858.

No. 143 *of* 1858.—The Right Honourable the Governor-General directs the publication of the two following despatches from the Honourable the Court of Directors, with the greatest satisfaction.

It will be seen that the Honourable Court fully approve and support the recommendation in respect of prize, which the Governor-General in Council has made in favour of the gallant troops composing the Field Force by which Delhi was captured.

It will also be seen that in respect of batta, the grant of six months' batta which has been already awarded by the Governor-General in Council, and beyond which the authority of the Government of India does not extend, has been increased by the Honourable Court to a grant of batta for twelve months, in favour of the Delhi Field Force and of the original garrison of Lucknow.

The Honourable Court have further ordered a donation of six

months' batta to be given to all those belonging to, or accompanying, the force under Major-General Sir H. Havelock, which entered the Residency on the 25th of September last.

R. J. H. BIRCH, *Colonel*,
Sec. to the Gov. of India, Mil. Dep., with the Gov.-Gen.

MILITARY DEPARTMENT.—No. 84 of 1858.

Our Governor-General of India in Council.

1. We have taken into our consideration the communications made in your military letters dated on the 10th December, 1857, and 3rd January, 1858, relating to the property captured at Delhi; and announcing the grant to the troops composing the Field Force employed against that city, of a donation of six months' batta in recognition of their services.

2. We most cordially unite with you in expressing the highest appreciation of the claims of the troops comprising the Field Force, by which, as observed by you, "Delhi has been nobly wrested from the hands of the mutineers and rebels; and by whose gallantry, signal punishment has been inflicted on the insurgents there." The grant of six months' batta to all the troops engaged in the operations against that city, as a donation in recognition of their services, has our approval.

3. We concur in the views announced in your General Order of the 27th November, 1857, on the question of claims on the part of the troops to have granted to them, as prize, the property belonging to the State, and that belonging to private individuals, recovered from the mutineers. We also fully approve of your recommendation, that property taken by the troops which is neither claimed on behalf of the State, nor claimed and identified by individuals who may establish their loyalty, should be considered to be prize. We shall, accordingly, as soon as we are informed by you of the necessary particulars, make application to the Crown, in the usual form, praying a royal grant of the same as prize.

4. We are further of opinion, that the troops are entitled to a special grant on account of the value of the stores and other property recovered by them on behalf of the State, and on behalf of private individuals who may establish their loyalty and identify their property; and we have now to announce to you that we have resolved to grant to the troops on this account, an additional donation of six months' full batta.

5. We trust that no time will be lost in sending us full particulars of the captures which we now propose to recognize as booty of war.

6. The whole of the despatches and orders relating to these important operations, have been published in the *London Gazette*.
We are, &c.,
Ross D. MANGLES, F. CURRIE, and eight others.
London, 31st March, 1858.

APPENDIX B.

General Orders by the Hon. the President of the Council of India in Council.

Fort William, 20th August, 1858.

No. 1,218 of 1858.—The following extract from the *London Gazette,* of the 16th July, 1858, is published for general information:—

GENERAL ORDER.

War Office, Pall Mall, 16th July, 1858.

Horse Guards, 16th July, 1858.

In consideration of the eminent services of Major-General Sir James Outram, G.C.B., of the East India Company's Service, in the recent operations in India, Her Majesty has been graciously pleased to command that he be promoted to the rank of Lieutenant-General.

By order of his Royal Highness the General Commanding-in-Chief.

G. A. WETHERALL, *Adjutant-General.*

BREVET.

Major-General Sir James Outram, G.C.B., of the service of the East India Company, to be Lieutenant-General in the army, dated 16th July, 1858.

F. D. ATKINSON, *Major,*
Officg. Sec. to the Gov. of India, in the Mil. Dep.

FROM THE "LONDON GAZETTE," 12TH OCTOBER.

Whitehall, 9th October.

The Queen has been pleased to direct letters patent to be passed under the Great Seal, granting the dignity of a baronet of the United Kingdom of Great Britain and Ireland unto Sir James Outram, G.C.B., Lieutenant-General of her Majesty's Indian Forces, and member of the Council of the Governor-General of India, and to the heirs male of his body lawfully begotten.

APPENDIX C.

C. Beadon, Esq., Sec. to the Gov. of India, to Lieutenant-General the Hon. Sir J. Outram, G.C.B.

Dated Council Chamber, 21st Sept. 1858.

HON. SIR,—I am directed by the Honourable the President in Council to transmit for your information, the accompanying extract, para. 2, of a Despatch No. 109, dated 4th August, 1858, from the Hon. the Court of Directors.

I have the honour to be, &c.,
C. BEADON, *Sec. to the Gov. of India.*

Extract from a Despatch from the Hon. the Court of Directors, No. 109 of 1858, dated 4th August.

2. We have also great satisfaction in forwarding to you, for communication to Lieutenant-General Sir James Outram, G.C.B., the following Resolutions of the Court of Directors, and of the General Court of Proprietors, which have likewise been approved and confirmed by the Right Hon. the Board of Commissioners for the Affairs of India, viz. :—

" At a Court of Directors held on Wednesday, 9th June, 1858.

" Resolved unanimously, That as a special mark of the high sense entertained by the East India Company of the services of Major-General Sir James Outram, G.C.B., in the course of his long and brilliant career, and more particularly those connected with the memorable defence of the Residency at Lucknow, the occupation and defence of the important post of Alum Bâgh, and the final conquest of Lucknow under the command of General Sir Colin Campbell, G.C.B.; and with the view of enabling him to maintain the dignity of a Baronet which Her Majesty has been graciously pleased to confer upon him, Sir James Outram be granted an annuity of £1,000 for the term of his natural life, commencing from the date of the final occupation of Lucknow, subject to the approval of the General Court of Proprietors, and to the approval and confirmation of the Board of Commissioners for the Affairs of India."

" At a General Court of the East India Company held on Wednesday, 23rd June, 1858.

" Resolved, That this Court approve the unanimous Resolution of the Court of Directors, of the 9th instant, granting, upon the grounds therein stated, to Major-General Sir James Outram, G.C.B., an annuity of one thousand pounds (£1,000), subject to the confirmation of another General Court.

" At a General Court of the East India Company held on Wednesday, 7th July, 1858.

" Resolved, That this Court confirm the Resolution of the 23rd ultimo approving the Resolution of the Court of Directors of the 9th ultimo, granting upon the grounds therein stated, an annuity of one thousand pounds (£1,000) to Major-General Sir James Outram, G.C.B., to commence from the date of the final occupation of Lucknow.

" Resolved, That the annuity of £1,000 granted to Major-General Sir James Outram, G.C.B., be continued to his eldest son."

(A true extract.)

C. BEADON, *Sec. to the Gov. of India.*

APPENDIX D.

EXTRACTS *from Speeches in Parliament* (as reported in " Hansard") *relating to the* INDIAN CAMPAIGN.

HOUSE OF LORDS.—*December* 3, 1857.

LORD CAREW.—Of General Havelock it is needless to speak. His achievements are too well known to your Lordships and to the country to require any mention of mine. I can only express a hope that he and the gallant Outram will reap the reward of their glorious efforts, and that they, as well as the garrison for whose succour they so nobly struggled, together with its gallant commander, are now enjoying that repose which their labours and their patient endurance so well deserve. I trust that no mischance has befallen them. The country looks out with the utmost anxiety for the next mail from India, which we hope will bring us the account that they are at length placed in safety. Our army there has been left in a state of

extreme peril. For some time the communications between
different portions of it have been altogether broken off. They have
been surrounded, and there is no means of communication between
the portion which is at Allahabad and the portion which is at
Lucknow. They are not only separated, but they are surrounded by an overwhelming force, and I earnestly trust that
the forces which have been despatched to their relief may not
arrive too late to effect that object. If India has been saved,
the work has been wrought by means of the gallantry and
perseverance of her military force. With their own brave
hearts, their own strong right hands, and their trusty swords,
they have won their way and acted well their part. With all
my heart I wish that the praise to which they are entitled may
not be grudgingly bestowed upon them, and that they may
receive at the hands of their country the rewards which they
so justly merit.

HOUSE OF COMMONS.—*December* 3, 1857.

Mr. C. W. MARTYN.—Need I point to the gallantry with
which, in another part of the country, Sir Henry Havelock,
alternately advancing and retreating, with daring only equalled
by his judgment, until he had attained his desired object of
throwing relief into beleaguered Lucknow, had gained im-
perishable laurels? Who has not admired the self-devotion
and chivalrous feeling with which Sir James Outram, though
the senior commanding officer, consented or rather offered to
accompany General Havelock in his civil capacity until he
perfected this great achievement.

HOUSE OF COMMONS.—*December* 8, 1857.

VISCOUNT PALMERSTON.—In recording the exertions of Sir
Henry Havelock, we must not forget the chivalrous conduct
of Sir James Outram. That gallant officer, when he joined the
force under Sir Henry Havelock, might from his superior
military rank have assumed the command, but with that delicacy
of feeling which is ever the concomitant of true courage, he
nobly abstained from doing so, and placed himself as a volunteer
under the orders of General Havelock, because he thought that
the man who had gone through such difficulties and dangers,
and who had made such great exertions to relieve Lucknow,
ought not to be deprived, by the arrival of a superior officer,
of an atom of glory, but that he ought to be left to finish that
which he had so well begun.

SIR JOHN PAKINGTON.—I am glad that the noble Lord has done justice to the great and generous conduct of Sir James Outram. There never was an incident more honourable to a British officer or more clearly showing that generosity which so much becomes the soldier, than the order of the day issued by that distinguished man, which we have lately had the pleasure of reading. When Sir James Outram arrived at General Havelock's position, he had, as senior officer, a right to claim the command, but he did not wish that General Havelock should be interrupted in his heroic career, and therefore he relinquished the command of the force which relieved Lucknow. Let it be our earnest hope and prayer that the next intelligence we receive from India may confirm our expectation of the safety of that gallant band, and inform us that General Havelock has entirely succeeded in his great object, and that the garrison of Lucknow is entirely relieved from the imminent danger which at present seems to surround it.

ADMIRAL WALCOTT.—Indeed, he knew not which most to admire—the rapid marches and glorious victories of General Havelock; the magnanimous self-denial of General Outram, who scorned to deck his own brow with the laurels due to his comrade; or the siege, assault, and capture of Delhi, in all of which the same bravery, the same sublime heroism, were displayed.

HOUSE OF LORDS.—*December* 8, 1857.

EARL GRANVILLE.—These reinforcements he received under the command of General Outram, who, I must remind the House, following the distinguished example of the late Commander-in-Chief, Lord Hardinge, in the Sikh campaign, most chivalrously and honourably to himself, confined himself to his civil office, and accompanied General Havelock as a volunteer, in order that that gallant officer might have the credit which so properly belonged to him, of having conducted the victorious troops under his command to the relief of the besieged city of Lucknow.

THE DUKE OF CAMBRIDGE.—It is but right that, while honouring General Havelock, we should also concede due honour to Sir James Outram, who upon this occasion waived his claim as a general officer of higher rank, and allowed to Sir Henry Havelock the distinguished honour of relieving Lucknow. It is gratifying also on such an occasion to be able to allude to officers of both services, that of the East India Company as well as that of Her Majesty.

HOUSE OF LORDS.—*February* 8, 1858.

LORD PANMURE.—The next commander I have to mention is Major-General Sir James Outram. That gallant officer had just returned from the command of the successful expedition in Persia, when he was called upon to render his services to his country in the suppression of the mutiny in India. In Persia he had achieved all that he was called upon to accomplish. Thence he came back with victory upon his crest, and was appointed to the civil and military command in Oude. Then it was that he found the gallant Havelock devising his plan for the first relief of Lucknow. With a chivalry which could be equalled only by his gallantry, Sir James Outram forbore to take out of the hands of his brother officer the command of those operations in which much had already been done by him towards the attainment of success. When, however, my Lords, the first relief of Lucknow was accomplished, General Outram assumed the direction of operations, and distinguished himself by the continuance of that defence which Inglis had so gallantly carried on. After the evacuation of Lucknow, he was left to maintain his position against a vastly superior force at the Alum Bâgh, and he has since greatly distinguished himself by the resistance which he has offered to the attacks which were made upon his position,—attacks which he repulsed with a vigour which inflicted an immense loss upon the enemy, while that which was sustained by his own forces was comparatively trifling. For achievements such as these, it is, my Lords, that I propose that the thanks of this House be given to Major-General Sir James Outram.

THE DUKE OF CAMBRIDGE.—Having said thus much in reference to Sir Colin Campbell, I may be permitted briefly to allude to the next name upon the list of those to whom your Lordships have been asked to pass a vote of thanks—I mean Sir James Outram. We are all aware of the mode in which he conducted the operations which he undertook in Persia. It is needless for me to say, that in my opinion they do him the utmost credit, and while giving expression to a similar opinion with reference to his achievements in India, I must not forget to notice the circumstance that when, as senior officer to Sir Henry Havelock, he might of right have laid claim to the command of the expedition for the first relief of Lucknow, he, with true soldier-like feeling, allowed his junior to retain the command, and, acting in subordination to him, brought the expedition to a glorious consummation.

HOUSE OF COMMONS.—*February* 8, 1858.

VISCOUNT PALMERSTON.—General Outram, too, after performing with great ability the service upon which he was sent to Persia, returned to India and was appointed to a command which entitled him to supersede General Havelock, who had been earning by repeated successes those laurels which now, alas! can only crown his monument. Yet Sir James Outram, with a spirit of chivalry equal to his gallantry and skill, with that generosity which is so often the accompaniment of true courage, declined to take from General Havelock the command of that force with which he had acquired such brilliant distinction, telling him that " until you have succeeded in relieving Lucknow, the object of your successive efforts, I will serve under you as a volunteer, and will not step in to deprive you of that glory which you so justly deserve." It is gratifying then to see that those who distinguished themselves in arms also show themselves to be endowed with the magnanimity so nobly displayed in this instance by General Outram.

HOUSE OF COMMONS.—*February* 8, 1858.

MR. DISRAELI.—Lucknow also produced a cluster of illustrious names not inferior to those to whom I have referred. They are contained in one of the votes which will come under our consideration this evening. All remember the charge of Outram, the chivalry of which was not more distinguished than the generous sentiment which placed him in a subordinate position.

ADMIRAL WALCOTT.—We may well be at a loss whether to admire most the rapid advance of the conquering Havelock, the generous self-denial of Outram, the storming of Delhi held by a maddened garrison, or the passive indomitable courage displayed in the heroic defence of Lucknow, a defence scarcely if ever surpassed in history; or the masterly advance, the admirable tactics, and the memorable retreat of Sir Colin Campbell, crowned by his victory at Cawnpore; but of this he was quite certain, that all these actions would conduce to one and the same end, the establishment on a sounder basis of the British supremacy in India.

SIR FREDERICK SMITH.—The successes achieved by our troops under such an overwhelming numerical disparity were perfectly marvellous, and this country shared in the glory which was reflected by such splendid exploits as the marches of Havelock and of Greathed, the marvellous relief of Lucknow by Sir James Outram, and the striking display of skill and energy made by Sir Colin Campbell.

HOUSE OF COMMONS.—*February* 12, 1858.

COLONEL FRENCH said, he would beg to ask the First Lord of the Treasury if he will lay on the table of the House the despatch of Sir James Outram, detailing the operations at Lucknow between the 25th day of September, when Colonel Inglis was relieved by him and General Havelock, and the 22nd day of November, when Sir Colin Campbell forced his way through the rebel army to the Residency.

MR. VERNON SMITH said, no official despatch had yet been received at the India House from Sir James Outram; when it was, it would be presented immediately to that House, as all former despatches had been and all future despatches would continue to be.

LORD HOTHAM said, he wished to advert for a moment to the answer which the right hon. gentleman the President of the Board of Control had given to the hon. and gallant member for Roscommon (Colonel French). The right hon. gentleman said no despatch had been received from Sir James Outram. But he (Lord Hotham) had a very confident impression, if not a positive conviction, that he had read that very despatch in a Calcutta newspaper; therefore he hoped the right hon. gentleman would make some further inquiry upon the subject. He must also add, that there had been published in this country, he did not say in the *London Gazette*, an order issued by the Governor-General of India, in which he bestows commendation upon the officers of that force, in consequence of their having been recommended in Sir James Outram's despatch. Now the country was naturally anxious to see the despatch itself, for he hoped he might say, without any intention to disparage the Governor-General, and certainly he would not join in the censures cast upon him the other night, that however gratifying it might be to the officers and soldiers concerned to be commended by such a high authority as the Governor-General, still it would be more satisfactory to the friends and relatives of those gallant men, as well as to the public at large, to see the commendations bestowed upon them by their commander, who was an eye-witness of their valour. He would therefore beg to inquire why no official announcement has been made in this country of any despatch or report from Major-General Sir James Outram, detailing what had taken place between the time of his assuming the command in Lucknow and the arrival of General Sir Colin Campbell; and whether there is any objection to this and any other despatch or report from Brigadier Inglis being made public.

MR. VERNON SMITH said he was much obliged to the noble

Lord for thus pressing the subject upon his notice. It had, however, been forced upon his attention both by the question which the hon. and gallant member (Colonel French) had put, and by the question the noble Lord had himself given notice of. He certainly was surprised that no despatch had been received; but he had made strict inquiries, and neither at the Board of Control nor at the India House had any copy of the despatch referred to been received. If it had appeared in the Calcutta papers, there certainly must have been some omission in not having sent it home. But there was much to be said for them owing to the extreme hurry and difficulties encountered in their duties there. He quite participated in the noble Lord's feelings, that it would be more gratifying to the friends and relatives of the officers and soldiers to see their names mentioned in the despatch of a general so distinguished, and so well able to appreciate valour, as Sir James Outram, than it would be to be named even in the orders of the Governor-General. It was his great care to supply every information as soon as possible, knowing the anxiety there was for the fullest information respecting India; but he thought the noble Lord would agree with him that it was not desirable to give non-official documents.

APPENDIX E.

East India House.

The General Quarterly Court of the East India Company was held on Wednesday, 23rd June, 1858, at their house in Leadenhall-street, and the meeting was made special, for the purpose of laying before the Proprietors, for their approbation, the unanimous resolutions of the Directors, passed on the 9th of June, granting annuities to General Sir John Colin Campbell, G.C.B., of 2,000*l.*; and to Major-General Sir James Outram, G.C.B., of 1,000*l.* The Chairman of the Company, Sir F. Currie, presided.

The Chairman read a letter from the Governor-General of India, acknowledging the resolutions of the General Courts, held on the 10th and 17th of January last. He then stated that the Court was made special, for the purpose of laying before the proprietors the two unanimous resolutions mentioned in the notice convening the meeting.

The resolution having been read awarding an annuity of 2,000*l.* to Sir Colin Campbell,—

The CHAIRMAN said he did not think it necessary to enter into any details of the services which had been performed by Sir Colin Campbell, as they were so generally known and so highly appreciated by the public. He could only say that he felt very great gratification personally in being the organ of the Court on the present occasion, having a personal knowledge of the excellent services which Sir C. Campbell had rendered to the East India Company. He had the good fortune to serve with Sir Colin in the year 1847 at Lahore, and he must say that he never saw a more statesmanlike individual, or a man who had the interest of the Company more at heart. He trusted that the resolution of the Court of Directors would be unanimously confirmed by the Court of Proprietors.

The DEPUTY-CHAIRMAN (Captain Eastwick), in seconding the motion, said that Sir Colin Campbell had fought himself into his present position by hard service; that no man had more efficiently supported the honour of the British name; and he trusted that he would long live to enjoy the rewards which had been conferred upon him by our gracious Sovereign.

After a few words from Mr. Lewin and Mr. Cooke,

Mr. CRAWSHAY said that before a reward was voted by citizens to soldiers, the citizens ought to satisfy themselves that the services for which the soldiers were engaged were great and had been honourably performed. Sir J. Outram had been engaged in operations which had led to the conquest of Scinde, but he had considered those operations unjust, and had refused to receive his share of the prize money. Now, if a soldier refused a reward because the service on which he was engaged was one of which his conscience did not approve, surely the citizen was bound in like manner not to sanction operations which he believed to be unjust by rewarding those engaged in such operations. After the relief of the garrison of Lucknow he believed the operations in Oude to have been unjust and unnecessary, and calculated to throw great difficulties in the way of maintaining British supremacy. He did not believe that British supremacy had been restored in Oude, and was convinced that these operations were destructive of British authority, and therefore must enter his protest against what had been done by moving the following amendment :—" That the military operations in Oude subsequent to the relief of the garrison of Lucknow have been unjust, unnecessary, calculated to increase the animosity which by previous injustice had been excited against British supremacy, and seriously to aggravate the difficulty of sustaining it. That this Court, therefore, acting as trustees for the people of India, declines to sanction these operations by assenting to the resolutions of the Court of Directors for rewarding the officers by whom they have been conducted."

Mr. JONES would second the amendment, if the original resolution expressed any approval of what had followed the capture of Lucknow.

The CHAIRMAN said the ground on which the annuity had been voted by the Directors was the information which had been communicated to them of the honour which her Majesty had conferred on Sir Colin Campbell. On receiving that information they thought it their duty to suggest the propriety of making a grant to the gallant officer who had so highly distinguished himself. The services which Sir Colin Campbell had rendered in India did not on the present occasion, so far as official records were concerned, go beyond the capture of Lucknow and the restoration of the British supremacy in that city. It was on account of Sir Colin Campbell's previous services, and his services up to the conclusion of the capture of Lucknow, that the annuity had been proposed to support the dignity which had been conferred by her Majesty on that gallant officer. (Hear.)

After a few remarks from Mr. PRINSEP, the amendment, not having been seconded, fell to the ground, and the original motion was agreed to.

The resolution awarding an annuity of 1,000*l.* to Sir James Outram having been read,—

The CHAIRMAN, in submitting it to the approval of the Court, said Sir J. Outram was one of the Company's own officers, and his career had been for a long time one of a very marked character. His services in Persia were well known. He considered it perfectly unnecessary to enter at any length into the services of Sir James Outram, inasmuch as they would be spoken to by the deputy-chairman, who was the personal friend of that gallant and distinguished man.

The DEPUTY-CHAIRMAN (Captain Eastwick) then said—I have peculiar satisfaction in seconding this motion. Having had the privilege of an intimate friendship with Sir J. Outram for many years, having served with him in India, and having enjoyed ample opportunities of witnessing and appreciating his great ability, his indomitable courage, and his untiring devotion to the public service, I most cordially unite in the proposition to confer upon him this special mark of the high sense entertained of his services by the East India Company, which has been awarded to only a few of their most distinguished servants, but which no one has earned more fairly than Sir James Outram. It is nearly 40 years since he landed in India, and from the earliest period of his brilliant career, he gave promise of future eminence and distinction. He showed that he possessed in a remarkable degree two qualities which fit a man for high achievements. He relied upon his own convictions, and had the courage to act upon them without dread of the responsibility. Whatever he had to do, he did with all his might, not with eye service as to men, but in singleness of purpose and with sole reference to the public good. He entered the Bombay army as a cadet in 1819, and was soon appointed adjutant of his corps. He saw service in the Myhee Kaunta, Kattywar, and the Southern Mahratta Country; but it was not until 1825 that an opportunity was afforded him of displaying, in an especial manner, that quickness of perception, that readiness of resource, and that promptness in action, which made him a marked man in his profession, and led to his selection for difficult and responsible employment. A rebel chief in Khandeish, with about 800 followers, plundered the town of Bhurtpore, and took refuge in a hill fort. There he raised the standard of the Peishwa, adherents flocked to him, and in a short time insurrection would have spread throughout the whole province. British troops were warned from every quarter, but Outram, with a small detachment of 200 sepoys, having made a forced march of 35 miles under cover of a false attack in front, escaladed the fort in the rear, killed the leader, and crushed the rebellion. Shortly after this brilliant exploit, Mr. Elphinstone, the Governor of Bombay, selected Lieutenant Outram to organize the Bheel Corps. Khandeish was at that period a scene of anarchy, rapine, and disorder. The Bheels were a proscribed race. Their hand was against every man, and every man's hand was against them. They were sunk in ignorance, debauchery, and crime, and it was thought by some in authority that their utter extermination could alone restore peace to the province. Mr. Elphinstone thought otherwise. He determined to make them the guardians of the peace they had so long disturbed, and in Lieut. Outram he found a fitting instrument. It would occupy too much time to trace the progress of an experiment alike honourable to our countrymen and country. Suffice it to state the results. In a few years Khandeish was pacified, not, however, without difficulties which, as Sir John Malcolm wrote, only Lieut. Outram's local influence and personal character could have overcome, " affording an example of what may be done by officers who add to a knowledge of their duty as soldiers an acquaintance with the habits, prejudices, and language of the natives, and who by conciliatory conduct to all ranks secure their confidence, and are thus enabled to effect objects which by military force alone they could never accomplish." To relate the romantic adventures and hair-breadth escapes of Outram's Khandeish career would fill volumes. Foremost in every expedition of danger, whether in pursuit of the wild beasts of the forest, or still wilder gangs of plunderers, he seemed to these " children of the mist" to bear a charmed life. In an expedition to the Dang jungle, out of 13 officers that accompanied him, he alone escaped the deadly jungle fever. I may remark, as a curious fact, that it is said he owed his safety to a precaution of always sleeping with a covering of fine gauze over his head and face, to the irksomeness of which "fever guard" others would not submit. In the hot weather of 1831 most alarming atrocities were perpetrated by the Bheel tribes, and we learn from official documents that Outram, with only 25 of his own Bheels and a few district police and horse, apprehended 469 desperate characters. He selected 158 of the more guilty for punishment, committed them for trial, for 30 gang robberies, with such full and clear evidence, that all but eight were convicted and sentenced. Thus by alternate vigour and conciliation, now penetrating into their most secure fastnesses, and crushing with iron hand those who defied his authority; at another time throwing himself unarmed and unattended amidst his recent foes, sitting at their feet, listening to their legends, joining in their games and hunting expeditions, he stole the hearts of those wild denizens of the forests, moulded them to his own ends, and gained new triumphs for progress and civilization. It is related of Washington, when travelling in the country of the Indians, that he was met by an aged chief, who had come a long distance to pay him homage, telling him that at the battle of Monongaheli, where Washington had been miraculously preserved, having had four bullets through his coat and two horses shot under him, he had aimed at him several times with his rifle, and had directed his gallant warriors to do the same, without effect, and that they had desisted, believing that Washington was under the guardianship of the Great Spirit, and was not destined to die in battle. We can recognize the hand of a special Providence reserving a great man for a great work on earth. But it is not difficult to imagine the magic influence that would attach to the name of Washington connected with such an incident in the minds of the untutored Indians. In the same manner the name of Outram became a household word amongst the Bheels. Never was the power of an individual mind more strikingly exemplified—never did moral superiority achieve a greater triumph. There is no mean lesson in statecraft to be derived from the study of this portion of Sir J. Outram's career. In it lies the whole secret of the marvellous rise and progress of our Indian empire. It is simply the art of governing the natives through themselves by the force of individual minds subjugating the wills and affections of the millions: from Clive and Hastings to Lawrence and Outram, a succession of heroes and statesmen has grown up equal to the great work. Recent events have proved that race is not extinct, if we only give them fair play. But of late years we have more and more sought to curb individual thought and energy, by check and countercheck, by petty interference and jealous mistrust, and by a repressive system of centralization. It was not thus we gained India—it is not thus we can hold it. Simplicity, promptness, and vigour in our machinery; justice and moderation in our measures, based on real superiority of character, alone can enable a handful of Europeans to rule millions of Asiatics. But to return to Sir James Outram. The disturbed districts of the Myhee Kaunta were the next scene of his labours. From thence, in 1838, he joined Lord Keane's force, and shared in the taking of Ghuzni and all the operations in Affghanistan. His capture of a Ghazee standard, his adventurous pursuit of Dost Mahommed, and his dispersion of the rebel Ghilzie chiefs, are well known. We next find him earning distinction as aide-de-camp to General Willshire at the siege of Khelat; and then followed one of those characteristic incidents which invest his career with the most romantic interest. After the fall of the fortress he undertook to carry the tidings through the heart of the enemy's country, a distance of 360 miles, which he traversed in native costume on a sturdy little Affghan pony in seven days and a half, exposed to all kinds of dangers and privations on the road, and finally escaping his pursuers only by a few hours. In 1840, Major Outram was appointed political agent in Lower Scinde. How he bore himself throughout those eventful years of mingled triumph and disaster, let Sir H. Lawrence and Mr. Elphinstone say. In the *Calcutta Review* for September, 1849, Sir H. Lawrence writes:—"In the year 1838, Outram carried to Affghanistan a character such as could not be paralleled by any officer of his standing in India. His services during the first Affghan war were second to those of no officer then and there employed, and had he remained in the Ghilzie country, or at Khelat, many of our disasters might have been averted. But it is by his civil management, first of Lower Scinde, and then of both the upper and lower provinces, and of all Beloochistan, that Outram has won our highest admiration. When the European inhabitants of Calcutta trembled for our Indian empire, when in the highest places men grew pale at the evil tidings from Affghanistan, Outram held his frontier post with a firm hand, brave heart, and cheerful tone, that ought to have been contagious. Vigilant, conciliatory, courageous, he managed with his handful of troops not only to prevent the Ameers from taking advantage of our disasters, but to induce them to aid in furnishing supplies and carriage for the relieving, then considered the retreating, army." And in a published letter of Mr. Elphinstone, dated 7th July, 1843, to Mr. John Loch, after recapitulating Colonel Outram's claims to higher distinction than had been awarded to him, Mr. Elphinstone goes on to say, "All this is written as if Colonel Outram was merely a military officer who had distinguished himself in the Affghan campaign, and who had again shared with many others in the services lately performed in Scinde. But you are well aware how far this is from Colonel Outram's real position. Besides his ample share in the planning and conduct of various military enterprises, his political services for several years have been such as it would be difficult to parallel in the whole course of Indian diplomacy." If I know anything of Outram's warm heart, this recorded testimony of the greatest of Indian statesmen conveyed more real satisfaction to his mind than any commendation he may have received throughout his brilliant career. About this time Major Outram was presented with a sword by the community at Bombay, including the most eminent civil and military servants, "for the intrepid gallantry which had marked his career in India, but more especially for his heroic defence of the British Residency at Hyderabad, in Scinde, on the 15th of February, 1843, against an army of 8,000 Beloochees with six guns." The venerable and pious Bishop of Bombay could not consistently join in the presentation of a sword, but, "as a mark of respect, he sent Major Outram a Book of Common Prayer and Holy Bible, with the appropriate inscription, 'Thou hast covered my head in the day of battle.'" While on this subject, I may mention that the present Pope caused a gold medal to be struck and transmitted to Sir J. Outram, "as a testimonial of gratitude for the kindness displayed by you to poor Catholics under your command or stationed within your Residency." I state these facts as evidences of Outram's generous and noble nature, large and liberal sympathies with his fellow-men, and of the universal estimation in which he is held by all classes. In 1843 Sir J. Outram came to England, but at the first rumour of war with the Sikhs returned to India. No war at that time occurred, and he was employed in the Southern Mahratta Country, where he earned the special approbation of Lord Hardinge, than whom no one was more capable of appreciating a good soldier. But I should trespass at too great length on the indulgence of the Court if I attempted to enter into details regarding the varied and distinguished services of Sir J. Outram in the high political appointments he held from 1843 to 1857. He was successively Resident at Sattara, at Baroda, at Aden, and at Lucknow. In 1856 he became the Governor-General's Agent and Chief Commissioner in Oude. At this period his health gave way under the burden of incessant toil. He came to England to recruit, and those friends who saw him bowed down by sickness and continual pain which almost entirely deprived him of sleep, little thought that he would be spared to render still greater services to his country. But, like an old war-horse, scenting the battle from afar, at the first sound of the trumpet of duty, his stiffened limbs resumed their wonted energy, and he started to take command of the expeditionary force to Persia. How successfully he carried out the instructions of the Government in those high operations is well known. He returned to Calcutta at the height of the mutiny to be entrusted by Lord Canning with an important command, where his first act was, with characteristic nobleness of disposition, to refuse to rob the lamented Havelock of the glory of relieving Lucknow. As a volunteer he charged with the yeomanry cavalry, and wherever the danger was the thickest there he was to be found. After what has been already said, it is not necessary to enlarge on the prominent part he bore in the first advance to Lucknow, in the subsequent defence of the Residency, in the occupation and defence of the important post of Alum Bâgh, and in the final conquest of Lucknow. In the enumeration of his claims on the gratitude of his country, I cannot omit his wise and strenuous advocacy of a generous policy towards the landholders of Oude, on which alone could hopes of tranquillity be based. On these grounds I cordially second this motion. It will be valued by Sir J. Outram, but not for its pecuniary advantages (for his own sake, and for his family's sake, he has, perhaps, cared too little for such considerations). As an instance, I may mention that from scruples of conscience he declined to appropriate to his own use his share of the Scinde prize money, but made over the whole amount (considerably more than 3,000l.) to charitable institutions. Col. French, of the Bombay army, was his almoner on this occasion, and told me the circumstance. Sir J. Outram would never have alluded to it. It may indeed be said of Outram, in the glowing words of Macaulay, that, "proud of his honourable poverty, after leading victorious armies, and after making and deposing kings, it was sufficient reward for him to feel that his name not only stood high in the list of warriors, but would be found in a better list—in the list of those who had done and suffered much for the happiness of mankind." It is right and fitting that this country should reward such men; for no institutions, no political contrivances, can supply their place in the administration of its affairs.

Mr. CRAWFORD and Colonel SYKES supported the resolution.

Mr. LEWIN said that in his opinion Sir J. Outram had erred most grievously in the course which he had pursued with respect to the annexation of Oude. If, instead of bending to the views of Lord Dalhousie, Sir J. Outram had declined being a party to that proceeding, he would have entitled himself to the unqualified approbation which the motion contained. Entertaining these opinions, he moved as an amendment, "That the conduct of Sir J. Outram with regard to the annexation of Oude disentitles him to the unqualified approbation expressed in the resolution."

Mr. JONES seconded the amendment, which, after a short

conversation, was put and negatived, and the original resolution was then agreed to.

Dr. BEATTIE moved that the annuity granted to Sir J. Outram should be continued to his son.

The CHAIRMAN intimated that, according to the bye-laws, such a motion could not be entertained without due notice.

Dr. BEATTIE then withdrew his motion, and gave notice of it in the regular form.

The CHAIRMAN, interrupting the hon. proprietor, observed that the Court of Directors were perfectly willing to present the protests to which reference had been made.

It was then agreed, on the motion of Mr. CRAWSHAY, that all protests of the Directors of the East India Company against the annexation of Oude should be immediately printed and published for the information of the Court of Proprietors.

On the motion of Mr. JONES, the consideration of the new India Bill was adjourned until Wednesday next.

APPENDIX F.

Presentation of the Freedom of the City to Lord Clyde and Sir James Outram.

On Thursday, October 7, a Court of Common Council was held for the despatch of public business, when Mr. CHARLES REED moved, " That the freedom of this city, with a sword of the value of 100 guineas, be presented to the Right Hon. Baron Clyde, Commander-in-Chief of her Majesty's Forces in the East Indies, in testimony of the distinguished services he has rendered to his country, and particularly for his decisive operations on Lucknow, which have resulted in the reduction and occupation of that important position, the dispersion of the rebel force from their great rallying point, and the undoubted confirmation of the ascendancy of the British arms."

Mr. REED said : My Lord Mayor,—I have to ask this Court to allow me the opportunity of stating that the delay which has arisen in bringing before their notice the resolution placed upon the paper of business some months since is not attributable to any other cause than an anxious desire to have the fullest means of forming a judgment upon the affairs of British India before considering the question involved in my motion. (Hear, hear.) It has been my duty upon two separate occasions, in deference to what seemed to be the general opinion of the Court, to postpone the introduction of the motion. It is presented to you to-day with the full conviction that you are prepared to discharge one of the highest and most noble functions of your corporate body: I mean the right of conferring upon such men as you may consider entitled to this mark of your distinction the freedom of this ancient city. (Hear, hear.) It is not in your power to decorate the breast with stars, nor is it yours to buckle the Garter on the knee. You cannot ennoble by title, or make a plain soldier into a peer of the realm; but you can give that which the sons of royalty are honoured by receiving, that which none but the truly great can wear. I ask you to-day to add to that roll of fame upon which stand inscribed the names of Clive, Abercrombie, Sidney Smith, Nelson, and Wellington, the names of two men to whom we owe very mainly, under God, the safety of our Indian Empire. (Cheers.) Very recently we voted the freedom of this city to a Lawrence, and, though called to twine the cypress with the laurel, we have not forgotten to leave our civic wreath to the memory of the noble Havelock. (Cheers.) The two other generals most distinguished in the history of the Indian mutiny are Campbell and Outram, and to them I ask you now to award the highest honour which it is in your power to confer. (Cheers.) Colin Campbell, sprung from an ancient family of Scotland, entered the army in 1808; consequently he has served his country for more than half a century. His earlier career is a matter not so much of memory in this assembly as of history. We first hear of him in 1808 at Vimiera. He then follows the fortune of Sir John Moore, and is with him at Corunna. He distinguishes himself at the surrender of Flushing, s mentioned at Barossa, Tarragona, and Tarifa, and is actively engaged under Wellington at Vittoria. He leads the memorable forlorn hope at San Sebastian, and leaves behind him in the record of that eventful campaign repeated proofs of his courage, judgment, and skill. (Cheers.) In 1814 he is engaged in America, and only leaves that country to quell a formidable revolt in Demerara. Achieving a signal success, he holds an important command in China, which he retains till 1848, when he is ordered to the Punjaub, under Lord Gough. At Rammuggur and Chillianwallah he evinces the cool intrepidity for which he is so eminently distinguished. In 1849 he is a brigadier-general in Affghanistan, and the record of his services there is too fresh in our memory to need even a passing reference. When the Russian war commenced, and everything assumed the state of inextricable confusion, there was one man whose presence in the Crimea gave the British people confidence and hope. Why Campbell did not hold a different position in that campaign, it is only for us to surmise. Of this we are assured, that no man deserved a higher post, and no man earned more real glory, than he did. (Cheers.) The victory of Alma belongs to those intrepid men who followed the leadership of him, who, when his horse fell under him, headed his regiment, crying out, "We'll hae nane but Highland bonnets here." He it was who turned the fortunes of the day at Balaclava; and, if not conspicuous at Sebastopol, he was there prepared to do his duty. (Cheers.) When the mutiny broke out in India, all eyes were turned to General Campbell; and, on the news of the lamented fall of Anson, the public learnt, with the highest satisfaction, of the nomination of his successor. Prompt and decisive in all his movements, he received his command and instantly left to assume it. Within twenty-four hours of his appointment, with scarcely time to communicate with his nearest relations, he was not only ready, but had actually quitted our shores. His arrival at Calcutta had a most tranquillizing effect, confirming constancy and devotion, and stimulating hope and fortitude. (Hear, hear.) Aware of the critical position of our interests in India, and resolved to strike his first blow at Lucknow, he gathered his forces for the rescue of those patriot warriors, Havelock and Outram, shut up within that important fortress. It is needless to describe to you the wonderful skill with which Sir Colin Campbell effected his approach and gained his victory at the very gates of the city. The meeting of those generals the artist and the poet may depict to future generations, I will not attempt to describe it. The men and their achievements have gathered around them the highest renown. To strengthen the position, to make good an evacuation, to escort in safety that gallant band of our fellow-countrymen with women and tender children, to bear them safely through the heart of a cruel and bloodthirsty host, and to house them in security in Cawnpore, were achievements of the profoundest skill and bravery; and though the planning of this is generously ascribed to Outram, it was effected by Campbell. (Hear, hear.) Retrieving the false step of Windham, gaining the bridge of boats, his object at Cawnpore being secured, Sir Colin hastens to join Outram at the Alum Bâgh, and by a combined attack to repossess themselves of Lucknow. We know how that work was accomplished—how, throwing off the officialism of the general, the commander of the noble army became a personal leader—how, exposing his own life, he covered the position of his men, sparing life everywhere. We know how he effected a complete and, speaking by comparison, a bloodless victory, gaining possession of one of the largest cities in India, and turning the retreat of the mutineers into a tumultuous flight. We know how he chased them in confusion to Rohilcund and Bareilly, and scattered them far up into the wild recesses of the Himalayas. (Cheers.) Gentlemen, I ask you, as a man of peace, as an earnest patriot, as a citizen of London, to do honour to a man who, in the terms of my resolution, has accomplished that which has resulted in the undoubted confirmation of the ascendancy of the British arms in India. (Loud cheering.)

Sheriff CONDER seconded the motion.

After a slight discussion, the motion was carried unanimously amid loud and prolonged cheering.

Presentation of the Freedom of the City to Sir James Outram.

Mr. C. REED: My Lord Mayor,—The public are less informed regarding the services of Sir James Outram than of the services of Lord Clyde, but I am convinced that his commanding talents and superior virtue are known and appreciated by this Court. (Hear, hear.) In the first instance I coupled his name with that of Sir Colin Campbell, but adopting the suggestion of a distinguished officer of the Indian army, I have felt it right to place them before you now in a separate form, and the resolution I have now to move is as follows: " That the freedom of this city, with a sword of the value of 100 guineas, be presented to Lieutenant-General Sir James Outram, K.C.B., in testimony of the signal services rendered by him in suppressing mutiny and rebellion in the East Indies, and in admiration of his high personal and public character, exemplified through a long period of military service in the East, as a brave, skilful, and patriotic soldier." Sir James Outram has been in active service nearly forty years in civil and military capacities. He entered the East India Company's service in 1819, and was sent out in that year to Khandeish. Full of youthful ardour, he headed a storming party at Kittoor, and in 1825 was engaged in suppressing an insurrection in Moolain. In 1826, he entered upon a work as perilous as it was important. The tribe of the Bheels were a wild band of robbers, infesting a district of which it had been resolved to dispossess them. Their system of plunder was so harassing that the doctrine of extermination had been openly preached, and Outram was selected to perform this service. The doctrine was as hateful to him as the means proposed to accomplish it were cruel, and he resolved to abandon both. He went in among them, and by his valour and kindness subdued these marauders, and won them over to his confidence. In less than eleven months he had formed them into a corps, and the very men who lived to rob and kill were enrolled to protect and defend the territory which had been the scene of de redation. So powerful a force did these Bheel Corps become, that Outram led them, at the outbreak of the rebellion, in the jungle of the Dang to quell that revolt, and there, upon the testimony of Sir J. Malcolm, he accomplished a work not less wonderful. Sir J. Malcolm publicly records his thanks " for the zeal, ability, and judgment Lieutenant Outram had displayed, to which is to be attributed the fortunate conclusion of the harassing service he has had to encounter;" and in a subsequent general order he observes that Outram had to encounter many difficulties which his local influence and personal character could alone have overcome, and he directed the attention of the army to him as one of those officers " who add to knowledge of their duty as soldiers, acquaintance with the habits, prejudices, and languages of the natives, and who, by conciliatory conduct to all ranks, secure their confidence, and effect objects which by military force alone they never could accomplish." His unparalleled activity and energy in preparing for the expedition to Affghanistan were highly eulogized. A late member of this Court, distinguished for services rendered as a professional man in India, and whose absence from our council we all sincerely deplore, testifies to this fact in the highest terms. He refers to the skill of Outram in quelling a mutiny, and narrates the history of this campaign, eulogizing the many virtues and profound knowledge of this remarkable soldier. In 1839, the Shah Shoojah, exposed to peril from a lawless banditti, finds a generous protector in Outram; and the Ameer of Scinde shortly after experiences in an English officer a generous conqueror. Sir John Keane had threatened to storm and sack the capital of the Ameer, unless terms of spoliation were instantly submitted to. Outram took charge of the expedition, and so successfully employed his opportunity, that the Ameer was won over to confide in the British power, and, dying, committed his sons to the care of Outram, saying, in words stamped with the sincerity of death, " You are to me as my brother; from the days of Adam no one has found so great truth and friendship as I have found in you." His services in Upper Scinde were so highly appreciated that Lord Auckland testified in the House of Lords, in 1842, that " to no man in a public office was the public under greater obligations than to Major Outram; a more distinguished servant of the Government did not exist, nor one more eminent in a long career." And Sir Charles Napier, at a banquet given to Major Outram when leaving for Bombay, used these words: " In the fourteenth century there was in the French army a knight renowned for his gallantry in war and wisdom in council. That knight was the Chevalier Bayard. Gentlemen, I give you the Bayard of India, Major James Outram, of the Bombay army." Few men have been entitled to or have received such a tribute of praise. Unable to leave for England, as he expected, Major Outram returned to Scinde under peculiar circumstances. It was known that he objected strongly to the policy of the Affghan war, and he had not hesitated in stating his dissent. This candour displeased Lord Ellenborough, and cost Outram great pecuniary loss, as well as deprived him of promotion. Yet as a soldier he obeys with military precision. He returns to

Scinde and does his duty, but, declining to receive his pay of 150*l.* per month, he leaves this protest, which is addressed to the very officer who had complimented him so highly. Writing to Sir Charles Napier, in 1843, just three weeks before the battle of Meeanee, he says,—" It grieves me to say that my heart and that judgment which God has given me unite in condemning the course we are carrying out for his Lordship as most tyrannical—positive robbery; and I consider that every life that may hereafter be lost in consequence will be a murder." This Court, looking at the events of that war, will see in this plain speaking the earnest utterance of sincere conviction and wonderful foresight in the writer. For the gallant defence of Hyderabad, Outram was selected to carry the news to Bombay, and arriving there in disguise, having passed through the heart of the enemy's territory, he received an ovation at the hands of the residents there. A sword of the value of three hundred guineas was presented to him in testimony of his gallant services. In 1843 Outram is in England, and is found spending his time in advocating the cause of the oppressed and despised princes of India. But at this juncture the revolution at Lahore requires the presence of an energetic man, and the Duke of Wellington sends Outram out with a letter recommending him for the service, and we have the testimony of an independent witness, himself an able administrator, who says:—" Fortunately for Government, the man they wanted was at hand. Forgetting past injuries and neglect, he volunteered to the rescue of the Government in their difficulties, and never was the magic power of the man's presence more striking than at Sawunt Waree. In addition to these testimonies, there are those of Sir R. Grant, Sir J. Carnac, and Lord Hardinge, which I now forbear to quote. Returning to Egypt for health, Outram pursued his career of incessant activity till called to return to India to assume the highest position the Indian Government could give him at Baroda. He only releases himself from this arduous service to take the command of the expedition to Persia, where he nominated the noble Havelock as his companion. No one here will regret the brief nature of that campaign, and these two men, though prepared for duty, triumphed rather in peace, though it brought a cessation to their occupation. Havelock having preceded him, Outram was sent out to command the Indian army. He landed there, without doubt, the fittest man for such a responsible charge. He knew every inch of ground—he knew the resources of the people—he knew the people themselves, and they knew well the courage and clemency of the Sahib Outram. Knowing the perilous position of Havelock—how with a small band he was breasting the full and swelling tide of mutiny in his attempt to reach Lucknow—he pressed forward to his friend. Perhaps no record in history exhibits a rarer proof of true magnanimity than the noble resolve of Outram to yield up the command of that column of relief to Havelock. "No," said he, "Havelock is entitled to all the glory. He shall lead to Lucknow, and not till then will I assume the command." He volunteered his services under Havelock. They passed the Ganges together, and the rolling tide of rebellion closed in behind them. There was nothing before them but Lucknow or death, and their brave hearts were prepared to bide the issue. You know how gloriously they achieved the rescue of Inglis and our imprisoned countrymen, and how in turn they were shut in for seven weeks, amid great privation, till the arrival of Sir Colin Campbell. That evacuation was the work of Outram, and in the dead of that November night, by a most skilful *ruse*, every one of the long-imprisoned garrison found safety in a retreat that will be long remembered in the annals of British history. Holding the Alum Bâgh, Outram was ready to join in the general attack upon the fortress of Lucknow. You know who headed the storming party, who gained the bridge, who made the breach in those walls, and who was the first to scale the heights and plant the British banner within its Residency—Outram was the leader. Though second, he was everywhere the first, and his daring secured for us the repossession of that stronghold, temporarily wrested from our hands. Sir James Outram has received a baronetcy and a pension. May we not hope that the Victoria Cross will yet be his? We cannot do more than confer our freedom—an ornament greatly coveted. Grant it this day to General Outram as a man of consummate skill and daring bravery—a man of true generosity, clemency, and humanity—a man worthy of the old chivalry of Europe—the true Bayard of India, *sans peur et sans reproche*.

Mr. DOLLOND seconded the motion, which was carried unanimously amid loud cheering.

[The compliments paid to Sir James Outram at the expense of Sir Colin Campbell were publicly disavowed by him in the following letter addressed to the town clerk of the city of London.]

MR. SERJT. MEREWETHER, *Town Clerk of the City of London*,

LIEUT.-GENERAL SIR J. OUTRAM presents his respectful compliments to the Town Clerk of the city of London, and begs to acknowledge his note of the 1st December, 1858, forwarding to him a copy of the resolution passed by the Court of Common Council on the 7th October last, voting him the Freedom of the City with a sword of the value of one hundred guineas.

Sir James Outram acknowledges, with feelings of the deepest

gratitude, these distinguished marks of the favour and approbation of the Common Council.

The honour of being enrolled as a liveryman of the first city in the world, is one that is coveted by every Englishman.

This honour is enhanced by the gratifying expression of the sense entertained of his military services, and by the valuable and highly prized gift by which it is accompanied.

The sword will remain with him through life as a gratifying memento of the honour conferred on him, and will be bequeathed to his descendants as an heirloom of unspeakable value.

Sir James Outram feels bound to take this opportunity to offer a few remarks on the discussion as reported in the *Times* of the 8th of October last, which led to the above resolution in his favour.

He feels most gratefully the generous warmth with which one honourable speaker eulogized his services; but he is in honour bound to disclaim much of the credit ascribed to him, which is due alone to his great commander—Lord Clyde. The withdrawal of the Lucknow garrison, the credit of which is assigned to Sir James, was planned by Lord Clyde, and effected under the protection of the troops immediately under his Lordship's command, Sir James Outram merely carrying out his chief's orders. In like manner were the operations which resulted in the capture of that city entirely planned by Lord Clyde, Sir James Outram merely carrying out such portions of the subordinate operations as were entrusted to him. Neither can Sir J. Outram claim the credit attributed to him of having "headed the storming party," "made the breach," or, being "the first to scale the heights;" and most earnestly does he disavow any title to be regarded as, on that occasion, " though second, everywhere the first."

Calcutta, Jan. 12, 1859.

APPENDIX G.

EXTRACT *from* the "History of the Service of the 78th Highlanders."

On the 26th of January the 2nd Brigade was paraded to witness the presentation of six good conduct medals to men of the 78th Highlanders, on which occasion Sir James Outram addressed the regiment in a most complimentary manner; the substance of his speech he conveyed in a letter to Brigadier Hamilton, of which the following is a copy:—

MY DEAR BRIGADIER, *Camp, Alum Bágh, 26th Jan.* 1858.

I should be very sorry that the 78th should attribute anything I said to-day to the excitement of the moment, and therefore somewhat more perhaps than what I would deliberately record. What I did say is what *I really feel,* and what I am sure must be the sentiment of every Englishman who knows what the 78th has done during the past year; and I had fully weighed what I should say, before I went to parade.

While fresh in my mind, I will here record what I did say, in case you may think my deliberately and conscientiously expressed testimony to the merits of your noble regiment of any value.

The following is the spirit, and I think almost literally what I said:—

" 78th Highlanders,—I gladly seize the opportunity of the brigade being assembled to witness the presentation of good conduct medals to some of your deserving comrades, to say a few words to you; to tell you of my high estimation of the very admirable conduct of the whole regiment during the year, completed to-morrow, that I have been associated with you in the field, commencing in Persia.

" Your exemplary conduct, 78th, in every respect, throughout the past eventful year, I can truly say, and *I do most emphatically declare,* has never been surpassed by any troops of any nation in any age, whether for indomitable valour in the field, or steady discipline in the camp, under an amount of fighting, hardship, and privation such as British troops have seldom, if ever, heretofore been exposed to.

" The cheerfulness with which you have gone through all this, has excited my admiration as much as the undaunted pluck with which you always close with the enemy whenever you can get at him, no matter what his odds against you are, or what the advantage of his position; and my feelings are but those of your countrymen all over the world, who are now watching your career with intense interest.

" I trust that it will not be long before the campaign will be brought to a glorious conclusion, by the utter destruction of the hosts of rebels in our front, on the capture of this doomed city, their last refuge; and I am sure that you, 78th, who will have borne the brunt of the war so gloriously from first to last, when you return to old England, will be hailed and rewarded by your grateful and admiring countrymen, as the band of heroes, as which you so well deserve to be regarded.

" Good and glorious as your conduct has been, 78th, your

goodness and your glory has been nobly emulated by all the troops of this division, which have shared your toils, your dangers, and your triumphs. To them also my acknowledgments are due, and they will be gratefully tendered when opportunity offers.

"Especially to the gallant 90th, now at your side, as they have ever stood by you, fought with you, and suffered with you, since we crossed the Ganges together. The great and brilliant services rendered by the 90th in the Crimean war, even they have been eclipsed by what it has already done in India.

"Nor must we forget, 78th, your gallant comrades of the 64th, though no longer with us, who served with you in Persia, served with you here, and have suffered as you have done. No, I shall not forget the 64th in a hurry, nor shall I forget you.

"Very sincerely yours,
(Signed) "J. OUTRAM."

To Brigadier Hamilton, Commanding 2nd Brigade,
Oude Field Force.

(True extract.)

G. D. BARKER, *Lieut. and Adjt., 78th Highlanders.*

www.ingramcontent.com/pod-product-compliance
Lightning Source LLC
Chambersburg PA
CBHW030544300426
44111CB00009B/855